5⁰⁰

D1109638

STRUCTURE
AND
PROCESS
OF ORGANIZATIONS

*Prentice-Hall
Behavioral Sciences in Business Series*

Herbert A. Simon, *Editor*

ARLYN J. MELCHER

Professor of Administrative Sciences
Kent State University

STRUCTURE
AND
PROCESS
OF ORGANIZATIONS:
A
Systems Approach

PRENTICE-HALL, INC., *Englewood Cliffs, New Jersey*

Library of Congress Cataloging in Publication Data

MELCHER, ARLYN J (DATE)
Structure and process of organizations.

(Prentice-Hall behavioral sciences in business series)
Includes indexes.
1. Organization. 2. Management. 3. Leadership. I. Title.
HD31.M395   658.4   75-11507
ISBN 0-13-855254-1

© 1976 by PRENTICE-HALL, INC.
Englewood Cliffs, New Jersey

Printed in the United States of America

10 9 8 7 6 5 4 3 2 1

Prentice-Hall International, Inc., *London*
Prentice-Hall of Australia, Pty. Ltd., *Sydney*
Prentice-Hall of Canada, Ltd., *Toronto*
Prentice-Hall of India Private Limited, *New Delhi*
Prentice-Hall of Japan, Inc., *Tokyo*
Prentice-Hall of Southeast Asia (PTE.) Ltd., *Singapore*

To Nyla, Jocelyn, Mike, and Teresa.
Their generation will need greater knowledge
to deal with our increasingly complex organizations.

A. J. M.

CONTENTS

4
WORK FLOW:
Specialization at the Operative Level   61

5
TASKS:
Degree of Complexity   91

6
SPATIAL-PHYSICAL FACTORS:
Barriers Within and Among Groups   117

III
SECONDARY STRUCTURAL VARIABLES:
Formal Authority Relationships

7
DELEGATION:
Distribution of Authority Among Levels   147

APPENDIX   182

8
DEPARTMENTATION:
Specialization and Grouping at the Supervisory Level   191

IV
SECONDARY STRUCTURAL VARIABLES:
Formal Control System

CONTROL SYSTEMS:
Institutional to Individual   219

9
STANDARDS:
Level of Formal Work Demands   224

10
REWARDS—PENALTIES:
The Focus of the Formal Incentives

V
LEADERSHIP STYLE

11
LEADERSHIP THEORY:
The Major Approaches

12
REPRESENTATION:
Balancing Conflicting Demands

13
RULE ORIENTATION:
The Reliance on the Formal System

14
PARTICIPATION:
Consulting with Subordinates

15
DIRECTION:
The Closeness of Supervision

16
INDUCEMENTS:
The Use of Rewards and Penalties

VI
CONCLUSION

17
SUMMARY AND APPLICATION:

APPENDICES

A

B

FOREWORD

When Louis Agassiz, the great biologist, acquired a new graduate student, his first concern was to train his student to see. His standard procedure was to confront the student with a dead fish, laid out on a plank, and ask him to observe the fish until he could describe it accurately. When the student, after some minutes of looking, reported to the teacher, Agassiz cross-examined him thoroughly, persuaded him that there were lots of things about the fish he hadn't seen, and sent him back to look again. This cycle was repeated many times. After some days, or weeks (the fish was pickled), the student satisfied Agassiz with his description. He could now see a biological specimen—as a trained biologist sees it.

Organizations are all around us. We are often born in them (hospitals), we earn our livings as their employees, we buy our food and furniture from them, return to them when we are seriously ill, and are finally buried by them. A large part of our waking behavior is organizational behavior—behavior as members or clients of organizations. That does not mean that we can see organizations—as a trained manager sees them.

Learning to see an organization means learning to interpret the behavior of the people around us in terms of their motives, their organization roles, the influences that the organization exerts on them. Learning to work effectively in an organization means learning what effects our behavior will have on the attitudes and behaviors of others.

As long as there have been human organizations, managers have studied them, and culled from their study important generalizations about how they operate—and sometimes advice about how to make them operate well. In recent years, however, this kind of practical understanding of organizations has been greatly broadened and deepened by careful scientific study, in the field and in the laboratory. We now have factual evidence to support some of the practical wisdom about organizations, and evidence to correct it where it was wrong, as practical wisdom sometimes is. Research has given us new ways of looking at organizations, especially in terms of the motivations of their participants, and new ways of predicting how organizations will react to external events, or to our attempts to redirect them.

In this book, Professor Melcher brings together some of this important knowledge, and applies it to describing organizations, diagnosing their problems, and, occasionally, prescribing for them. His emphasis is upon seeing and understanding, however, rather than prescribing; for it is dangerous for us to tinker with anything as complex as an organization until we have a thorough understanding of how it works. To aid his readers in "seeing" organizations, Professor Melcher has set forth in each chapter operational perceptual measures that define the principal variables discussed in the chapter.

Organizations can be viewed either in terms of their structure ("anatomy") or their processes ("physiology"). This book gives systematic attention to structural factors and leadership processes affecting behavior. Other approaches provide an understanding of such specific methods as T-groups, training and counselling, which orient one to deal directly with organization processes and behavior. Both approaches are useful, and they complement each other.

Much of the new scientific knowledge of organizations is psychological in nature, concerned, for example, with how people react to various kinds of incentives on the job, or to different styles of leadership. Information about individual behaviors, however, is to the design of organizations as information about the tensile strength of steel is to the design of buildings. One needs to understand not only the basic components, but also the ways for putting them together.

It is this concern for the relations of the parts that distinguishes a book on organizations, like this one, from a book on social psychology. Nowadays, when we wish to emphasize these relations, we often refer, as the author does, to a "systems approach" to organizations. At its simplest, a systems approach means that we don't try to diagnose organizational problems, or design improved organizations, in terms of single factors, viewed independently of all the others with which they interact. At its most sophisticated, a systems approach means that we try to use orderly, systematic procedures for analyzing social interactions in organizations.

Professor Melcher does not promise any magic from "systems thinking," but he does provide two important tools for helping us understand organizations: a useful review of what is known today, from scientific study, about human behavior in organizations, and a systematic framework for putting that knowledge to use in the description and analysis of organizational problems. If one wants to learn to see organizations, and then to operate effectively in them, it is with such knowledge and skills that he must begin. Professor Melcher has included in each section of the book a set of discussion questions, many of which call for the application of basic knowledge about behavior to concrete organizational situations. Examining these questions in depth will help readers develop the skills of analyzing an over-all organizational system in terms of the important underlying factors.

We hear much, nowadays, about man's "alienation" from society, and about the contribution of organizations to his "dehumanization." Organizations don't have a very good press today. The evidence reviewed in this book goes a long way toward putting such claims in perspective, and providing a balanced view of what organizations do to man, and what they do for him. If there are important imperfections in the organizations of modern society, and there surely are, then we must look to a better understanding of organizational behavior as a means of remedying them. There is no sign that we are going to live without organizations, or that we should want to. The quality of life in the future will depend very much on our success in improving them.

Herbert A. Simon
Pittsburgh, Pennsylvania

ACKNOWLEDGMENTS

My students and colleagues at Kent State University have been partners in the formulation of this model, and the writing of this book. The stimulation provided especially by my colleagues Joseph Schwitter and Buddy Myers were invaluable at early stages in the project. Joe has been my severest critic and strongest supporter. Many ideas were hammered out in discussions with him. Buddy has been a germinal source of ideas at several critical points in this effort. Both have been and are valued professionals and friends. I've used the model regularly in my classes at the undergraduate and graduate levels. The questions raised and observations made have been essential in testing its utility and refining the approach.

The field studies of many students have contributed to the assessment of definitions, measurements of the variables and provided insights into problems of applying the model in practice and its usefulness as a research tool. The complex projects of Bonita West, Thomas Kayser, David Hawk, Daniel Roby, Joseph LaTona and Andres Bermudez were especially helpful. David Cabel worked with me as a teaching assistant and research assistant for three years and contributed in numerous ways to the project. Many others have worked with the model, critiqued it, or applied it in diagnostic and research studies. Colleagues and students at the University of South Florida have pressed both its diagnostic and research value over several years.

Several reviewers have partially oriented me in the writing of this book. Herbert Simon has provided useful criticism and suggestions on stylistic quirks, awkward writing style, ambiguities in the material and encouragement in the project. George Strauss' critique of an early proposal was insightful. Reviews by Alton Bartlett and James McNaul provided useful criticism for clarifying the material at a later stage.

Bea, my wife, has tolerantly listened to my discussion of the literature. She has ignored the coming and going of unmet deadlines and accepted new ones without wry comment. She has been a help and stimulation as a wife, companion, and colleague.

The final typing was ably coordinated by Mrs. Cecilia Gambaccini and done by Laurie Sharkody, Gloria Tronge, and Nancy Hall. They have interpreted my scribbling and produced readable drafts and a clean final manuscript.

I am responsible for the final version of the manuscript. Despite the helpful orientation of students, colleagues and reviewers, I've accepted only part of their suggestions and criticism.

STRUCTURE
AND
PROCESS
OF ORGANIZATIONS

I

THEORETICAL BACKGROUND

1

INTRODUCTION

This book is concerned with understanding the determinants of behavior in complex organizations. The goal is to provide a framework for dealing with behavioral problems on a rigorous analytical level whether one is involved in diagnosing, predicting, or devising measures to influence behavior. The orientation is to provide general theory that is applicable regardless of institutional setting—industrial, educational, hospital, governmental, prison, or other context.

The approach is broadly integrative, drawing upon both the contributions of the behavioral sciences as well as traditional human relations and management literature. It seeks to tie together the diverse contributions of those who focus upon a limited number of the factors that influence behavior and to put in perspective the respective contributions of those who focus upon different conditions, dimensions of formal structure, and different elements of leadership.

There is no easy way of avoiding the methodological underpinnings of this work. The emphasis is upon cause and effect relationships. As a minimum base to proceed, the independent and dependent variables—that is, the causes of behavior and the dimensions of behavior itself—must be defined precisely and in a way that permits systematic analysis. A careful attempt has been made to define the variables so that the causal variables are independent of each other as well as of behavior they affect. Care has been taken to define terms operationally: students should be able to describe and analyze organizations in terms of the concepts presented.

The chapters present the theory—that is, generalizations of cause and effect relationships. The emphasis is upon theory that is applicable in different institutional settings and organizations of different size. The orientation is to develop what is common rather than unique among organizations, emphasizing explanations rather than prescription. While principles of organizational behavior are not presented, the student who masters the analytical approach and the theory can then formulate principles that are applicable for dealing with specific problems. If one can explain the causes of behavior, he then is able to prescribe how to change or modify what exists.

The relations are largely dealt with qualitatively rather than quantitatively. This choice, to a large extent, reflects the stage of development of the area. As further refinements are made, the approach lends itself to more precise quantitative treatment. The analysis provides the basis for determining the direction of the influence that the variables exert over behavior. The literature emphasizes the direction of influence, but provides relatively little information on the weighting of the variables when two or more interact in the same or opposite directions. This is an important problem. Some suggestions will be offered both upon methods of weighting and on some of the actual weights that can be assigned using the limited data available at this time. There is likely to be considerable gain as the model is quantified.

The framework provides a basis for systematic analysis of causes of behavior in complex cases or actual organizations. The text provides a statement of relevant theory. The field manual that accompanies the text provides guidelines in applying the framework to the analysis of complex cases and of diagnosing causes of problems in actual organizations.

The theory and application to cases, or actual field situations, supplement each other. The cases offer the opportunity to apply the theory for diagnostic purposes and for testing the generalizations that are set forth in the text. If, for instance, the research findings indicate that the use of broad participation by management motivates and stimulates employees, this generalization provides a basis for diagnosing a case; the data in the case provide a basis for testing whether the generalization holds. If contrasts exist on the use of participation among departments or the use of participation changes over time (or both), the theory should enable the student to predict the consequences for behavior. If it does not, a question is raised about the analysis of the case or the soundness of the theory.

Complex cases provide a bridge between the statement of the theory and its application in ongoing organizations. The theory has relevance to the extent that it helps the student to understand, predict, and specify the means to influence behavior in an organization. When the student tests and applies the theory to the cases, he gains practice in dealing with the operational problems of applying theory in an ongoing organization. The student thus has a basis for determining to what extent the theory enables diagnosis of an actual organization, prediction of behavior patterns, and a basis of prescribing the way in which behavior could be changed. This is the ultimate marriage of theory and practice.

The book's approach invites the instructor and student to assume a critical posture. The model provides the basis for systematic analysis of the determinants of behavior. The research summarized in the text describes how the variables affect behavior. Where the framework is applied to analyzing cases, or where field studies are undertaken by students, situations are provided for applying and testing the usefulness of the theory.

Nearly all individuals have had personal experience in organizations that can be interpreted using the model. If the student's experience challenges the generalizations set forth in the text, this should raise questions to be pursued. It may provide a basis for reinterpreting that experience, or it may provide an insight into the limitations and qualifications that need to be added to the generalizations developed in the book. A critical perspective should help in exorcising absurd and misleading generalizations that have often won broad acceptance. To the extent that the instructor elicits a critical dialogue with the students, there is a broad basis not only for developing valuable skills but also for learning and subsequent reading.

We are faced in the study of organizations with a dilemma. An overall understanding of organizations is necessary to understand completely the influence of a particular variable. But the overall understanding, in part, turns upon understanding each variable. There seems to be no easy solution to this problem. The best approach is to take the model step by step and then to review how the entire framework provides a unified view of the multiple influences that shape behavior.

The chapters are organized around a similar format. Generalizations that are commonly accepted by practicing managers and broadly taught in traditional textbooks are briefly summarized. This material is then tested against carefully designed field studies and experimental work done in a laboratory setting. Where a particularly cogent summary or theoretical statement exists showing how the variables influence behavior, this material has been excerpted and presented in the original format. The field progresses partly by closely reasoned statements on expected relationships, partly by carefully designed research projects in a field or laboratory setting, and partly by the integration and synthesis of the accumulated work. The approach is to try to provide the best of each area. The student should gain a perspective on the way in which theory gradually unfolds through the efforts of many research workers and also a critical perspective that is useful in interpreting the results of specific research projects.

Chapter 2 presents the overall analytical model used to integrate the research on organization behavior. It is sketched out briefly; the components are developed in detail in subsequent chapters. Section II develops the effects of primary structural factors over behavior. The focus is on the way size of the organization, spatial-physical barriers, work flow, and task complexity induce predictable patterns of behavior. Section III presents the way in which secondary structural variables influence behavior. Two dimensions of formal authority relationships and two aspects of control systems are explored and their influence over behavior developed. Section IV explores the way in which five elements of leadership style affect behavior. Section V concludes the analysis with a brief summary and an application to an organization.

The student should be forewarned that comprehension of the total model develops only gradually. By the end of the book, he should have a good understanding of the multiple influences that shape behavior. Initially, little of this understanding is intuitively obvious. The use of research articles rather than popularized versions, and drawing upon the work of a wide variety of specialists also may cause some initial difficulties. The approach offers the possibility, however, of a quantum jump in one's understanding of organizations. It can be an exciting look at the order that exists in complex organizations.[1]

[1]A more comprehensive version of the model was presented in Anant Negandhi and Joseph Schwitter (ed.), *Organizational Behavioral Models* (Kent, Ohio: Comparative Administration Research Institute, Kent State University, 1969), pp. 109–38.

2

A SYSTEMS MODEL FOR ANALYZING ORGANIZATION BEHAVIOR

DIMENSIONS OF ORGANIZATION BEHAVIOR

Among the factors affecting the overall effectiveness of an organization are the behavior patterns that emerge. Two organizations may be operating in a similar environment, using parallel equipment, and possessing similar mastery of technology; the personnel may have a common background, skills, and professional education. Still, one organization may be more innovative, efficient, and effective in achieving its goals. The behavioral patterns that develop may largely explain these differences.

Several aspects of behavior are important in the functioning of an organization: individual behavior patterns, vertical relations, and intragroup and intergroup relations. At the lower levels in an organization, supervisors are concerned principally with individual and intragroup behavior. However, at higher levels, intergroup relations become increasingly important.

Several important elements of individual behavior are job involvement, commitment to meeting standards, initiative to improve methods and to solve problems, orientation to improve oneself, work goal commitment, sense of achievement or frustration, absenteeism, and turnover. These dimensions of behavior cover what Katz refers to as three types of behavioral requirements essential for the functioning of the organization.[1]

1. People must be induced to enter and remain within the system.
2. They must carry out their role assignments in a dependable fashion.
3. They must be innovative and spontaneously active in achieving organizational objectives that go beyond the role specifications.

[1]Daniel Katz, "The Motivational Basis of Organization Behavior," *Behavioral Science*, 19 (April 1964), 131–46.

The functioning of complex organizations is also affected by the relations that develop within groups and among groups. Some significant dimensions of lateral relations within and among groups are extent and nature of interaction patterns, confidence and trust, accuracy and completeness of communication, degree of cooperation, cohesiveness, and group loyalty. The vertical relations between superiors and subordinates are also relevant. The trust and confidence of superiors in subordinates and vice versa, the accuracy and completeness of communication where superiors request information, and the degree to which subordinates initiate communication upward are

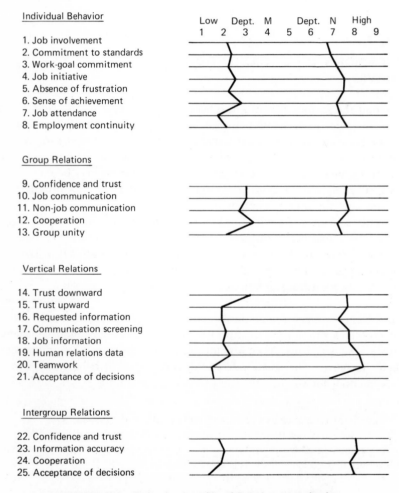

Individual Behavior

Low Dept. M   Dept. N High
1   2   3   4   5   6   7   8   9

1. Job involvement
2. Commitment to standards
3. Work-goal commitment
4. Job initiative
5. Absence of frustration
6. Sense of achievement
7. Job attendance
8. Employment continuity

Group Relations

9. Confidence and trust
10. Job communication
11. Non-job communication
12. Cooperation
13. Group unity

Vertical Relations

14. Trust downward
15. Trust upward
16. Requested information
17. Communication screening
18. Job information
19. Human relations data
20. Teamwork
21. Acceptance of decisions

Intergroup Relations

22. Confidence and trust
23. Information accuracy
24. Cooperation
25. Acceptance of decisions

FIGURE 2-1.   Behavioral profile of Rehclem organization

important. Other intergroup behavior patterns that affect the functioning of organizations are the degree of cooperation, teamwork, loyalty, and acceptance by subordinates of decisions made by supervisors or specialists groups outside the department.

These behavioral patterns are important to the organizations since they affect:

1. The degree of cooperation and coordination among individuals and groups that perform specialized tasks
2. The degree of spontaneity in personal relations that permits efforts to be directed to task requirements rather than to group maintenance functions such an mediating conflict
3. The degree to which current information—needed to make daily decisions on the job, short-term planning, and policy formulation—is collected and exchanged among those who have the data and those who need it
4. The extent that ideas are exchanged and technical and professional training pooled to solve both unanticipated, unique, and regular recurring problems
5. The amount of attention and effort directed to organizational goals rather than the self-interest of individuals and groups

These behavior patterns can be measured and a behavioral profile developed that shows changes through time or contrasts among units. For example, assume that the behavior of individuals in two units in an organization has been measured and the profile in Figure 2-1 has been generated, showing sharp behavioral differences in two departments. A practical problem is to determine the causes of the differences in behavior patterns. Thus, if the day shift is highly productive and the night shift erratic and inefficient, or a department trouble-free at one point in time but trouble-ridden later on, management must seek the causes of the differences. The next section introduces the analytical factors that may cause differences in behavior.

BEHAVIORAL PROFILE

The measurement of behavior in an actual organization can be done by observation, interviewing, or by questionnaire. A questionnaire has been devised to provide measures of the perceived state of behavior. It is filled out by all members of the formal units that are studied. The questions are worded so that a profile emerges where low values (0–10 percent) represent undesirable behavioral patterns; high values (90–100 percent) represent the other polar extreme of desirable behavior patterns. Some questions, however, are reversed. These are constructed in this manner to provide a check on employees' carefulness in filling out the questionnaire.

INSTRUCTIONS

Below are questions on the behavior of work groups. Please fill in the space on the answer sheet which best describes your behavior and that of your group. For example, on the first question the number is filled in on the answer sheet that best describes your level of commitment on the job.

1. JOB INVOLVEMENT. To what extent are you committed to your work (like trying to do the job well and taking pride in your work)?

1	2	3	4	5	6	7	8	9
10% or	20%	30%	40%	50%	60%	70%	80%	90%
less of the				of the time				or more of
time you				you feel				the time
feel com-				committed				you feel
mitted to				to doing a				committed
doing a				good job				to doing a
good job								good job

Individual

1. JOB INVOLVEMENT. To what extent are you committed to your work (like trying to do the job well and taking pride in your work)?
2. COMMITMENT TO STANDARDS. What percentage of the time do you try to meet work standards, or other measures of a full day's work?
3. WORK-GOAL COMMITMENT. To what extent do you automatically increase your work pace and shorten work breaks as work pressure increases?
4. JOB INITIATIVE. To what degree do you assume job responsibility (such as trying to improve methods and solve work problems)?
5. FRUSTRATION. What percentage of the time do you feel frustrated in trying to do your job?
6. ACHIEVEMENT. To what degree do you have a sense of achievement in performing your job (such as getting a kick out of doing good work)?
7. ABSENTEEISM. What percentage of the time are you on the job regularly enough that the group can count on you to be there?
8. (Reversed) TURNOVER. To what extent do you think of leaving your job (that is, quitting or asking for a transfer)?

Intragroup

9. CONFIDENCE AND TRUST. What percentage of the members in your work group do you have confidence in and trust?
10. JOB-RELATED COMMUNICATION. To what degree do you have useful discus-

sions with other group members on *job-related* subjects (such as on work problems, how to resolve personal conflicts, and so forth)?

11. NON-JOB-RELATED COMMUNICATION. To what extent do you have discussions with other group members on non-job-related subjects (such as politics, sports, etc.)?

12. COOPERATION. What percentage of the time do members of your group help you when assistance is needed without being asked?

13. GROUP UNITY. To what degree do you identify with your work group (such as by showing a sense of unity, feeling part of the group, and wishing to remain in the group)?

Vertical

14. TRUST DOWNWARD. To what extent does your *supervisor* show he has trust and confidence in you?

15. TRUST UPWARD. To what degree do you have trust and confidence in him?

16. REQUESTED INFORMATION. When information is requested by your supervisor, to what extent do you provide accurate and complete data?

17. (Reversed) COMMUNICATION SCREENING. What percentage of the time is it necessary for you to withhold and distort information from your supervisor for your own self-protection?

18. JOB INFORMATION. To what extent do you bring job problems to his attention?

19. HUMAN RELATIONS INFORMATION. To what degree do you volunteer useful information to him on personnel problems, group conflict, and other types of human relations problems?

20. TEAMWORK. To what extent do you have a sense of being a part of your supervisor's team?

21. ACCEPTANCE OF DECISIONS. What percentage of the time do you accept decisions of your supervisor? (For example, do you implement his orders and requests by interpreting both what his intention is as well as what he actually says?)

Intergroup Relations:

The following questions deal with the relation that your work group has to the others listed below. Fill in the space on the answer sheet that best describes what your relation is to these groups. For example, questions 1–5 ask, "What percentage of the time is there confidence and trust in each of these other groups?"

A "1" on the scale indicates that 10% or less of the time there is confidence and trust; in contrast, a "9" shows that 90% or more of the time trust and confidence exists. Question 1 deals with the relation of your work group to the group listed under A; Question 2 looks at how your work group is related to group listed under B; and so forth.

Please answer all questions.

Relation of your group (particularly how you feel) to each of the following:

Intergroup Variables

Behavioral Patterns

	A*	B*	C*	D*	E*
1–5 What percentage of the time is there trust and confidence in each of these groups?	1	2	3	4	5
6–10 What percentage of communications with each of these groups is accurate and complete?	6	7	8	9	10
11–15 In the normal working relationship called for by the job, what percentage of the time does each of these groups readily cooperate and provide assistance?	11	12	13	14	15
16–20 When your group is affected by decisions made by these other groups, what percentage of the time are these decisions accepted with good will (such as where necessary adjustments are made without protesting)?	16	17	18	19	20

*The researcher writes in the groups before the questionnaire is handed out.

THE CONTEXT: STRUCTURAL ELEMENTS OF ORGANIZATIONS

The general thesis is that individual, intragroup, and intergroup behavior is caused by identifiable factors. An individual moves into a structured context and his behavior is partly the product of the forces that flow from the context and, partly, a consequence of his personality. We cannot yet identify all variables that affect behavior, understand completely their interaction, or know precisely what weights to place on them. Still, we can identify many of the factors that exert a pervasive influence on behavior in all institutional contexts.

These variables are classified under three main headings: *structural variables, leadership style,* and *personality*. The structural variables, which are further classified as primary and secondary variables, are set forth in Figure 2-2. Each variable is defined along a continuum, so that the structural features of any organization can be described in terms of these variables and the features that make organizations similar or dissimilar identified. Thus, two hospitals may be very different but a hospital and an industrial organization quite alike in terms of these analytical dimensions.

Organizations that lie mostly on the left ends of the continua may be called *simple*; those on the right, *complex*. Most organizations lie between these extremes. An organization may be quite large and yet be relatively simple if there is little specialization (independent work flow) and few spatial-physical barriers among personnel. The authority relationships, controls, and information system may be only partially formalized and detailed. Whatever the combination, in any case, it is possible to develop a profile of the organization and of the forces associated with the variables at particular points on the continua.

The analysis and survey of the literature will show how each of the factors affects behavior. Some difficulties in doing this exist since it is a rare project that explores the three dimensions of individual, group, and intergroup behavior. We will need to draw upon many studies to provide an integration of the multiple effects of each of the variables.

LEADERSHIP STYLE

At middle or lower level management, the structural variables—both primary and secondary—are largely fixed. Over a period of time, managers at these levels may be able to make some changes, but to a large extent the variables define the environment within which the manager operates.

© King Features Syndicate, 1973.

FIGURE 2-2. Structural factors affecting behavior in organizations

A. Primary Structural Variables

	Simple Organization							Complex Organization	
	1	2	3	4	5	6	7	8	9
1. Size:	Small .... Large
2. Work Flow:	Independent .... Interdependent
3. Tasks:	Programmed .... Unprogrammed
4. Spatial-Physical Barriers:	Concentrated .... Dispersed

B. Secondary Structural Variables

	1	2	3	4	5	6	7	8	9
1. Formal Authority Relationships:	Diffuse .... Specific
a. Delegation:	Decentralized .... Centralized
b. Departmentation:	Interdependent .... Autonomous
2. Formal Control System:	Institutional .... Individual
a. Standards:	Low .... High
b. Rewards:	Undifferentiated .... Differentiated
3. Formal Information System:	Spontaneous .... Rationalized
a. Networks:	Complete .... Single
b. Channel Density:	Multiple .... Restricted

Leadership is defined by the way in which a supervisor relates to his superiors and other groups and the way in which he deals with subordinates. A number of important aspects of leadership directly affect the individual, intragroup, and intergroup behavior patterns. A supervisor may encourage or discourage participation; his direction may be laissez faire, general, or close; he may permit broad deviation from rules and policies or demand exact adherence; he may place emphasis upon representing the interests of subordinates to superiors or other groups or, contrarily, assume actively the role of spokesman of the views of higher management and staff groups; he may rely primarily on rewards to motivate subordinates and others, or he may emphasize the use of penalties.

Each of these elements of leadership influences the behavior of subordinates and other groups. Any supervisor can be described in terms of these leadership characteristics to define his leadership style or profile. The overall profiles of three alternative styles can be referred to as *democratic, mixed,* and *directive,* as indicated in Figure 2-3.

FIGURE 2-3.   Elements of leadership style

	Democratic			Mixed			Directive	
	1 2 3		4	5	6	7	8 9	
Participation	Extensive						Restrictive	
Direction	Loose						Close	
Rule Adherence	Lax						Strict	
Representation	Upward						Downward	
Inducements	Rewards						Penalties	

The consequences to the individual, intragroup, and intergroup behavior of each aspect can be explored. We will review the literature broadly to unravel what effects each of these has on behavior. Understanding the effects of a particular leadership style—a given point on each scale and the relative weight of each dimension—provides a basis for prediction. While high precision is not obtainable at this time, much is known about the relations of leadership style to behavior.

PERSONALITY DIMENSIONS

The structural variables and leadership patterns create the context within which individuals move. A typical behavioral response is likely from a set of forces created by the context. Most individuals, for instance, will react similarly when under increased stress. It is clear, though, that there will be both a mean response and a range around that mean. The many experiments on the influence of group consensus over individual opinions illustrate both a norm and a range of responses to the same context.

To achieve greater predictability of response, personality must be introduced. Where personality isn't explicitly introduced, the normal or typical reaction is emphasized implicitly in tracing out the effects of structural and leadership variables.

"*. . . I told the chef what you said about the soufflé . . .*"

Cartoon courtesy *Better Homes and Gardens.* © Meredith Corporation, 1973.

SUMMARY OF SYSTEMS MODEL

Figure 2-4 provides an overall perspective. In summary, our focus is upon individual, group, and intergroup behavior and the factors that influence their development significantly. Structural variables, leadership, and per-

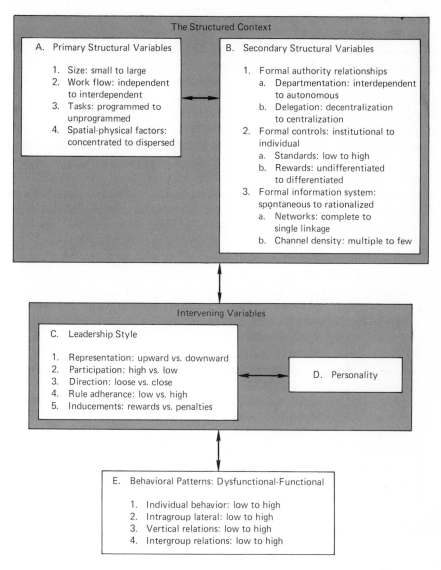

FIGURE 2-4. Framework for analyzing determinants of behavior in organizations

sonality are identified as important sets of influences affecting behavior. Our concern is both with the way in which each factor influences behavior and with the interaction of the variables. Ultimately, we aim to develop an overall understanding of these interactions.

THEORETICAL RATIONALE
FOR THE MODEL

Structural Variables. If an organization is viewed as a behavioral sytem, the primary variables contribute to forces as we move along the continua to the right. Complexity of a group increases with larger size, greater interdependence in work flow, less programmed tasks, and increased physical-spatial barriers. The factors of increased organizational size, more interdependent work flow, less-programmed tasks, and increased physical-spatial barriers exert forces toward dysfunctional aspects of individual behavior, and intragroup and intergroup relations. Typical symptoms are reduced commitment, breakdown in communication, and increased conflict. The spontaneous methods and interpersonal interactions that are adequate for coordination and motivation in simple organizations break down with increased complexity.

These forces may be offset by changes in the secondary variables. As the organization increases in complexity, formal provisions aid in achieving coordination; consequently, authority relationships are specified. Managers are appointed to coordinate and supervise group efforts (formal groups are broken into smaller units and levels are introduced into the organization); an attempt is made to restrict individual decisions to a common set of premises (policies, procedures, and rules that restrict the discretion of members to make decisions are set forth); that is, the organization moves toward centralization.

Problems of coordination increase as the organization becomes more specialized. Specialized functional departments are replaced by autonomous groupings that place different specialists in major project groupings to shift problems of coordination to the smaller formal units. This added complexity provides the rationale for establishing a set of formal authority relations to supplement and partially replace informal understandings.

Similarly, increased complexity creates a need for a formal system of controls. In a small group, personal relations, high interaction possibilities, and the relative ease with which members can identify with overall goals provide informal support and satisfactions. These conditions contribute to individual motivation and incentive for participation and commitment. These factors rapidly lose their influence as an organization increases in complexity. Formal controls take the place of the informal system. Explicit individual and group standards must be set, an evaluation system created to determine whether the standards are met, and a formal system introduced to reward those who meet the standards and apply penalties against those who don't.

Furthermore, it becomes necessary to provide formally for communication since the informal system of communication breaks down as complexity increases. A situation where all individuals have equal access to all other individuals is replaced by more rationalized and restricted contacts (i.e., movement from a complete network toward a single linkage). Informal face-to-face communication breaks down because the multiplicity of paths for communicating among the centers causes overloading, queuing, and break-down of flow of information; informal face-to-face and telephone contacts are sharply restricted and replaced by more specific means such as formal written memos and reports (decreased density of channels is imposed). In sum, informal spontaneous methods are replaced or supplemented by formal provisions for communication.

In review, as the primary variables move to the right along their continua, they create forces toward disintegration of the organization. The secondary variables of explicit authority, control systems, and the information system are formal provisions for offsetting these forces. If they are poorly designed, the mediating variables will add to the disintegrative influences on the organization. This point may be further clarified by Table 2-1 where the focus is upon the interaction between the primary and secondary variables.

TABLE 2-1. Organizational Types

		Values on Primary Structural Variables		
		Low (1–3)	Medium (4–6)	High (7–9)
Values on Secondary Structural Variables	Low (1–3)	11 Simple	12	13
	Medium (4–6)	21	22 Intermediate	23
	High (7–9)	31	32	33 Complex

Some organizations try to retain the same formal structure, control systems, and information systems as they move from cell 11 to 13. This is likely to cause increased behavioral problems and decreased organizational effectiveness. Cell 13 is illustrated by collegial-type structures that are identified by their lack of formal authority, formal controls, and formal information systems. This type of organization exists in many universities and in mental hospitals that attempt to create a "milieu environment." These environments probably require that several of the primary factors be held at a low or medium level (cells 11, 12, 21, or 22) to maintain viable behavioral relations.

When the organization is simple, little need exists for formal secondary relations; if these are introduced, the formal provisions are likely to cause undesired behavioral reactions.

Leadership. When a supervisor moves into a structured context, he may be able to offset partially the forces created by the structural variables. The way in which the leadership functions are carried out determines how far they will contribute to or adversely affect the ability of subordinates or others to be effective. The supervisor, for instance, may be able to introduce some flexibility into a situation that is rigid and nonadaptable to the conditions.

In top management, a set of decisions in the past may have created a structured context that has highly negative effects on behavior. Here, one test of leadership will be whether the structural variables can be redefined to create a more favorable working situation. Some situations are probably structured in such a way that no supervisor, regardless of his level of skill, could be effective. He may be restricted from making the changes that would permit essential innovations. There certainly are instances where this extreme situation occurs. More typically, though, the situation has both favorable and unfavorable aspects. The effectiveness of the supervision at all levels of management also rests on the manner in which the functions of leadership are carried out.

Considerable interaction probably exists between the context and leadership style. If we look at the different combinations of structure and leadership in Table 2-2, it is likely that different leadership styles would be appropriate

TABLE 2-2. Combinations of Organization Types and Leadership Styles

| | | Organization Types | | |
		Simple	Intermediate	Complex
	Democratic	11	12	13
Leadership Style	Mixed	21	22	23
	Directive	31	32	33

for different contexts. Probably, democratic leadership is highly functional in simple organizations (cell 11) but becomes less effective as organizations become more complex (movement from cells 11 to 13). In turn, movement from democratic to directive leadership (cells 11 to 31) would be expected to produce adverse consequences under simple organizations but functional effects under complex organizations (movement from cells 13 to 33). Section

V appraises the research to determine the extent to which these interaction effects occur.

Personality. As with leadership, we are likely to find some interaction between personality types and context. It appears reasonable that in highly structured contexts—cells 31, 32, and 33 of Table 2-1—one who is low on independence and high in authoritarian qualities would find these restrictions acceptable. Contrarily, he would most likely be uncomfortable in the contexts of cells 11, 12, and 13 of Table 2-1. Similarly, where context and leadership style are combined, as in Table 2-2, certain personalities are likely to be more receptive to the open situation of 11, and quite different personalities to condition 33. Whether formal systems are appropriate to the context or not, some individuals are more concerned than others with clear statements of what to do and what not to do. The former will seek or at least accept readily the formal restrictions of a tightly defined context and authoritarian leadership style.

General and Unique Job Characteristics

Baldamus distinguishes between the general physical conditions of the work environment and the specific characteristics of the job.[2] He develops the thesis that the worker gradually adapts to the physical conditions that are common to all the workers but becomes more sensitive to the special characteristics of his job. (In our frame of reference, the latter are the structural variables.) "Specific factors" refer to the concrete type of work; "conditions of work" identify the general physical environment of a job. In an iron foundry, types of work such as floor moulding, bench moulding, metal pouring, and cleaning of castings each have specific characteristics. The conditions of heat, dust, and noise are general in the shop.

This distinction between specific and general, or between type of work and conditions of work, is important in the context of motivation because we are going to show that it matters a great deal to a worker whether he is a floor moulder or a bench moulder, while he is indifferent to heat and dirt. To demonstrate this point more clearly, we shall assume that the worker's willingness varies with his emotional attitude towards work: *if*, for instance, he dislikes his job, this will influence his effort unfavorably. Our problem is then reduced to showing that workers maintain distinctive likes and dislikes with regard to the type of work, but that the conditions of work do not produce any definite emotional attitudes.

---

[2]W. Baldamus, "Type of Work and Motivation," *British Journal of Sociology*, 2 (1951), 45, slightly abridged.

Why this is so will readily be seen if the psychological process of adaptation is taken into account. Most of what is known of adaptation was found inadvertently, chiefly in the course of studies concerned with the effect of working conditions on capacity where adaptation effects appeared as a by-product, undesired but difficult to eliminate. If, however, we are dealing with willingness (and attitudes), these effects are important; they refer to the fact that a worker, in time, is getting used to the conditions surrounding his job. Many observations have been made, and it is also common experience that distasteful general conditions affect the attitude of newcomers but are rarely objected to by the seasoned workers.

On the other hand, there is no evidence that emotional attitudes toward the specific characteristics of the type of work are similarly subject to the wearing-off effects of adaptation. On the contrary: not only is there no adaptation, but the opposite process takes place; specific differences between jobs become in time more and more crystallized into very definite and consistent notions of like and dislikes. While distasteful general conditions of work tend, subjectively, slowly to lose their distinctive features and merge into a vaguely familiar if not homey atmosphere, the specific details and peculiarities inherent in a given type of work may gradually become more articulate and more accentuated in the worker's mind. We must therefore conclude that the specific conditions inherent in the type of work are more decisive to the study of motivation than the general conditions.

Qualifications to the Approach. Several additional factors may explain differences in behavior, even where the more significant factors affecting behavior have been identified. Perhaps the most important additional factor is multiple membership. A description of the structured context is usually carried out within a single organization, such as the work organization. But individuals belong to multiple groups and organizations—family, social, fraternal, religious, service, professional, and educational—as well as work groups. Each of these groups exerts forces upon the individual; each demands that the individual allocate a portion of his time, attention, and energy to it and that he follow a particular path. Since time, energy, and resources are largely fixed, they must be allocated among competing demands. Those forces that are most diffuse, easiest to evade, or result in the least penalty are likely to be sacrificed. A priority list will be established, and those forces having the least short- and long-term consequences probably will be evaded first. The behavior of a member of multiple groups may be less predictable than that of a person who belongs to only a few groups.

In our society, priority is usually given to the demands of the work organization. Success or failure in this context has implications throughout an individual's life. His sense of personal adequacy, his income, his status in other groups (including his family, community, and religious groups) typically are tied closely to his status in the work organization. Thus, where adjustments must be made to multiple demands, they are likely to be made in secondary organizations such as religious, social, or community groups. This means that forces created by structural and leadership styles in work organizations probably affect behavior most pervasively. If we identify a set of forces exerted by the structural contexts and leadership of social organizations, the ability to predict behavior from them is probably less than in work organizations.

Our model could be expanded to include a systematic assessment of the influence of secondary organizations. This should be particularly useful where two or more organizations exert conflicting pressures on an individual. In industrial organizations, labor unions often exert forces that complement or contradict the influence of management. This may be true particularly for people at the operating level. At the management or staff levels, professional associations may establish policies that support or offset the influences of the administration. In an organization such as a hospital, for instance, the American Medical Association may establish a set of influences on doctors as demanding as those emanating from the hospital administration. Where two or more organizations exert influence on individuals in the work setting, this is likely to affect the ability to predict behavioral patterns unless both sets of forces are identified.

Although individuals are more likely to respond to the influences of a work organization than to the forces of secondary organizations, persons in certain roles may be more subject to influences from other groups. Working wives with children may be more responsive to family demands than those of the work organizations. Students are more likely to react to the demands of the classroom than to those of their part-time jobs. Highly religious individuals may set higher priorities on meeting the demands of their churches than of their jobs; the new immigrant to a city from a foreign land or the rural South may react more directly to influence of peers, or community groups such as gangs, than to the job. In most cases, though, the bulk of blue- and white-collar workers will be more responsive to demands of the work organization than of secondary organizations.

Another factor not included, but relevant particularly where short-term effects are observed, is the nature of the ongoing group, such as its cohesiveness and accepted norms. The nature of intragroup relations partly determines, for instance, how external forces are handled. Suppose, for example, group incentives are replaced by individual incentives. A group that is highly cohesive may be able to maintain the old relationships, even though a set of forces has been created to break these down. The group norms may be more important in influencing the group's behavior than the external reward-penalties applied by management. In a group where cohesiveness is low, the possibilities of change are usually greater. Implicit in our approach is that the character of the ongoing relations or existing behavioral patterns are modified rapidly by the forces created by structural and leadership factors.

Our model does not include environmental differences that exert demands on an organization. It is assumed that these factors are directly relevant to organizational effectiveness but of less importance in the behavioral patterns. It is evident, though, that certain behavior dimensions (such as turnover and absenteeism) are affected by the state of the labor market. If jobs are easy to obtain, turnover is likely to be greater—other factors being equal. At one point, these factors will have to be considered.

An underlying thesis of our approach is that we can arrive at viable generalizations that apply to any institution in any cultural context. If there is a similarly structured context in the United States and Japan, we predict that the same behavior patterns will emerge. This, of course, remains to be seen; we will review some evidence that supports this viewpoint and some that questions it. On a logical basis, though, the values associated with work organizations vis-à-vis other organizations probably differ in different societies. In developing societies, for instance, there may be greater response to the demands of the family or tribe than to those of the work organization. It is likely, though, that generalizations made are applicable at least to industrialized societies.

It is useful to keep a perspective of what is covered by the approach and what is not. We take the context, leadership, and personality as given and consider the influence they exert over behavior. This analytical simplification reduces the complexity of the problem. In practice, structural variables influence leadership and vice versa; multiple factors determine the personality types that predominate in an organization, including selection procedures, methods used to induce members to stay, and methods used to force out undesired members. While structural variables, leadership style, and personality influence behavior, the influence process also operates in the opposite direction. Emerging behavioral patterns partially affect the formulation of structural variables and development of leadership style. Further, since behavior isn't unidimensional, one aspect of behavior affects another. One can explore any of these relationships. Part of the complexity of the literature of organizations is that these questions are being explored by different researchers, who often propose their emphasis as *the* key to unlock the puzzle of organizations. The approaches are complementary, but it takes a well-developed analytical model to identify their complementarity. We will only be concerned with one aspect of the many relations that could be developed.

One can also explore the path that behavior takes as it moves over time from one equilibrium to another. As size of a group increases, for instance, it is relatively easy to develop the behavior patterns in one time period and compare them with the patterns in a second time period. It is more complex to trace the path of change between these two points. This form of dynamic analysis would be useful but is beyond the scope of this book.

This is a behavior model and not an effectiveness model. The emerging behavioral patterns presumably are directly relevant to the effectiveness of the organization. In some organizations, such as hospitals, they may be highly related to the organization's output. In other organizational contexts, the emerging behavioral patterns have relatively little impact on effectiveness. For instance, it may be that in governmental agencies concerned with placing unemployed handicapped workers, this goal is principally affected by inter-organizational relations with referral agencies, training centers, private and public placement agencies, and employers. If the units are able to achieve good interorganizational relations, they may perform well in placement. Besides the behavioral patterns, the nature of equipment, capital, resources, the general permissiveness of the environment such as economic conditions and other external variables influence the effectiveness of an organization. Our attention is restricted to setting forth a set of structural factors and leadership systematically and developing how each affects behavior.

Several substantial benefits are associated with the model, of which several deserve emphasis. Presenting a set of variables in model form imposes an analytical discipline in defining variables rigorously and defining them so that they are complementary. This is associated with other advantages. It increases sharply the additivity of studies. The use of the model permits empirical work to be systematically compared. This contrasts with the situation up to this time where it has been difficult to integrate the findings of different researchers.

The approach increases the possibility of doing controlled studies when one or more variables are systematically explored. In doing field studies, one can describe the context and then select units where, at most, only a few variables contrast. In laboratory studies, an awareness of the multiple factors that may affect behavior provides the analytical framework to vary systematically only the factors being explored. This contrasts sharply with the situation where researchers do not have a theoretical basis for rejecting the charge that other factors may be causing the results rather than those that they are identifying.

The explicit statement of the variables that affect behavior contributes to the ability to review critically, assess, and integrate the literature. Critical review is aided by an explicit statement of the factors that affect behavior but are not recognized by the author. Contradictions in the literature often can be reconciled and integrated. An article by Miller and Hamblin illustrates the value of a larger perspective.[3] Reviewing over twenty previous studies, they were able to identify two variables that were affecting the results, whereas the researchers thought they were dealing with only one. Miller and Hamblin's framework permitted them to reconcile the results of more than a score of studies.

The model also places the determinants of behavior in a larger perspective. There are two questions, in particular, that a model highlights:

1. What weights must be placed on each of the factors that influences behavior, i.e., what is the relative influence of each variable?
2. Are there linear, curvilinear, or discontinuous relationships as one moves along these scales?

When variables are analyzed alone, it is possible to talk about the general directions of influence and gloss over the absolute amounts of influence. When the variables are interacting, specific judgments must be made upon both directions and amounts. For instance, spatial concentration contributes to intra- and intergroup cohesion. An individual incentive system contributes to intra- and intergroup disintegration. These statements only suggest the general direction of influence. When an individual incentive system is applied to a group that is spatially concentrated, these two variables exert influence in opposing directions. If one is to diagnose or predict the outcome of these two influences, he must determine the relative weight of each. Even though we cannot provide definitive answers to these two problems, something is gained by directing attention to them, and some research provides partial answers.

Finally, the identification of variables affecting behavior provides handholds for the practitioner. The model expressly identifies multiple variables that may influence behavior, thus providing the leverage necessary for achieving change. In many cases it identifies the parameters that restrict changes—also a valuable thing to know.

PART I

DISCUSSION QUESTIONS

1. Katz refers to three types of behavioral requirements essential for a functioning of the organization. What are they?
2. Melcher lists a number of aspects of vertical and intergroup relationships that he

[3]Keith Miller and Robert L. Hamblin, "Interdependence, Differential Rewarding, and Productivity," *American Sociological Review*, 28 (1963), 768–78.

contends also are important for the functioning of organizations. In what way are these behavioral patterns important to the functioning of the organization?

3. In Melcher's framework, what role does personality play in predicting behavior?

4. You have been asked to present to a group of supervisors the way in which they can influence behavior in their organization. Explain to them the "Melcher" perspective on these issues.

5. What are some of the factors that reduce the degree one can predict behavior using Melcher's structural-process model?

6. How would you use this model to explain differences in behavior among departments in an organization? To explain changes in behavior through time?

7. Suppose you are appointed as supervisor of a department where individual behavior and intragroup relations are sharply dysfunctional: commitment is low, frustration high, absenteeism, and turnover are high; cooperation, communication, and interaction among group members is poor. How would this model help you to identify what could be done to change and improve these behavioral patterns?

8. Melcher calls this a systems model. Can this be justified since he doesn't include aspects of the environment within which an organization operates? In what way do all system approaches set limits on their analysis?

II

PRIMARY STRUCTURAL VARIABLES

3

SIZE:
The Pressures from Numbers

INTRODUCTION

The size of a group or an organization is of broad significance to behavioral patterns. There is little that is intuitive about the way in which size of a group exerts influence. Nevertheless, it is difficult to escape from the pressure created by size of the unit.

The history of earliest times suggests that getting a large number of people to share in a common task is difficult. The practical difficulties of managing increases rapidly as the number of persons rises. The task of managing 1,000 people or more, for instance, is more than twice as complex as managing 500.

Historically, organizations have been small. At the end of the fifth century, one of the largest employers in Greece had 120 men making shields.[1] The eighteenth century produced the modern factories with the steam engine harnessed to the loom for the first time. Despite an abundance and cheapness of labor, and the lack of restrictions on how it was used, factories in the mid-eighteenth century employed less than 600 persons—about the size of the maintenance staff in some plants today.[2] By the end of the century, the Soho works of Boulton and Watt, regarded by Lyndall Urwich as the first scientifically managed enterprise of modern times, employed 1,000.[3]

Organizational subgroups tend to be small. In one study of the board of directors of a bank, the size range depended upon whether it was an action or a nonaction subgroup.[4] The average size of the action-taking groups was

---

[1]R. W. Revans, "Human Relations, Management and Size," in E. M. Hugh-Jones, ed., *Human Relations and Modern Management* (Chicago: Quadrangle Books, 1959), p. 183.

[2]Ibid.

[3]Ibid., p. 186.

[4]John James, "A Preliminary Study of Size Determinant in Small Group Interaction," *American Sociological Review*, 16 (1951), 474–77.

"Many hands make light the work."

Drawing by O'Brian; © 1971 The New Yorker Magazine, Inc.

6.5 while the nonaction groups' was 14. Size of subcommittees in the U.S. government range from 2 to 12 with 5.4 the average in the Senate and from 3 to 26 with an average of 7.8 in the House. In a survey of the size of groups that spontaneously form in a broad variety of contexts, over 97 percent had only four members or less.[5] While this type of data is hardly conclusive, it is suggestive of the stresses that occur as group size increases.

Caplow has provided an intuitively appealing way of classifying different size groups,[6] based on interaction possibilities. In *small primary groups*, which ordinarily range in size from two to about twenty, each member interacts with every other member. In the *medium group*, one or more members may establish pair relationahips with all of the others, but most members only develop pair relationships with some of the other members. Under ordinary conditions, the medium group ranges from about fifty to perhaps one thousand members. In the *large group*, one or more members may be recognized and may interact with all of the other members, but with only one-way recognition; i.e., a key member may be recognized by all others but may not recognize all of them. The large groups range from about one thousand members to an upper limit of ten thousand. The *giant group* is too large to permit direct contact of any individual with all of the others. However, certain personalities may be recognized by all other members, with the aid of mass communication. A giant group has ten thousand or more members.

Measuring the Size of Units

Caplow's method of classifying groups is simple and intuitively appealing. An alternative to this is provided, with each level scaled separately. Thus, a group at the bottom of the organization may be scaled the same as the plant or division. This is a less intuitive measure but should be analytically more useful.

The size of a formal unit is defined by the number of subordinates formally assigned to that unit. In other terms, it is the number of employees for which the supervisor or executive is responsible. This includes those directly reporting to him and those at lower levels in his group. Thus, the size of groups varies, depending on the level or organization (the higher the level, the greater the number) and absolute number of each level.

---

[5]Ibid., pp. 474–76.

[6]Theodore Caplow, "Organizational Size," *Administrative Science Quarterly*, 1 (1957), 486–87.

Operationally, the size is defined in terms of a scale. The absolute numbers are interpreted into an analytical scale by specifying approximately where stress for subgroupings sharply increases.

Size Scale

Small								Large
1	2	3	4	5	6	7	8	9

Table 3-1 provides the data for classifying a unit along the scale. Levels are defined from bottom beginning with first-line supervisor.

TABLE 3-1. Number of Individuals in a Formal Unit and the Corresponding Values on a Size Scale

No. of Levels	Size Scale								
	Small 1	2	3	4	5	6	7	8	Large 9
First	1–5	6–10	11–15	16–20	21–25	26–30	31–35	36–40	41–
Second	1–30	31–60	61–90	91–120	121–150	151–180	181–210	211–240	241–
Third	1–125	126–250	251–325 ...					...	1125–

NATURE OF THE LITERATURE

There are a number of good surveys of the literature on size.[7] The research literature can be broadly classified by the size of the unit and by the

[7]"Class Size," *Encyclopedia of Educational Research*, 1941, pp. 197–200; Robert F. Bales, A. Paul Hare, and Edgar F. Borgatta, "Structure and Dynamics of Small Groups: A Review of Four Variables," in Joseph P. Gittler, ed., *A Review of Sociology* (New York: John Wiley & Sons, 1957), pp. 391–422; A. Paul Hare, "Group Size," *Handbook of Small Group Research*, 1962, pp. 244–45; Theodore Caplow, "Organizational Size," pp. 484–505; Bernard P. Indik, "Organizational Size and Member Participation: Some Empirical Tests of Alternative Explanations," *Human Relations*, 18 (November 1965), 339–50; Lyman W. Porter and Edward E. Lawler III, "Properties of Organizational Structure in Relation to Job Attitudes and Job Behavior," *Psychological Bulletin*, 64 (July 1965), 34–43; Roger C. Barket et al, *Big School, Small School: Study of the Effects of High School Size on the Behavior and Experiences of Students* (University of Kansas: Midwest Psychological Field Station, 1962), pp. 42–70.

relations being explored. Many of the authors regard an organization as a black box and relate how the size of the box is correlated with particular structural characteristics;[8] others develop the relation of size to output or behavioral patterns.[9] Other field studies focus upon small groups within an organization such as sections, or work groups, and are typically concerned with how size affects group processes.[10]

Our principal attention is on some of the better field studies that have been done on major subunits such as plants or branches, subgroups in these units, and laboratory experiments of small groups. Our emphasis in the chapter moves from explaining effects associated with size to a partial understanding of the group processes associated with those effects.

THE SIZE EFFECT: FIELD STUDIES

The literature consistently finds that as size increases, absenteeism, turnover, accident rates, and conflict rise. Size adversely affects the quality of work, efficiency, and productivity of units. This holds true whether one is studying coal mines, factories, hospitals, or other organizations. Table 3-2 contains most of the key studies. The type of organizational unit studied, the size range of the unit, the dependent variable, and the relationship that was found are summarized.

[8]Frederick W. Terrien, "Too Much Room at the Top," *Social Forces*, 37 (1958–59), 298–305; Frederick W. Terrien and Donald L. Mills, "The Effect of Changing Size upon the Internal Structure of Organization," *American Sociological Review*, 20 (1955), 11–13; Mason Haire, "Size, Shape, and Function in Industrial Organizations," *Human Organizations*, 14 (1955–56), 17–22; Richard H. Hall, J. Eugene Haas, and Normal J. Johnson, "Organizational Size, Complexity, and Formalization," *American Sociological Review*, 32 (December 1967), 903–12; Peter Blau, Wolf V. Heydebrand, and Robert E. Stauffer, "Structure of Small Bureaucracies," *American Sociological Review*, 31 (April 1966), 179–91; Peter M. Blau and Richard A. Schoenherr, *The Structure of Organizations* (New York: Basic Books, 1971); D. S. Pugh et al, "The Context of Organizational Structures," *Administrative Science Quarterly*, 14, No. 1 (March 1969), 91–114; Peter M. Blau, "A Formal Theory of Differentiation in Organizations," *American Sociological Review*, 35 (1970), 201–18. See also Marshall W. Myer, "Constraints in Analyzing Data on Organizational Structures," *American Sociological Review*, 36 (1971), 293–97; Lawrence G. Hrebiniak and Joseph A. Alutto, "A Comparative Organizational Study of Performance and Size Correlates in Inpatient Psychiatric Departments," *Administrative Science Quarterly*, 18 (September 1973), 365–82.

[9]Sergio Talacchi, "Organization Size, Individual Attitudes and Behavior: An Empirical Study," *Administrative Science Quarterly*, 5 (1960–61), 398–420; Joseph W. Scott and Mohamed El-Assal, "Multi-university, University Size, University Quality and Student Protest: An Empirical Study," *American Sociological Review*, 34 (October 1969), 375–86; Norbert J. Esser and George B. Strother, "Rule Interpretation as an Indicator of Style of Management," *Personnel Psychology*, 15 (1962), 375–86; Paul Lazarsfeld and Wagner Thielens, Jr., *The Academic Mind* (Glencoe, Ill.: Free Press, 1958), pp. 18–26.

[10]Edwin J. Thomas and Clinton F. Fink, "Effects of Group Size," *Psychological Bulletin*, 60 (1963), 371–84.

TABLE 3-2. Studies Exploring Effects of Size of Major Subunits on Behavior and Output

Author	Type of Organization Unit	Size Range of Units	Dependent Variables	Correlation of Size to Dependent Variable
Worthy (1950)	Retail Stores	Not stated	Morale	Negative
Katzell (1961)	Warehouses	13–85	Efficiency	−.24
			Quality of Work	+.12
			Turnover	−.07
Baumkartel and	Airline Offices	172–283;381–639	Absenteeism	Curvilineary
Sobol (1959)	Hospitals	1330–1554;3174–3205	Accident Rates	Positive
Revans (1959)	Coal Mines	10–2500+	Absenteeism	Positive
		10–1000+	Accident Rates	
			British Mines	Positive
			American Mines	Curvilineary
	Factories	70–3500	Absenteeism	Positive
	Gas Works	67–3430	Tardiness	Curvilineary
	Coal Mines	Below 500 to 2500+	Absences and Accidents	.91
			Strikes	Positive
Georgopolos and	Delivery	15–61	Vertical Communication	−.46
Tannenbaum (1961)	Branches		Intragroup Relations	−.48
			Job Satisfaction	−.47
			Absenteeism	−.53
Indik (1965)	Auto Dealerships	25–132	Vertical Communications	−.35
			Intragroup Relations	−.33
			Job Satisfaction	−.11
			Meeting Attendance	−.34

TABLE 3-2 (cont.)

Author	Type of Organization Unit	Size Range of Units	Dependent Variables	Correlation of Size to Dependent Variable
Tannenbaum (1957–58)	Voluntary Organizations	101–2 + 989	Vertical Communication	–.30
			Intragroup Relations	–.13
			Job Satisfaction	–.30
			Meeting Attendance	–.42
Cleland (1955)	Manufacturing	100–5000+	Turnover and Absenteeism	Positive
			Strikes	Positive
			Commitment	Negative
			Superior/Subordinate Relations	Negative
Marriott (1949)	Groups in Manufacturing Plants	10–50+	Productivity	Negative
Revans (1959)	Coal Mines	250–1500+	Productivity	Negative

Little empirical work was done on the effects of size until 1950. James C. Worthy, a sociologist working in an applied research capacity for Sears and Roebuck, published his findings on the factors that were related to morale in the firm's stores.[11] He concluded that there probably is no more important influence on attitudes and morale than sheer size of organization. Morale declines with increasing size, even though the same personnel and management policies are applied. The reason for higher morale in smaller units is that employees have a better opportunity to know each other. Cooperation between individuals and departments can develop on a more personal, informal basis and not be dependent on impersonal systems and administrative controls. In a large mail-order plant, those who control an inventory of thousands of items and those who handle the merchandise must work in close coordination with each other. However, the large number of people in each group means few personal relations develop across divisional lines, so coordination between the separate but related activities must be accomplished through a complex system of procedures. In a small retail store, the situation is different. Sales people, office clerks, and the few employees in the receiving and shipping rooms know each other on a first-name basis; cooperation between them is a matter of close associates working together. Cooperation develops spontaneously; it doesn't require orders or a system of formal procedures. An organization such as this operates primarily through face-to-face relationships and only secondarily through impersonal, institutionalized relationships.

In the smaller organization, employees see where they fit into the organization and the significance of their jobs in the larger picture; knowing where they fit supports cooperation. In large, complex organizations, cooperation depends on a status system that defines working relationships in functional terms. In such organizations, interaction is more segmented than in smaller, simpler structures where people know each other and where cooperation involves a larger part of their personalities. The record clerk in a mail-order plant has difficulty seeing beyond her routine task of processing inventory control cards; stockmen and order fillers are a world apart. The clerk in a small store can see the relationship between her work and that of other employees and the manner in which all their efforts dovetail into the overall task of serving the customer. Each individual job takes on more meaning and importance because it is a necessary part of this larger function and because that relationship can be seen and appreciated by all members of the group.

A further advantage of smaller organizations is that the regular contacts between the executives and workers result in friendlier, easier relationships.

[11]James C. Worthy, "Factors Influencing Employee Morale," *Harvard Business Review*, 28 (1950), 268.

The "big boss" is not some remote, little-known personage but an actual, flesh-and-blood individual who can be evaluated through personal acquaintance. This contributes to a better understanding of each other's problems and points of view and facilitates working out difficulties that arise.

In summary, the smaller organization represents a simpler social system than does the larger unit. There are fewer people, fewer levels in the organizational hierarchy, and less subdivision of labor. It is easier for the employee to adapt himself to the simpler system and win a place in it. His work is more meaningful, both to himself and to his associates; they can see its relation and importance to other functions and to the organization as a whole. The closer relations between the employee and higher executives are only one aspect—but an important one—of the simple and better integrated social system of the smaller organization.

SIZE, ABSENTEEISM, PUNCTUALITY, AND ACCIDENT RATES

Studies have explored the relation of size to absenteeism in warehouses,[12] airlines offices,[13] coal fields,[14] plants where electrolytic products and chemicals are manufactured,[15] gas plants in the London area,[16] and gas plants in Great Britain.[17] Size is directly correlated with absenteeism rates. Revans concludes that on the basis of the studies that he reviewed, absenteeism and size can be described by a logarithmic relationship; that is, the percentage increase in the size of the firm is correlated with the percentage increase in the average *absenteeism rate*.[18] The only study that did not support this relationship was by Katzel, Barrett, and Parker. The warehouses they explored operated under standard work methods and procedures and ranged from thirteen to eighty-three employees. In a simple correlation analysis, they found no relationship between size and turnover $(-.07)$.[19]

Punctuality as well as absence shows a size effect. Table 3-3 summarizes

[12]Raymond S. Katzell, Richard S. Barrett, and Treadway C. Parker, "Job Satisfaction, Job Performance, and Situational Characteristics," *Journal of Applied Psychology*, 45 (April 1961), 65–72.

[13]Howard Baumgartel and Ronald Sobol, "Background and Organizational Factors in Absenteeism," *Personnel Psychology*, 12 (1959), 431–43.

[14]R. W. Revans, "Human Relations, Management and Size," p. 198.

[15]Ibid., pp. 198–99.

[16]Ibid., p. 196.

[17]Ibid.

[18]Ibid.

[19]Katzel, Barrett and Parker, "Job Satisfaction, Job Performance, and Situational Characteristics," p. 67.

the employees' tardiness record in five randomly selected gas works in London.[20]

TABLE 3-3. Times Late per Man by Length of Service and Size of Plant at Five Gas Works London (1952)

Size of Works by No. of Men	Below 1 Year	1–5 Years	5–10 Years	10–15 Years	15–20 Years	Over 20 Years
			Length of Service in Years			
67	3.4	1.4	1.7	0.8	0.0	0.1
240	5.2	4.3	7.1	1.9	2.8	2.3
460	15.5	10.6	3.8	8.4	3.2	2.7
790	10.2	9.3	5.9	5.0	3.3	3.4
3430	9.2	9.9	7.4	6.6	5.2	2.7

Tardiness generally increases with plant size, but a curvilinear relationship exists, with tardiness going up to the highest figure for medium-size plants of 460 for those employed five years or less. A sharp reduction in the tardiness occurs with longer service in all size plants. This sample is only of five plants but is suggestive of a close relationship among tardiness, plant size, and length of service.

The accident rate was computed in random samples of American hospitals for 1953.[21] The larger the hospital, the greater the incidence of accidents per man-hour worked. In units employing nineteen or less, the accident rate was 3.2 per million man-hours worked. This rose steadily to 13.5 for hospitals ranging from 1,000 to 2,499 and then declined to 12.4 in hospitals 2,500 and over.

Paralleling these results, Figure 3-1 shows that compensable accident rates among miners and quarry men in Britain vary directly with the size of the mine. This contrasts somewhat with American mines, where a curvilinear relationship exists with rates rising until about 900 employees and then falling.[22]

SIZE AND CONFLICT

Revans also analyzed the relationship between size and strike incidence in coal mines in two coal fields. He computed the average tons *lost* per man

[20]R. W. Revans, "Human Relations, Management and Size," p. 199.
[21]Ibid., pp. 196–97.
[22]Ibid., p. 178.

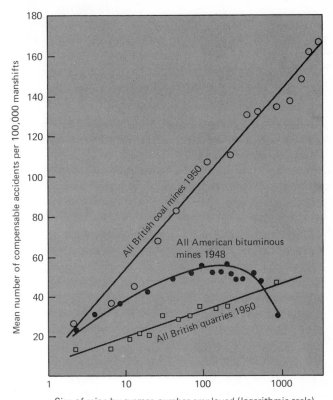

FIGURE 3-1. Relation between mean accident rate and mean group-size of all British coal mines and quarries 1950 and of all American bituminous coal mines 1948

(which takes into account both the number and the length of disputes) and found that production losses steadily became worse ranging from 9.69 tons per man for mines employing 500 or less to 23.39 tons in mines employing 1,500 to 2,000 men in the South Wales coal field. In the Yorkshire coal field, 5.94 tons per man were lost in mines below 500; this rose to 16.39 tons per man in mines employing 1,001 to 1,500 men, declined to 12.82 tons per man in the 1,501–2,000 category, and rose steadily to 22.7 tons per man for mines employing 2,500 or more.[23]

The data suggest that the willingness to strike goes steadily up with the size of mine. In pursuing the thesis further, Revans explored the relationship

[23]Ibid., p. 201.

of size to type of nonmonetary issues on which conflict centered.[24] These were grouped as follows:

1. Arguments with the management on personnel including disputes over other men being dismissed, reprimanded, or suspended; objection to attitudes of particular officials, questions of personal allowances, promotion, grading, and miscellaneous matters
2. Impatience at mechanical breakdowns followed by wildcat strike
3. Criticism of the organization, including disagreements over tasks or methods and refusal to accept alternative work in emergencies
4. Objections to mine conditions, including refusal to complete work left over from the previous shift

The relation of size of the mine to the nature of dispute is summarized in Table 3-4.[25]

TABLE 3-4. Percent of Nonmonetary Issues Officially Reported Causing Strikes

	Nature of Issue			
Size of Mine	Personnel Problems	Impatience on Breakdowns	Organizational Challenges	Mine Conditions
Small	19.7	3.1	45.0	35.2
Medium	8.6	6.1	50.4	34.0
Large	7.3	13.0	46.3	35.7

The disputes over personnel issues, such as allowances, and job classification declined from about 20 to 7 percent as size of mines increased. Contrarily, impatience with mechanical breakdowns accompanied by walkouts rose from 3 to 13 percent as mine size increased. There was little change in the extent other issues were in dispute with different size mines.

SIZE AND BEHAVIOR

Indik summarizes the results of three studies—one on a delivery organization, an automobile dealership, and a voluntary agency.[26] Among other factors, he explored how size affected vertical communication, intragroup relationships, job satisfaction, and an index of member participation (absen-

[24]Ibid., p. 203.
[25]Ibid.
[26]Bernard P. Indik, "Organizational Size and Member Participation," p. 346.

teeism for the delivery organization, turnover for the auto dealership, and average meetings attended for the voluntary association). He computed the degree of correlation between size and these factors. In the delivery organization, size was negatively related to vertical communication ($-.46$), intragroup relations ($-.48$), absenteeism ($-.53$), and job satisfaction ($-.47$). In the auto dealership and volunteer organization, the same relations existed except to a lesser degree.

Cleland compared eighty-two plants in a community to obtain the relation of size to several dependent variables including turnover, work force cohesiveness, the incidence of strikes, and susceptibility to unionization.[27] The major findings of this study were:

1. Plants under 500 had a smaller number of job applicants and the employees had lower wages and fringe benefits, but the plants still had the lowest turnover.

2. One of the major advantages of small size is the plant atmosphere. The small plant usually was described as being "informal" or "first name" or having a "family atmosphere." The small plant size allows the intimate contact necessary to know one's workers, and there is greater opportunity to provide the workers with a variety of personal services.

3. A small plant is more likely than a large plant to have a cohesive work force. The use of internal recruitment encourages father–son teams and outside friendships. Also, the personal contact in the small plant helps to tie the work force together.

4. Plant size was related to unionization. In an area where the incidence of union organization was high, all of the unorganized plants were small.

5. Strikes were more prevalent in the larger plants. The larger the size of the plant, the more likely it was to have a strike. Plant size appeared to be a more significant variable in a plant's past strike history than the union affiliation or the nature of the industry.

SIZE AND PRODUCTIVITY

Marriott, in a fifteen-month study of two car factories in Great Britain, found that the size of groups was closely related to productivity. The average productivity declined from an index of 133.8 for groups of ten or under to 126.1 for groups of forty to forty-nine; with groups of fifty and over there was a slight increase in productivity to 127.1 again.[28] In contrast, where the

[27]Sherrill Cleland, *The Influence of Plant Size on Industrial Relations* (Princeton, N.J.: Princeton University, 1955), 346.

[28]R. Marriott, "Size of Working Group and Output," *Occupational Psychology*, 23 (January 1949), 47–57.

focus is on entire organizations, this may not hold. Revans's analysis of the relationship of size to efficiency in the coal mines shows that the productivity in British pits rose steadily nearly 19 percent as pits increased from 250 men to 2,000 men. In larger coal mines, productivity declined nearly as much, as size increased to 3,000 men and over.[29]

The Problems of Identifying Size Effects

Thomas and Fink, in their review of the literature on small groups, comment on some problems of separating the effects of size from other factors.[30] Their points apply even more so where the researchers have investigated larger organization units.

Nondependable intervening variables are those that are affected by changes in group size only under certain conditions. Almost any social or psychological condition influencing group process or outcome may be a nondependable intervening variable. There are numerous examples: the time allowed for group discussion may be held constant while group size is increased, thereby reducing the opportunity to participate; a group payoff may be held constant in cooperative groups of different sizes, thus varying the amount of reward that each member may possibly get when the payoff is divided among them; expectancy of reward may decrease with increasing size of a competitive group; the relative contribution of each member in cooperative groups may decrease with size, thereby decreasing the individual's sense of importance and worth in the group; the interdependence of the members may be high, thus increasing the likelihood that with increasing size there will be at least one individual who will perform poorly and hinder the group's progress; the cost in time and money represented by each additional group member may eventually exceed the possible gain to be derived from having more individuals work on the problem; and the complexity of the cognitive field may become great with increasing size to the extent that members try to attend to impinging social stimuli.

Most of the observed effects of size reviewed here appear to be contingent upon the operation of one or more of these nondependable intervening variables. Where such mediating variables are affecting an outcome, the proper focus for explanation should be on the theoretical

---

[29]R. W. Revans, "Human Relations, Management and Size," p. 203.

[30]Edwin J. Thomas and Clinton F. Fink, "Effects of Group Size," *Psychological Bulletin*, 60 (1963), 382–83. Copyright 1963 by the American Psychological Association, and reproduced by permission.

framework, of which the intervening variable is part and only secondarily on size.

SUMMARY OF FIELD STUDIES

Worthy concluded that "there is no more important influence on attitudes and morale than sheer size of organization." Morale "declined sharply with increasing size." Revans stated that absenteeism rate rises proportionally with size of the organization. Accident rates also are related to size of the unit: in a study of general hospitals, they rose from 2.5 per million man-hours worked in units employing 19 or less to 10.3 for those employing 2,500 or more. Accident rates in British coal mines and quarries rose proportionately with size of the organization unit; similar trends existed in American coal mines up to units employing about 100, but then accidents declined to about one-half the rate as the mines increased to 1,000.

Other behavior elements also are affected by size of the unit. Indik found as size increased, vertical communication and job satisfaction declined along with intragroup relations. The correlation coefficients were all small, though, ranging from −.11 to −.48 (that is, about 1 percent to 23 percent of the variance is explained by size).

The degree of conflict between unions and management and the nature of the disputes are partially related to the size of the units. Revans found little relationship between the number of disputes and size, but the severity of the disputes rose sharply with size: in one coal field, tonnage lost per man due to strikes increased 240 percent when mines below 500 were compared with mines in the 1,501–2,000 range. In another coal field, tonnage lost per man was 382 percent greater in mines over 2,500 as compared to mines below 500 employees. The nature of the nonmonetary issues on which strikes centered was also partially related to size: personnel problems such as challenges to discipline and job allowances declined in importance with larger mines from about 20 to 7 percent of the issues. Walkouts over mechanical breakdowns increased with mine size from about 3 to 13 percent. Other issues were unrelated to mine size.

These findings were further supported by Cleland in an intensive study of eighty-three firms. Small plants were more likely to have a cohesive work force and fewer strikes and to be nonunion. He concluded that one of the major advantages of the small-size plant is that it contributes toward a plant atmosphere that supports close contact with workers and generally a personal approach by management.

Contradictory findings exist on relationship of size and productivity.

Marriott, in a study of groups in an automobile factory, found productivity inversely related to size of work groups. Productivity in groups of forty to forty-nine was 5 percent less than in groups of nine or smaller. Marriott did not compile absenteeisms or tardiness data, but it seems reasonable that tardiness and absenteeism rate could affect this degree of difference in productivity. In contrast, Revans found that average productivity of coal mines in British pits rose about 19 percent as mines increased in size from 250 to 499 employees to the 1,500–1,999 level; productivity then declined as size increased to 3,000 or over. There was little difference in productivity of the smallest and the largest mines but considerable differences for the mines in between. Here, we don't know whether there were any differences in the size of work groups as mines increased in size; if there were differences, this might enable us to reconcile the findings of the two studies.

It is apparent that size has an influence over the functioning of an organization. These studies are too gross in character to unravel the precise relationships. The next section attempts to analyze in more precise form what happens in small groups, as their size changes.

Working in the Large Organization

Shepherd Mead, in his satire on business organizations, highlights some elements that enable the charlatan to be successful.[31] *One of these elements is the size of the firm.*

How To Apply for a Job

Let us assume you are young, healthy, clear-eyed, and eager, anxious to rise quickly and easily to the top of the business world.

You can!

If you have education, intelligence, and ability, so much the better. But remember that thousands have reached the top without them. You, too, can be among the lucky few. . . .

Choose the Right Company

This is the first essential, neglected by so many. There are thousands and thousands of "right" companies. Find them. Make sure *your* company fits these easy requirements:

1. *It must be BIG.* In fact, the bigger the better. It should be big enough so that nobody knows exactly what anyone else is doing.
2. *It should be in a Big City.* This is not essential, but it helps. New York City is best, but many others will qualify. . . .

[31]Shepherd Mead, *How to Succeed in Business Without Really Trying* (New York: Simon & Schuster, 1952), pp. 3–4, 8–11, partially abridged.

Seize Your Opportunities

Though you, as a keen young man, must plot a straight course and an accurate one for your business career, leaving little to chance, you must nevertheless be ready on an instant's notice for the knock of Opportunity.

This is particularly true in the early stages before you make your connection.

Suppose, for example, you happen to run into the head of a large corporation:

Suppose you happen to run into the head of a large corporation.

"Oops, sorry, Mr. Biggley, didn't mean to knock you down!"
"You blasted idiot!"
"I was just coming to ask you for a job, sir—"
"Dammit, you imbecile, what do you think we have a personnel man for?"

Seize your opportunity! Go to the personnel man:

"I was speaking to J. B. Biggley only this morning."

"Biggley *himself*?"

"He said to see you."

"Not old J. B.!"

"Oh yes. Just happened to run into him."

"Well, well, Mr. uh—"

"Finch. Pierrepont Finch."

"Well, this may be over my level Mr. Finch. Perhaps you ought to see Mr. Bratt."

And so, in one way or another you will have stormed the gates and the company of your choice will be quick to grant you that important interview.

THE EFFECTS OF SIZE:
LABORATORY EXPERIMENTS

The laboratory experiments have considerable advantage over the field experiments, since the size of the group can be systematically changed. The focus of the laboratory research, however, has characteristically been upon small groups of seven or under. There are a few studies where the groups go up to a dozen members but practically no studies where the effects of larger numbers are explored.

A laboratory study offers the advantage of exploring in a systematic way the functioning of a group as the size changes. The laboratory studies also tend to be valuable since they more typically focus upon theoretically significant dependent variables rather than those of immediate interest to management. Table 3-5 summarizes four studies.

INTERACTION OF GROUP SIZE AND
NATURE OF DECISION

Ziller sought to determine what happens to the quality of decisions (as measured by error level), satisfaction with group decisions, sense of group unity, and the extent that communication is inhibited as a group increases from one to six members.[32] He designed an experiment where members of military air crews were assigned two tasks on which a range of errors could be made. On one task, where the members estimated the number of dots that was flashed on the board, a broad range of errors could be made. In the second task, the group was given a human relations problem where the number of errors was limited. Fifteen alternatives were presented, four of which were correct. In the dot experiment, the error levels went down sharply as size increased from one to three members but then rose in the four- and five-member group; errors then fell off sharply for the six-member group. In the human relations problem where a limited set of choices existed, the relation of size to error level was inversely related—the larger the group, the lower the error level.

Apparently a high interaction between nature of task and size of group exists. The reactions of members to these different size groups changed as the group moved from four to five members. Satisfaction with the group's decision increased slightly as size rose from two to four and then steadily fell off

[32]Robert C. Ziller, "Group Size: A Determinant of the Quality and Stability of Group Decisions," *Sociometry*, 20 (1957), 165–72.

TABLE 3-5. Effects of Size in Four Laboratory Studies

Author	Group Size	Nature of Group Members	Task Assigned	Dependent Variables

Ziller (1957)	1–6	Military air crews	Group decision: task with restricted alternatives compared with numerous alternatives	Error levels
				Satisfaction
				  With group decisions
				  Participation levels
				Sense of group unity
				Inhibition of communication

Hare (1952)	5 & 12	Boy Scouts	Group decision on choice of equipment for a simulated survival task	Group consensus Satisfaction with level of participation Subgrouping
Bales and Borgatta (1966)	2–7	Hired college students	Group decision on solving a human relations problem	Group processes: Problem-solving activities Intragroup relations
Slater (1966)	2–7	Same group used by Bales and Borgatta	Same task	Optimum size of group Sources of dissatisfaction as group changed from optimum size

as the group moved up to six members. The same held with their sense that the group adequately considered their opinions. The group worked well together in a group of two or three with a slight falling in the feeling of unity as the group became larger. Members felt they were freer to question suggestions and proposals of the other members in two-member groups; this sense of freedom declined as the group moved up to five members.[33]

EFFECTS OF INCREASING SIZE ON INTERACTION AND CONSENSUS

In another study, Hare explored the way in which groups of five and twelve affect the nature of interaction and consensus.[34] He studied Boy Scouts in a summer camp who were involved in a camping game. The groups had to choose ten pieces of camping equipment that would be needed if an individual were lost and had to find his way back to civilization alone.

As the group increased from five to twelve members, the amount of consensus decreased. The importance of the leader varied with group size. In groups of five, the more active the leader, the less movement there was toward consensus. Contrarily, in groups of twelve, the active leader achieved a greater degree of consensus. Only 3 percent of the followers in the small groups reported they had too little time for discussion; 22 percent in the larger group complained they had too little time. The actual time used for discussion supported this point. The average time used in discussion by the small groups was 14.8 minutes compared with 18 minutes with large groups; six of the larger groups used the full 20 minutes for discussion. There was a higher degree of agreement on the decisions in the small groups than in the larger groups. In the groups of five, nearly all members agreed with the decision, while 83 percent agreed in the larger group. In the larger groups, 21 percent felt their opinions were less important, while 9 percent of those in the small groups had this impression. There was a tendency for subgrouping into two and three factions in the groups of twelve members.

SIZE EFFECTS ON PROBLEM SOLVING AND INTRAGROUP RELATIONS

A systematic investigation of group processes was undertaken by Bales and Borgatta in groups that ranged from two to seven members.[35] Bales

[33]Ibid., p. 169.

[34]Paul Hare, "A Study of Interaction and Consensus in Different Sized Groups," *American Sociological Review*, 17 (June 1952), 261–67.

[35]Robert F. Bales and Edgar F. Borgatta, "Size of Groups as a Factor in the Interaction Profile," in A. Paul Hare, Edgar F. Borgatta, and Robert F. Bales, eds., *Small Groups*, rev. ed. (New York: A. A. Knopf, 1966), p. 499.

used a method of "interaction process analysis," where every observed act of verbal and nonverbal communication between members is classified into twelve categories. These are measures of problem solving, expressions of support, and symptoms of withdrawal in groups. Problem solving consists of questions asking for orientation, opinion and suggestions, or comments giving orientation, opinion, and suggestions. In expressing support or withdrawal of support, members are classified as showing agreement, tension release, and solidarity, or disagreement, tension, and antagonism.

In an experiment, groups from two to seven were assigned the task of discussing a human relations case using limited data. They were to explain why the people in the case were behaving as they did and decide what action should be recommended to solve the problem. Table 3-6 summarizes the nature of the group processes as group size moved from two to seven.[36] The contrasts are illustrated in Figures 3-2 and 3-3.

TABLE 3-6. Group Processes in Different Size Groups*

	Group Size					
Behavior	2	3	4	5	6	7
Expressions of Support						
Shows Solidarity	9.2	9.1	10.3	9.7	11.2	10.5
Shows Tension Release	11.2	11.4	12.8	14.2	18.4	16.6
Shows Agreement	27.2	27.0	22.3	23.1	21.6	21.3
Problem-Solving Activities						
Gives Suggestions	14.3	13.5	13.7	15.9	18.4	19.2
Gives Opinions	31.7	34.0	35.0	32.0	32.1	31.2
Gives Information	25.3	23.3	23.7	26.6	24.1	25.7
Asks Information	12.0	10.2	10.5	10.2	10.2	10.1
Asks Opinion	9.8	8.5	8.2	8.5	7.4	7.1
Asks Orientation	5.2	5.9	5.0	6.4	4.6	5.9
Expressions of Conflict						
Shows Disagreement	10.2	15.6	19.9	14.5	17.7	16.4
Shows Tension	12.4	8.6	10.0	9.1	6.3	6.6
Shows Antagonism	1.0	3.5	5.2	3.3	3.9	3.8

*The profile of each individual is the sum over four sessions of his raw profile in each session, converted to a percentage profile and transformed to arcsine equivalents. The higher the number, the greater the element of behavior.

[36]Ibid., p. 500.

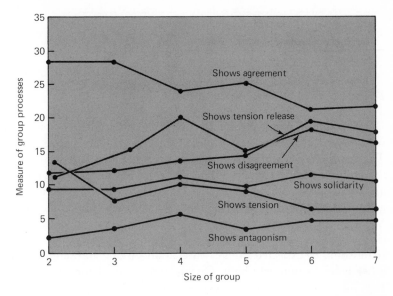

FIGURE 3-2.   Expressions of support and conflict in groups varying from 2 to 7

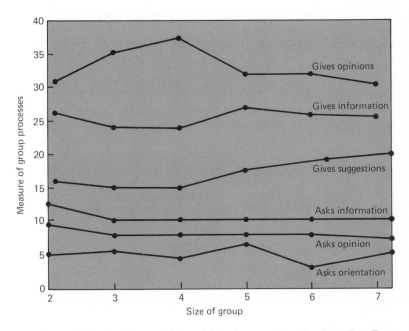

FIGURE 3-3.   Problem-solving activities in groups varying from 2 to 7

Unique Processes in Two-Person Groups

When a group contains only two members, it has some unique aspects. Bales and Borgatta summarize the results of their research.[37]

Inspection of Table 3-6 for the possibility that any given size may show unique characteristics strongly suggests that size two is unique. The mean profile for groups of this size has a notably high rate of showing tension, and at the same time low rates of showing disagreement and antagonism. Asking for orientation is uniquely high, and although giving orientation is not uniquely high, it is somewhat higher than would be expected from extrapolating the trend for the remaining group sizes. Similarly, giving opinion, although not uniquely low, is lower than would be expected from extrapolation. Asking for opinion, on the other hand, is uniquely high. Giving suggestions is somewhat on the high side in the sense that it deviates from an otherwise perfectly clear and consistent trend seen in the remaining group sizes.

Most, if not all, of the unique features of the interaction profile of the two-person group may be associated with one major feature which distinguishes it from groups of all other sizes. This is the fact that in a group of two it is impossible to form a majority except by unanimity. Either person in the dyad possesses power to influence the decision by withdrawal or veto. Neither person is able to influence the other by bringing a majority to bear against him. In this sense there is no public opinion or group sanction to which either can appeal. Similarly, there is no officer, mediator, or arbitrator who can reconcile the differences. Consequently, each person is under pressure to behave in such a way that the other will not withdraw and will continue to cooperate even though he may have to yield a point at a given time. Essentially, this is the problem of allowing the co-participant to "save face" when he does yield a point. The dominant person is thus under pressure to avoid the implication of superiority, and to persuade the other by gentle and self-effacing means.

The low rates of showing disagreement and antagonism and the high rates of asking for information and opinion are reasonably associated with the necessity of a gentle, persuasive approach. The high rate of showing tension is probably associated both with the delicate

[37]Ibid., pp. 501–502, slightly abridged.

balance the dominant person tries to maintain and with the tendency to withdraw used as a power device by the less dominant person. The concentration on giving orientation and relative avoidance of giving opinion may be a device used for the neutralizing of the evaluative implications of what is said or suggested, by sticking to that which is most self-evident and incontrovertable. The relatively high rate of giving suggestion, if indeed the rate is high, may reflect the development of procedural suggestions to handle the high tension. It is of some interest that there is a high rate of asking for opinion and that this is not accompanied by a correspondingly high rate of giving opinion. This suggests, again, the hesitancy to respond in terms which are evaluative.

Table 3-6 indicates that when size of the group increases, tension release and giving suggestions sharply rise. Solidarity goes up somewhat, and when groups of two are considered separately, giving information also increases. Tension rises sharply as the group becomes larger; this is associated with a decrease in showing agreement and asking for opinion. Again, if groups of size two are disregarded, giving opinion declines with larger groups.

The authors interpret the results as affected by two factors:

The first is that the relative talking time available per member decreases as size increases. The second is that each person is confronted with an absolutely larger number of persons as size increases. Each is under pressure to maintain a more or less adequate relationship with each other. Thus, as size increases, each member has more relationships to maintain and less time to do so.[38]

Time restrictions mean that more persons must participate at lower rates. Those who are inclined to participate in a minimal way tend to be forced even more so to a passive role such as listening, showing tension, withdrawing, nervous mannerisms, or other acts that don't compete for time.

There apparently is a tradeoff between asking for and giving opinion. Giving suggestions is a more direct response to the demands of the task than

[38]Ibid., p. 500.

is giving opinions. When time is at a premium, members may feel under pressure to take the direct approach.

Even numbered groups (with the exception of group size two) are high in showing disagreement and antagonism, and low in asking for suggestions. They tend to be higher than odd-numbered groups in showing solidarity and lower in showing agreement. Even-numbered groups probably persist in deadlocks, whereas odd-numbered groups can break into a majority and minority and arrive at a decision. Disagreement and antagonism are overt manifestations of conflict; the relative lack of asking for suggestions and showing agreement is consistent with this state of conflict. There is no obvious reason, however, why showing solidarity should be higher in even-numbered groups.

Slater examined the same data from a complementary perspective.[39] He was concerned with finding what the optimum size of the group was from the perspective of the members and what their sources of dissatisfaction were in groups that were larger or smaller than the optimal size of five. Members of larger groups felt that their group was disorderly and wasted time and that its members were too pushy, aggressive, and competitive. Despite indications that there was an established and accepted hierarchy, some called for more central control over the discussion, while others grumbled over the highhandedness with which some members dominated the discussion.

In smaller groups, the members inhibited more acts that could lead to conflicts, such as giving suggestions. There was an emphasis upon expressed agreement and avoidance of controversial subjects. This was most striking in groups of two but also applied to the other size groups.

This suggests that in a larger group, physical freedom is restricted while psychological freedom is increased. The member has less time to talk, more points of view to adjust to and integrate, and a more elaborate structure to fit. At the same time, he is freer to ignore these viewpoints, to express his own feelings and ideas in a direct and forceful fashion, and to withdraw without loss of face.

A further analysis of the data provides support for this thesis. An index of inhibition varied directly with the size of the group. There was greater reluctance in expressing oneself directly in group size two; this declined until group size six, where it leveled off. When the groups were studied through time, there was relatively little decline in degree of inhibition in small groups over the four sessions the groups met. In the larger groups, there was a substantial decline in the degree of inhibition in the four meetings.

[39]Philip E. Slater, "Contrasting Correlates of Group Size," *Sociometry*, 2 (1958), 129–39.

SUMMARY

The four studies reviewed in this section provide a profile of the changes in group processes as a group expands from two to twelve members. The studies suggest some factors that change as membership expands to twelve members. Group size two is fairly unique. It has its own special dimensions apparently because of the difficulty in dealing with conflict in a systematic manner. As the group increases to five members, the group on balance improves its overall relationships. Individuals are satisfied with their decisions, their level of participation, and the other members.

As a group grows beyond seven members, the degree of consensus, intragroup relationships, and general satisfaction with the group tend to decline. Subgrouping occurs and role differentiation increases. As the group expands. the roles tend to be more restricted, but the sense of psychological freedom increases. Individuals have less time to present their views, there is a greater diversity of viewpoints to integrate and adjust to, and a more elaborate structure in which to fit. At the same time, one is freer to ignore the views of others, to express one's ideas directly, or to withdraw into a passive role.

The field studies and laboratory studies provide an overall perspective of relation of size to organization processes and behavior. Figure 3-4 summarizes some of the basic changes that take place as group size changes. As a unit increases in size, greater complexity of relationships develop (1). Simply, a greater number of individuals, relationships, and roles must be coordinated. Partly associated with this complexity and partly a direct product of the larger number, there is a greater sense of depersonalization, a reduced level of participation, greater role specialization, centralization, a rise in irrelevant information, and overloading of channels and queuing of messages, all of which result in communication blockages.

As a group expands, a sense of depersonalization rapidly develops as individuals' feelings of being noticed and sense of importance decline (2). There are more individuals but less time for each; there is less familiarity with the personal goals, problems, and personalities of others; and individuals relate more to others only in the formal role or job that they perform in the group.

On balance, participation levels of most members *must* decline (3). To the extent that some individuals maintain their involvement, the participation levels of others must be even more sharply reduced. If any form of central task exists, it is necessary to specialize roles (4), centralize by imposing parameters upon the decisions of individuals, and generally reduce duplication of effort and obtain coordination (5). The increased complexity of relationships is associated with communication blockages (6). This is noticeable in

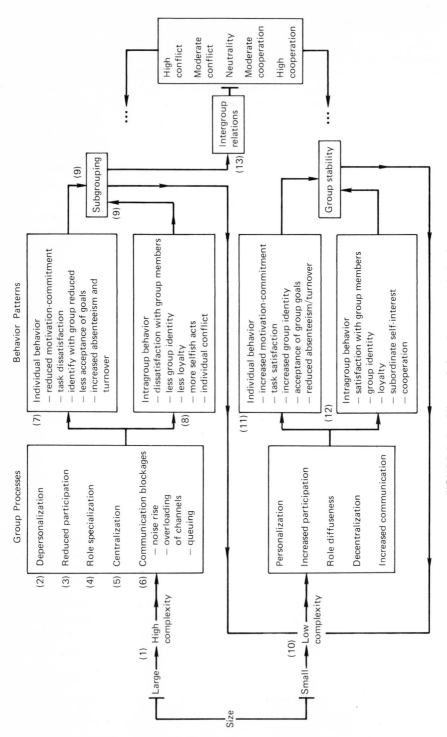

FIGURE 3-4. Effects of size of group on behavior

any gathering where the communication has not been rationalized. The general noise level rises in the sense that more talk at the same time; a great deal of selective listening occurs as each member necessarily is forced to choose what to tune into. Since the communication is principally verbal, channels are quickly overloaded; to the extent that rationalization takes place, rapid queuing develops as individuals wait their turn to make their point.

These factors, in turn, influence both individual (7) and interpersonal (8) behavior. On balance, as a consequence of the increased complexity, individual behavior patterns deteriorate. There is less motivation and commitment, greater task dissatisfaction, reduced identity with the group, less acceptance of group goals, and greater tendency to withdraw by being late, absent, or leaving the group entirely. There is likely to be greater dissatisfaction with members, a reduced sense of group identity and loyalty, and a greater tendency to suboptimize in terms of individual acts. Both the group processes and the behavioral patterns that develop contribute to subgrouping, i.e., a breaking into two or more groups (9).

In subgrouping, we move from formal specification of groups to behavioral definition of groups. That is, management organizes individuals into formal units such as sections, departments, and project teams. But when a formal group is expanded beyond a critical size, behavioral units form. These are usually referred to as cliques, informal groups, or other terms that indicate a high degree of interaction and cohesion among selected individuals. They may be friendship groups or political units where individuals band together to exert greater influence and control in the organization. Melville Dalton and others have provided detailed descriptions of these groups in operation.[40]

Subgrouping, in turn, creates two processes that work in opposite directions—intragroup cohesion and intergroup rivalry. The smaller subgroups now have changed relationships among members in each group (10). The sharply reduced size and complexity of relationships influence a higher degree of personalization, greater potential participation, less specialization, and increased communication. This is likely to be associated with both positive individual (11) and intragroup (12) behavior patterns. But the formation of smaller subgroups or cliques creates intergroup relations (13).

The degree of cooperation or conflict among groups is largely determined by factors other than size. The subgroupings create the conditions that permit variables such as standards, rewards, and leadership to exert a powerful influence over behavior. A common task and an interdependent work flow,

[40]Melvin Dalton, *Men Who Manage* (New York: John Wiley & Sons, 1959); Edward Gross, "Some Functional Consequences of Primary Controls in Formal Organizations," *American Sociological Review*, 18 (1953), 368–73; Leonard R. Sayles, *Behavior of Industrial Work Groups: Prediction and Control* (New York: John Wiley & Sons, 1958).

for instance, are likely to be associated with a degree of tension and conflict among the subgroups, but if specialists are grouped so that each group's work is independent of other groups, the relations among groups are likely to be neutral in character.

In this chapter our emphasis has been on understanding the way in which one variable—size of groups—influences group processes and behavior. In later chapters, we explore the influence of other variables on these processes.

4

WORK FLOW:
Specialization at the Operative Level

INTRODUCTION

One of the basic thrusts in industrialization is to increase the degree of specialization. This occurs both in the larger society with organizations performing specialized activities and within organizations where individuals are assigned narrowly defined tasks. Specialization sharply increases the degree of complexity both in society and in organizations.

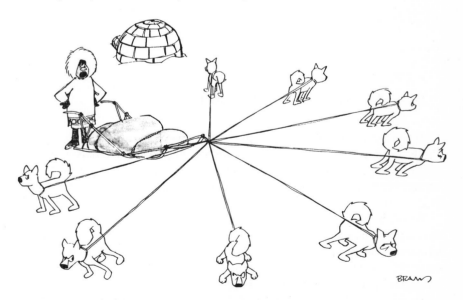

"I wish all of you would settle your differences before you come to work."

Drawing by Herb Brammeier; © *The Rotarian* Magazine, 1972. Courtesy of *The Rotarian* Magazine.

Within an organization there may be variation in the amount of specialization ranging from little specialization to an intensive degree. In the first case, each individual performs most of the functions involved in a complete task. In a job shop, for instance, one may start with the blueprints supplied by the customer and perform all steps in the manufacturing operation to end up with the finished product. The craftsman is dependent only upon himself to complete the manufacturing operations. Contrarily, in the case of a high degree of specialization, each office is assigned narrowly defined duties. In this case the product must be acted upon by several people before the finished product is obtained.

The immediate effect of specialization is to create interdependency among workers and groups. Each specialist must fulfill his responsibilities so that the overall job can be done. In a classroom, for instance, if group projects are assigned, members may decide to divide the task to share the workload. This immediately results in each member becoming dependent upon the others if the project is to be successfully completed. This holds true in any organization. A completely interdependent relationship is created where the output of one position becomes the input of another, and each unit cannot proceed until it receives its input. Graphically, Figure 4-1 represents such a situation.

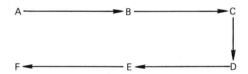

FIGURE 4-1. Interdependent work flow illustrated

In steel making, for example, the work moves in several steps, charging the furnace with materials, heating, adding additional materials at appropriate times, and then tapping the furnace. In some furnaces, a new cycle cannot begin until the old cycle is complete. In this case, the failure of any individual to perform his task results in a breakdown in the total task.

As might be expected, this interdependence creates a strain on the relationship among members. A form of interdependence that exerts particular stress on relationships is where a position serves a number of others. A secretary, for instance, may have a multiple relationship in that she works for several persons, as indicated in Figure 4-2.

In this case, the work arrangement contributes to a competitive relation among those seeking assistance and places the secretary in a difficult position, particularly if she is of lower rank than those utilizing her services. A maintenance unit in a plant that serves several production units is in a position

FIGURE 4-2. Interdependent work flow with high stress

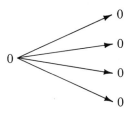

similar to our secretary illustration. Where services are involved, two ways of reducing the stress are by providing flexibility in the amount of available resources and establishing rules lining up the work in a queue. In the first case, additional help may be recruited such as calling in other part-time women to assist in typing or aid the service personnel in the shop. The second method is to establish priorities, but this still leaves the service unit under pressure since some of those wanting service may not accept the priority system and may exert pressure for the service unit to ignore the official policies.

Where there is a physical flow, such as when an item is being assembled along a line, inventories provide a method of reducing the degree of inter-dependence. In Figure 4-3 below, each position is independent as long as it can produce for or draw from inventory for its supplies.

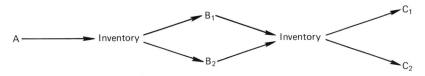

FIGURE 4-3. Degree of integration among positions as affected by an inventory buffer

In an assembly line, for instance, if each individual draws from a reserve of parts and can queue his output, he achieves some degree of short-term independence.

In an organization, the work flow among specialized positions—in con-trast to the formal authority relationships—is readily observable on the fac-tory floor, in the hospital, and in other organizations. Somewhat more subtle but still easily observable is where personnel move around the organization, performing specialized operations on the work unit. Two basic ways in which the work situations are tied together into a common work flow are:

1. *The work station is constant*—Activities are performed at each station, but the work is moved among the stations. The product may be a material

commodity, such as a car on an assembly line; it may be documents or reports such as are performed at each desk in a consulting firm as the project moves among the specialists; or it may be information, as in a telephone company, where on a long distance call activities of dialing the next exchange are performed at two or more stations in sequence.

2. *Items to be worked are constant*—The item to be worked is constant, but personnel flow to each work station. For example, maintenance personnel typically go to where there is a breakdown in an assembly line; a doctor moves among a series of rooms where the patients are located; students move to classrooms; and the like.

An Illustration of Specialization and Its Effects

The restaurant, while relatively small, typically specializes to a high degree. William F. Whyte describes how changes in degree of specialization have broad ramifications for the social system.[1]

The restaurant is a combination production and service unit. It differs from the factory, which is solely a production unit, and also from the retail store, which is solely a service unit.

The restaurant operator produces a perishable product for immediate sale. Success requires a delicate adjustment of supply to demand and skillful coordination of production with service. The production and service tie-up not only makes for difficult human problems of coordinating action but adds a new dimension to the structure of the organization: the customer-employee relationship.

The problems of coordination and customer relations are relatively simple in the small restaurant, but they become much more difficult as the organization grows. This may be illustrated structurally in terms of five stages of growth.

In the first stage, we have a small restaurant where the owner and several other employees dispense short orders over the counter. There is little division of labor. The owner and employees serve together as cooks, countermen, and dishwashers.

In the second stage, the business is still characterized by the informality and flexibility of its relationships. The boss knows most customers and all his employees on a personal basis. There is no need for formal controls and elaborate paper work. Still, the organization has grown in complexity as it has grown in size. The volume of business is

[1]William F. Whyte, "Social Structure of the Restaurant," *American Journal of Sociology*, 54 (January 1949), 302–303.

such that it becomes necessary to divide the work, and we have dish-washers and kitchen employees, as well as those who wait on the customers. Now the problems of coordination begin to grow also, but the organization is still small enough so that the owner-manager can observe directly a large part of its activities and step in to straighten out friction or inefficiency.

As the business continues to expand, it requires a still more complex organization as well as larger quarters. No longer able to supervise all activities directly, the owner-manager hires a service supervisor, a food production supervisor, and places one of his employees in charge of the dishroom as a working supervisor. He also employs a checker to total checks for his waitresses and see that the food is served in correct portion and style.

In time, the owner-manager finds that he can accommodate a larger number of customers if he takes one more step in the division of labor. Up to now the cooks have been serving the food to the waitresses. When these functions are divided, both cooking and serving can proceed more efficiently. Therefore, he sets up a service pantry apart from the kitchen. The cooks now concentrate on cooking, the runners carry food from kitchen to pantry and carry orders from pantry to kitchen, and the pantry girls serve the waitresses over the counter. This adds two more groups (pantry girls and runners) to be supervised, and, to cope with this and the larger scale of operation, the owner adds another level of supervision, so that there are two supervisors between himself and the workers. Somewhere along the line of development, perhaps he begins serving drinks and adds bartenders to his organization.

Stage Five need not be diagrammed here, for it does not necessarily involve any structural changes in the individual unit. Here several units are tied together into a chain, and one or more levels of authority are set up in a main office above the individual unit structures.

This expansion process magnifies old problems and gives rise to new ones.

The particular problem of the large restaurant is to tie together its line of authority with the relations that arise along the flow of work. In the first instance, this involves the customer relationship, for here is where the flow of work begins. The handling of the customer relationship is crucial for adjustment of the restaurant personnel, and a large part of that problem can be stated in strictly quantitative interaction terms: Who originates action for whom and how often? In a large and busy restaurant a waitress may take orders from fifty to one hundred customers a day (and perhaps several times for each meal) in addition to the orders (much less frequent) she receives from her supervisor. When we add to this the problem of adjusting to service-pantry workers, bartenders, and perhaps checkers, we can readily see the possibilities

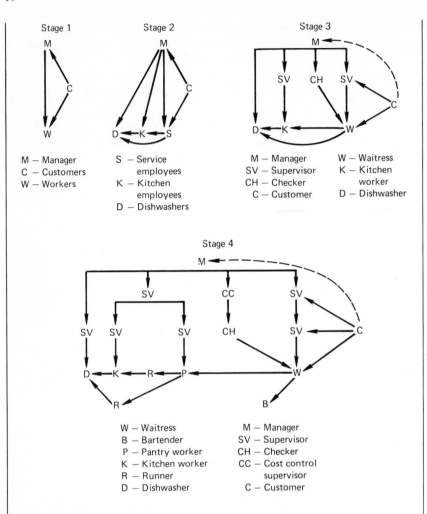

Stage 1

M — Manager
C — Customers
W — Workers

Stage 2

S — Service
    employees
K — Kitchen
    employees
D — Dishwashers

Stage 3

M — Manager   W — Waitress
SV — Supervisor   K — Kitchen
CH — Checker   worker
C — Customer   D — Dishwasher

Stage 4

W — Waitress   M — Manager
B — Bartender   SV — Supervisor
P — Pantry worker   CH — Checker
K — Kitchen worker   CC — Cost control
R — Runner   supervisor
D — Dishwasher   C — Customer

of emotional tension—and, in our study, we did see a number of girls break down and cry under the strain.

Our findings suggested that emotional tension could be related directly to this quantitative interaction picture. The skillful waitress, who maintained her emotional equilibrium, did not simply respond to the initiative of customers. In various obvious and subtle ways she took the play away from customers, got them responding to her, and fitted them into the pattern of her work. She was also more aggressive than the emotionally insecure in originating action for other waitresses, service-pantry people, and supervisor.

While in the rush hour, the waitress works under a good deal of tension at best, the supervisor can either add to or relieve it. Here again we can speak in quantitative terms. In one restaurant we observed a change in dining-room management when a supervisor who was skillful in originating action for customers (thus taking pressure off waitresses) and who responded frequently to the initiation of waitresses was replaced by a supervisor who had less skill in controlling customers and who originated for the girls much more frequently and seldom responded to them. This change was followed by evidences of increased nervous tension, especially among the less experienced waitresses, and finally by a series of waitress resignations.

The customer relationship is, of course, only one point along the flow of work which brings orders from dining-room to kitchen and food from kitchen to dining-room. In a large restaurant operating on several floors, this is a long chain which may break down at any point, thus leading to emotional explosions on all quarters. The orders may go from waitress to pantry girl and then, as the pantry girl runs low in supplies, from pantry girl to pantry supplyman, from pantry supplyman to kitchen supplyman, and from kitchen supplyman to cook. And the food comes back along the same route in the opposite direction. Where drinks are served, the bar must be tied in with this flow of work, but there the chain is short and the problem less complex.

We have here a social system whose parts are interdependent in a highly sensitive manner. Thus the emotional tension experienced by waitresses is readily transmitted, link by link, all the way to the kitchen.

An extensive literature exists of a popular nature and to a lesser extent of a scientific character.[2] Our review focuses first upon those studies that explore the effects of specialization at the worker level. In Chapter 8 we will review a second group of studies that develop the effects of specialization and grouping at the first supervisory and higher levels.

[2]Four reviews of the area refer to a substantial part of the empirical work that has been done: A. C. MacKinney, P. F. Wernimont, and W. O. Galitz, "Has Specialization Reduced Job Satisfaction?" *Personnel* (January-February 1962), pp. 8–17; Norman R. J. Maier, *Psychology and Industry*, 2nd ed. (Boston: Houghton Mifflin Co., 1955), pp. 339–74; Charles L. Hulin and Milton R. Blood, "Job Enlargement, Individual Differences, and Worker Responses, "*Psychological Bulletin*, 69 (1968), 41–55; and Delbert C. Miller and William H. Form, *Industrial Sociology*, rev. ed. (New York: Harper & Row, 1964), pp. 630–32.

Essays of interest are: Daniel Bell, "Adjusting Men to Machines," *Commentary*, 3 (January 1947), 79–88; Robert Dubin, "Industrial Workers' Words: A Study of the Central Life Interest of the Industrial Workers," *Social Problems*, 3 (January 1966), 132–42; Nathan Glazer, "The Alienation of Modern Man," *Commentary*, 3 (April 1947), 378–85; Harold Wilensky, "Varieties of Work Experience," in Henry Borow, ed., *Man in a World of Work* (Boston: Houghton Mifflin Co., 1964), pp. 125–254; Harvey Swados, "The Myth of the Happy Worker," in Eric and Mary Josephson, eds., *Man Alone: Alienation in Modern Society* (New York: Dell, 1962), pp. 106–13; and Byron E. Calame, "Wary Labor Eyes Job Enrichment," *Wall Street Journal* (February 26, 1973).

Engineering Emphasis in Job Design.   At the beginning of the twenti-
eth century, Adam Smith was one of the first to expound on the merits of
specialization.[3] In a famous pin example, he stated that a workman who had
little training could make up to twenty pins a day where he performed each
step in the process. But where operations were divided into eighteen distinct
steps and performed by different employees, workmen could produce twelve
pounds of pins a day or average forty-eight hundred pins for each worker.[4]
Smith attributed the increased output to increased dexterity of each workman, saving of time moving from one task to another, and the invention of
machines that aided and assumed part of the labor. He contended that a loss
of time occurred as one moved from one task to another, and this was amplified since it was man's nature to dally somewhat as he completed one task
and started another.

> A man commonly saunters a little in turning his hand from one sort
> of employment to another. When he first begins to do work he is seldom
> very keen and hardy; his mind, as they say, does not go to it, and for
> some time he rather trifles than tries to good purpose. The habit of
> sauntering and indolent careless application, which is naturally, or
> rather necessarily, acquired by every country workman who is obliged
> to change his working tools every half hour, and to apply his hand in
> twenty different ways almost every day of his life renders him almost
> slothful and lazy and incapable of any vigorous application, even on the
> most pressing occasions.[5]

In 1832, Babbage summarized the advantages economists saw as supporting the use of extensive division of labor.[6]

1. *Ease of training*—A workman can be trained faster to carry out one or two specific
    operations than an apprentice can be trained in all the operations required to
    manufacture a product. Specialized training saves materials that an apprentice
    would waste in learning his trade.

[3]Adam Smith, *An Inquiry into the Nature and Cause of Wealth of Nations,* Edwin Canon, ed.
(London: Methuen & Co., 1904), pp. 3–12.
[4]Ibid., pp. 4–5.
[5]Ibid., pp. 8–9.
[6]Charles Babbage, *On the Economy of Machinery and Manufacturers,* 2nd ed. (London:
Charles Knight, 1832), pp. 166–73.

2. *Less lost time*—More productive time is achieved by reducing movement from one operation to another and from one tool to another.
3. *Greater skill*—In carrying out a specific operation repeatedly, the workers develop greater speed in their movements.
4. *Improvements in methods*—By devoting their entire effort to one operation, engineers are able to simplify and improve the method—the first step in developing a multioperational machine.
5. *Selection of labor*—As a final advantage, the division of labor allows the manufacturer to select men for operations for which they are best suited.

Criteria Used in Job Design

In the excerpt by Louis Davis and Ralph Canter,[7] we find that the idea that increased specialization generally increases efficiency has been broadly accepted by engineers who typically design jobs and plant layout. Davis and Canter summarize some of their findings on the factors engineers considered in designing jobs in industrial firms.

In the interviews all of the companies were asked what factors they normally take into consideration in assigning tasks to workers and in combining the tasks to make specific jobs. All of the companies considered it very important to:

1. Break the job into the smallest components possible to reduce skill requirements.
2. Make the content of the job as repetitive as possible.
3. Minimize internal transportation and handling time.
4. Provide suitable working conditions.
5. Obtain greater specialization.
6. Stabilize production and reduce job shifts to a minimum.
7. Have engineering departments, whenever possible, take an active part in assigning tasks and jobs. (In all the companies the line foreman or supervisor was directly involved in carrying out these activities.)

General comments indicated that the majority of companies believed in limiting the content of the individual jobs as much as possible. This means limiting the number of tasks within the jobs and limiting the variations permitted in tasks or jobs. This further indicates that specialization of work was a primary consideration. Another indication of this was obtained in the last section of the questionnaire, which asked the

---

[7]Louis E. Davis and Ralph Canter, "Current Job Design Criteria," *Journal of Industrial Engineering*, 6 (1955), 6–8. Reprinted with permission from the *Journal of Industrial Engineering*. Copyright by the American Institute of Industrial Engineers, Inc., 25 Technology Park/Atlanta, Norcross, Georgia 30071.

respondents to report any indications they might hold concerning the relationship between job content and productivity. The pertinent comments made in this section are summarized as follows:

1. Tasks with too many elements of work reduce productivity.
2. Combining elements provides individual responsibility for those elements which usually improve quality and productivity.
3. Productivity is improved by revising tooling to reduce the possibility of errors and to reduce fatigue.
4. The greater the number of tasks assigned to an individual, the longer the training time required and the lower the output. In general, productivity will remain low.
5. Experience has indicated that job content does not appreciably affect productivity.
6. Job content is not as important as employee attitude. Mental attitude is the most important consideration. ". . . We specify job content to fit our facilities—then sell it."
7. Productivity was found to be higher when job content involved horizontal assignments (all elements at approximately the same skill levels).
8. Best results have been obtained by combining relatively few tasks into jobs for average workers. Overspecialization has not proved effective. Workers who show high aptitude and desire for diversified work are transferred to jobs in repair, or special products departments.
9. Simpler jobs result in higher output and make the workers happier. The company believes in simplification and elimination of rotation for job satisfaction.
10. In general, the greater the degree of specialization, the higher the productivity. When specialization becomes so refined that the job becomes unbearably monotonous, productivity tends to decline; however, the monotony and decline in productivity are off-set to some extent by the ever-present challenge of the incentive system.
11. A change to an assembly line increases productivity.

The Human Relations View. The engineer's approach to job design has not gone unchallenged. According to Peter Drucker, there is evidence that the use of the worker as a single-purpose tool is a wasteful use of man in the production process. It is poor engineering that leads to tension, frustration, and dissatisfaction. Drucker feels that the principle of specialization is productive and efficient when applied to machinery, but it is dubious whether we know how to apply the principle to people. He asks, is specialization "a social and individually satisfying way of using human energy and production. . ." ?[8] His position is that it is not.

Walker and Guest have arrived at conclusions that have won broad popularity among a human relations contingent in the area.[9] Their studies focused upon mass production processes and the extent of alienation of the workers who perform specialized tasks on the assembly line. The elements of job designs that lead to alienation of individuals from their job, their fellow workers, the management, and the firm are summarized as follows:

1. *Factors leading to the anonymity of the individual worker*—The job is designed so that virtually everything that might be of personal value to the worker is eliminated:

—The worker has no control over his work pace.
—His job is repetitive and requires little skill because of the simple movements required.
—Methods and tools are completely specified and changes are introduced without his knowledge or control.
—He never works on more than a fraction of the product. He has no identity with the product or process.
—The job demands require only surface attention, not enough to allow him to become absorbed in his work.
—Men on the line work as individuals without identifying as a work group.

2. *Factors leading to the depersonalization of the job*—There are no means for job progression through a series of distinct steps. Simplified tasks have all but eliminated skill differences from one job to the next.

Authors such as Behling, Argyris, and Herzberg theorize *why* specialization may be dysfunctional. Behling contends that specialized work leads to dissatisfaction because our present civilization is able to satisfy our lower level needs and this in turn moves higher level needs to a priority position. The higher level needs are frustrated under job simplification, so dissatisfaction with the organization develops.[10]

Argyris provides a more involved theoretical basis for his ideas.[11] He con-

[8]Peter Drucker, *The New Society* (New York: Harper Bros., 1950).

[9]Charles R. Walker and Robert H. Guest, *The Man on the Assembly Line* (Cambridge, Mass.: Harvard University Press, 1952), pp. 38–65.

[10]O. C. Behling, "The Meaning of Dissatisfaction with Factory Work," *Management of Personnel Quarterly*, 3 (1964), 11–16.

[11]Chris Argyris, "The Individual and the Organization: An Empirical Test," *Administrative Science Quarterly*, 4, No. 2 (1959), 145–67.

tends that human beings develop as they move from infant to adult: they change from a state of passivity to increasing activity, dependence upon others to relative independence, quixotic interest to deeper interests, limited to wide-range behavioral patterns, short to longer time perspective, from a subordinate position to that of an equal or superior, from a lack of awareness to an awareness of self, and from being controlled to controlling one's own behavior. Consequently, when healthy people are placed into work situations that require them to be dependent, submissive, and to use only their superficial abilities, they become frustrated and leave or adapt by becoming defensive and apathetic and accepting the lack of growth; the job is considered only as a means to make money. Argyris believes the remedy for this is to restructure the organization so that it is consistent with higher level needs of man. One basic approach is job enlargement.

Herzberg contends that two distinct sets of job-related variables operate within the work environment: job content variables (motivators), and job context (hygiene) variables.[12] The motivators include achievement, recognition, performing interesting and challenging work, responsibility, advancement, and personal growth, which are *intrinsic* to the job. The hygiene factors are *extrinsic* to the job and include company policy and administration, the worker's relationship with his boss and his peers, working conditions, and salary and fringe benefits.

Herzberg contends that the motivators are primarily responsible for job satisfaction. If the hygiene factors are present in sufficient quantity to meet workers' expectations, or even exceed workers' demands, the result is limited to "no job dissatisfaction." However, if the management wants to motivate workers, it must concentrate on improving their jobs. In applying Herzberg's theory to job enrichment plans, managers make workers more productive by changing job content so that the workers are able to receive recognition, achievement, and the other intrinsic motivators.

Job Enlargement: Eliminating Problems of Specialization? The human relations approach contends that job enlargement results in less absenteeism and turnover, greater personal satisfaction, and a rise in efficiency. These conclusions largely have been built on several early studies of assembly lines in production plants.[13] The studies' conclusions have been supported by

---

[12]A good review of two-factor theory is Frederick Herzberg, "One More Time: How Do You Motivate Employees?" *Harvard Business Review* (January-February 1968), pp. 53–67.

[13]Studies that have won wide attention are George Friedman, *Industrial Society* (New York: Free Press, 1955); Charles R. Walker, *Toward the Automatic Factory* (New Haven, Conn.: Yale University Press, 1957); Walker and Guest, *The Man on the Assembly Line; F. L. Richardson and C. R. Walker, *Human Relations in an Expanding Company* (New Haven, Conn.: Labor and Management Center, Yale University, 1948).

various managers and personnel specialists who have written about job enlargement in their plants.[14]

In one of the first studies, Richardson and Walker at Yale studied job changes in an IBM plant.[15] Along with changes in formal organization, production layout, supervisory training, and other areas in the plant, a program of job enlargement was undertaken. The jobs of machine operators were expanded from operating the machines to also preparing the parts for the machining and having responsibility for inspection. The company reported that this resulted in products of better quality, less idle time for both machines and operators, and greater variety and responsibility for the worker. Presumably, everybody profited, with the company receiving better quality work with lower costs, the employee increased satisfaction, and the consumer an improved product.

The Yale group followed up their study of IBM by exploring behavior on assembly lines in automobile production plants.[16] They concluded that most individuals, regardless of the time involved in the plant, were alienated from their job, their fellow workers, management, and the company in general. Guest also reported on other case studies where management expanded the scope of the job.[17] In the field of nursing, reduced specialization resulted in greater meaningfulness of the job to the nurse, improved patient care, and greater efficiency. Enlargement of clerical jobs in an insurance company reportedly resulted in greater satisfaction, reduced turnover, and improved quality of work.

Worthy also reported similar advantages associated with job enlargement at Sears and Roebuck.[18] Elliott provided further testimony on the happy consequences of job enlargement at Detroit Edison.[19] Combining tasks of

[14]Some of these are Douglas Elliott, "Increasing Office Productivity Through Job Enlargement," *The Human Side of the Office Manager's Job*, Office Management Series no. 134 (New York: American Management Association, 1954), pp. 3–15; John Maher et al, "Enriched Jobs Mean Better Inspection Performance," *Industrial Engineering*, 2 (November 1969), 23–26; Greylan Tuggle, "Job Enlargement," *Industrial Engineering*, 2 (1969), 26–31; William E. Reif and Peter P. Schoderbek, "Job Enlargement: Antidote to Apathy," *Management of Personnel Quarterly*, 5, No. 1 (1966), 16–23; Raymond F. Pilissier, "Successful Experience with Job Design," *Personnel Administration* (March-April 1965), pp. 12–16; Robert M. Monczka and William E. Reif, "A Contingency Approach to Job Enrichment Design," *Human Resource Management*, 12 (Winter 1973), 9–17.

[15]Richardson and Walker, *Human Relations in an Expanding Company*; Charles R. Walker, "The Problem of the Repetitive Job," *Harvard Business Review*, 28 (1950), 54–58.

[16]Walker and Guest, *The Man on the Assembly Line*.

[17]Robert H. Guest, "Job Enlargement: A Revolution in Job Design," *Personnel Administration*, 20, No. 2 (1957), 12.

[18]James C. Worthy, "Organizational Structure and Employee Morale," *American Sociological Review*, 15 (April 1950), 169–79.

[19]Elliott, "Increasing Office Productivity Through Job Enlargement," pp. 3–15.

making out customer bills and checking them, expanding job classifications so that individuals were responsible for running several machines rather than one, giving first-line supervisors broad authority over their work group rather than simply implementing staff decisions, and combining work groups performing sequential tasks reportedly resulted in lower costs, better quality, and more satisfied employees.

"I know what we need, Hartford, honey . . . we need a change of pace . . . that's what we need . . . we need a change of pace . . . it just came to me . . . we need a change of pace . . . what do you think about that . . . I mean about a change of pace . . . don't you think we need a change of pace?"

EFFECTS OF SPECIALIZATION: RESEARCH STUDIES

The assembly line studies are of limited use in evaluating the merits of specialization. An assembly line is a complex, highly structured system. It incorporates many other features besides specialization, including a fixed demanding pace set by moving belts; continuous production run rather than batching of work; rigid schedule for work breaks; detailed specification of work methods; little control over flow of supplies, parts, or quality of the total product; physical dispersion along a line so that interaction is typically restricted to those on each side of work stations; a mixture of reward-penalty methods—sometimes an individual piecework system, sometimes group incentives, and often hourly pay; and supervisory styles that vary widely. An assembly line is important to describe and analyze, but its effects must be related to more factors than specialization and repetition.

Illustrative case reports by management have suggestive value, but they have limited scientific merit. Regardless of complexity of changes, the typical report attributes the effects to one variable such as job enlargement. We must rely principally upon systematic investigations of specialization to evaluate its effects.

Measuring the Degree of Interdependence of Work Flow

A way of measuring the degree of work flow within formal units is set forth in the following excerpt. In Chapter 8, the complementary measure is presented on the degree of work flow among formal units. The two together constitute a measure of work flow within and among formal units in an organization.

The interdependence of work flow is defined by the extent of input-output relationships among positions within each formal unit. The degree of interdependence within groups is determined by the degree of specialization, the existence of buffers, and the extent to which there is a simple or complex interdependence among positions. The degree of interdependence within a group is operationalized by averaging the following factors:

Interdependence Scale within a Group

	1	2	3	4	5	6	7	8	9
1. Functional Specialization	Little							Extensive	
2. Interdependence Complexity	Low							High	
3. Buffers	Extensive							Few	

1. *Functional Specialization*—The members of a group may each perform specialized tasks such as on an assembly line; thus, each member
is dependent on others to perform their jobs properly to take the next
step. Contrarily, there may be little specialization and little interdependence among positions. What degree of specialization exists in your
group?

1	2	3	4	5	6	7	8	9

Little Specialization	Some	Moderate	Considerable	Extensive Specialization

2. *Interdependence Complexity: Low vs. High*—Where an interdependent
work flow exists, positions may be serially related in that each position
provides services or generates inputs for only one position, e.g.:

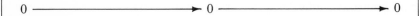

Contrarily, a position may serve a number of others, such as where a
secretary works for several persons, e.g.:

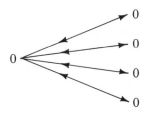

How many people do you work for in that they are dependent upon
your services or output?

1	2	3	4	5	6	7	8	9

None (Don't pro- vide inputs for other group members)	Some (Two or more)	Moderate (Four or more	Considerable (Six or more)	Many (Eight or more are dependent upon the output)

3. *Buffers Between Positions*—Where interdependence exists among
positions, there may be different levels of inventory or other buffers
between positions that permit individuals to continue to work even

when breakdowns occur or when others are absent. To what degree are there ways of reducing the immediate dependence among positions?

1	2	3	4	5	6	7	8	9
Extensive (Many ways of making daily or weekly adjustments to breakdown in workflow)	Considerable		Moderate			Some		Few (Little that can be done when breakdown in work flow occurs)

Skill Levels and Job Satisfaction.　One line of research examines the degree of job satisfaction associated with different skill levels. There are problems of interpretation since level of skill and degree of specialization don't necessarily go together; even where they do, the question arises of whether the job creates the attitudes and degree of satisfaction or the workers bring to certain types of jobs the attitudes and approaches that are often found. It may be, for instance, that unskilled workers have lower educational levels and are less integrated into the society than those at higher skill levels, and the attitudes in their work are traceable to these factors. Even so, it is useful to examine the results of these studies. They are mostly consistent with one another, so one study will be used to illustrate their findings.

Shepard, in a carefully designed study, contrasted the degree of job satisfaction of three groups of workers—control room monitors in an oil refinery, assembly line workers, and journeymen engaged in maintenance work in an automobile assembly plant.[20]

A direct relationship existed between the degree of specialization and low job satisfaction, sense of being powerless, meaninglessness of the work, and feelings of low autonomy and little responsibility. The greater the degree of specialization, the more adversely the individuals were affected. However, some anomalies exist in the relationships. Eighty-six percent of the assemblers indicated they had low job satisfaction, but only 73 percent reported that the work was meaningless. Only 13 percent of the craftsmen indicated low job satisfaction, while 42 percent reported that the work was meaningless. Evidently some other factor was contributing to job satisfaction besides the degree of specialization. Similarly, a difference existed between the sense of

[20]John M. Shepard, "Functional Specialization and Work Attitudes," *Industrial Relations*, 8, No. 2 (1969), 185–94.

being powerless and the workers' sense of autonomy and responsibility, although these would reasonably seem to be opposite sides of the same coin. Ninety-three percent of the assemblers expressed a sense of being powerless, but only 81 percent indicated a low degree of autonomy and responsibility. Similarly, 19 percent of craftsmen indicated a sense of being powerless, while only 11 percent reported a low degree of autonomy and responsibility.

These studies suggest that a high correlation exists between specialization and negative behavioral patterns, but they also indicate that other factors confound the relationship. These factors are to some extent sorted out in a number of other studies. Conant and Kilbridge highlight some of the variables that may change as one moves from specialized, low-level skilled jobs to those with a higher level of skills and greater variety.[21] The authors explored the effects of expanding jobs in a large plant manufacturing laundry equipment. The Maytag Company had restructured a number of jobs including one where the change was from a conventional assembly line to a bench job approach, where the individual workers were assigned responsibility for making complete assemblies. The changes made on a water pump assembly illustrate the approach. A water pump composed of twenty-seven parts was originally assembled by six operators on a line, with each operator performing an average of six work elements. The company changed this so that each worker assembled an entire pump. Further, each operator determined at least within a broad range his pace and method used to assemble the pumps and was responsible for quality. This change, however, was associated with several other changes. The pacing that was previously done by a conveyor belt was eliminated; a group incentive plan was replaced by an individual incentive plan; higher standards were established as the company capitalized on the shrinkage of nonproductive time and better balance in work load among positions that resulted from the redesign of the work. This is another way of saying that the standards were tighter under the new system but justified because previously nonproductive time had been eliminated. Further, with the new arrangements, spatial and physical barriers were erected between individuals. Because bench positions were stationary and parts didn't arrive by conveyor belt, increased space was required to store parts at each position. The result was that workers were on an average nearly twice as far apart as before, their view of other work spaces was blocked, and they were more remote from aisle traffic. The majority preferred the

[21]Eaton H. Conant and Maurice D. Kilbridge, "An Interdisciplinary Analysis of Job Enlargement: Technology, Cost, Behavioral Implications," *Industrial and Labor Relations Review*, 18 (April 1965), 377–95; Maurice D. Kilbridge, "Turnover, Absence, and Transfer Rates as Indicators of Employee Dissatisfaction with Repetitive Work," *Industrial and Labor Relations Review*, 15 (1961), 21–32; Maurice D. Kilbridge, "Reduced Costs Through Job Enlargement: A Case Study," *Journal of Business*, 33 (1960), 357–62; and J. F. Biggane and Paul A. Stewart, *Job Englargement: A Case Study*, Research Series, no. 25 (Iowa City: State University of Iowa, 1963).

self-pacing associated with bench work, the freedom to leave the bench, working on a complete subcomponent rather than only a part, responsibility for quality of the product, and the larger variety of tasks. On the other hand, they preferred the social interaction associated with the line and the shorter learning time associated with mastery of the job.

Defining Job Enlargement and Its Practical Limits

Kilbridge defines job enlargement and develops some practical limitations on the degree jobs can be expanded in this brief excerpt.[22]

True job enlargement requires, first, an increase in the variety of tasks performed, not merely adding more of the same kind of tasks. This is only "job extension" and does not accomplish the purpose of job enlargement. Wharton provides an example of job extension at IBM:

"A dramatic example concerns wiring the electric calculator's panel —a unit about the size of a Scrabble board, to which 2,331 small wires have to be connected precisely. Formerly one girl connected all black wires, another all yellow wires, another all red, green, and violet wires. The panel moved from girl to girl on the line. . . . Now each girl wires a whole panel, connecting all 2,331 wires."

If connecting black wires is boresome, why should connecting black and yellow wires be less so? This is not an enlarged job. An enlarged job contains a variety of kinds of tasks, such as connecting, soldering, testing, etc., not just more of the same task.

With respect to giving the worker responsibility for pace, quality, and method—such responsibility can only be relative, never absolute. This can easily be seen for the pace of work. Industrial workers are paced to a large extent by the system itself. The interdependence of work operations and the need to maintain a constant flow of work in order to avoid shortages and meet production schedules imposes a work tempo on the entire factory that the individual worker cannot escape. In addition, management, to insure that schedules are met and to have a basis for the equitable distribution of work, usually establishes output requirements for individual jobs.

How, then, is the worker left any freedom of pace? In the flow production of manufactured goods where conveyors are used, he has virtually none, except if a bank of work is accumulated at each conveyor station; in this case he has a slight amount of freedom. Normally, however, he must meet the pace of the line, and this is constant throughout

---

[22]Kilbridge, "Reduced Costs Through Job Enlargement," pp. 358–59.

the day. On the other hand, where work is done in batches, the worker has considerable freedom of pace in the short run. This "short run" is usually either the time it takes to complete his operation on a batch of product or a work day, whichever is shorter. The batch worker, since he is not linked directly to other workers depending on him for a steady flow of product, can slow down or speed up at will so long as his average productivity is adequate. Thus, if production quotas or standards are set on a daily basis, for example, the batch worker can, if he pleases, work fast in the morning and slow in the afternoon. The most commonly used technique for enlarging jobs by increasing freedom of pace is that of converting from line to batch-type work.

Responsibility for checking quality, like freedom of pace, can also only be relative. In typical industrial operations workers do not inspect their own production. Although theoretically they are held responsible for the quality of their work, they are not asked to inspect it themselves. This is done by inspectors. Human nature being what it is, some form of other-person inspection of the final product is still considered essential. However, it is feasible in many industrial situations to transfer intermediate inspection operations to the production workers themselves. The worker also may be required to rework unsatisfactory pieces and to stamp his identifying mark on the finished items. Quality errors then become more easily assignable. The worker's pride in his work is enhanced. This form of job enlargement returns to the worker a sense of responsibility for, and involvement in, the functionality of the product.

Discretion for method also cannot be absolute. Industrial work methods are largely dictated by the nature of the product and the machines and tools available to make it. The manufacturing process fixes work methods to a high degree. However, minor decisions can be left to the workers rather than usurped by management. There is frequently room for choice in the order in which a sequence of tasks is performed and in the motion pattern used. Different persons have different ways of doing things, and these individual differences can be respected by allowing the workers some discretion in work methods.

Job enlargement, therefore, involves giving the worker more to do and more freedom in doing it.

Short-Term Effects of Job Enlargement. Arthur Marks investigated the short-term effects of job enlargement in a production department of a biological and pharmaceutical firm with about 700 employees.[23] The produc-

---

[23]Arthur R. Marks, "An Investigation of Modifications of Job Design in an Industrial Situation and Their Effects on Some Measures of Economic Productivity" (Ph.D. diss., University of California, Berkeley, 1954), summarized in Louis Davis and Ralph Canter, "Job Design Research," *Journal of Industrial Engineering*, 7 (1956), 275–82.

tion line assembled medical first aid packs, where high-quality standards had to be maintained. Twenty-nine women and one man working on the line assembled the packs in a sequence of nine steps. They were assisted by four table workers, one supply man, one inspector, and were supervised by two foremen. Employees working on the production line were paced by a belt and assembled the medical kits. Two additional features were that the productivity level was rated and the percentage of expected standard was posted every two hours; employees also rotated among jobs every two hours.

The experimental design involved these changes:

1. *Group Design*—In a separate room, a group of four employees was assigned responsibility for assembling the kits on a table; the line pacing was eliminated. After the initial group set up, two workers were rotated into the positions every day so that each employee had two days' experience under the group design. Employees were told by management to work at their regular pace.

2. *Individual Job Design in a Separate Room*—Each worker was assigned responsibility for assembling complete kits. Workers were rotated into the room for two days and told to work at a normal pace.

3. *Individual Job Design in Main Production Rooms*—The same design as in number 2 was repeated except work stations were returned to the main work room. Sixteen of the twenty-nine workers worked under this design for six days, five for five days or less, and eight not at all.

The effects on productivity and quality of the three changes are summarized in Table 4-1.[24] An 11 percent decline in productivity occurred for enlarged jobs performed under the group design, and about a 5 percent

TABLE 4-1. Effects of Three Variations in Job Design Over a Short Period of Time

	Line Job Design	Group Job Design (2 days)	Individual Job Design	
			Separate Room (2 days)	Main Room (6 days)
Index of productivity	100.0*	89.0	91.7	95.3
Quality before sterilization	4.2**	3.5	2.1	1.6
Quality index after sterilization	2.4	3.1	2.3	1.4

*In computing the productivity index, average productivity under assembly line was used as the base.
**Quality scale varied from 0 to 5 with high quality on the zero end of the scale.

[24]Ibid., p. 83.

decline when individuals performed the entire task. The decline was partly related to short time on the task and apparently to the lack of specific output standards. Quality was evaluated before and after sterilization; it was lowest under assembly line job design and highest under individual job design.

Figure 4-4 indicates that average productivity rose as workers gained experience under the method, starting from around a 10 percent drop and rising to productivity levels achieved under the original line-paced method.[25]

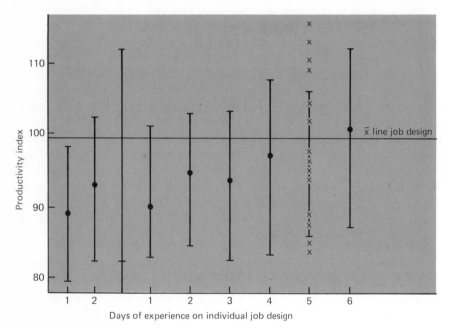

Days of experience on individual job design

● Average of individual productivity indexes
x Individual productivity indexes on 5th day of 2nd individual job design
I Limits of one standard deviation

FIGURE 4-4. Productivity each day under job enlargement compared with line job design

The work by Cox and Sharp in Great Britain supports Marks' findings.[26] In experiments at a radio factory, the unit work cycle was increased from two to four minutes for a team of eight workers; production initially fell, then recovered to four-fifths of the old rate within a week. However, four of the eight workers asked that the old cycle be reinstated, and the experimenter complied. Then twelve new workers were placed on the longer work cycle;

[25]Ibid., pp. 82, 88.

[26]David Cox and K. M. Dyce Sharp, "Research on the Unit of Work," *Occupational Psychology*, 24 (1951), 90–108.

but by the end of the week eight of the twelve asked to return to the shorter cycle, and that experiment was discontinued.

One worker took on the job of making the entire radio set—a twenty-minute cycle. Her output fell initially, but by the ninth week had reached a normal level; from the tenth to twenty-third week, she averaged 18 percent higher than the average production rate of the other workers. The quality of her work also fell at first and then rose above the average of the other employees.

While these studies are far from definitive, they do show considerable variability among workers in their reaction to specialization and job enlargement. A few authors have specifically explored the degree of variability and factors associated with differences.

ROUTINE AND MONOTONY: VARIATIONS AMONG INDIVIDUALS

Early studies highlighted the fact that individuals vary widely on the extent they find routine work monotonous and boring. Wyatt and Langdon, in a survey of 355 employees who worked at routine jobs in four plants in Great Britain, found their reaction ranged from "freedom from boredom" to "always bored."[27] About as many indicated they were only slightly bored as those who suffered severely from boredom. Table 4-2 summarizes the data.[28]

TABLE 4-2. The Incidence of Boredom in Four Factories Expressed as a Percentage of the Total in Each Group

Factory	Number in Group	Slightly Bored	Severity of Boredom			Always Bored
		0–1	1–2	2–3	3–4	4–5
A	142	1%	26%	43%	28%	2%
B	102	3	42	37	16	2
C	81	5	39	33	19	4
D	30	3	13	37	30	17
Average	–	3	33	38	23	3

In a further analysis, the workers were grouped into three classes of most bored, intermediate, and least bored. Table 4-3 summarizes the choices of factors most important to the most and least bored groups.[29]

[27]S. Wyatt and J. N. Langdon, *Fatigue and Boredom in Repetitive Work*, Report no. 77 (London: Her Britannic Majesty's Stationery Office, 1937), p. 2074.

[28]Ibid., p. 44. Reprinted with permission of the Controller of Her Britannic Majesty's Stationery Office.

[29]Ibid., p. 62. Reprinted with permission of the Controller of Her Britannic Majesty's Stationery Office.

TABLE 4-3. Relative Importance of Conditions of Work of the Most and Least
Bored Workers

| | Factory A | | Factory B | | Factory C | |
	Most Bored	Least Bored	Most Bored	Least Bored	Most Bored	Least Bored
Opportunity for promotion	5.3	3.4	6.1	2.5	4.9	3.3
Security of employment	7.2	8.1	7.3	8.1	7.5	8.3
Good supervisor	4.5	5.7	5.9	6.3	6.2	6.4
Pleasant working companions	4.1	5.7	5.0	5.7	5.4	6.1
High wages	4.4	4.7	4.8	4.8	3.1	4.2
Short hours	3.3	3.4	2.3	3.0	2.0	2.2
Opportunity to use own ideas	5.3	3.4	4.8	2.5	4.7	3.0
Comfortable working conditions	5.4	6.0	4.8	6.6	6.2	6.4
Work that makes you think	5.0	2.5	4.3	2.1	5.1	1.2
Work that needs no thought	0.2	1.8	0.2	3.4	0.6	3.7

Little difference existed among workers on importance of security, good
supervision, pleasant companions, comfortable working conditions, wages,
and hours. The workers who were most bored placed higher value on work
that makes one think, opportunity to use one's own ideas, and opportunity
for promotion.

Turner and Lawrence have developed the thesis that effects of specialization turn upon the nature of an individual's orientation.[30] They propose
that those raised in a rural work setting are dissatisfied with specialized
repetitive jobs and react positively to job expansion. In contrast, workers
from cities react in an opposite manner! They like repetitive work and
dislike variety, autonomy, and other features usually considered as desirable.

Hulin and Blood's idea is that blue-collar workers raised in cities have
different values than those raised in small towns.[31] They are more likely to
reject middle-class norms such as belief in hard work, striving for responsibility and achievement, and work-related aspects of the Protestant ethic.
They instead develop a set of values more consistent with industrial life.

[30]A. N. Turner and P. R. Lawrence, *Industrial Jobs and the Worker: An Investigation of
Response to Task Attributes* (Boston: Harvard University Graduate School of Business
Administration, 1965).

[31]Charles L. Hulin and Milton R. Blood, "Job Enlargement, Individual Differences, and
Worker Responses," *Psychological Bulletin,* 69, No. 1 (1968), 41–55.

In a secondary analysis of data collected by Patricia Smith on twenty-one plants, Hulin and Blood relate aspects of the plant setting, including factors such as extent of slums, urbanization, and population density, to behavior and attitudes of the workers. They found a significant difference among workers' orientation in contrasting environmental settings. Further, work satisfaction was inversely related to the level of the job in "alienated"-type communities ($r = -.50$) but positively related in "integrated" communities ($r = .40$).

Goldthorpe provides a more direct challenge to the human relations perspective than either Hulin and Blood or Lawrence and Turner.[32] Goldthorpe found that in an automobile assembly line in Great Britain, the assemblers derived little satisfaction from their work, with 69 percent complaining about monotony, 48 percent complaining of tiredness, and 3 percent working at too fast a speed. Eighty-seven percent wanted to move off the line to different jobs with higher skill, more responsibility, greater variety, and more freedom. Most of the workers stayed because of what they could earn: 31 percent reported that level of pay was the only reason they remained, and another 43 percent indicated this was one of several reasons for staying. Six percent said they stayed because they liked the work. Goldthorpe contends that the tendency of assembly line workers to regard the job simply as a means for making a living is a product of their values rather than of the job creating the values.

SUMMARY

In summary, the amount of specialization may vary broadly from very little to an intensive degree. The degree of specialization is directly correlated with the scope of the job and interdependence of individuals. Little attention, however, has been given to the effects of the interdependence. Researchers have been principally concerned with individual reactions to a broader scope of the task, i.e., job enlargement.

Up to about World War II, the technological thrust was to narrow the scope of the job. The assumptions of engineers and economists had been that specialization saved training time, reduced waste materials during training, eliminated time moving from one operation to another or from one tool to another, built up speed in carrying out each step, increased the opportunity to simplify and improve methods, and aided in hiring and placement of men in operations for which they were best suited.

Davis found that engineers used these guidelines to minimize the number of elements in each task. The engineers assumed that any adverse effects of specialization could be offset by an individual incentive system, rotation of

[32]John A. Goldthorpe, "Attitudes and Behavior of Our Assembly Workers: A Deviant Case and Theoretical Critique," *Business Journal of Sociology*, 17 (1966), 227–44.

personnel on these jobs, transferring high-aptitude workers to other jobs, highlighting the benefits of the job, or hiring those with appropriate mental attitudes.

The human relations view has been critical of specialization for ignoring the basic character of individuals—their desire for independence, autonomy, creativity, and self-control. Engineers designed out of the job all that was satisfying by eliminating skill requirements, specifying methods and tools, having workers concentrate on a fraction of a product, and assigning work that requires only surface attention. The result was passive, submissive individuals or frustrated people who adapted by defensive, apathetic, or instrumental views of the work.

The engineers' perspective has been challenged broadly by researchers in loosely designed studies and by personnel specialists and managers relating the results of job enlargement in their organizations. The keynote study was by Richardson and Walker in 1940 at IBM. Numerous changes occurred in the plant, among which was job enlargement. The result was a happy combination of better quality, lower costs, and greater work satisfaction. Subsequent work by them in assembly line plants was carefully designed in the planning stage where special features of assembly lines were identified. Unfortunately, when the authors have generalized from these studies, they have largely attributed the effects to a high degree of specialization. Reports by Guest on various organizations, Worthy on Sears and Roebuck, Elliott on Detroit Edison, and numerous other authors on different organizations have taken up the popular theme.

The few research studies with some scientific rigor reveal that a set of other changes are typically associated with job enlargement. The careful project by Conant and Kilbridge on job enlargement at the Maytag Company found improvements in efficiency, reduced costs, and improved quality under an enlarged task. The authors, however, detail other changes that also were made at the same time, including movement from pacing by conveyor belt to self-pacing, change from group incentive to an individual incentive, and tighter standards. Each of these is a powerful variable as we will discuss in later chapters and could easily have caused the results attributed to job enlargement.

A number of researchers have assumed that higher skilled jobs are less specialized than lower skilled positions. Shepard contrasted three skilled-worker groups and found that the lower the level of the worker, the less the satisfaction, the greater the feeling that the work is meaningless, and the greater the sense of being powerless and of having a low degree of autonomy and responsibility. But even a casual examination of different skilled groups reveals contrasts in other variables such as degree of delegation of authority, the nature of the control system and the information system, and very probably the nature of leadership. The conclusions that specialization results in these effects is at best an oversimplification.

Marks' experiment showed that the short-term effects of job enlargement are an 11 percent initial drop in productivity and then a gradual increase so that by the end of a week previous work levels are achieved. He found an immediate increase in quality with a greater improvement under individual job design than group design. Marks' results paralleled those by Cox and Sharp, who studied workers in Great Britain. In this case, workers had the choice of discontinuing the experiment and did so typically within a week. They apparently were paid on an incentive rate and were penalized by drop in production. In one exception, the immediate effects were a substantial drop in productivity and quality; but within ten weeks, previous levels of productivity were achieved, and subsequently both productivity and quality increased 18 percent.

Broad variation exists in individual reactions to job enlargement. The early work by Wyatt and Langdon showed broad variations among individuals in their reaction to specialization. There was approximately a normal distribution of satisfaction-dissatisfaction with specialized jobs within three of the factories; in the fourth factory, attitudes heavily weighted toward the dissatisfied end of the scale. A further analysis of three of the factories showed that the nature of the work was of varying importance to the most and least bored workers. Those who were most bored placed higher value on work that makes one think, opportunity to use one's own ideas, and opportunity for promotion. Those least bored placed higher values on security of employment, supervision, working conditions, wages, and short hours.

Turner and Lawrence and Hulin and Blood developed the thesis that those raised in an urban environment were more likely to have values that rejected middle-class norms and in turn to find specialization and limited opportunity as being acceptable. Goldthorpe has further contended that a self-selection develops whereby those who value autonomy and self-satisfaction in their jobs choose other types of work. He found that car assemblers were instrumentally oriented and placed low values on job fulfillment.

Despite the broadly held opinions on pros and cons of specialization at the worker level, few systematic studies have been done. Those that have been done suggest:

—Broad differences exist among individuals in their reactions to specialization.

—Short-term effects of reduced specialization are a drop in quantity and adverse behavioral reactions. It appears that output exceeds previous levels and adverse behavioral reactions are reversed after a learning period, and performance then rises above previous levels.

—Many of the effects attributed to specialization are probably caused by factors often associated with—but not necessarily a part of—specialized jobs. These factors include a high level of work demands, pacing by moving belt, blocked opportunity in the organization, rigid and detailed specification of how the job is to be done, and changes made in the job without consultation or consideration of views of workers on the job.

—The improvements in productivity attributed to job expansion may be related at
least in part to less dead time rather than to greater employee satisfaction and
commitment. The variability among workers, the difficulty of establishing an
average pace, and the tendency to work a varying rate hour by hour create
problems in line balancing. It is simpler to balance work among positions with
longer work cycles.

—The quality of the work tends to improve where the worker has a longer work
cycle since there is more opportunity to make corrections and it is easier to establish responsibility for errors.

—It is probable, but there is no evidence, that intragroup conflict increases with
greater specialization. Chapter 8 notes some effects on intergroup conflict.

Figure 4-5 further summarizes and extrapolates some of the effects of
variations in work flow. High specialization (1) with the resulting interdependence creates high task repetition (2) and high stress among positions (3).
The task repetition is associated with few requirements for skills, and they are
limited to a narrow area. In the short term (5), this has the advantage of
minimizing the learning period for new employees and minimizing waste
motion, material scrappage, and misuse of tools (6). The job is mastered with
minimal costs. It also simplifies and reduces recruitment costs since lower
aptitude and skills are required. In the short term, higher quality, efficiency,
and earnings are achieved (7).

In the longer term, the consequences differ. The narrow scope of the job
and high repetition contribute to boredom and monotony (9). The reaction
to boredom and monotony varies with the personality type. Given personality types generally represented in rural areas where individuals broadly subscribe to the Protestant ethics of hard work, achievement, and the intrinsic
satisfaction of work (10), workers find the highly specialized job frustrating,
unfulfilling, and associated with dissatisfaction with the work, fellow workers,
supervision, and the company (11). This dissatisfaction may be expressed in
many ways, including high rates of grievances, absenteeism, and turnover
either by workers quitting or being fired (12). These actions, in turn, result
in relatively low quality and efficiency (13).

On the other hand, these consequences may not occur where the employees have an instrumentally oriented personality type (14). The monotony
and boredom of specialized jobs are acceptable where workers value high
wages, security, comfortable working conditions, and good supervision.
Intrinsic job challenge and promotional possibilities are of less interest and
may be rejected. These personality types are more prevalent in urban settings, and they reject the Protestant ethics of work and its meaning (14).

With these personality types (14), the routine and boredom of the specialized job are accepted as costs of wages and security. They are satisfied
with the routine job and are likely to find their fellow workers compatible
and to value the company as a good place to work (15). They are content

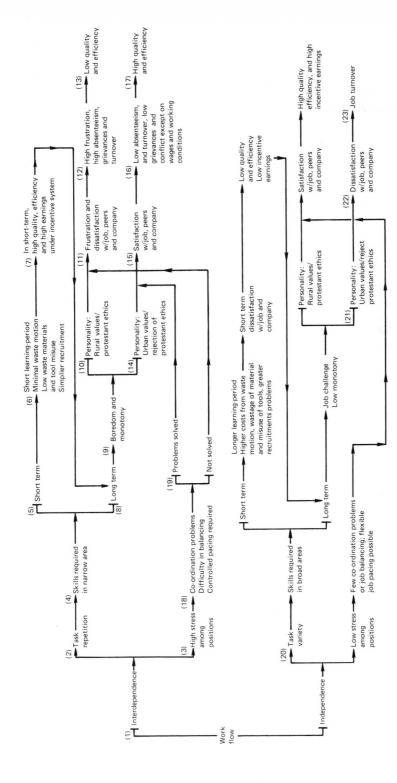

FIGURE 4-5. Effects of work flow on behavior

except for continual striving for higher wages and improved working conditions—the important things for them in the job. Absenteeism is relatively lower; turnover either from quitting or being fired is also relatively low (16). Quality and efficiency should be relatively high since this is part of the effort-wage bargain this group of workers accepts (17).

The analysis up to this point has focused only on task repetition and its consequences. A second factor associated with high specialization and the consequent job interdependence is high stress among positions (3). The interdependence means that interposition tension and stress are part of the job design. A close working interface is necessary, difficult to achieve, and easily upset. The illustration of the restaurant illustrates the job design. The emotionality and instability of the behavioral patterns among waitresses, cooks, supervisor, and customers show the consequences of breakdown in the close interface. The interdependence is associated with problems of coordination, balancing work among each position to avoid bottlenecks when any one point is overloaded, and controlled pacing so that under average conditions, all can keep up in their operation (18).

If these problems are solved (19), it contributes to satisfaction with the job, fellow workers, and the company. Anyone who has participated in team sports such as basketball, baseball, or football may have experienced the satisfaction of working in close harmony with others on a team (15). In contrast, if the problems of coordination are not solved, the normal stress of interdependence is multiplied, and the experience is frustrating; as a result a person feels a low sense of self-worth, anger at fellow members, and dissatisfaction with the position and the team or company (11). These frustrations are expressed in varying ways, including grievances, absenteeism, and turnover, as individuals quit or are terminated from the group (12). Both aspects of the specialization—the routine and the interdependence—contribute to long-term lowering of quality, efficiency, and effectiveness (13).

When we look at the opposite side of the coin and examine consequences of low specialization, job enlargement, and task variety (20), most of the relationships are the opposite of those developed above. The job design is simpler, and long-term effects are greater efficiency, higher quality, and greater effectiveness. The part of the relationships that has little research basis for support or rejection is the reaction of urban personality types to job challenge. The limited evidence we have suggests that where even short-term earnings are adversely affected, workers reject job enlargement and request the narrow job design. It may be that they also prefer the simpler, nonchallenging tasks of the more specialized jobs. In any case, the logic of our schematic suggests that the urban personality type will be dissatisfied with the enlarged job and with fellow workers who like it and its challenge (22) and will either quit or be fired as this dissatisfaction is expressed (23).

5

TASKS:
Degree of Complexity

INTRODUCTION

An important aspect of the context in which individuals operate is the complexity of the problems with which they are faced. On the one hand, problems may be unsolvable if people lack the knowledge of the way in which the solution can be obtained or if the state of knowledge is such that there is no solution. On the other hand, problems may be of a nature whereby the

"I'd like to see old Ho-Ho-Ho try to assemble one of these damn toys."

Drawing by Stevenson; © 1968 the New Yorker Magazine, Inc.

solutions or procedures for arriving at solutions are well known and it is a simple matter of applying these skills. We have called this variable "tasks," and it ranges from unprogrammed to programmed in character. The complexity of tasks is the predictability of the consequences of the methods used to arrive at solutions rather than the degree that procedures are defined for dealing with the problems.

The complexity of tasks is closely associated with the search procedures necessary to solve problems and make correct decisions. If the consequence of particular actions is predictable, the generation and selection among alternatives (the search procedure) is routine and systematic. While the problem may be intricate, the individual can systematically work out the solution. An engineer constructing a bridge typically uses methods that are well developed; this appears to be the situation for many of the tasks facing professionals and technicians—chemists, surgeons, engineers, etc.—as well as operating employees in most dimensions of their jobs.

Tasks: Programmed to Unprogrammed

The measurement of the task variable is briefly presented. Task complexity is in terms of the predictability of outcome of actions or decisions. This may vary from predictable to unpredictable.

Predictable   Unpredictable

1	2	3	4	5	6	7	8	9

The variable is operationalized by averaging the answers to two questions on (1) the knowledge each individual has in carrying out assigned tasks and solving problems, and (2) the resources from which he can draw for help.

	Task Scale								
	1	2	3	4	5	6	7	8	9
Predictability of actions	99%	88	77	66	55	44	33	22	0–11%
Availability of help from others	99%	88	77	66	55	44	33	22	0–11%

Task Question

1. In some jobs things are fairly predictable–if you do something, you know what will happen. In others you often are not sure whether something will work. What percent of the time are you sure whether something you do will work as expected?

Almost always		Usually		Often		Sometimes		Seldom
99%	88	77	66	55	44	33	22	0–10

2. Sometimes, even though you don't know how to handle a problem, you can go to someone else in your group or elsewhere for reliable help. In other cases, nobody else is likely to be able to provide any reliable help. What percent of the time can you go to others for reliable help when you are at a loss on how to solve a problem?

Almost always		Usually		Often		Sometimes		Seldom
99%	88	77	66	55	44	33	22	0–10%

Systematic attention has been directed to this variable by Charles Perrow, a sociologist. In a set of essays, he developed the concept, pulled together the literature where other authors have dealt with the variable under different names, and underscored its importance.[1] Perrow's general thesis is that the behavior patterns, the goals of the organization, and the form of structure are directly related to the knowledge available for processing the raw materials in that organization whether the raw materials are people, products, or intangibles such as information.

[1]Charles Perrow, "Hospitals: Technology, Structure and Goals," in James P. March, ed., *Handbook of Organizations* (Rand McNally & Co., 1965); Charles Perrow, "A Framework for the Comparative Analysis of Organizations," *American Sociological Review*, 32 (April 1967), 194–208; Charles Perrow, "Reality Adjustment: A Young Institution Settles for Humane Care," *Social Problems*, 14 (summer 1966), 69–79; Charles Perrow, "Technology and Organization Structure," in *Industrial Relations Research Association Proceedings* (New York: Harper & Bros., December 1966), pp. 156–63; Charles Perrow, "The Analysis of Goals in Complex Organizations," *American Sociological Review*, 26 (1961), 854–66; Charles Perrow, "Goals in Power Structures: A Historical Case Study," in Eliot Freidson, ed., *A Hospital in Modern Society* (Glencoe, Ill.: Free Press, 1963), pp. 112–46.

PARTIALLY UNPROGRAMMED TASKS

Situations of Over- and Understimulation

A variety of field studies and laboratory experiments have been carried out where individuals were faced with unsolvable problems or situations where they found it difficult to orient themselves. Autobiographical material on individuals lost at sea or placed in other high-stress situations reveals some of the effects of an unprogrammed context.[2] The ability to survive in these contexts is related, in part, to the capacity for dealing with an unfamiliar situation.

In cases of isolation at sea or in the polar night, the first exposure causes the greatest fear and impediment to productive acts. Sailors crossing the ocean in a small boat find that the first days out of port are the most dangerous with initial reactions of awe, humility, and acute fear of the sea. Alan Bombard, one of these intrepid individuals, stated that if the fear of the first week can be overcome, one can survive. Some become paranoid during this period and either try to commit suicide or murder their fellow passengers.

In experiments where the opposite condition of no stimulus exists, individuals find themselves quickly disoriented. In one study the subjects were suspended in a tank with masks for breathing and with the water temperature at a level where there was no sensation. In this condition the sound was maintained low enough so that only their breathing and faint water sounds of the piping could be heard. After several hours, subjects found it difficult to carry on organized thinking, and suggestibility sharply increased. They developed an intense desire for stimuli and action; they had periods of thrashing around in an attempt to satisfy these needs. Somewhere between twenty-four and seventy-two hours, most subjects couldn't stand it any longer and stopped the experiment. For those who stayed longer than two days, hallucinations and illusions developed.

Effects of "Loss of Anchor in Reality"

Torrance, in generalizing on a variety of studies, develops how an unstructured situation creates stress as a result of a "loss of anchor in reality." [3]

The distinctive element in stress is to be found in the lack of structure or loss of anchor in reality experienced by the individual or group as a

---

[2]John Lilly, "Illustrative Strategies for Research for Psychopathology in Mental Health," *Group for the Advancement of Psychiatry, Symposium No. 2,* (June 1966), pp. 13–20.

[3]From "A Theory of Leadership and Interpersonal Behavior Under Stress," by E. Paul Torrance, in *Leadership and Interpersonal Behavior,* edited by Luigi Petrullo and Barnard M. Bass. Copyright © 1961 by Holt, Rinehart and Winston, Publishers. Reprinted by permission of Holt, Rinehart and Winston, Publishers.

result of the condition labeled "stressful." In the group situation, this lack of structure or loss of anchor in reality makes it difficult or impossible for the group to cope with the requirements of the situation and the problem of leadership and interpersonal behavior becomes one of evolving or supplying a structure or anchor and of supplying the expertness for coping with the demands of the situation.

Any of several sets of circumstances may make it difficult for the perceiver to structure the situation, or to cope with the situation after structuring has occurred. The situation may be unfamiliar to the group or require rapid shifts in customary activities. The group may not know what to do and, even if they know what must be done, they may not know who should do what with whom. The situation may also constitute a dangerous threat to central values of the group as a group, or of group members. This may blind the group to some important realities of the situation. Loss of structure may be occasioned by the instability of the situation or of group members or by confusion concerning the demands of the situation. There may be lack of cues or too many cues. The changes may be too rapid to process adequately or the requirements may overwhelm the group because it has inadequate skills for coping with them.

Studies of groups in unfamiliar, stress situations provide some understanding of the effects of the lack of structure on behavior. A fundamental element of a stressful situation is its demand for a level and type of activity that sharply departs from customary behavior patterns. This often demands the use of skills that have previously been of minor importance in the group's normal task performance. Adjustment to the stressful situation is aided by factors that reduce the abrupt nature of the change, such as readiness of the group to accept the emergency, good communication, and willingness to experiment with new types of organization.

CRISIS SITUATIONS WITH FAILURES IN LEADERSHIP

Torrance has made a number of studies of enlisted men in the military under a wide variety of emergency conditions.[4] In one project, twenty airmen were assigned to take ten days of air survival training where they had to

---

[4]E. Paul Torrance, G. Rolfe LaForge, and Raigh Mason, *Group Adaptations in Emergencies and Extreme Conditions,* Technical Memorandum Off-Tm-56-4 (Randolph Air Force Base, Texas: Air Force Personnel and Training Research Center, Air Research and Development Command, December 1956).

hike a considerable distance over rough ground. They were organized into three formal groups with instructors assigned to leadership positions. On the second day of the hike, while traveling over difficult and dangerous terrain, a severe blizzard struck with heavy blowing snow and freezing temperatures. Soon after the blizzard hit, the three formal groups broke into seven informal subgroups. Three of these rapidly adjusted to the new conditions while four of the groups failed to adapt.

The adaptable groups quickly evaluated the seriousness of the situation and made preparations to deal with the storm such as building adequate shelters and fires, preparing hot food and drink, drying out foot gear, and taking other essential steps to avoid frostbite and maintain their morale. The nonadaptable groups failed to recognize the seriousness of the situation, so they did little to prepare when the blizzard hit. On the second day, the severity of the conditions dawned upon them, and they attempted to adjust to the conditions by a burst of activity. But by the third day, they had become demoralized and failed to take even elementary steps necessary to avoid frostbite and death. By the end of the fifth day, six of the ten individuals had developed frostbite, were demoralized, and had to be evacuated by helicopter.

Several factors contributed to the relative performance of the two groups. The nonadaptable groups delayed accepting the realities of the situation until adjustments became difficult. A history of conflict between the official leaders of the group and the trainees reduced their ability to adjust to the unexpected conditions. Under stress, the formal groups broke down and subgroups replaced them. Instructors failed to execute expected leadership acts: they kept to themselves, stopped giving briefings, and failed to communicate their plans, provide the opportunity for the trainees to communicate with the leader, or respond to the initiatives or suggestions of the members. These factors, in turn, caused the trainees to rebel and refuse to follow instructions even when given.

The subgroups even failed to communicate with each other. Some of the groups, for example, were not aware that others had dug into snow, built fires, and made other preparations when the blizzard hit. The behavior within the groups was self-enforcing, with the nonadaptable groups communicating low morale, fear, and passiveness while the members of the adaptive groups supported each other by encouraging, communicating, and providing psychological assurance. In summary, this study shows some of the effects of a loss of structure and the conditions contributing to this situation.

Two types of structure define task complexity: structure of the field and structure of the group. Structure of the field is the degree of clarity with which paths lead to the goal. Group structure is the degree to which behavioral patterns and linkages have been stabilized. Organizations normally provide a high degree of structure. Combat flyers, for example, are accustomed to structured situations in which both the goal structure and group structure are well defined. Each individual is given certain functions that to a large extent automatically define the frequency and kind of interaction he has with the others. When a survival situation arises, however, unusual problems occur where past goal and group structures often are inappropriate. Members may not know what they must do to survive. This often results in a random, trial-and-error type of behavior and a feeling of hopelessness that decreases the chances for survival.

Effects of Unprogrammed Situations over Time

Torrance has generalized on the effects of an unstructured situation over time.[5] He draws mostly upon his work with many different military groups operating in a variety of unstructured conditions.

To the extent that we have been able to assess group performance under stress along a time continuum, the data appear to conform quite closely to the process described by Selye for physiological adaptation and by J. G. Miller for psychological adaptation. When there is mastery of stress, this process may be represented schematically by the theoretical curve shown in Figure 5-1. In other words, when the stress is suddenly encountered, there is an initial shock or resistance to accepting the seriousness of the situation. This lag is followed by a rapid overcompensation and recovery with a leveling off of performance as control is gained.

If the stress is continued long enough, regardless of the intensity of the stress and strength of the group, fatigue occurs and ultimately there will be collapse or breakdown. There may be vast differences, however, in the length of time required for different groups under different intensities of stress to reach a "breaking-point." Before the breaking-point is reached a variety of both positive and negative effects may be manifested. There may be confusion, inefficiency, recklessness, apathy, fatigue, hostility, changes in leadership, and the like. In fact such actions may occur almost until the break appears. In such cases, the

---

[5]From "A Theory of Leadership and Interpersonal Behavior Under Stress," by E. Paul Torrance, in *Leadership and Interpersonal Behavior*, edited by Luigi Petrullo and Bernard M. Bass. Copyright © 1961 by Holt, Rinehart and Winston, Publishers. Reprinted by permission of Holt, Rinehart and Winston, Publishers.

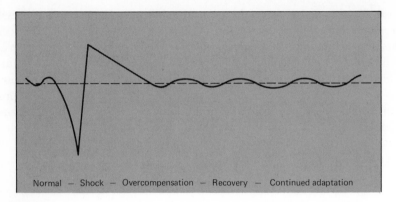

Figure 5-1. Theoretical curve of group performance under stress over time in case of mastery of stress.

break may seem sudden. Prior to the break, the signs of approaching breakdown may have been denied or ignored. Usually after the break has occurred, the warning signs can be recalled.

An Unstructured Social Context: Racial Conflict.   Cone and Williams have explored the effects on individuals in an unfamiliar interpersonal situation.[6] They investigated the way in which customers, workers, and owners of small restaurants and taverns in the South reacted when faced with a demand to serve black patrons. The researchers staged a confrontation by having the blacks enter and press to be served. The manager typically was caught in a dilemma. On the one hand, it was illegal to refuse to serve blacks, but the managers apparently feared that if they did serve the blacks, their customers would object. Where this type of demand was partially but not entirely novel, the parties usually defined the situation in terms with which they were familiar. They sought clues that would indicate that the blacks either did not realize that they were not welcome or were intent upon making trouble. In these cases, there were past patterns to follow. In the more extreme cases, the participants became confused. Either the situation was so far outside the range of their experience or it had such a wide variety of definitions that they were unable to react in any systematic way.

Cone and Williams observe that in an unpatterned situation, an individual elicits at least one of two reactions: (1) he is *confused* about what behavior to expect from others and what action to take, or (2) he has a reasonably

[6]Robert M. Williams, Jr., and Melvin Cone, "Situational Patterning in Intergroup Relations," *American Sociological Review,* 21 (1956), 164–74.

definite idea of how others will act and how he should act himself, but these are contradictory. In the first case, when the individual is confused, he actively seeks clues from others on the way in which to respond to the situation. If there is a formal leader, the participants turn to him for guidance. If those in leadership positions are confused on how to react, then the overt action on the part of any individual sharply influences the orientation of the other members. If no one defines what to do, then there is intense confusion. In the second case, when individuals see two or more alternatives that are contradictory actions or definitions of the situation, they define the situation as atypical. Thus, they view the event as being special and unique—for example, the black wishing service is "different from other blacks"—and they can then typically make accommodations to the confrontation.

UNPROGRAMMED SITUATIONS

Behavior Effects and Methods of Adaptation of Physicians. Another study has explored the behavior of physicians in a highly unstructured context.[7] All physicians are confronted with problems of uncertainty. Some of these result from the physicians' own imperfect mastery of available medical knowledge while others grow out of difficulties in distinguishing between personal ignorance and the limitations of medical science. Fox investigated a ward that had been set up to do research on little-understood diseases. In a fifteen-bed metabolic research ward in a small teaching hospital, diseases were studied that were not well understood and could not be effectively controlled by the current state of medical science. Eleven physicians in this ward had the responsibility to care for the patients and to conduct research upon them.

The group, in part, actively created some of the uncertainties with which they worked and, in part, uncertainty was defined by the context. Their tasks were to devise, explore, and appraise new methods, procedures, and drugs. They were faced with uncertainties regarding fundamental biochemical and physiological mechanisms underlying the conditions they studied, uncertainties connected with the experimental compounds and procedures with which they worked, uncertainties on the laboratory techniques they were developing, and clinical ambiguities on diagnosis and treatment of patients' illnesses.

They were also faced with the fundamental contradiction that actions that contributed to medical research often were in opposition to actions that might have relieved the patient immediately from some pain or stress or might have protected the patient's life. A set of professional ethics define the

[7]Renee C. Fox, *Experiment Perilous: Physicians and Patients Facing the Unknown* (Glencoe, Ill.: Free Press, 1959).

boundaries of professional conduct, but these provide only broad outlines on what is permissible and consistent with professional norms. In the administration of new drugs, for example, controlled tests require both the application and the withholding of these drugs from different patients. The dilemma was, on the one hand, their use or withholding of a drug often put them in a position where a patient's welfare was jeopardized. On the other hand, what they did to help these patients or protect them impaired their research results. As one researcher reported:

> Being a clinical investigator has its problems. A lot of the research you do is of no benefit to the patients, and there is a real possibility that you can do them harm; so in order to do research, you've got to close your eyes to some extent, or at least take calculated risks with the patients on whom you run the experiments. . . . [8]

The factors of uncertainty, the difficulty of resolving problems on the ethics of human experimentation, the moral ambiguity of selecting which patients to experiment on, the conflict between standards of rigorous investigation and those of good medical practice each contributed to the stress on the physicians. At times, the members of the group also had to deal with the fact that a high percentage of patients died or that the group wasn't learning anything except what didn't work.

In many respects the situation is unusual but not unique. The physicians voluntarily placed themselves in a highly unstructured, stressful situation where their ability to predict was low. The group was relatively small and homogeneous in their professional orientation and training. Its unique features were that human beings sometimes died or patients' welfare was adversely affected if the physicians made mistakes. The group developed a number of ways of dealing with the unprogrammed character of the situations. These included emphasizing the long-term gains that were obtained by conducting the research, providing mutual support by joking or betting on the results, and providing special treatment and attention to the patients. And lastly, the doctor could withdraw from the group and concentrate on normal medical practice.

The emphasis upon research provided a logical-rational way of dealing with the uncertainty. To the extent that knowledge was gained, this made the short-term cost to the patients justifiable. The group members provided broad support for one another. The degree of common commitment, problems, goals, and shared stress contributed to a unity that enabled broad exchange of opinions and feelings and sense of shared responsibility. By openly expressing their limitations of knowledge and understanding and by admitting their limited ability to help many of their patients or to reconcile

[8]Ibid., p. 55.

good medical practice and good research, they were able to reduce their tension, frustration, and disquietude. The sharing of these feelings with colleagues gave them "a lift" and provided support from other members of the group on decisions even when there was no scientific basis for the choice.

Humor and placing the events in a gambling context also helped de-emotionalize the stresses. As one doctor expressed it, "Our humor is a kind of protective device. If we were to talk seriously all the time and act like a bunch of Sir Galahads or something, we just couldn't take all of this."[9] Joking reduced the discomfort of the situation by enabling the group to express in unemotional terms some of the tension that they felt. The more serious the situation, the more of a tendency to joke about it, as if by laughing at the events, they accepted the conditions as inevitable. Similarly, by betting on the outcomes of highly ambiguous situations, they were saying their ignorance was so great that they had little more control than in a lottery. They could make reasonable guesses, but it was more a matter of luck than knowledge. In this way, physicians wryly acknowledged that their efforts were often confounded by unpredictable chance elements. This dissipated their sense of responsibility for outcomes.

Laboratory Studies: Contradictions to One's Perception. Many situations exist where one's sense of correctness is dependent upon judgment rather than systematic reasoning or testing of evidence. What happens in a situation where one's judgment is directly challenged by those around him? In a classic experiment, Ash explored the influence that the majority has upon an individual, or a minority in a context where it is possible to make definite judgements but not to verify those judgements.[10]

The experiment placed an individual in a context where his judgment and perception were directly contradicted by those around him. A group of eight individuals was instructed to match the length of a line with one of three unequal lines. Each member announced his judgments publicly. The group, however, with the exception of a naive member, had received instructions to respond at certain points with wrong answers. Thus, a minority of one made a judgment upon a clearly perceptible relationship, but he was contradicted by all others.

Considerable variability in reactions occurred.[11] Ninety-three percent of a control group where judgments were private made no errors. In the experimental groups, on twelve critical trials in which the responses of the majority were incorrect, three-fourths of the subjects moved toward the majority position. Among these who moved, a broad variability occurred with one

[9]Ibid., pp. 76–77.
[10]S. E. Asch, "Effects of Group Pressure Upon the Modification of Distortion of Judgments," in Eleanor Maccoby, Theodore M. Newcomb, and Eugene L. Hartley, eds., *Reading in Social Psychology*, 3rd ed. (New York: Holt, Rinehart & Winston, 1958), pp. 174–83.
[11]Ibid., p. 177.

individual moving eleven out of twelve times to the majority position and thirteen others moving seven to ten times toward the majority position. Only one-fourth of the subjects were completely independent. One-third displaced their estimates toward the majority position on one-half or more of the trials. Even those who didn't modify their judgments toward the direction of the majority were under stress. While some of the subjects remained confident throughout the experiment, others became disoriented, doubt ridden, and expressed a desire to be like the majority. Some demonstrated confidence in their perception and experience even though they were aware of the group pressures. A different group maintained its independence but paid an emotional cost in differing from the group consensus. Of those who yielded to the majority, a few subjects' were influenced so completely that they believed the majority estimates were correct. One individual who moved toward the position of the majority eleven out of twelve times had the sense that the experiment involved an illusion *but that they, not he,* were the subject of the experimental manipulations. Most subjects, however, felt that the majority were probably correct; so, they joined the majority on the basis that they lacked confidence in their own judgment.

Some subjects felt they were correct but yielded to the majority because they didn't want to be different. The social basis of this position was emphasized by one of the later experimental variations where a single member was instructed to deviate from a position that was taken by the others, but in this case the majority reactions were the object of the experiment. The members of the majority reacted to the lone dissenter with amusement; they found him odd and hilariously funny to be so dumb. This amusement, however, quickly gave way when one or more members supported the dissenting member. In a number of variations on this experiment, the support of one or more individuals sharply changed the influence of the majority. When one's judgment is supported by someone else, it enables most individuals to maintain their independence.

Conflicts in Irreconcilable Demands.   Another unprogrammed context involves an individual caught between two sharply conflicting demands that cannot be reconciled. Stanley Milgram conducted a series of experiments where he placed subjects in a high-conflict context.[12] The experiment was ostensibly designed to determine whether punishment contributes to learning. Subjects from a broad variety of backgrounds were paid $4.50 to participate in a learning experiment. Upon arrival at the laboratory, they

---

[12]Stanley Milgram, "Some Conditions of Obedience and Disobedience to Authority," *Human Relations,* 18 (1965), 57–76; Stanley Milgram, "Technique and First Findings of a Laboratory Study of Obedience to Authority," *Yale Scientific Magazine* (November 1964); Stanley Milgram, "Behavioral Study of Obedience," *Journal of Abnormal and Social Psychology,* 67 (1963), 371–78; Stanley Milgram, "Dynamics of Obedience: The Experiments in Social Psychology," mimeographed report, *National Science Foundation* (January 25, 1961). The experiments are also discussed by Phillip Myer, "If Hitler Asked You to Electrocute a Stranger, Would You?" *Esquire,* 73 (February 1970), 128–32.

drew lots—which were rigged so that the subjects would become teachers—and they were introduced to the learner. He had been specially selected and trained—an innocent-appearing gentleman, fiftyish, an accountant, a little overweight, very mild and harmless looking, who believed he has a heart condition. The naive teacher was told that his task was to teach the learner a list of paired words, to test him on this list, and when he made errors to punish him with increasing levels of shock.

The learner was then strapped into a chair in another room behind an opaque glass panel, and the teacher was placed before a control panel to administer the shocks. The shock panel had descriptions ranging from slight shock at the left-hand side to dangerous, severe shock at the far right.

Unknown to the naive teacher, a series of errors had been programmed, and the learner increasingly protested the shocks. The responses of the learner had been standardized on tape, with each level of shock coordinated with a particular level of response. Starting with 75 volts, the learner began to grunt and moan; at 150, he demanded to be let out of the experiment; at 180, he cried out that he could no longer stand the pain; at 300, he refused to provide any more answers, insisting he was no longer a participant and had to be freed.

When the teacher refused to administer the next-higher shock level, the experiment was ended. If the teacher wished to stop, the experimenter told him that he had to continue. The teacher was thus placed into a context where he was instructed to give increasing levels of punishment to another individual who, in turn, became more insistent and pleading that the shocks could not be tolerated and, finally, who demanded that the experiment be discontinued. Many situations exist where individuals are caught in the dilemma of conflicting demands, so the situation in the experiment was general rather than specific in its features.

Teachers might have been expected to break off as their consciences dictated. Under various conditions, from one-third to two-thirds of the subjects did break off the experiment rather than continue to the final level of giving the maximum shock. Both those who quit the experiment and those who continued it to the end were caught up with powerful emotional strains and high tensions. Many of them sweated, trembled, stuttered, bit their lips, and groaned as they found themselves increasingly implicated in the conflict. Some of them verbally refused to go on with the experiment but, when told they had to continue, did in fact follow through and give the learner higher shocks. Many developed nervous laughing fits. Seventy-one of the 160 subjects started smiling or broke out into nervous laughter. Fifteen of these were seized by uncontrollable laughing fits. On one occasion, a forty-six-year-old salesman was caught up with such a violent convulsive laughter, the experiment had to be halted. The majority of the subjects were highly nervous and tense, and some of the subjects showed a high hostility toward the individual whom they were shocking.

In summary, where individuals were placed into an unprogrammed context with sharply conflicting demands, they reacted in a highly emotional manner showing high levels of tension, nonproductive adaptive reactions, and inability to reconcile the conflicting demands.

Reactions to Unsolvable Problems. Hamblin and Wiggins have explored the effects of three-man groups when faced with unsolvable problems.[13] The experimental task was to have the groups play a modified shuffleboard game for thirty minutes where they had to discover the rules by trying out different ideas and watching a light-board. A red light flashed when a rule was violated and a green light when a score was made. The groups were told they were competing with high school students; their accumulative scores were posted along with what they thought were average high school scores. They were informed further that the game illustrated the ability to analyze complex situations and that mature college students were expected to do better than high school students.

The competitive condition resulted in a high level of commitment, with members rushing about shouting commands, showing visible satisfaction as they mastered the rules and their scores began to exceed those of high school students. As the first half of the experimental period ended, the players had learned most of the rules and were performing successfully as indicated by the green lights and increased lead over high school scores. The participants were self-satisfied and confident.

Unknown to the members, the rules of the game were abruptly changed. Permissible procedures were now against the rules; prohibited acts were now acceptable. As the participants saw it, they were suddenly receiving red lights for doing the same things for which they had been receiving green lights. Then, as soon as they learned the new rule, it was changed. The net effect was that they were unable to earn a single score in the last three periods, their leads vanished, and they soon fell behind their high school rivals. This elicited an extreme level of frustration, and the situation was seen as threatening. The participants became more aggressive and hostile; even after the experiment was over, it took a long permissive session to reduce the level of anxiety and hostility.

The structure of the groups changed under stress. Those who had initially assumed a leadership role as measured by giving suggestions and having them accepted tended to lose this influence. Those who were second in influence tended to move into the most influential role, displacing the original dominant member. In the crisis groups, three-fourths of the leaders were replaced. Hamblin generalizes that unless the leader can solve a crisis, he is displaced by someone else.[14]

[13]Robert L. Hamblin and James A. Wiggins, "Suggestibility, Imitation, and Recall During a Crisis," *Midwest Sociologist*, 20 (1957), 26–32.

[14]Robert L. Hamblin, "Leadership in Crisis," *Sociometry*, 21 (1958), 322–35.

Hamblin followed this experiment up with more attention to what happens to intragroup relationships when the group is faced with an unsolvable problem.[15] The teachers were again placed into a game situation where they learned the rules by trying out different methods. Similar to the previous study, under the pressure of the crisis created by the falling scores and confusion on how to make their points, both individual and intragroup behavioral patterns sharply deteriorated. Helping-type behavior to aid team members to do better sharply declined as refusals to help increased. Self-oriented behavior such as trying to dominate or becoming dependent, seeking status in the eyes of the group, or releasing tension by such acts as nervous laughter or expressions of hostility or self-disgust also rose sharply. Supportive acts such as where individuals praise one another declined, and expressions of antagonism increased.

In summary, disintegration increases when a group is faced with a difficult-to-solve problem. Pulling together breaks down and mutual support takes a more passive form. As one solution after another fails, frustration mounts, with group members overreacting to things that irritate them. This reaction may take the form of antagonism and hostility, but these are normally inhibited by social norms. Withdrawal of help and failure to provide positive support are more subtle and less risky forms of aggression. Also, expressing self-oriented behavior such as disgust and anxiety is not a direct threat that typically causes repercussions from other members.

Mediating Effect of Group Structure When Faced with Unsolvable Problems. One of the factors that mediates the way in which unprogrammed tasks affect behavior is the extent to which the groups are stable and cohesive. Thirty years ago, French designed an experiment where 16 six-man groups were given three problems to solve.[16] They were instructed to work as a group on any one of those problems but could switch to another if they found it too difficult. The problems were unsolvable, although this was not apparent either on initial examination or after working with the problems.

The groups were instructed to solve the problems as fast as possible but were limited to forty-five minutes to solve all of the problems. The group was told that the solution of one problem in the shortest possible time depended partly on knowing which problem to choose and when to shift to another problem. The three puzzles were (a) The Four's Problem, (b) The Disc Problem, (c) The Ball and Spiral Problem. The first was primarily intellectual in nature, the ball and spiral largely a motor skill task, while the disc task involved both intellectual and motor skills. The problems were more

[15]Robert L. Hamblin, "Group Integration During a Crisis," *Human Relations,* 11 (1958), 57–76.

[16]John R. P. French, Jr., "The Disruption and Cohesion of Groups," *The Journal of Abnormal and Social Psychology,* 36 (1941), 361–77. A more extensive report of the studies is in John R. P. French, Jr., "Organized and Unorganized Groups Under Fear and Frustration," *University of Iowa Studies in Child Welfare,* 20 (1944), 229–308.

complex than they appeared and increased in difficulty as a solution was approached.

The eight unorganized groups were composed of unacquainted undergraduate students. Five of the organized groups were members of basketball or football teams from dormitories, and the other three were clubs from a neighborhood house that was organized for athletic and social purposes. Some changes were made in the experimental design after six groups had gone through the exercise, so quantitative data were available only on the last ten groups—five organized and five unorganized.

The groups reacted to the frustrations of the situation with considerable variability. The results of nine groups are summarized in Table 5-1, where the average rating is given on a eight-point scale on motivation, frustration, identity with the group, and working together as a group.[17]

TABLE 5-1.

Rank Order by Behavior of Organized and Unorganized Groups

Motivation		Frustration		Team Identity		Group Coordination	
Group	Means*	Group	Means*	Group	Means*	Group	Means*
Highest Scores							
Org O^3	6.50	Org O^4	6.14	Org O^1	6.28	Org O^4	7.74
Org O^4	6.29	Org O^3	5.92	Org O^2	5.78	Org O^3	7.38
Org O^2	5.31	Org O^2	5.32	Org O^4	5.53	Org O^2	6.98
Medium Scores							
Unorg U^1	4.97	Org O^5	5.05	Org O^3	5.46	Org O^1	6.33
Org O^1	4.00	Unorg U^2	4.08	Unorg U^2	4.58	Unorg U^2	5.48
Org O^5	3.79	Org O^1	4.02	Unorg U^1	4.10	Org O^5	5.30
Lowest Scores							
Unorg U^4	3.51	Unorg U^1	3.92	Unorg U^5	3.75	Unorg U^3	4.40
Unorg U^3	3.29	Unorg U^5	3.20	Unorg U^3	3.35	Unorg U^4	4.14
Unorg U^5	3.26	Unorg U^4	2.94	Unorg U^4	3.09	Unorg U^5	3.96

*Average values of two observers on a 0 to 8 scale judging degree of motivation, frustration, identity with team, and working together as a group.

Three of the organized groups had the highest motivation and three of the unorganized groups the lowest. The pattern was reversed for the midvalues, with the two unorganized groups having higher motivation than the organized groups. Four of the five organized groups showed a higher level of frustration and coordination of effort than the unorganized groups. The members in the organized groups had more of a sense of identity than the unorganized groups; the differences were fairly distinct between the top and bottom three groups in each category.

[17]Ibid., adapted from p. 262.

This description of the groups is complemented by the observers' descriptions of a number of acts that were problem oriented, expressing friendship, aggressing against others, complaints about the problems, downgrading of oneself, and withdrawal from the task and group. All but one organized group had a relatively high number of problem-solving acts. In contrast, considerable variation existed on the extent that the unorganized groups concentrated directly on accomplishing the task. Two of the unorganized groups had the highest problem-directed acts and two had the lowest problem-directed acts.

Somewhat unexpectedly, the interpersonal relations were more constructive in the unorganized groups than in the organized groups. Higher incidence of aggressive acts toward others occurred in all except one of the organized groups. In contrast, aggressive acts against others were low in unorganized groups, except in one group. Both the organized and unorganized groups accepted the problems as solvable and were frustrated with one another but not the situation. A relatively high incidence of attempts to escape from the problem by withdrawing occurred, but little consistent difference between organized and unorganized groups developed.

The organized and unorganized groups moved in different directions on the degree of participation. Early in the experiments, several individuals in unorganized groups typically contributed little to the solution of the problem but increasingly participated as the period progressed. In the organized groups, on the other hand, all members participated to a high degree at the start, but frequently one or two individuals subsequently assumed more of the problem-solving role as the group functioned.

In summary, the posing of unsolvable problems to groups—who are under the impression that the problems are solvable—contributes toward high frustration and pressure on interpersonal relationships with hostile withdrawal being common. The degree to which the groups have had a previous experience with one another and have developed group structure affects partially the way in which members respond. There is a high degree of expression of hostility and withdrawal in the organized groups, but they have a greater ability to reorganize in order to again attack the problem. The unorganized groups are less likely to express the hostility or withdrawal but have a lower capacity to deal with the problem if relationships break down.

CONTRASTS IN PROGRAMMED AND UNPROGRAMMED CONTEXTS

The Medical and Surgical Floor in the General Hospital. Two studies have highlighted the way in which task complexity in a hospital determines the behavior patterns between doctors and patients and between nurses and patients.[18] Both studies compare the way in which medical and surgical wards differ. Burling, Lentz, and Wilson focus on the way in which nurses relate to one another and to patients, and the relationship that develops among patients. A surgical nurse commented, "I always hated it on medical. Even when they [the patients] get better, you don't always know how much you have had to do with it. Maybe it was just all the bedrest." In contrast, a medical nurse observed, "I am definitely not interested in surgery. It's too mechanical a type of work, like running a lathe."[19] The authors observe that medical floors look, sound, and have a different feeling than surgical floors. Medical floors are quiet while the dominant note on surgical floors is one of activity and bustle. Surgical floors are characterized by camaraderie—the patients entertain one another, play games, joke with one another, and help others with minor needs. In contrast, on the medical floors, many patients are querulous and often have the emotional stability of children.

Two technical developments have influenced the nature of activity on medical floors and surgical wards. The advent of antibiotics has sharply reduced the number of serious cases such as acute infections on medical floors. In surgical areas, the trend toward early ambulation has revolutionized the work of nurses. The patients are thrust into early activity shortly following surgery rather than being waited upon in bed, and their hospital stay is typically relatively short. There is also a variety of patients since automobile accidents, inflamed appendixes, and general surgery affect the whole population. Medical floors, in contrast, have a higher percentage of elderly patients with heart and circulatory diseases, diabetes, cancer, and other chronic diseases. Many of these cases respond slowly to treatment, their prognosis is poor, and they require considerable care such as baths, changes of bed linens, and other personal services.

Differences in behavior are closely related to the nature of illness and treatment. On surgical floors, the nurses and doctors concentrate on the patient's incision and don't concern themselves with the patient's larger needs. The patient typically assumes that once his operation is over, his crisis has passed. This releases him from much of his worry and anxiety and enables him to turn to his neighbors. In contrast, on the medical floor, the patient usually has no such clean transition point. The medical patient is typically ill, worried, and less likely to be concerned with his neighbors. When he starts feeling better, he characteristically goes home for further recuperation.

[18]Temple Burling, Edith M. Lentz, and Robert N. Wilson, *The Give and Take in Hospitals* (New York: G. P. Putnam's Sons, 1956), pp. 244–59; Rose L. Coser, *Life in the Ward* (East Lansing: Michigan State University Press, 1962), pp. 129–47. This article is also summarized in Rose L. Coser, "Authority and Decision-Making in a Hospital: A Comparative Analysis," *American Sociological Review*, 23 (1958), 56–64.

[19]Burling, Lentz, and Wilson, *The Give and Take in Hospitals*, p. 255.

On the surgical floors, patients typically recover at a predictable speed and in a standard way. Further, in surgical wards, it is relatively simple for the head nurse to assign her most expert workers to the sickest patients and give each nurse a reasonable amount of work. The competence required for different aspects of surgical nursing can be clearly graded. It is relatively easy to determine the level of skills of nurses and student trainees and the skills required to aid patients.

Medical floors contrast with this degree of predictability and the nature of the task. The patient's progress often fluctuates more because of factors such as the nature of the disease, variable reactions to drugs, and the psychological state of the patient. Patients' days vary from good to bad, and nursing needs are somewhat upredictable. It is more difficult to interest student nurses and other auxiliary helpers since they find themselves often "making beds while the graduates do all the interesting things." This happens since the graduate nurses care for the seriously ill such as the acute cases while chronic illnesses are assigned to the care of students and other helpers.

These two kinds of cases require widely different care. Chronic cases are heavily laden with custodial-type duties such as bed making, carrying water, and other service activities. Patient care is more subtle and interpersonal than medically defined. From the nurses' perspective, on the surgical floors they could be systematic, but on medical floors they couldn't. When a patient would come in, he would be operated on the next day, and five days later, he would be up and around. The nurses could plan their work ahead, and the doctor could understand what they were doing. The doctor could see that the nurses were following a system. On the other hand, on medical floors and on general surgery, the nurses dealt with a variety of patients and doctors. They didn't get acquainted with any of them, and it was more difficult to organize their work.

The differences in the nature of the wards also affect the relation of the doctors to the interns and the doctors and interns to the nurses. Coser, in her study, paid particular attention to these relationships. On the surgical wards an apparent anomaly exists between the degree of delegation by doctors to interns and by doctors and interns to nurses. The chief resident and the visiting doctors make the decisions in the surgical wards and neither delegate nor consult much with the interns. Important operations are carried out by the chief resident, chief of staff, or a visiting surgeon. In contrast, authority is broadly delegated to the nurses on surgical wards. This comes about for several reasons. When surgery is being performed, the entire surgical staff is in the operating room for a large part of the day. Only one intern is on duty. Since little authority is delegated to an intern, it is difficult for him to assume the role of chief of staff. The relation to the surgical nurses and the doctors is profiled by the comment of a surgical nurse: "The doctors want to be called in an emergency only if they know you and they feel you know what you are doing."[20] As a consequence of her higher prestige and greater authority, the surgical nurse often gives suggestions to doctors on treatments for patients and is less concerned with the rules and regulations. The doctors, in turn, seek qualities in nurses that are decision oriented, such as "foresight," ability to provide "quick, reliable assistance," and "intelligence."

On the medical wards, in contrast, the chief resident consistently delegates authority down the line to interns, but there is little delegation to nurses. The chief resident may say to the interns: "You make the final decision, he's your patient."[21] Decisions in medical wards are often made by consultation and consensus among doctors and interns. In diagnosing illness and choosing among different courses of treatment, difficult problems exist that exert pressure for careful thinking, consultation, and deliberation among the team members. In teaching medical students, the emphasis is upon thinking and reflection, while on surgical wards, it is on action and exact performance.

Unlike on the surgical wards, relatively little authority is delegated to the medical nurses. In the medical wards, nurses participate only in morning rounds with the chief resident but not in rounds with the visiting doctor. In the surgical ward, she either participates in both rounds or is approached by the visiting doctor for information. A medical nurse is pressed more into a clerical role in these rounds, while a surgical nurse assumes a more direct participative role in commenting on the patients' conditions and suggesting treatments. Nurses on the medical wards more often cling to rules, are less likely to think independently or act innovatively, and are more procedurally oriented. Doctors seek nurses on the medical wards who have qualities such as sympathy and understanding rather than decision-making qualities.

In summary, we find a complex mixture in the degree of delegation by doctors to interns and by doctors and interns to nurses on the surgical and medical wards. This complexity, however, is patterned when we examine the division of labor, and the degree treatment has a programmed character. In surgery there is a major difference in complexity of tasks between surgery and postoperative treatment. Surgery requires a high level of skill and knowledge. While it can be acquired by the neophyte, the skill must be at a critical level before the intern can apply this skill on major cases. Initially, practice is on minor surgery with observation and assistance on major surgery. Consequently, typically little authority is delegated from the surgeon in charge to the intern.

In contrast, postoperative care is of a more programmed character. The surgical incision and aftereffects heal at a fairly predictable pace. It is also easier to divide up the tasks depending upon the severity of the operation,

[20]Ibid., p. 10.
[21]Ibid., p. 135.

condition of the patient, and stage of recovery. Since the doctors and interns are occupied in surgery a good portion of the day and the tasks are more programmed and divisible into degrees of severity, it is reasonable to expect a broad delegation of authority to the nurses in the surgical wards. In the medical wards, the situation is basically different. Continuing diagnosis and treatment are closely interwoven; the initial diagnosis and treatment are tentative and subject to revision depending upon developing symptoms of the patient. Both steps are compounded by psychological factors since symptoms and patient recovery are influenced by the patient's state of mind and attitudes.

Chronic cases such as arthritis, bad heart, or diseases of old age are relatively simple to diagnose, but there is little that can be done for the patient except professional care. Acute cases, on the other hand, have a high degree of unpredictability about them. They are difficult to diagnose and treat. Given the broad variability in reactions to drugs and other forms of treatment, there is a need for close observation and reevaluation as the patient reacts through time.

It is understandable why the doctors delegate less to the nurses and why the graduate nurses delegate less to the student nurses on acute cases. One would expect greater delegation on chronic cases, since there are few decisions to make and a great deal of custodial care to undertake. The student nurses find themselves assigned to handling these chores while the "interesting cases" are assumed by the skilled graduate nurses. As in the case of interns in surgery, a critical level of skill has to be obtained before care of more serious cases can be delegated to the neophytes.

Summary and Conclusion. We have been exploring the implications that the degree of complexity of tasks has for behavior. The focus has been on the degree to which solutions can be worked out systematically and outcomes predicted.

Sailors, soldiers, and college students who are placed in unstructured contexts, such as when they are faced with an overwhelming barrage of stimuli or a complete absence of stimuli, react with high stress and inability to deal productively and systematically with the problems. Individuals experience high frustration and often have hallucinations and illusions.

As an unprogrammed situation develops, pressure is exerted that adversely affects individual behavior patterns and intragroup relations. Individuals lose their orientation and develop a sense of inadequacy and dissatisfaction with themselves and with group members, which, in turn, contributes to intragroup conflict. Groups faced with unsolvable problems displace their leaders, show a breakdown in interpersonal relationships, and increase self-oriented behavioral patterns.

The degree to which tasks are programmed has broader effects including the type of individual who is valued, degree of delegation of authority, and general working climate. The contrasts in medical and surgical wards in a hospital illustrate these effects. Surgical wards with their more structured tasks create two different climates for patients, doctors, interns, and nurses. Patients are more optimistic and interaction oriented; doctors delegate greater authority to nurses, prize the nurses' independence and initiative, and consult with them about patients. The medical ward, with its pervasive, complex problems where diagnosis and treatment are tentative and the progress of a patient difficult to assess, have different patterns. Patients are pessimistic, less active, and more self-oriented; doctors seldom delegate authority or consult with nurses; nurses are more rule oriented and exercise less initiative. The pervasive difficulties associated with medical wards create a less pleasant, more subdued environment and different interpersonal relations.

Table 5-2 lists some of the factors that affect the degree to which tasks are programmed.

TABLE 5-2. Factors Affecting the Degree of Task Complexity

Factors	Programmed	Unprogrammed
Clarity and consistency among multiple goals/demands	Clearly understood, complementary goals/demands	Unclear, contradictory goals/demands
Clarity of structure and relationships	Stable structure, good relationships	Unstable structure with history of conflict
Nature of problems	Solvable	Unsolvable
Training	Trained	Untrained
Anticipation of problems	Anticipated/ planned	Unanticipated/ emergencies
Stability of stimulus	Constant	Sharp change (increase or complete withdrawal)

Survival studies reveal the different forms of reactions that develop when individuals are faced with inconsistent, multiple goals such as choosing between actions that contribute to survival or saving a buddy. The conflicting demands often throw the parties into a quandary over what to do. Torrance relates many examples in which the men failed to act and were drowned, captured, killed by the enemy, lost, or frozen in severe weather. Torrance also relates examples where individuals were at a point of collapse when a plan was formulated: the exhaustion and disorientation evaporated immediately. Keys to survival were good training, familiarity with what to do, and well-defined goals. That is, to the extent that members could create structure in these ambiguous situations, they sharply increased their ability to survive.

Groups that were stable and well-structured—i.e., members had confidence and trust in one another, actions were predictable, constructive behavior had occurred in the past, and the members were oriented to act in the group interest rather than only for themselves—were able to deal with the emergencies, high stress, and fluid situations. Where these factors were absent, the group relationships adversely affected the ability to deal with the problems.

Experimental studies illustrate the difficulties of dealing with problems with contradictory demands where group support is lacking. The Cone and Williams study of blacks demanding to be served in the South in public restaurants placed the proprietors in the situation where they were pulled between what they interpreted as the expectations of the customers and the expectations of the blacks, who were backed by the law. The physicians studied by Fox were caught between the need to serve the patients and the need to do research that required actions that often weren't in the patients' interest. The experiments by Milgram placed individuals in a context where they had to either disobey the experimenter or increase the punishment of a pleading man.

The Asch experiments placed individuals so that their perception of a clear object was challenged by all others in the group. Many modified their judgment to avoid the stress of having a different opinion than the others. Even those who maintained their independence were anxious and tense about their judgments. In this situation, the members were able to make a clear distinction with their own eyes. In many of life's problems, the right and wrong are difficult to objectively determine, so the stress is probably even greater. The slightest form of support—only one member agreeing with the deviant individual—gave the individual enough confidence and assurance to maintain his position and reduce the stress of the majority challenge.

These cases varied in the degree to which contradictions existed and in the immediacy of the demand to deal with those contradictions. Even so, each of the conditions caused high stress, with the proprietors looking for clues from customers or others to define how to react and the physicians justifying their behavior and relieving tension by joking, emphasizing the long-term gains of research, giving special treatment and attention to patients, and relying heavily upon group support for their action.

These contexts are stressful largely because the individual loses the usual structure and anchor to reality that guide his decisions and actions. While all members initially may be fearful, anxious, and immobilized, this is quickly overcome in integrated groups. Positive actions are taken to support one another and deal with the situation.

The physicians had an ideal context in which to deal with the stress in that the group was homogeneous and had common goals. Milgram's subjects, in contrast, were faced with the need to deal with problems without help; their only recourse was to withdraw from the experiment—i.e., refuse to follow the orders of the experimenter to exact greater punishment on the subject, who was already showing intense reactions to each level of punishment.

A history of factional conflicts or distrust or where the members have acted selfishly and independently of the interest of others also reduces the probability of the group dealing with problems. When these conditions occur, problems of maintaining relations at a stable level dominate group activities. Any panic, apathy, exhaustion, or collapse is communicated to the other members and, in turn, reinforces adverse behavior patterns.

Intragroup conflict further contributes to loss of group structure and stability. When the relationship among members is either undefined or inappropriate to the situation—such as when the group members fail to develop complementary roles or when leaders fail to perform leadership tasks—this contributes to further disorientation of members. If one or more members react in an unpredictable or distraught manner or if valued members leave the group, this also adversely affects the ability of the group to deal with problems.

French's exploration of the degree to which the past experiences of the members influenced their reactions found that organized groups showed higher motivation and frustration, as well as a greater sense of identity and working together. However, some minimal level of past group cohesion must exist before it mediates the influence of an unprogrammed task. In this experiment, only the extremes in behavior were related to previous cohesion of the group. A more reliable measure of group cohesion than past interaction would probably show cohesion to be a consistent mediating influence with the level of stress.

Personality is likely to be a mediating factor that affects the influence that structure or lack of it exerts, but no studies were found that examined this relation. The size of the group, the degree to which work flow is interdependent, spatial-physical barriers, and the level of standards probably interact with complexity of the task in their impact on behavior. The larger the group, the more vulnerable it is to an unprogrammed situation, since strains already exist in large groups. Similarly, where interdependent work flow exists within and between groups, unprogrammed problems elicit a greater impact than where the groups are not interdependent. Their interdependence already contributes to stress, and task complexity adds to difficulties in a compounded basis. Spatial-physical barriers also reduce the ability of the members to check their judgments and to receive support from group members. In a similar way, a high level of work demands combined with an unstructured problem situation creates higher stress than the two factors changing separately.

The schematic summary clarifies some of these effects. Figure 5-2 focuses on completely unprogrammed tasks, such as where problems are unsolvable,

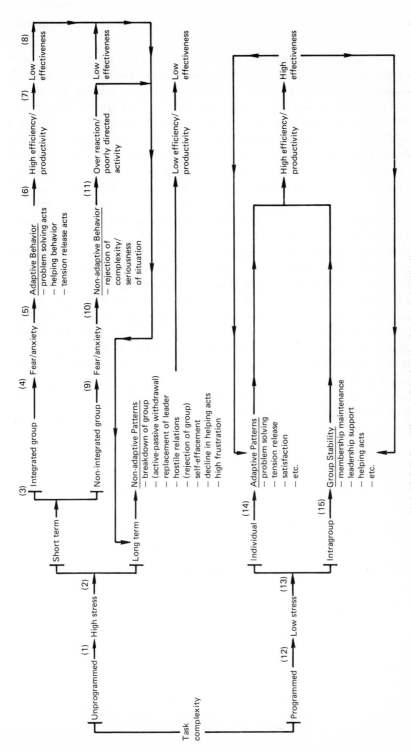

FIGURE 5-2. Effects of task complexity on behavior

and the completely programmed situation. Where tasks are unprogrammed (1), this leads to high stress (2). In the short term—and this may be only a few hours or days—the reactions vary depending upon existing group relations. Where the group has a stable structure and has operated in an integrated manner (3), anxiety and fear occur (4). This, however, is directed toward problem-solving acts, helping behavior, and tension release (5). The study of physicians dealing with partially unprogrammed situations and armed service personnel in life and death situations indicates that a group can function without breaking down. Initially, the group is efficient and productive (6). If the problems are solvable, the behavior is reinforced. If they are unsolvable, the low effectiveness of the group (7) results in collapse and long-term nonadaptive behavior (8).

Nonintegrated groups also become fearful and anxious (9), but they initially reject the seriousness or complexity of the situation (10). When they realize later that action is needed, they give a burst of poorly organized and poorly directed activity (11). When this fails, they lapse into passive acceptance of failure or catastrophy. In life and death survival situations, they panic and die; in other situations, they fail to deal with the problems. Where problems are solvable, they fail due to lack of effort and direction.

With programmed tasks (12), stress is low (13). Individual and group behavior is constructive and stable (14 and 15), with the result of high efficiency and effectiveness. The high effectiveness, in turn, reinforces individual and intragroup patterns.

6

SPATIAL-PHYSICAL FACTORS:
Barriers within
and among Groups

INTRODUCTION

Considerable attention has been given to the relation of spatial-physical barriers to behavior. Two strands have developed, one of which focuses on the way in which spatial-physical barriers influence behavior patterns. The second theme is on the way in which individuals use space and barriers to build cohesion or to maintain differences.[1] The perspectives on both the way in which spatial-physical barriers influence behavior and the way in which individuals and groups use spatial-physical barriers to support ongoing behavioral patterns are useful.

Pitney Bowes used the illustration on the next page to focus upon the handling of paper flow in an office. It also provides an overview of spatial-physical barriers in an office and the use of space and barriers. The walls separate the personnel among offices. Within each office the physical arrangements of furniture support or discourage interaction. Observe the arrangements of the manager's office. He is physically screened by walls and by his secretary (3) from visitors. But if they are admitted, the chair arrangement supports interaction but with clear social distance maintained.

[1]Constance Perin, *With Man in Mind: An Interdisciplinary Prospectus for Environmental Design* (Boston: M.I.T. Press, 1970); Robert Gutman, "Site Planning and Social Behavior," *Journal of Social Issues*, 22 (1966), 103–15; Humphrey Osmond, "Function as the Basis of Psychiatric Ward Design," *Mental Hospitals* (April 1957), pp. 23–29; Robert Sommer, *Personal Space* (New York: McGraw-Hill, 1969); William B. Cameron and Raymond H. Wheeler, "Physical Setting and Intellectual Climate," *School and Society* (February 25, 1961); William Griffin, Joseph H. Mauritzen, and Joyce V. Kasmur, "The Psychological Aspects of the Architectural Environment: A Review," *American Journal of Psychiatry*, 125 (February 1969), 1057–62; Henry Sanoff and Sidney Cohn, eds., *Proceedings of the 1st Annual Environmental Design Research Association Conference* (1970); Oscar Newman, *Defensible Space* (New York: Macmillan Co., 1972); James P. Batchelor and George R. Goethals, "Spatial Arrangements in Freely Formed Groups," *Sociometry*, 35 (1972), 270–79; Clark McPhail and David Miller, "The Assembling Process: A Theoretical and Empirical Examination," *American Sociological Review*, 38 (1973), 721–35.

Reproduced by permission of Pitney Bowes. Copyright © 1974 by Pitney Bowes.

Would it influence the sense of approachableness if his chair was on the opposite side of the desk?

Contrast these arrangements in the mail room. Positions 1, 5, and 6 are designed to minimize interaction by their use of space and physical orientation of the desks. Observe the locations of the doors. Do they minimize or support interaction among offices?

The use of space and physical objects to support interaction within groups is illustrated in the other two offices. At position 2 and 4, small groups face each other around a desk and table.

This chapter first reviews the studies on the way that spatial-physical barriers affect behavior and the mediating factors that amplify, reduce, or reverse the behavioral effects. Next, a brief exposition is given of the way existing relationships influence the use of spatial-physical barriers. The chapter concludes with a summary of these two strands of literature.

Spatial-physical barriers cover several aspects:

1. *Separation by distance.* This is the number of feet individuals or groups are apart. A subdimension is the degree to which individuals are located

face to face and are able to have direct eye contact without turning their heads or bodies.

2. *Separation by semifixed features.* This is where individuals or groups are separated by objects such as desks, bookcases, tables, filing cabinets, chairs, and similar objects. These are movable but typically are regularly ordered in a specified manner.

3. *Separation by fixed features.* Attention here is on separation by walls, location on different floors, or buildings. The transparency of the windows, height of the walls, location of doorways, hallways, stairways, and connecting walks are relevant features of fixed dimensions.

Spatial-physical barriers directly affect interaction patterns and the nature of the relationships that develop. Moving individuals or groups apart or together exerts pressure on their interaction patterns; simply placing them back to back or face to face exerts pressure to reduce or increase their contacts with each other. The location of barriers, whether they are bookcases, filing cabinets, tables, or walls, exerts a pervasive influence on relationships. The positions in which doors and passageways are placed affects the extent to which individuals meet one another and develop personal relationships. The location of service facilities such as cafeterias, restrooms, drinking fountains, or other central services determines, in part, the development of intra- and intergroup relationships.

Osmond refers to those factors that discourage interaction and personal relationships as sociofugal in character, while sociopetal arrangements support and encourage development of personal relationships.[2] Spatial-physical barriers along with other factors such as noise, lighting, traffic, and temperature are sociofugal characteristics of lobbies in large metropolitan airports that encourage travelers and visitors to move to side areas. Some of these such as shops, short-order restaurants, and newsstands encourage individuals to look, purchase, and leave. Others such as bars, restaurants, and lounges are designed for comfort, relaxation, and support of small-group interaction to encourage longer stays.

A dynamic relationship exists between barriers and the individual's use of space. The physical arrangement of chairs and tables, for instance, exerts an influence on behavior, but where people are free to move the furniture, they tend to rearrange it to support preferred interaction patterns and minimize those they wish to avoid. Even when they don't physically relocate the chairs and tables, they often sit where it aids interaction with some and discourages it with others. At the same time, the tendency is to accept the physical arrangement as a proper sense of order. If chairs are neatly lined along

---

[2]Humphrey Osmond, "Function as the Basis of Psychiatric Ward Design," *Mental Hospitals* (April 1957), p. 28.

the sides of a hallway or waiting room, for instance, this discourages interaction. Those who work in the building typically consider it their job to
maintain the orderly arrangement even when those in the room continually
rearrange the chairs to support interaction. Social scientists, architects,
hospital administrators, physicians, and managers often are in a position to
design and direct spatial-physical arrangements but typically do so with
little understanding of the effects they are creating.

Measuring Spatial Physical Barriers

*The excerpt sets forth the measurement of spatial-physical barriers that exist among
individuals. The same approach is applied to measure barriers between groups.*

The spatial-physical factors refer to the extent to which individuals
are grouped or separated by distance, spatial orientation or physical
barriers. On one extreme, individuals are close together and positioned
so they are face to face. An example would be where individuals sit
around a table with no physical barriers between them. At the other
extreme, individuals are separated by distance, or physical barriers
such as separate rooms or floors.

This is operationalized by averaging the following items:

SPATIAL-PHYSICAL SCALE: INTRAGROUP

Concentrated							Dispersed	
1	2	3	4	5	6	7	8	9

Talking Distance   _____

Eye Contact   _____

1. *Physical Relation of Group Members*—What percentage of members
of your work group are located close enough to you to carry on a normal conversation regularly without shouting or going out of your way?

TALKING DISTANCE AMONG GROUP MEMBERS

1	2	3	4	5	6	7	8	9
Extensive: most members are within talking distance	Some		Moderate: half are within talking distance			Considerable		Few: practically nobody is within talking distance

2. *Direct Eye Contact*—What percentage of members do you have direct eye contact with without turning around or moving from your regular work position or office?

EYE CONTACT AMONG GROUP MEMBERS

1	2	3	4	5	6	7	8	9

Direct:	Partial:	Indirect:
most members	side-by-side	back-to-back
are located	relationship	relationship
face-to-face	among most	among most
	members	members

THE INFLUENCE OF SPATIAL-PHYSICAL BARRIERS ON BEHAVIOR

Spatial-Physical Factors in the Community. Spatial-physical barriers exert a pervasive influence on the way in which the community develops. The importance of the physical features is emphasized by Floyd Hunter:

The community. . . can be measured, charted, and plotted. It has a "reality" in a stronger sense than many other materials with which social scientists must work. The physical features are part of the social

DRAWN BY PENNY WILLIAMS

Aramco World Magazine, vol. 25, no. 4 (July-August 1974).

structure in that they help to regulate and routinize the behavior patterns of men around which physical features are built. There is, therefore, an interaction between the physical characteristics of the community and the patterned actions of men. The physical structures once created act as passive barriers of channels for the dynamic actions of men.[3]

Stouffer develops the thesis that spatial factors are part of the explanation of why people go to a particular place to get jobs, trade at a store, commit a crime in a particular neighborhood, or marry the spouse they choose.[4]

Distance and the transportation links are important determinants of the structure of a city. The maximum distance between homes and service centers, for instance, is partially determined by the extent that distance can be traveled using available transportation. The slower the means, the smaller the range of the community. Where there is a dependence upon walking, oxcarts, or animals, for example, such as in villages in rural India or China, the range of the community is sharply limited.[5]

Studies that have examined the relationships between distance and partners selected in marriage show an inverse relationship between the distance separating potential partners and the number of marriages. In New Haven, 76 percent of the marriages in 1940 were between persons living within twenty blocks and 35 percent between persons living within five blocks of each other.[6]

Studies of American suburbs have found that where residents are located so that they can see neighbors, this lays the foundation for initial contact among them. This is important in determining relations during the early stages of living in the neighborhood, and the interactions are likely to develop into an enduring pattern when the parties have a homogeneous set of values.[7]

Housing Studies: Distance and Interaction. In a housing project study, distances as small as twenty to thirty feet played a major part in determining friendship patterns.[8] The most friendships developed with next-

[3]Floyd Hunter, *Community Power Structure* (Chapel Hill, N.C.: University of North Carolina Press, 1953), pp. 23–24.

[4]S. A. Stouffer, "Intervening Opportunities: A Theory Relating Mobility and Distance," *American Sociological Review*, 5 (1940), 845–67.

[5]R. D. McKenzie, "Spatial Distance and Community Organization Pattern," *Social Forces* (1927), pp. 623–27.

[6]R. H. Abrams, "Residential Propinquity as a Factor in Marriage Selection," *American Sociological Review*, 8 (1943), 288–94; R. Kennedy, "Pre-Marital Residential Propinquity," *American Journal of Sociology*, 48 (1943), 580–84.

[7]Herbert J. Glans, "Planning and Social Life," *Journal of American Institute of Planners*, 27 (1961), 134–40; Herbert J. Glans, "The Balanced Community," *Journal of American Institute of Planners*, 27 (1961), 176–84.

[8]Leon Festinger, Stanley Schachter, and Kurt Back, *Social Pressures in Informal Groups* (Stanford: Stanford University Press, 1950), pp. 33–59.

door neighbors, with 41 percent reporting friendship patterns; friendships declined to 22 percent with those living two doors away; those three doors away to 16 percent; and four doors away to 10 percent. While neighboring apartments were only twenty-two feet apart and apartments at the opposite ends of the same floor about eighty-eight feet, these small differences were major determinants of whether friendships formed. Similarly, living on different floors directly affected friendship patterns. The separation of floors sharply reduced the interaction, with 21 percent of those one apartment unit apart showing friendship choices; this declined to 5 percent where they were four units apart.

Another housing study supported the thesis that spatial-physical barriers affect both the nature and degree of interaction. One group of whites who lived close to black tenants in the same building was compared with whites who lived in all-white buildings.[9] Among the five residents they knew best, two-fifths of the women in the integrated buildings knew at least one black resident compared with none for the women in nonintegrated buildings. Over one-half of the white women from integrated buildings had developed a social cohesion that included one or more activities of visiting back and forth, helping each other, participating in informal club activities, and going out together; less than 3 percent of the white women in segregated housing had developed these forms of social cohesion. Almost half of the women in integrated housing believed their friends would favor friendly interaction with blacks compared with 4 percent in nonintegrated buildings. In respect to adherence to stereotypes, about four-fifths of the women in integrated housing felt that the blacks were much the same as the whites living in the housing complex; this contrasts with three-fifths of the women in segregated housing.[10]

Modifying Influence of Status. Barnlund and Harland's findings partially qualify these conclusions. While spatial differences partly explained different levels of interaction among a group of sororities, differences in prestige also affected relationships.[11] Interaction among sororities was closely bound by their relative prestige: high-status sororities communicated with one another; moderate-status groups interacted with one another, etc. The principal exception was where one of the sororities with moderate status had extensive communication with sororities at the same status level and with higher status groups. In this case, the sorority was rapidly moving up the status hierarchy.

[9]Daniel M. Wilner, Rosabelle P. Walkley, and Stewart W. Cook, "Residential Proximity and Intergroup Relations in Public Housing Projects," *Journal of Social Issues*, 8 (1952), 45–69.

[10]Ibid.

[11]Dean C. Barnlund and Carrol Harland, "Propinquity and Prestige as Determinants of Communication Networks," *Sociometry*, 26 (1963), 467–79.

The authors conclude that the physical setting in which people interact sets limits upon and determines the frequency of communication in the early stages of interpersonal relations. Once a social system evolves, though, and status differentiation occurs, communication centers on high-status figures. The influence of the physical setting may be then reinforced, modified, or reversed by the influence of status.

Physical Separation and Intergroup Relations. A study of a college dormitory revealed some of the sociofugal-sociopetal qualities of a nine-story complex. The main floor was divided into a lobby, library, and three multiple-purpose rooms. Twenty-four students per floor were divided among twelve rooms on each of the eight dormitory floors. A common bathroom served each floor. The floors were sociopetal in character since the residents were physically divided from other floors and had a common functional facility of the bathroom. Each floor tended to develop into a cohesive social group. In contrast, the large size and high ceilings of the lounge and library area, lack of privacy from the entrance hall, and formality of furniture arrangements created sociofugal contexts. The facilities were seldom used by the students.[12]

Richards and Dobyns identified the way in which changes in physical arrangements in an office affect intragroup and intergroup relations and relationships of a group to supervisors.[13] A small unit that varied from six to nine employees in a bank was located in a small enclosed work area; access was through two doors, one of which permitted exit to the outside of the building. Those outside the unit could not see into the room, and locks on the door made it impossible for visitors to enter without special admission. The group of workers had developed a high degree of cohesion, a well-structured social system, and a sense of special status and of working in a friendly atmosphere.

In a reorganization move, the work unit was shifted to another floor to a similar room except that one wall was open to view from the outside, and it didn't have a door leaving the building. The unit was still enclosed with a steel mesh defining the boundary. In the new unit, entrance and exit from the cage were possible only through one door that led through another work group. This combination resulted in the unit coming under direct supervisory observation and being exposed to the larger work group. The substitution of the steel mesh for a wall enabled the supervisor who was physically outside the room to exercise close control over the workers. Special customs such as having an afternoon snack were soon brought to the attention of the

---

[12]Sim Van Der Ryn and Murray Silverstein, "Berkeley: How Do Students Really Live?" *Architectural Forum*, 127 (1967), 93–95.

[13]Cara B. Richards and Henry Dobyns, "Topography and Culture: The Case of the Changing Cage," *Human Organization*, 16 (1957), 16–20.

supervisor and the other workers outside the cage. The customs were then either restricted by the supervisor or made available to all so that the cage lost its special privileges.

Increased stress, less satisfaction, more absenteeism, passive resistance to instructions, a greater degree of overt opposition, and decline in efficiency developed in the unit. Part of these factors could be attributed to the close supervision and elimination of the unit's special status, but both had been made possible by the removal of barriers.

Structuring the Context with Spatial-Physical Arrangements

Robert Sommer has given systematic attention to the importance of spatial-physical factors. In the excerpt he develops the importance of these factors and identifies the assumptions that often underline the determination of spatial-physical arrangements.[14]

We find ourselves being arranged by impersonal environments in lecture halls, airports, waiting rooms, and lobbies. Many aspects of the proximate environment, including furniture and room dividers, have been placed for ease of maintenance and efficient cleaning with little cognizance to their social functions. These principles will be of most help in an institutional setting such as schools, hospitals, public buildings, and old folks' homes where the occupants have little control over their surroundings. The straight-row arrangement of most classrooms has been taken for granted for too long. The typical long narrow shape of a classroom resulted from a desire to get light across the room. The front of each room was determined by window location, since pupils had to be seated so that window light came over the left shoulder. However, new developments in lighting, acoustics, ventilation, and fireproofing have rendered invalid many of the arguments for the box-like room with straight rows. In mental hospitals, the isolation of schizophrenic individuals can be furthered by sociofugal setting which minimizes social contact, or reduced through sociopetal buildings aimed at reinforcing social behavior. The former approach is valid if one wants to provide an optimal environment in terms of the individual's present needs, the latter if society desires to shape the patient's social behavior to facilitate his return to society. It is mindless to design mental hospitals without taking cognizance of the connection between physical environment and social behavior. The study of small group ecology is important not only from the standpoint of developing an adequate theory

---

[14]Robert Sommer, "Small Group Ecology," *Psychological Bulletin,* 67 (1967), 150. Copyright 1967 by the American Psychological Association. Reprinted by permission.

of relationships that takes into account the context of social relationships, but also from the practical standpoint of designing and maintaining functional contexts in which human relationships can develop.

SEMI-FIXED FEATURES

Spatial Physical Barriers: Effects in the Factory. The classic study at Western Electric Company provides evidence on the effects of spatial arrangements on formation of groups. One stage of the research focused upon the behavioral patterns of a shop group. Three functional groups, made up of wiremen, soldermen, and inspectors, were moved into a 200- by 400-foot room. Three wiremen and a solderman worked as a unit on an electrical device; their work was reviewed by an inspector. Seven benches were positioned along the length of the room with the workers positioned around the benches. Two groups formed with one at each end of the room. Of the three wiremen in the center of the room one was a member of one group and the other a partial member of the other. The other wireman and solderer in the middle of the room were excluded from both groups.[15]

Conant and Kilbridge[16] studied the Maytag Company when it restructured a job from assembly line to a bench approach, where each worker assembled a complete item. Under the new arrangements, material was stored at each work station, which required greater space and created physical barriers among individuals. Workers were nearly twice as far apart as before, their view of other workspaces was blocked, and they were removed from aisle traffic. Interaction fell sharply.

A study of an automobile plant in Detroit that moved from an assembly line to a highly automated method identified changes in behavior. Faunce interviewed 125 workers in four large machine departments who had been transferred from similar jobs in older plant fifteen months earlier.[17] In the old plants the average working distance was somewhat under ten feet between work stations; in the new plant it was around twenty feet.[18]

Over 80 percent of the workers had been able to talk "very often" with

[15]F. J. Roethlisberger and William Dickson, *Management and the Worker* (Cambridge, Mass.: Harvard University Press, 1939), pp. 459–510.

[16]Eaton H. Conant and Maurice D. Kilbridge, "An Interdisciplinary Analysis of Job Enlargement: Technology, Costs, Behavioral Implications," *Industrial and Labor Relations Review*, 18 (1965), 377–95.

[17]William A. Faunce, "Automation in the Automobile Industry: Some Consequences for In-plant Social Structure," *American Sociological Review*, 23 (1958), 401–407.

[18]Ibid., p. 403.

men with whom they had worked in the old plant compared to 45 percent in the new job. The new plant sharply reduced the interaction occurring every few minutes from 43.6 to 18.5 percent; further, only 13.7 percent of the workers interacted only once a day or less under the old plant compared with 24.5 percent under the new job.

The group formation also varied. Under the old plant, the workers along the line usually belonged to overlapping groups. In the new plant, however, groups were structured so that they tended to form smaller separate units. About 55 percent indicated four or fewer in the group in the old plant, and 79 percent in the new plant. Friendship patterns followed a similar pattern. Forty-seven percent reported they had had more friends in the old plant compared with 13 percent in the new plant.

Other factors also changed from the old plant to the new plant including a requirement for greater degree of attention under the new job, less control of work pace, greater machine noise, and fewer jobs involving team work. Still, one of the major variables affecting the behavior patterns was the greater distance.

Spatial-Physical Factors and Previous Cohesion. Another study contrasted the interaction patterns of the laundry and the housekeeping employees in a hospital.[19] Considerable difference existed between the two groups in their morale, satisfaction with their fellow workers, and turnover. The laundry employees had more favorable patterns than the housekeeping group. The laundry workers spent their days within a large room divided up by the equipment: the washing machines were located on one side, the mangles in the middle, and the hampers on the other side of the room. The pattern of relationships paralleled these divisions, with press operators and mangle girls each forming their own friendship groups. Further, everyone in the room knew one another by their first names and had conversational relationships.

In the housekeeping department, in contrast, the workers were spread over the entire hospital. Even when two or more women were assigned to one floor, they usually divided the work so that they did each room separately. One exception among the wards indicates that spatial barriers may be overcome. A group of wall cleaners, some on the job as long as twenty-five years, had developed a high degree of cohesiveness and professional pride in their work. They always worked as a team in either fours or eights in cleaning a room. The cohesion among this one group in the housekeeping department indicates that other factors may offset the disintegrative influence of spatial barriers if members are permitted a choice of whether to work to-

---

[19]T. Burling, E. Lentz, and R. Wilson, *The Give and Take in Hospitals* (New York: Putnam's Sons, 1956), pp. 182–98.

gether or alone. Perhaps a supervisor emphasized and supported working together at one time and a cohesive group developed.

Classroom Design and Interpersonal Relations. A number of studies show that spatial-factors affect interaction both in face-to-face discussion groups and in classroom situations. Steinzor observed in one of the early studies that the spatial factor in face-to-face discussion affected the degree of communication.[20] He noticed that when individuals were face to face, their ideas and statements were supported by gestures, posture, and various subtle clues that provided a total physical impression. Byrne and Buehler found that classroom seating patterns affected relationships where the class met for one hour, three times a week, for fifteen weeks. The average acquaintanceship among class members grew from 8 to 21 percent while acquaintanceship of neighbors developed from 3 to 74 percent.[21] These findings were supported even where there were distinct differences among members.[22] In a boarding school in France, despite differences in school, class background, and the length of time students had been in school, acquaintanceships were heavily influenced by seating, especially for students who sat next to each other. Nearly all isolated subjects were in a corner at the end of a row with only one immediate neighbor.

Byrne found that varying the time from three and one-half to seven and fourteen weeks affected relationships where students were assigned particular seats.[23] Three and one-half weeks was not long enough for physical location to affect relationships. Neighbors did become acquainted to a greater degree during the seven- and fourteen-week periods. The other side of the coin is how fast friendships break down when physically separated. Where friends were separated, the intensity of friendship was maintained for the three and one-half week period; but this declined where individuals were separated for seven- and fourteen-week periods.

The work of Leavitt and Bavelas further illustrates the influence that position in a group has on interaction patterns, satisfaction, and intragroup relationships.[24] Leavitt used groups of five subjects who were seated at a table but separated from one another by vertical partitions. Centrally located

[20]Bernard Steinzor, "The Spatial Factor in Face-to-Face Discussion Groups," *Journal of Abnormal and Social Psychology*, 45 (1950), 552–55.

[21]Donn Byrne and John Buehler, "A Note on the Influence on Propinquity Upon Acquaintanceships," *Journal of Abnormal and Social Psychology*, 51 (1955), 147–48.

[22]J. Maesonneuve, "Selective Choices and Propinquity," *Sociometry*, 15 (1955), 135–40.

[23]Donn Byrne, "The Influence of Propinquity and Opportunities for Interaction on Classroom Relationships," *Human Relations*, 14 (1961), 63–69.

[24]H. J. Leavitt, "Some Effects of Certain Communication Patterns in Group Performance," *Journal of Abnormal and Social Psychology*, 46 (1951), 38–50; A. Bavelas, "Communication Processes in Task-Oriented Groups," *Journal of the Acoustical Society of America*, 22 (1950), 725–30.

individuals moved into leadership roles and enjoyed the task the most; in contrast, those in the side positions enjoyed it least.

The Influence of Position vs. Importance of Leadership. Another study provides some basis for evaluating the degree of influence spatial relations have compared with leadership style in affecting participation in a group.[25] In an experiment, five members and a trainer discussed ways in which to improve group activity. They sat around a square table with the trainer and one member on one side, two members along one side, and two members at the side opposite the trainer.[26] Two forms of leadership were used. In the nondirective approach, the trainer was available to the group when members initiated a request for help. His principal objective was to encourage the group to assume responsibility for improving its performance. Under the directive style, the trainer took an active role in giving critical analysis of past performance and urged the members to modify their ways and future behavior.

Under the nondirective leadership, the spatial position was paramount in determining the degree of participation, with the individuals in the central position contributing substantially more and those on the side positions contributing lesser amounts. In contrast, under the directive leadership, the individuals beside the trainer and opposite him participated the most while the others made fewer comments. The experiment suggests that forceful leadership exerts a stronger influence than position in the group, but under nondirective leadership, physical position is the most important influence.

Spatial-Physical Factors Versus Previous Friendships. Gullahorn observed the interaction among twelve women who worked in one part of an office of a large firm.[27] They were organized into three rows of four women each, with each row separated by file cabinets. The files were low enough so that the women could look over them to see and talk with those in the next row, but not as easily as they could talk to those within their rows. Most of the women had previously worked in two separate offices and had been reorganized into a single work group about a year and a half before. Their behavior was recorded four times an hour for two weeks. Table 6-1 summarizes the interaction patterns. These were principally within each row with few exceptions:[28] Baldwin (row 1) and Lenihan (row 3) interacted, and Rafferty (row 2), Casey, Carey, and O'Malley (row 3) also interacted to a considerable degree.

---

[25]Gordon Hearn, "Leadership and the Spatial Factor in Small Groups," *Journal of Abnormal and Social Psychology,* 54 (1957), 269–72.

[26]Ibid., p. 270.

[27]John Gullahorn, "Distance and Friendship as Factors in the Gross Interaction Matrix," *Sociometry,* 15 (1952), 123–34.

[28]Ibid., p. 125.

TABLE 6-1. Interaction Patterns Among 12 Office Women Located in Three Rows Separated by Filing Cabinets

		Row I				Row II				Row III			
		Baldwin	*Fahey*	*Rioux*	*Murray*	*Doherty*	*Rafferty*	*Hall*	*Donovan*	*Casey*	*Carey*	*O'Malley*	*Lenihan*
Row I	Baldwin	–	53	23	8	0	5	2	2	0	1	1	16
	Fahey	53	–	26	9	0	2	3	0	2	1	0	1
	Rioux	23	26	–	75	1	4	1	2	2	1	0	0
	Murray	8	9	75	–	0	2	1	3	1	1	1	1
Row II	Doherty					–	24	26	18	4	8	7	2
	Rafferty					24	–	6	30	20	19	21	3
	Hall					26	6	–	51	7	5	3	2
	Donovan					18	30	51	–	3	7	1	1
Row III	Casey									–	46	42	20
	Carey									46	–	69	30
	O'Malley									42	69	–	53
	Lenihan									20	30	53	–

While distance was the principal determinant of interaction patterns, the patterns were also mediated by age of the members, friendship patterns developed in the previous offices, and sex. Rafferty's interaction outside of her row may be partially explained by her prior experience in working with both Casey and O'Malley. Both Baldwin and Lenihan had high interaction between rows, apparently carried over from their acquaintanceship in the previous office. Doherty, however, had not worked with Carey before and yet developed a high-interaction pattern. Interaction data were not presented on the men, but the authors observed: "It was found that among them, business matters were the most important influence on the rate of interaction, except for one man who talked excessively."[29]

Spatial-Physical Factors and Health of Individuals. Sommer and Dewar reported on an exploratory study on a ward for elderly people.[30] The ward had been renovated with cheerful colors, a spacious dayroom, new chairs, television, air conditioning, and other improvements. A striking feature was that little interaction developed in the ward. The designers caused this unknowingly by arranging the furniture along the walls of the room and stationing three islands of chairs back to back. The furniture for a corridor that was used by visiting relatives was organized similarly. Every

[29]Ibid., p. 133.

[30]Robert Sommer and Robert Dewar, "The Physical Environment of the Ward," in E. Freidson, ed., *The Hospital in Modern Society* (New York: Free Press, 1963), pp. 319–42.

morning, however, the visitors moved the chairs into small groups so they could face each other comfortably. This never happened in the ward since the patients were less willing or unable to tamper with the physical environment.

In the hospital context, the physical environment is particularly important to the patient since he is captive, sick, and to some extent helpless. The healthy person is able to modify his environment to suit his preferences—he can move the furniture in his home or, if he doesn't want to go to that trouble, avoid the setting. He can minimize the effects of an unpleasant environment or change it. The patient in the hospital isn't in a position to do either.

Spatial Physical Barriers and Conflict. Sherif, in an experimental study, highlighted the way in which spatial factors interact with group goals to affect intragroup and intergroup conflict.[31] Experiments were carried out in 1948, 1953, and 1954. The 1953 experiment illustrates the approach used in developing the group identity. Twenty-four young boys about twelve years old were invited to a summer camp to study camping methods and procedures. The boys were initially placed in a large bunkhouse for two days; then they were split into two groups that were separated from each other. Each group was assigned activities such as hiking, cookouts, and building projects. This combination of group projects and physical separation resulted in the groups developing cohesive structured units by the seventh day.

Subsequently, the groups were placed into competitive situations. The combination of physical separation and competition caused the groups to develop high degrees of rivalry, hostility, and adverse stereotypes about the other groups. The two factors also contributed to a high degree of cohesion, sense of identity, and interaction within each group. In the 1948 and 1954 experiments, when the researchers attempted to reduce the rivalry and conflict by bringing the groups together, it precipitated overt challenges between them. Physical proximity enabled the groups to express overt aggressive acts. Sherif only found two methods that effectively reduced the level of conflict. One was to have an outside group challenge the entire camp to a contest. In the second method, the researchers set a "superordinate" goal that could only be achieved through the pooling of resources and cooperation of the teams.

The Sherif study is instructive in that he identifies preconditions that must be met before close physical relations will result in favorable relationships. The other studies that have been reviewed have focused mostly upon how individuals who were previously unacquainted were affected by physical proximity. Sherif carries this one step further by creating both intragroup

[31]Muzafer Sherif, B. J. White, and O. J. Harvey, "Status in Experimentally Produced Groups," *American Journal of Sociology*, 60 (1955), 370–79.

cohesion and intergroup conflict. Once the conflict develops, the relationship becomes an important factor influencing the subsequent relationship. Physical proximity then enables conflict and aggression to take place directly. Other methods apparently have to be utilized to achieve the commonality of approach and viewpoint that enables physical proximity to influence the nature of interactions constructively.

THE USE OF SPACE AND BARRIERS

The discussion up to now has been centered on the way in which spatial-physical factors influence interaction patterns. This approach assumes that individuals do not control these barriers. To a large extent this is true: walls are not typically knocked down or offices designed with attention to the way in which physical arrangements support desired interaction patterns. But in many situations, individuals are in a position to structure the way in which they physically relate to others. This is referred to as "the use of space." Both Sommer and Patterson have summarized much of the literature on this subject.[32]

Drawing by Honeyset, © 1974, *Punch.*

[32]Sommer, *Personal Space;* Sommer, "Small Group Ecology," *Psychological Bulletin,* 67 (1967), 145–52; Miles Patterson, "Spatial-Factors in Social Interactions," *Human Relations,* 21 (1968), 351–61.

Using Spatial-Physical Barriers to Maintain Privacy. An underlying factor affecting an individual's use of space and physical barriers is the need for privacy.[33] Privacy can be conceptualized as ranging from solitude to intimacy. Solitude exists when an individual or a group is alone and free from observation from others and sensory stimuli such as noise. Intimacy exists when two or more individuals or groups such as families have close interpersonal relations with each other but are free from observation and sensory input from others. A midpoint on the range is where individuals or groups are in a public setting so they can be observed but are anonymous.

Privacy serves several functions including limiting communication, maintaining personal autonomy, permitting self-evaluation, and enabling emotional release. The use of distance and physical barriers establishes a psychological distance to encourage or limit communication. In intimate relations, these barriers are reduced or eliminated; in neutral or antagonistic relations, they are increased.

A study of a large college dormitory indicates how privacy needs determine the use of space. Students were irritated with built-in furnishings, even closets, since they wanted to rearrange their personal space both for variety and to increase privacy. In joint-occupancy rooms, two out of three women students faced their desks to a wall and in other ways tried to escape their roommate's field of vision. Room arrangements by men, however, tended to be more varied.[34]

Sommer develops the importance of privacy in a study of a main library. In the large study areas, individuals generally positioned themselves to minimize interaction by either sitting alone or diagonally across from others when the tables were occupied. Students protected their privacy both by offensive and defensive means. Defensively, they would sit at the far end of the table, place objects on chairs, scatter papers on the table, and try to be the first to take a table or room. Offensively, they would take a center position at the table and project an attitude that they wished to remain alone, such as looking annoyed when others indicated they might sit down.[35]

Patterson, Mullens, and Romaro found that subjects developed a number of defenses to maintain their privacy when personal space was intruded upon. Students sitting at tables in the library were approached at varying distances by the experimenter (one, two, and three seats away and across from the student). When the intruder positioned himself at the closer dis-

[33]This is a modification of the ideas presented in A.P. Westin, *Privacy and Freedom* (New York: Atheneum, 1967), cited by Proshansky, Ittelson, and Riulin in "Freedom of Choice and Behavior in a Physical Setting," in Harold M. Proshansky, William H. Ittelson and Leanne G. Riulin, eds., *Environmental Psychology* (New York: Holt, Rinehart, & Winston, Inc., 1970), pp. 176–77.

[34]Sim Van Der Ryn and Murray Silverstein, "How Do Students Really Live?" p. 93.

[35]Robert Sommer, "The Ecology of Privacy," *The Library Quarterly*, 36 (1966), 234–48.

tances, students had a greater tendency to lean or slide away, or to block the intruder from view by turning away or using a hand to screen him out.[36]

Factors Affecting Spacing : The Nature of the Relationship.   Hall suggests that the way in which space is used varies under different conditions.[37] He postulates that individuals are comfortable with given distances under conditions of intimacy, friendship, and social and public relationships. With an intimate relationship, people seek and accept distances from 0 to 18 inches that combine visual and olfactory cues and sensations of warmth that signal involvement with another's body. Personal distance is from 18 inches to 4 feet and is maintained among individuals who are familiar with each other but not on an intimate basis. "Social distance," varying from 4 to 12 feet, includes usual social contacts, while "public distance" of 12 feet or more is maintained where no attempt is made to become meaningfully involved with others.

Albert and Dabbs found the extent that distance was varied (1–2, 4–5, 14–15 feet) when a speaker approached a listener influenced the latter's perception of the speaker and degree of communication. At 4–5 feet, the speaker was attributed as having a greater degree of expertness, with most attention paid to the message and least to physical appearance. At 1–2 feet, listeners paid least attention to the message and most to the speaker's appearance.[38]

Patterson and Sechrest also found that people rate others, in part, on the basis of the distance that individuals maintain.[39] The students were told to interview individuals and secretly rate them on traits of friendliness, aggressiveness, dominance, extroversion, and intelligence. Those being interviewed were in fact confederates who approached the interviewers at from 2 to 8 feet and gave standard answers to questions. Less favorable ratings were given, the further the two people were separated. In the closest condition, attempts were made to increase the distance by moving the chairs back slightly. Even the confederates who were aware of the experiment and were trying to remain neutral were obviously uncomfortable at the closest distance.

In another study along the same lines, Garfinkel had each student in his class select a friend or acquaintance with whom he violated the distance

[36]Miles L. Patterson, Sherry Mullens, and Jeanne Romaro, "Compensatory Reactions to Spatial Intrusion," *Sociometry*, 34 (1971), 114–21.

[37]E. T. Hall, *The Silent Language* (New York: Doubleday & Co., 1959), and *The Hidden Dimension* (New York: Doubleday & Co., 1966).

[38]Stuart Albert and James M. Dabbs, Jr., "Physical Distance and Persuasion," *Journal of Personality and Social Psychology*, 15 (1970), 265–70.

[39]M. L. Patterson and L. B. Sechrest, "Impression Formation and Interpersonal Distance," (manuscript, 1967), reported in Patterson, "Spatial-Factors and Social Interactions," pp. 354–55.

that would be typically maintained.[40] In the course of conversation, he brought his face close to the other person's face. Typical patterns were avoidance, bewilderment, and acute embarrassment, particularly between males. When it was later explained that this was an experiment, the subjects still were alarmed and wanted to know why they were chosen to be in the experiment.

Other Factors Influencing Spacing Patterns. A number of other factors determine the distance individuals place between them. Some of these are culture, sex, size of the room, status, competitiveness, and personality. Hall suggests that Arabs stand closer to each other than do Americans.[41] This has been supported by controlled observation by Watson and Graves.[42] Arabs in pairs confronted each other more directly than Americans; they moved closer together, frequently touched each other while talking, had greater eye contact, and talked in louder tones.

Sommer reported that nationalities differed somewhat on the degree distance indicated intimacy. University students in each of five countries—America, England, Sweden, Netherlands, and Pakistan—were asked to rate the degree of intimacy of two persons in five different seating arrangements around a table. Students agreed that the degree of intimacy ranged from side by side, on either side of a corner, sitting across from each other, to the greatest distance possible at the table. The most intimate was the side by side position with the distant position as least intimate. The Dutch students attributed slightly less intimacy to side and corner positions than did the other students. The Dutch and Pakistani students felt the "across" position was of lesser intimacy than the other students.[43]

Sex also affects the use of distance.[44] Several investigators have found that females more often sit side by side than males. This is the most intimate of all seating arrangements for those already acquainted. The status of people affects the distance they maintain. Lott and Sommer found that subjects chose seats more distant from another when that individual was described as having high or low status.[45] Sommer found that high status individuals in

[40]H. Garfinkel, "Studies of the Routine Grounds of Everyday Activities," *Social Problems,* 11 (1964), 225–50.

[41]E. T. Hall, "A System for the Notation of Proxemic Behavior," *American Anthropologist,* 65 (1963), 1003–26.

[42]O. M. Watson and T. A. Graves, "Quantitative Research in Proxemic Behavior," *American Anthropologist,* 68 (1966), 971–85.

[43]Robert Sommer, "Intimacy Ratings in Five Countries," *International Journal of Psychology,* 3 (1968), 109–14.

[44]Al Elkin, "The Behavioral Use of Space" (Master's thesis, 1964); G. A. Norum, "Perceived Interpersonal Relationships and Spatial Arrangements" (Master's thesis, 1966); R. Sommer, "Studies in Personal Space," *Sociometry,* 22 (1959), 247–60.

[45]B. F. Lott and R. Sommer, "Seating Arrangements and Status," *Journal of Personal Social Psychology,* 7 (1967), 90–95.

small discussion groups sit more at the head position at rectangular tables.[46] This is also supported by Strodtbeck and Hook, who observed in a study of jury deliberations that those of the managerial and professional classes selected the head chair more than the individuals of lower status.[47]

The degree of competitiveness among the individuals affects the way in which they relate physically. Sommer and Norum have studied the way in which individuals position themselves at a rectangular table under competitive conditions.[48] Competing pairs sat across from each other; cooperating pairs sat side by side; conversing pairs sat corner to corner; and co-acting individuals sat so they were at considerable distance from each other. Rosenfeld found that when females were instructed to seek or avoid approval of another female, they maintained differences in the distance.[49] When they sought approval, the average distance was 57 inches; when they maintained a neutral relationship, the mean distance was 94 inches. King found that the number of unfriendly acts committed by a child toward another influences the average distance the latter maintains in a free-play situation. A prize toy reduces this distance.[50] Personality mediates the use of distance. Hare and Bales found that dominant subjects choose central seats and do the most talking.[51] Extroverts typically approach the interviewer closer than introverts and talk longer when responding to questions.[52]

The interaction between semifixed furniture arrangements, the tendency of a fixed pattern of usage, and influence of furniture arrangements on interaction patterns are explored in a study of three homes for the elderly in Britain.[53] Chairs were located around the perimeter of a large rectangular room. In one of the rooms, chairs were also positioned in rows in the center to form two U's, with one U facing a piano and the other facing a television set. Nearly all residents laid claim to a chair: they sat in that chair nearly all the time and protected it from invasion by other residents. In choosing their chairs, the members divided into two groups that reflected their former

[46]R. Sommer, "Studies in Personal Space," pp. 247–60.

[47]F. L. Strodtbeck and L. H. Hook, "The Social Dimensions of a Twelve-Man Jury Table," *Sociometry*, 24 (1961).

[48]G. A. Norum, "Perceived Interpersonal Relationships and Spatial Arrangements" and R. Sommer, "Further Studies in Small Group Ecology," *Sociometry*, 28 (1965), 337–48.

[49]H. M. Rosenfeld, "Effect of Approval-Seeking Induction on Interpersonal Proximity," *Psychological Reports*, 17 (1965), 120–22.

[50]M. G. King, "Interpersonal Relations in Pre-school Children and the Average Approach Distance," *Journal of Genetic Psychology*, 108 (1966), 109–16.

[51]A. P. Hare and R. F. Bales, "Seating Position and Small Group Interaction," *Sociometry*, 26 (1963), 480–86.

[52]W. D. Leipold, "Psychological Distance in a Dyadic Interview as a Function of Interversion-Extroversion, Anxiety, Social Desirability, and Stress" (Ph.D. diss., 1963).

[53]Alan Lipman, "Building Design and Social Interaction," *The Architects Journal*, 147 (1968), 23–30.

status of "roughs" and "respectables," indicating their blue-collar and white-collar backgrounds. The principal interaction was with members of their own chair circle. Friendship patterns developed between those who sat next to each other or across corners. An underlying hostility existed between the two groups. About one-fourth of the exchanges were unfriendly in character and had an emotional quality to them. In smaller rooms, in contrast, a lower level of hostility was expressed, and this was more individually than group directed.

In summary, status factors were important initial determinants of whom one sat next to in the room. The claiming of chairs along with reluctance to disturb the furniture arrangement exerted an important influence on interaction and friendship patterns that emerged.

Little research has focused on the way in which *groups* relate to each other on a spatial-physical basis. It is likely that cohesive groups or cliques in organizations establish buffer zones. In turn, individuals probably observe a buffer zone in their approach to cliques; one does not normally casually wander into a social group unless invited or sponsored by a group member; to do so would be considered gauche. The use of space and barriers is probably affected by the nature of relations between the groups, the extent they interact on a functional basis, culture, and other factors.

SUMMARY AND CONCLUSIONS

In summary, spatial-physical barriers have two aspects. On the one hand, spatial-physical barriers between individuals or groups affect interaction. On the other hand, existing relations affect the way in which people relate to one another spatially and physically. The influence of spatial-physical factors has been explored in many different contexts.

Spatial physical factors may be sociofugal or sociopedal in nature. Whether planned or unplanned, spatial-physical configurations exert a pervasive pressure on intragroup and intergroup relations. It is not a powerful variable, and its influence can be countered by other factors including individual or group status, leadership style, superordinate goals, functional elements that encourage traffic patterns, sex, race, nationality, and other factors. The elements, however, may work in the same direction as spatial-physical factors.

Existing relationships are reinforced where people can choose the spatial-physical configuration. Antagonism and neutral relations are maintained by greater distance and physical orientation that reduces eye contact. Friendship and social patterns are reinforced by minimizing spatial-physical barriers. This is illustrated by the varying distance maintained in intimate, friendship, social, and neutral and antagonistic relationships. Some variation exists with each relationship depending upon sex, nationality, and cultural patterns, but these only slightly modify the use of space.

Figure 6-1 summarizes the effects of varying spatial-physical barriers between individuals or groups and the way existing behavior patterns affect the use of spatial-physical barriers. Increasing barriers between individuals exert pressure for reduced interaction (1). The relationship that exists may be cooperative, neutral, or in conflict. Whatever the relations, greater barriers with the accompanying reduced interaction reduce the intensity of that relationship (2). If a neutral relationship exists, this is maintained. Generally, reduced cooperation is associated with less satisfaction, greater frustration, and less commitment by the individual (3); this, in turn, causes individuals to place greater space between them and to erect physical barriers that reinforce the behavioral pattern (4). Reduced conflict exerts influence in the opposite direction (5).

The influence of spatial-physical barriers between groups has a different impact on intragroup and intergroup relationships. The erection of barriers between groups (6) increases the probability of interaction within each group (7); the increased interaction, in turn, amplifies existing relations (8). If a high degree of cooperation and group cohesiveness exists, the barriers between groups contribute to an even greater group identity, cohesion, and sense of belonging (9). If a high level of conflict exists, the increased interaction results in even greater conflict (10).

In contrast, barriers between groups reduce interaction between units (11). This, in turn, contributes toward the breakdown of existing relationships (12). If cooperation previously existed among groups, the barriers reduce the level of cooperation (13); if conflict existed, the barriers reduce the level of conflict (14). The effects of reduced cooperation or lowered conflict among groups are mediated by the extent to which the groups are dependent upon one another. Where an independent work flow exists, reduced cooperation among groups has little implication in getting the job done since the groups don't depend on one another. However, a failure to cooperate is likely to be regarded as an act of rivalry or hostility and contributes to the group drawing together to face the common threat (15).

In contrast, with an interdependent work flow, reduced cooperation among groups quickly affects the level of frustation among group members and reduces their sense of cohesion (16). They become angry at other groups for not providing resources needed in the work flow sequence, and they are frustrated with one another as their ability to deal with the situation is thwarted. This, in turn, contributes to greater use of spatial-physical barriers both among members of groups and between groups.

The research studies have indicated the way in which barriers influence the nature of interaction and the intensity of these patterns. Other factors can outweigh the influence of these barriers, but unless offset, interaction patterns are directly affected. The emerging behavior patterns, in turn, affect the way in which individuals and groups use space and barriers. Higher conflict or

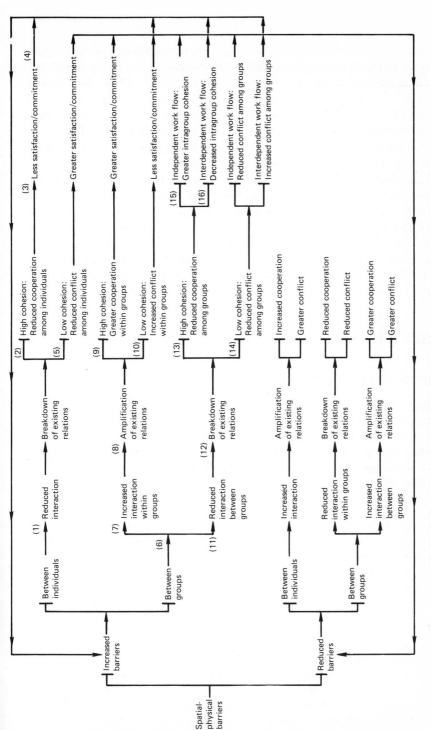

FIGURE 6-1. Effects of spatial-physical barriers on behavior and effects of behavior on use of spatial-physical barriers

reduced cooperation within or between groups results in individuals and groups separating themselves spatially or physically. In contrast, reduced conflict and greater cooperation reinforce the tendency to reduce distance and eliminate physical barriers. This analysis suggests that spatial-physical arrangements are influential ways of affecting relationships, particularly where neutral or friendly relations initially existed. But where friction or conflict already exists, other variables need to be brought to bear to moderate or reverse the conflicts within or among groups.

Spatial-physical barriers have a high degree of permanency when incorporated into buildings and designs. Semifixed items such as furniture and movable walls can be modified, but the same pattern is generally maintained, particularly in institutional contexts such as prisons, hospitals, and work layouts in the office and factory. Consideration should be given to the behavioral implications of these patterns when the structure and work place are designed. If not then, the patterns should be reevaluated and modified where design exerts pressure for inappropriate behavior patterns to develop.

SECTION II

DISCUSSION QUESTIONS

A) *Size*
1. A group may be defined in formal terms (structurally), or in behavioral terms (process). How do you know when you have a formal group? How do you know when you have an informal group? Illustrate, by using your class as an example, the difference between formal and informal groups.
2. How large must a formal group grow before subgrouping characteristically occurs?
3. If a group was expanded in size from 5 members to 10 members, indicate the effects this would have upon the group processes of degree of personalization, participation rate, specialization, and communication among members and the way these group process affect individual and intragroup behavior. What research studies supports these relationships?
4. Critically comment on the problems of generalizing on studies that relate size of total organization to various behavioral processes. Would studies of formal subunits (plants, departments, sections) lead to more reliable conclusions than size of total organizations? Would laboratory studies of different size groups provide a better basis for understanding how size affects group processes?
5. Melcher summarized the results of the way in which size is related to various aspects of behavior in Table 2 of the size chapter. What do the following relations of size to behavior mean?
    a. Size of a store is negatively correlated with morale.
    b. Size of a warehouse has an $r = -.24$ with efficiency.
    c. Size of airline offices is curvilinearily related to absenteeism.

6. Develop the effects that size of an organization has over the following aspects of behavior: Absenteeism, tardiness, accident rates, strikes, intragroup relations, and productivity. What research studies support your position?

B) *Work Flow*

1. In reviewing the evidence on the influence that specialization exerts over behavior, what are the limitations of the "assembly line" studies? Of the studies that contrast the behavior of individuals at different skill levels?

2. Develop the short-term and longer-term effects of reducing specialization upon productivity and boredom of workers. What studies support your positions?

3. If you were designing a job, how would the relative importance of quality and costs per unit affect the degree you broke the task into specialized parts? What studies support your position?

4. Job enlargement is broadly believed to contribute to higher employee morale, greater efficiency, and productivity of workers. Evaluate the merits of this belief and refer to the research that supports your thesis.

5. Explain how degrees of specialization and extensiveness of buffers affect the degree of interdependence of work flow within groups.

6. What is the distinction, if any, between "the need for cooperation in an interdependent work flow" and "the influence work flow exerts for cooperative patterns to develop?"

7. You have been invited by the management of a small manufacturing firm to review their production facilities. They are especially concerned about obtaining a smoother flow of production and improving the relationships and cooperation among groups.
   a. What relevance, if any, does a high degree of interdependence among groups have for need for cooperation and degree of cooperation elicited?
   b. What relevance, if any, does the amount of inventories between interdependent groups have for intergroup relations?
   c. If management accepted an order that reduced the tolerances for error on component parts (i.e., required higher quality of the product) what effect, if any, would this have upon intergroup relations?
   If you were identifying stress points where conflict is probably high in the production system, where would you look? Would this conclusion apply in other organizations such as hospitals, or public accounting firms?

C) *Task Complexity*

1. Indicate the degree the following tasks are relatively programmed or unprogrammed and briefly explain your position:
   a. Engineer designing bridges.
   b. Mathematician working through proofs.
   c. Assembly line workers in an automobile plant.
   d. Top management assessing the relevance that changing technology has to the amount of expenditures to allocate to long-term research.
   e. A child learning to speak.
   f. A surgeon making heart transplants.

2. A group is manufacturing electronic tubes. Unknown to them, the gas being used in the tubes is being randomly contaminated. It is causing the tubes to be rejected at the following rates:

Time periods	t_1	t_2	t_3	t_4
Percentage of tubes that are rejected	1%	20%	60%	90%

They have no instruments to reveal why the tubes aren't performing adequately. Predict the form of behavior that would emerge from t_1 to t_4. Focus on aspects of individual behavior, intragroup and vertical (supervisory-subordinate) relationships. Refer to relevant studies that support your position.

3. If individuals are placed in an unstructured situation, develop the effects this has upon intragroup relations, delegation of authority, influence that the majority have over a minority, and degree of anxiety and stress. Refer to research studies that support your position on these relationships.

D) *Spatial-Physical Barriers*

1. What is the distinction between sociofugal and sociopetal spatial-physical contexts? Provide examples of each.

2. Develop the following distinctions and provide examples of each:
   a. Spatial distance.
   b. Spatial orientation.
   c. Physical barriers.
   d. Functional facilities.

3. Discuss the way in which spatial-physical barriers, spatial orientation, and functional facilities affect interaction patterns among members of an organization. What studies support your position?

4. What distinction is there between the way spatial-physical factors influence relationships and the way past and emerging relationships influence the use of spatial-physical barriers?

5. Look around you in your class. What patterns of interaction do you predict will arise, based upon the spatial physical design of the room and distribution of the chairs, desks, and/or tables?

6. Again look around you. What can you tell about the relationships that exist among the students and between the students and teachers by the use that has been made of spatial-physical barriers?

7. In your classes, residence, and work place, observe how you and others use spatial-physical barriers to support or discourage interaction. Be prepared to discuss your observations in class.

8. Discuss the way in which past relationships, cultural factors, and status of individuals influence the use of spatial-physical patterns. What research studies support your position?

9. You have been brought in as a consultant to review the spatial-physical design of the recreational area in a rest home. The room is for the use of the 300 residents and their visitors. The residents are from a diversity of backgrounds—blue and white collar workers, different educational levels, occupations, nationalities, religions, political backgrounds, and they vary in age from 60 to 98. Three fourths are single or widowed and 60% are women. They vary widely in degree of mental and physical infirmity with most of them able to take care of themselves,

move about, and interact. You are provided the following sketch of the recreational room. You are asked to provide recommendations on:

a. What type of intragroup and intergroup behavior would be optimal for the residents.

b. Analyze whether the present spatial physical arrangements and recreational

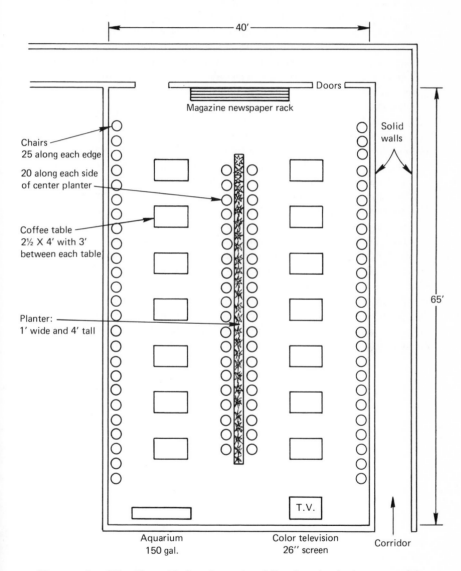

The room has 20' ceiling with three large chandaliers hanging in the center of the room.

Recreational room in rest home

facilities in the room support this optimal behavior patterns. Observe both the influence the design exerts over behavior and the way residents are likely to use the spatial-physical arrangements to support desired patterns and minimize undesired patterns. If the spatial-physical arrangements are not appropriate, design them so that they contribute to this optimal end. You are free to modify the internal arrangements of the room in any way, including erection of walls, placement of doorways, replacement of solid walls by windows or glass, removal of present furniture and replacement with new. You are constrained only in that the total room size is fixed, any changes must be justified (i.e., you must develop the way the design contributes to the desired behavior patterns) and you are to consider *only* the design of the room and the recreational facilities to place in it. Other arrangements are being reviewed by other consultants.

E)   *Application: All Variables in Section II*
Develop how you would set up group or groups to achieve high quality or pride and satisfaction in a task. You are to consider *only* the following factors:

1)   You are working with 10 men and 10 women of similar ages but with diverse racial, religious, political, social, and economic backgrounds.

2)   The project can be broken down to 20 steps or steps can be combined in any sequence including having each individual completing the entire project.

3)   Spatial-physical factors can be established in any manner.

4)   They are working with materials that vary widely in quality with the result that 50% of the items may be rejected as being faulty anywhere from 10% to 90% of the time depending on quality of the material and care that is taken in working with the material.

Specify the nature of intra- and intergroup relations that you want to develop. Develop how your design contributes to the group relations specified and the high pride satisfaction and quality of work. What studies support that your recommendations would influence behavior in the predicted direction?

III

SECONDARY
STRUCTURAL VARIABLES:
Formal Authority Relationships

7

DELEGATION:
Distribution of Authority among Levels

THE NATURE OF DELEGATION

Two aspects of the degree of delegation are the level at which decisions are made and the degree of discretion the individual has in making a decision when it is referred to his level.[1] In the first case, the most restrictive set of rules simply says all decisions must be referred to the top manager for decisions. Discretion isn't permitted on the part of lower level managers or operational personnel. They are simply involved in implementing actions ordered by the superiors. Under decentralization, the decisions are moved to lower levels. The extreme is abdication by the central manager—operating personnel are given the authority to make all decisions without any guidelines or restrictions.

More characteristically, some degree of centralization is provided. The amount is determined by the policies, procedures, and rules. While the higher level executives could restrict the right to make any decisions, it is more feasible to provide a statement of policies that provide the framework or premises within which decisions are made. In this manner, lower level supervisors and employees make the decisions but within the parameters of the policy and procedure specifications. The supervisor in a centralized organization is in a situation similar to that of the driver of an automobile in a city. He makes the decisions of driving, but the traffic rules and regulations provide the restrictions that he is expected to observe.

[1]The span of control and concentration of physical facilities are sometimes also regarded as defining degree of centralization. These are treated as separate variables in this book, since both may vary independently of degree of delegation of authority. An organization may be centralized or decentralized and have either a narrow or broad span of control. Physical facilities may be partially concentrated or broadly dispersed. With either case, the organization may be centralized or decentralized.

Degree of participation and delegation are also treated as separate variables. This point is developed in chapter 14.

Extreme Case of Centralization: An Analogy

The extreme case highlights central features. Under high centralization where policies, procedures, and rules specify what to do and how to do it in detail, little discretion exists in making decisions. If these formal provisions are internalized into belief systems, behavior assumes a stable and rigid pattern.

An analogy illustrates the character of high centralization. In the animal, bird, or insect world, instinct is the dominant factor determining behavior. Instinct is a form of imprinting that occurs before birth, or soon after, that directs actions. Behavior in lower forms of life are principally defined by patterns that are imprinted before birth. Higher forms of life have some degree of instinct and a good deal of behavior that is imprinted at an early stage. A duck, for example, reacts to the immediate stimulus that it receives as it emerges from its egg. It will willingly follow a dog, a man, or its mother around depending upon what it sees when it emerges from the egg. The species cannot learn the new techniques if it is born with the instincts, or if behavior is imprinted soon after birth. Bees, ants, and birds must follow the set of programs that they are born with or learn soon after birth.

Behavior is programmed in the same way that a computer follows the instructions of the programmer. Birds build nests in a special manner—they cannot make adjustments if given materials are not available and use substitutes, or make a different type of nest. Tent caterpillars are programmed to follow the silk thread laid down by the leader. If the silk thread is placed in a circle the caterpillars will go round and round until they collapse and die. In beehives, activities are highly specialized —building combs for holding the honey, extracting pollen from flowers, processing pollen into honey, keeping the hive the proper temperature, and maintaining guard over the hive. Even the mating is programmed with the queen bee flying to the lowest point on the horizon and the drone bees rising in the sky and flying to the identical spot. The problems of coordination are completely solved by these built-in programs. There's no need for formal authority systems, control systems, and little need for information systems, or leadership. Problems are solved by instinct that programs performance in a specific way.

Organizations aren't governed by instinct and behavior of human beings isn't determined by imprinting at birth. However, where policies, procedures, and rules are specified to a high degree, and reward-penalty systems reinforce the training and indocrination programs, these formal restrictions tend to be internalized and adapted as part of belief systems. As a consequence, stable, predictable patterns of behavior emerge. The behavior pattern is maintained whether or not it is appropriate to the conditions analogous to our tent caterpillars.

Bureaucracy as a Centralized Organization

A number of consequences of extensive rules and regulations that are associated with bureaucracy are developed in an essay by Merton.[2] Following is a brief summary.

The bureaucracy exerts constant pressure upon the official to be methodical, prudent, and disciplined. If coordination is to be achieved, the behavior of the individuals must achieve a high degree of reliability and conformity to prescribed patterns of action. Those operating in a bureaucratic organization often develop strong sentiments which entail devotion to duty, and a sense of the limitation of their authority, and a necessity to methodically perform routine activities. The effects of these characteristics leads to a transference from the aims of the organization to adherence to the details and rules.

While rules are originally conceived as a means to achieving ends, they become transformed into the ends themselves regardless of effects upon the goals. The behavior moves in the direction of formalism and ritualism with insistence upon close adherence to formalized procedures. Where the original circumstance changes, or unanticipated conditions develop, the office holder is unable to adjust his perspective from rule observation to adjustment to the new conditions.

[2]Robert K. Merton, *Social Theory and Social Structure*, rev. ed. (Glencoe, Ill.: Free Press, 1957), pp. 195–206.

Table 7-1 outlines four combinations of focus of decision and degree of specification of policies that define the degree of centralization.

TABLE 7-1. Organization Types

Level for Referring Decisions not Covered by Policies	Policies, Procedures, and Rules	
	Few Policies/Broadly Defined	Many Policies/Narrowly Defined
TOP—Headquarters personnel	11 *Autocracy*/Highly Centralized. Few decisions are made by lower level personnel, and these are governed by broad policies. Most decisions must be referred to higher level management.	12 *Bureaucracy* / Centralized. Decisions are made by operating personnel within the framework of restrictive policies, procedures, and rules; problems not covered must be referred to higher levels for decisions or policy clarification.
BOTTOM— Operating personnel	21 *Collegial*/Highly Decentralized. Most decisions are made at lower levels without policy restrictions; other decisions made at lower levels within the framework of policies.	22 *Bureaucracy*/Decentralized. Most decisions are made at lower levels within the framework of the policies; personnel have discretion on problems *not* covered by policies.

The centralized bureaucracy is illustrated by the military branches, governmental agencies, and many large organizations (cell 12). These have extensive written policies, procedures, and rules that restrict the degree of discretion. In a centralized bureaucracy, problems not covered by policy must be referred to higher level personnel. Decisions are made at all levels, but the degree of discretion at lower levels in the organization is sharply restricted. The loan officer in a bank, for instance, may make most of the decisions but within the parameters of the criteria established by higher level officers. He may have little discretion in what loans to make or reject. Cell 22 describes a bureaucratic decentralized structure. Given considerable variability in types of problems, a moderate degree of decentralization exists since the lower level personnel have the discretion to make decisions where the policy and procedures are not applicable. This structure probably is widespread in large organizations, since it is difficult to delineate policies that cover all problems, and it is impractical to refer all problems not covered by policies to higher levels for decisions.

The autocracy is often found in smaller organizations that are headed by authoritarian-type leaders (cell 11). Few regulations are specified, and even these are inadequate guidelines for decisions. Where customary practice doesn't apply, as in new situations, decisions have to be referred to those at the top of the organization. A collegial structure is where rules only broadly limit decisions and the lower level personnel have the authority to make decisions on areas not covered by policies (cell 21). This form of organization exists in many universities, professional organizations, and small and moderate-size complex organizations faced with varying conditions.

Types of Policies

The establishment of policies, procedures, and rules restricts the area of discretion and provides the degree to which the individual has freedom to act. Policies provide a defined area to move around in, and within this framework one can do the job in his own way. They provide an impersonal and objective method of coordination.

Three types of policies are those specifying objectives, those developing rules of reason, and those detailing what must be done and what is prohibited. In the first case, objectives are defined and general considerations are set forth; that is, the general framework for making decisions are stated. In the second case, policies that set forth rules of reason provide restrictions on what is to be done, but the context is that if good reasons exist for deviating from the policies, it is appropriate. The third set of policies are rules of duty. These provide little discretion for action and are stated as imperatives on what must be done, or isn't permitted. The greater the specification of rules of duty, the less discretion individuals have and the greater the centralization.

DETERMINING DEGREE OF DELEGATION IN COMPLEX STRUCTURES

One of the complications in determining the degree of centralization is that it is determined separately at each level and within each department. Considerable authority may be delegated down to the divisional or vice-presidential level; but *within* each division, wide variations may exist in the degree of decentralization. A second complication is that the degree of centralization in large organizations that have specialists at the headquarters level is determined, in part, by how these specialists are related to lower level personnel. In a centralized organization, the specialists at the headquarters level are given the authority to command in their specialized areas. Personnel specialists, for instance, instruct lower level personnel on personnel activities; industrial engineers specify plant layout, equipment specifications, and general physical arrangements of the plant. Similar relationships exist for the other specialists in purchasing, design engineering, law, and accounting, with line managers retaining only residual authority. If the specialists are placed in an advisory role, broad decentralization can take place down to the divisional manager level and below within each division.

In more complex organizations, staff specialists exist both at the headquarters and divisional level, as indicated in Figure 7-1.

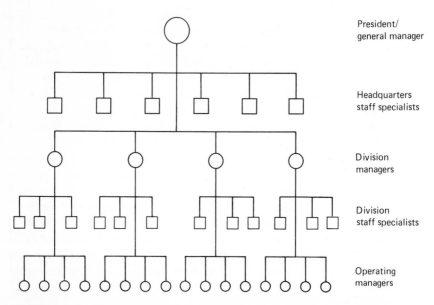

President/
general manager

Headquarters
staff specialists

Division
managers

Division
staff specialists

Operating
managers

FIGURE 7-1. Staff specialists and line managers in a complex organization

In this case, the relation of the specialists at headquarters to division managers determines the degree of delegation down to the divisions. The relation of the specialists at the divisional level with the operating managers determines the degree of decentralization within the divisions. Giving specialists authority to make decisions defines a centralized organization; limiting their authority provides a decentralized structure. We will examine a couple of cases later where these variations in structure exist.

Operationalization of Delegation

Degree of delegation is measured at each level in the organization by three factors: (1) the percentage of decisions requiring consultation with, or approval by immediate, or higher level, supervisors; (2) the degree of discretion that the policies, procedures, and rules permit in making decisions; (3) the level at which decisions are made relative to the point where problems arise.

The first question measures the extent of delegation where policies, procedures, and rules have been only partially codified (i.e., formalized), or not at all. The second measures the degree of discretion where policies, procedures, and rules are codified. The third measures the level decisions must be referred to for a decision when personnel aren't authorized to make the decision.

DELEGATION SCALE

	Decentralized							Centralized	
	1	2	3	4	5	6	7	8	9
Percentage or decisions that can be made without approval of higher level supervision									
Degree of discretion permitted by policies, procedures, and rules									
Level at which problems must be referred for a decision									

A. What percentage of decisions is the group permitted to make in regard to their responsibilities without checking with or obtaining approval of higher level supervisors?

Decentralized							Centralized	
1	2	3	4	5	6	7	8	9
99%	88%	77%	66%	55%	44%	33%	22%	0–11%

B. What best describes the degree of discretion that is left to the group by the policies, procedures, and rules laid down by higher level management and staff groups?

Extensive	General	Moderate	Some	Restricted
1 2	3 4	5 6	7 8	9

(1). *Extensive discretion*—Individuals have broad discretion in making decisions; general flexibility exists to adjust to local conditions and special situations and to implement one's ideas in performing the job assignment; higher level supervision broadly relies upon judgment, general competence, and adherence to professional or trade standards to orient the individual in doing his job properly.

(5). *Moderate discretion*—Policy and procedure statements and rules cover most of the important decisions in the job; however, some discretion exists to adjust to local conditions, special situations, and opportunity to implement new ideas in performing the job assignment; some reliance is upon the judgment, general competence, and adherence to professional or trade standards to orient the individual in doing his job properly.

(9). *Restricted discretion*—The policies, procedures, and rules limit discretion in decision making to routine details; no leeway is permitted to adapt to local conditions, special situations, or to apply new ideas in performing the job assignment; little reliance is placed upon judgment, general competence, and adherence to professional or trade standards to orient the individual in doing his job properly.

C. To what level must problems that aren't covered by policies or procedure be referred for a decision?

1	2	3	4	5	6	7	8	9
Decisions made at point where problems occur		Problems must be referred to immediate supervisor		Problems must be referred to middle management		Problems must be referred to central staff		Problems must be referred to the president for decisions

CONTRASTING PERSPECTIVES OF HEADQUARTERS AND LOCAL UNITS

An analysis by Feld of military organizations reveals some of the factors that contribute to problems of a centralized and decentralized structure.[3] He develops the different perspectives of personnel at the local level and headquarters level and the complex situation facing those supervisors who are in between. The differences in perspectives are summarized in Table

[3]M. D. Feld, "Information and Authority: The Structure of Military Organizations," *American Sociological Review*, 24 (1959), 15–22.

7-2. The orientation of the headquarters is with the general conditions facing the organization and developing broad strategy and detailed plans to deal with these general conditions. In contrast, the personnel at the operating level are concerned with *local* conditions and tactics that will enable them to deal with these problems. Those at the headquarters level concentrate on maintaining a unified plan, advancing toward common objectives, and maintaining the organization as a whole. In contrast, those at the local level are attuned to overcoming local obstacles and maintaining their group as

TABLE 7-2. Contrasting Perspectives of Headquarters and Local Personnel

Organizational Dimensions	Organizational Level	
	Headquarters	Operating Level/Local Units
Scope of concern	General conditions facing the organization/local units	Particular conditions faced by the local unit
Nature of planning	Concern is with broad strategy and a general plan to deal with common conditions	Concern is with developing tactics to deal with conditions faced by the local unit, i.e., to overcome *local* obstacles/solve *local* problems
Relative stability and calmness of decision/planning environment	Relatively stable, calm environment for planning and decision making	Relatively unstable, hectic environment with pressure for immediate decisions
The organizational perspective	To maintain and promote the organization as a whole even at the expense of some of the local units	To maintain themselves as a cohesive, viable unit even if this isn't in the interest of the entire organization
Focus of coordination	To maintain order and consistency of direction among units and to advance common objectives	To maintain order within the local unit and to advance its objectives
Physical and emotional relation to local problems	Physically separated and emotionally detached from problems	Physically near problems; emotionally involved in the urgency of solution
Scope of available information	The higher the level, the broader the scope and access to information; data are generated both from local units and from other sources	The lower the level, the more specific and unique the information that is directly available to the operating personnel; dependent upon higher level personnel for general information

a cohesive, viable unit. While it may be beneficial to the entire organization to sacrifice the interests of particular local units, the local perspective is to maintain its integrity, to survive and prosper in the organization. The thrust of the central headquarters unit is to maintain internal order and obtain a coordinated effort toward organizational goals. The local unit is concerned with mastering local problems and dealing with its external stresses.

Those at headquarters level usually are physically and emotionally removed from the local conditions. In contrast, those at the local level are both physically near and emotionally involved in trying to deal with these problems. The scope of information available to headquarters is usually broad and general. The higher the level, the broader the access to the information since data are obtained from the local units and from sources directly gathered by the headquarters unit. In contrast, the lower the level, the more specific and unique the information that's available.

These two varying perspectives generate different approaches in the use and meaning of the formal organization. From headquarter's standpoint, the emphasis is to clarify formal authority relationships, define the chain of command, specialize by function, and plan a rational, coordinated organization. In commanding, or attempting to influence, the emphasis is on the use of the formal structure.

In contrast, at the local level the degree of specialization and authority definitions are diffuse and plans are only partially formulated. Ad hoc decision making is emphasized over planning: Faced with problems that require immediate decisions and with limited time to reflect, the emphasis is on pragmatic action rather than delaying decisions for additional information. Less reliance is placed on the formal structure with its chain of command, specialized functions, and authority derived from the office. Greater reliance is upon leading and setting examples by resolute action and enthusiasm. To the degree that the organization is centralized, the perspectives of those at headquarters dominate the decisions. The degree of decentralization determines if the perspectives of those at the operating level will prevail.

CONSEQUENCES OF VARYING DEGREES OF DELEGATION

The advantages and disadvantages associated with varying degrees of delegation are discussed in nearly all textbooks of management and administration.[4] These conclusions are from the introspection of practicing man-

---

[4]David R. Hampton, Charles E. Summer, and Ross A. Webber, *Organizational Behavior and the Practice of Management*, rev. ed. (Glenville, Ill.: Scott, Foresman & Co., 1973), pp. 430–52; Henry H. Albers, *Principles of Organization and Management*, 3rd ed. (New York: John Wiley & Sons, 1969), pp. 195–211; Billy J. Hodge and Herbert J. Johnson, *Management and Organizational Behavior: A Multidimensional Approach* (New York: John Wiley & Sons, 1970),

agers, observations of organizational theorists, and some systematic research. Table 7-3 summarizes the effects of centralization on organizational processes, behavioral patterns, organizational vulnerability, and change. The effects of decentralization are not stated since they can be extrapolated from the table.

TABLE 7-3. Consequences of Centralization on Organizational Processes

	Consequences	
	Advantages	*Disadvantages*
Organizational Processes		
Coordination	Greater coordination through central direction and uniform policies	Uniform policies apply regardless of the degree to which local conditions vary
Decision making: perspective	Company as a whole is considered in decisions when made by top management and staff personnel and where lower level managers make decisions within the parameters of policy statements issued by headquarters	The company perspective is likely to ignore the special features/problems of divisions, departments, and work units
Decision making: speed	In emergencies, central staff and management can mobilize the information and make decisive decisions without delay	The normal decision process results in delays; flow of information up and flow of orders/policies down take time; central personnel are often overloaded so decisions are further delayed

pp. 404–12; Wilfred Brown, *Organization* (London: Heinman Educational Books, 1971), pp. 143–51; Gerald G. Fisch, *Organization for Profit* (New York: McGraw-Hill Book Co., 1964), pp. 79–91; Robert T. Golembiewski, *Organizing Men and Power: Patterns of Behavior and Line-Staff Models* (Chicago: Rand McNally & Co., 1967), pp. 247–60; Ernest Dale, *Organization* (New York: American Management Association, 1967), pp. 104–30; Franklin G. Moore, ed., *A Management Source Book* (New York: Harper & Row, 1964), pp. 248–76; Louis A. Allen, *The Management Profession* (New York: McGraw-Hill Book Co., 1964), pp. 198–216; Theo Haimann and William G. Scott, *Management in the Modern Organization* (Boston: Houghton Mifflin Co., 1970), pp. 256–79; James L. Gibson, John M. Ivancevich, and James H. Donnelly, Jr., *Organization Structure, Processes, Behavior* (Dallas: Business Publications, 1973), pp. 135–45; Harold Koontz and Cyril O'Donnell, *Principles of Management: An Analysis of Managerial Functions*, 4th ed. (New York: McGraw-Hill Book Co., 1968), pp. 349–76; Alan C. Filley and Robert House, *Managerial Process and Organizational Behavior* (Glencoe, Ill.: Scott, Foresman & Co., 1967), pp. 239–56.

TABLE 7-3 (Cont.)

| | Consequences | |
	Advantages	Disadvantages
Organizational Processes		
Communication	The policies, procedures, and rules provide a standard set of communications on making decisions; this is an efficient means of communication downward	The reliance upon formal channels, reduced opportunity for feedback, and the greater number of communication centers through which messages flow reduce accuracy of upward and interdepartmental communication
Behavioral Patterns		
Initiation and motivation of management and staff	Higher initiative and motivation of top management/staff	Lower initiative and motivation of lower level management
Satisfaction with job, company, and decisions	Higher level personnel are more satisfied with their jobs and the company since they are involved in challenging work	Lower level personnel are dissatisfied with their jobs and the company
Vulnerability of the Organization		
Development of personnel	Develops breadth of experience and general perspective of top management and staff personnel	Inhibits development of lower level management personnel. They do not develop the scope, judgment, and orientation to make decisions
Dependence upon top management	The loyalty, ability, and experience of only a relatively few top management line and staff personnel are needed for a successful organization	If the top management or staff personnel become sick, die, age, decrease in ability, or leave the firm, the functioning of the organization is adversely affected
Change: initiation and implementation	Changes can be rapidly initiated	Implementation of centrally initiated changes are likely to be actively resisted or, at the minimum, passively resisted

A Skeptical View of Organizational Structure and Processes

The brief passage points up some of the problems associated with both centralization and decentralization.

The Well-Organized Factory: Centralized

a. An employee detecting machine failure reports to foreman.
b. Foreman reports to shop superintendent.
c. Shop superintendent reports to the department manager.
d. Department manager gets in touch with the factory manager.
e. Factory manager gets in touch with the industrial engineers.
f. Industrial engineers refer the problem to maintenance.
g. Maintenance goes to the foreman of department concerned.
h. Foreman informs maintenance of the problem and takes him to machine.
i. Maintenance finds the machine is now working.
j. Maintenance takes rest of day to complete forms reporting what he didn't do.

The above example highlights the dilemma of centralization. We live in an age of wonder drugs and cdrealls, and organizational structure has one, too—decentralization. Let's delegate some authority and see what happens to our "well-organized" factory.

The Well-Organized Factory: Decentralized

a. President states policy: "All employees have the authority and the responsibility to fix their own machines."
b. Industrial engineers notify the factory manager of the policy.
c. Factory manager calls in department managers to discuss the way to implement the policy so that everyone is aware of his authority and responsibility on machine maintenance and repairs.
d. Department managers and foremen hold meetings with employees to discuss their responsibilities on machine maintenance and repairs.
e. A machinist reports his machine isn't working.
f. Those near the scene—industrial engineers, factory manager, department managers, foremen, and employees—all grab repair tools. Everyone shouts, pushes, bumps, and stumbles trying to fix the machine.
g. If they are lucky, the machine begins to run by itself, or the individual who reported it fixes it after the others leave.

COORDINATION, DECISION MAKING, COMMUNICATION, AND ADJUSTMENT TO LOCAL CONDITIONS

One of the major advantages of centralization is that it provides unity of direction and coordination. Decisions are either referred to those at the top of the organization, or the policies, procedures, and rules sharply restrict the discretion of those lower in the organization when they make decisions. As a consequence, greater uniformity of direction and a larger degree of coordination are obtained.

Another positive feature is that where important tradeoffs must be made, an optimal decision can be reached when decisions are retained at the general management level. Pricing decisions, for example, made above the level of manufacturing, marketing, and research managers are likely to be superior; while each of these managers can contribute his perspective, the optimal decision must reflect the firm's welfare as a whole rather than that of each department.

One of the advantages of *decentralization* is the ability to make appropriate adjustments to a wide diversity of conditions. Each manager in a decentralized unit can take into account the special characteristics of the situation that he is facing. The local buyer, for instance, can buy for his clientele according to their special tastes, whether the preferences are in sizes, fashion, age, or fad in the community. While it is possible for a central buyer to do this also, he is unlikely to have the information, understanding of the diversity of conditions, or orientation to make these judgments about diverse clientele. This normally requires personal contact and knowledge of the local conditions.

Decisions that require a broad overview of the organization are of better quality when made by top management and staff personnel. At times it is necessary to suboptimize a particular area for the overall benefit. For example, the steps that might increase sales might also raise substantially the cost of production. A rapid growth of one division may be at the expense of another since resources of man and material are usually limited. On the other hand, decisions that require a close familiarity with local conditions tend to be of lower caliber when made on a centralized level whether the management prescribes the policies that govern the decisions or actually makes the operating decisions. The central management and staff personnel obtain information from multiple sources but are separated from the day-to-day information and operating problems. They are in a good position to sort out broad trends, long-term developments, and evaluate implications of particular strategies but in a poor position to make appropriate decisions on heterogeneous local situations.

Under decentralization, the lower level managers make decisions in terms of the variables and problems with which they are most familiar. These are within their unit and only incidentally those of the larger unit, whether it is the plant, division, or the company as a whole. Melcher found that in contract negotiations and interpreting the contracts, the perspective of local officials was narrower than that of national union personnel.[5] The latter were more concerned with company-wide, industry-wide or interindustry-wide negotiations. The local union officials were principally concerned with the departmental, interdepartmental, and plant considerations. While the adjustments between local union officials and local management may work out for the particular conditions, precedents may be established for other plants that cause difficulties. Granting seniority provisions where most workers are young and have little seniority may have little implications for costs in that plant; but in other plants where the ratio of senior people is greater, a provision to grant special privileges may have serious cost consequences and sharply reduce management's flexibility.

Cleaveland's study of the U.S. Bureau of Reclamation covering a period of about fifty years provides some evidence of how the degree of centralization affects coordination and adjustment to local conditions.[6] In 1925, the major activity of the bureau, to build single-purpose dams for irrigation, was changed to building multiple-purpose dams. The projects were to be justified on the basis of irrigation, power generation, and recreation. These broad projects covered basin-wide and region-wide territory and were more expensive, diversified, and technically complicated. The multiple-purpose projects were more difficult to design and construct, required extensive basic data on entire regions, and were more political, as the comprehensive projects affected the economy of entire regions. Basin-wide planning required close contact with numerous federal, state, and local governmental agencies, and representatives of major groups in the areas.

Before 1925, the Washington office established a broad policy, and the Denver office was given broad authority to coordinate and execute the programs authorized in the various regions. The Denver office, in turn, operated a highly centralized operation with its specialists acting as operating heads on the various projects. As the Bureau of Reclamation undertook multiple-purpose projects, it still operated with essentially this organizational structure.

In the early forties, the bureau was reorganized as Congress and the Washington office pressed for an organization form that would make the bureau more responsive. Essentially, the organizational changes moved the Denver office and its specialists into advisory roles on planning, operations, and maintenance of the projects and retained line authority for the

---

[5] Arlyn Melcher, "Central Negotiation and Master Contract: An Analysis of their Implications for Collective Bargaining," *Labor Law Journal*, 16 (June 1965), 352–58.

[6] Frederic Cleaveland, "Administrative Decentralization in the U. S. Bureau of Reclamation," *Public Administrative Review*, 13 (1953), 17–29.

design and construction of the projects. This effectively decentralized the *continuing* activities to the regional level and retained *one-time* activities to the Denver office; broad policy making was retained in the Washington office. From the regional perspective, a substantial decentralization of authority was accomplished.

Decentralization created internal pressures to bring the regional directors into policy formulation. The Washington office responded by setting up a formal mechanism to increase the degree of consultation and input from them. An annual policy conference was held where the regional directors, functional divisional specialists, and the commissioner's immediate staff in Washington met for several days to work out major policy problems. This enabled a closer interface between the policy group in Washington and the regional groups responsible for implementation. The consultation elicited inputs from regional offices on resources, political pressures, and regional needs. The regional directors became key figures as they brought to bear knowledge of their regions and practical insights from being an operating official in the field. At the same time, participation in the discussions of the national program provided for them a broader perspective of the interface of the regional interests with the national interests.

In one area, the Bureau of Reclamation remained centralized. The design and construction staff in Denver had retained authority over the design and construction of new projects. Further, the chief engineer represented the Washington office in contract negotiations and administration. This degree of centralization had several consequences. The construction engineer who headed a particular project had both the regional director and the chief engineer out of Denver as line supervisors. This created conflicts in instructions but, more important, the project heads found they had to continually clear proposals both with the chief engineer's office and the regional office to be sure a common understanding existed on approach. While overt incidents seldom developed, the uncertainty impaired morale and sapped the efficiency of the project team. Second, the regional director was held responsible for the features of the project and had to deal with the water users, but he didn't have the control over the design or the construction of the project. He couldn't add desirable features or delete unnecessary elements to hold down costs.

In summary, decentralization enabled those at the field level to make adjustments to problems in each region and on each project and effected a clearer unity of command. Further, it had the consequence of increasing the inputs into the policies formulated at the Washington level. Where centralization was retained on design and construction of projects, initiatives from the project directors had to be cleared with both line and staff personnel. This slowed down decisions and impaired morale.

Accuracy of Communications. Among the factors affecting the degree of communication accuracy are the reliance upon the formal channels, the opportunity for feedback, and the number of communication centers through which the information flows. Under centralization, each of these factors adversely influences the completeness and accuracy of vertical and lateral communication. Centralization reduces the potential for feedback, one of the most single important factors improving communication. When the sender is able to obtain direct feedback from the receiver, he understands better if the receiver comprehends and accepts the message.

Under centralization, orders and decisions are usually formalized and written. Since there is relatively little opportunity for direct feedback, the sender has to rely on third persons to monitor whether the message is understood. One weakness in this is that the third person may not see this as his role, or he may have reasons for screening out misinterpretations of the messages. It generally is in the interest of lower level personnel, for instance, to screen and block information flowing to the central levels on adverse local developments. Personnel also may be reluctant to bring to their superiors' attention that they have been ineffective in communicating with them. Further, the social distance between the sender and receiver is greater under a centralized organization than a decentralized one—which also reduces the feedback.

A field study throws some light on the relationship of delegation of authority to intra- and interdepartmental communication. In a study of sixteen health and welfare agencies, Hage, Aiken, and Merritt[7] related several variables including an index of formalization—which can be regarded as a measure of centralization—to the frequency of formal meetings and unscheduled informal meetings.[8] The trend was that with an increasing degree of centralization, fewer intra- or interdepartmental meetings were held either of a formal or informal character, and when held, fewer personnel attended. Possible reasons were that the differences in power and status among organizational members inhibited communications. The social distance between organizational levels reduced free flow of information in centralized organizations. The threat of penalties also discouraged frank discussion of problems and reduced upward communications.

The degree of centralization also influences the speed of communication and decision making. Under centralization, the local manager can make

[7]Jerald Hage, Michael Aiken, and Cora Merritt, "Organization Structure and Communications," *American Sociological Review*, 6 (October 1971), 860–71.

[8]The index of formalization was a measure of the degree to which a complete job description existed for each member and the degree to which specific procedures were defined for various contingencies. This would be an approximate measure of the degree of centralization as defined in this text. They also refer to a variable that they call centralization but which operationally is an element of leadership in this text.

decisions quickly *if the policies and procedures have been formulated.* Routine and reoccurring decisions can be readily handled since the criteria for decision making are spelled out. In a stable situation, a centralized organization can be efficient in communication and decision making. The limitations of centralization in respect to decision making develop where conditions are unstable, or where the policies and procedures haven't been formulated because of management inaction or management's desire to make each decision. When the regulations don't apply, or haven't been formulated, decisions are delayed. The local manager must wait until central management either makes a decision or formulates the regulation to govern the decision. In both cases, communications that report problems and conditions at lower levels must travel every level in the hierarchy to the decision-making point and back again for implementation. This process is typically slow, incomplete, and vulnerable to distortions. The formality of the communication and the number of communication centers the message must be sent through in going up and down the hierarchy contribute to poor communication.

In contrast, under decentralization the manager can assess and make the decisions without the delays in communication associated with going up and down the line. The manager who is close to the situation can collect information readily, process it, and arrive at a decision. Implementation of the decision can follow closely upon a commitment to action. Further, even in those areas where authority is retained by higher level management, decisions can be more readily considered. Since the bulk of decisions are made at the point at which they arise, the amount of paperwork that must go up and down is reduced. There's less chance of overloading either the higher level executives or the communication systems. This results in a quicker reaction and a better understanding of company policies that are centrally determined.

Centralization in Industrial Relations

The effects of the degree of centralization have been studied in the industrial relations area. On the company side, the degree of centralization influences the relationship of staff and line personnel at headquarters level with plant personnel. On the union side, it influences the relation of national officials with local representatives.

One aspect of negotiations is whether they physically take place at the plant level, or at headquarters level. This effects the scope of the negotiations, whether they are plant- or company-wide, and the degree to which local and/or national officials are involved. A second structural aspect of negotiations is whether local contracts are signed with each plant or a master contract is agreed upon that covers all the plants. The issues of central versus local negotiations and master versus local contracts are issues of centralization versus decen-

tralization. Melcher studied the collective bargaining of the three dominant firms in the agricultural implement industry—John Deere, International Harvester, and Allis Chalmers.[9]

Master contract and central negotiations are important to the parties for a number of reasons. They are important partly because they increase national control and participation in collective bargaining and partly because they facilitate development of a close-knit intracorporate council. Each of these factors in turn contributes to attainment of such goals as interplant and interindustry uniformity.

Master Contract

A master contract enables the national union and the company's central office to become key parties in the bargaining relationship. The agreement is between the general office of the company and the national union, although local representatives may also be signatory parties. Under a plant contract the agreement is between the plant management and the certified agent who may be the local, the national, or the local and national jointly. These variations have a number of implications for collective bargaining as outlined in Figure 7-2.

FIGURE 7-2. Effects of a master contract

1. Union can more easily appeal decisions at the plant level.
2. Arbitration awards apply to all plants.
3. Contributes to unity of the union.
4. Facilitates organization of new locals.
5. Increases contract control.
6. Assures central negotiation.

A master contract is associated in the minds of the company and union officials with an additional "half step" in the grievance procedure; that is, the right of locals or the national union to appeal decisions on grievances made by plant management to central office for review. A master contract is also identified with the right of union representatives to take a problem directly to top management. Under the plant contract this is less possible since the formal relationship is with the plant management. If the firm chooses, it can insist that the union deal only with local management. At times it is of strategic interest to take this position.

Under a master contract, any arbitration award rendered in one plant automatically applies to the others. From the union's point of

[9]Arlyn J. Melcher, "Central Negotiations and Masters Contract," pp. 353–57.

view, this largely solves the problem where the company delays the application of arbitration decisions to all the plants. It also tends to enable the national union to participate to a greater degree in screening grievances. Decisions automatically affect the contracts of all the locals and firmer controls are usually needed and accepted.

A master contract also provides an additional factor binding the union council together. Where an intracorporate council exists, locals are normally bound by the majority decision on common policy that is established. However, if each plant has its own contract, and the council is sharply divided on the issues, there always remains the possibility that one or more locals may enter into local negotiations and sign their own contracts with the company. Where a master contract has been and is being negotiated, this alternative is less available to any local.

Where a master contract is in effect, the union is in a better position to negotiate a clause which states that any subsequent units that are organized automatically come under the contract. This tends to simplify the negotiation of an initial contract. It also is an important provision in facilitating the organization of new units in a plant chain, particularly where sharp discrepancies exist between the organized and unorganized plants.

A master contract also provides better contract control both for the national union and for the company. Where there are individual contracts, particularly where the national union is not a party, there is always the possibility of locals making agreements with their respective plant managers who, from the union or management's point of view, may set poor precedents elsewhere. This possibility is not altogether eliminated with a master contract as the local union and management may make verbal agreements, but the latter have less possibility of serving as leverage in other plants.

A master contract usually assures central bargaining. Under local contracts the company has the right to discontinue central bargaining and return to local bargaining, although the form of central bargaining may have been followed for a number of years. Under the stress of stalled negotiations, the company may take this action to bring pressure on the union. If the firm were to carry out this threat, the national union would normally find it more difficult to hold the locals together. Under a master contract, the company has less of an alternative on bargaining procedure.

These are some of the main changes facilitated by a master contract. If the national union obtains these leverages through other means, the master contract is less important to it. For example, if the company deals with the national union as a matter of course in contract negotiations and administration, accepts central negotiations, and regularly applies arbitration awards to all the plants, there is little need for a master contract. This is particularly true if the national union has tight control over the locals at negotiations and during contract administration. The national has the advantages which tend to accrue to it under a master contract and therefore does not need the formal arrangement.

Central Negotiations

Where a master contract exists, central negotiations will surely be used. The converse is not necessarily so, as illustrated by John Deere and Allis Chalmer's experience. It is fruitful to consider what advantages the national union obtains with central negotiation. These are outlined in Figure 7-3.

FIGURE 7-3. Effects of central negotiation

1. Increases unity of the union.
2. Facilitates national control of a minority.
3. Enables greater national control over communication at negotiations.
4. Permits greater union control over the pace of negotiations.
5. Contributes to interplant uniformity.
6. Facilitates whipsawing of management's negotiation team against top management.
7. Dramatizes and publicizes settlements.

Central bargaining characteristically increases the unity of the intracorporate council and makes it a more effective body in coordinating negotiations and contract administration. Exchange of information on local practices and problems is facilitated. Greater participation interest and identity with the council programs can be expected to follow. There is an increased awareness of the need for central control in screening grievances. The role of national officials normally increases as they act as general spokesmen in the negotiating committee.

A minority can be brought into line more easily since the attitudes of the other locals and national representatives can be brought to bear more easily and continuously. Appeals for unity, threats of discipline, persuasion, and arguments can better be directed at locals that are wavering from the majority position. Under central negotiations responsibility of local unions to their membership is more diffuse as each local has only its per capita vote in decisions. Negotiations are normally physically removed from most of the plants, and as a consequence central negotiation places local pressures in the background. These factors contribute to the susceptibility of local leaders to pressure and persuasion from national officials.

Better control over union reports on the progress of negotiations is possible. In central negotiations the negotiating committee characteristically issues the only reports, thus providing a better framework for maintaining unity at the local level. The company may have a communication program of keeping the employees informed on the offers and counteroffers. However, a collective bargaining situation is normally so fluid, the negotiations so technical, the actual progress often so unclear that the union may have considerable success in discrediting information that management disseminates. The union may claim that "the company gives with one hand what it is taking back with the other" or "the principle is settled but the proper contract language remains to be worked out" and the like. There usually are many local demands on the table which also can be used to explain why a settlement is delayed.

In addition, central negotiation enables better control of the pace of negotiations. Under local negotiations the problems of holding the council together are multiplied where the company is willing to press the locals hard. With a single negotiating committee, negotiations can be more easily delayed or accelerated by the use of recesses, selection of local or national issues to be discussed, and timing of concessions.

When the union can control the pace of negotiations in each company, it is in a better position to probe and explore at which point in the industry pressure is most likely to pay off in a good pattern-setting package. Negotiations can be carried on simultaneously at the different companies in the industry. Once a choice is made on which point to apply pressure to, negotiations in the other companies can be delayed. In this way the union can avoid settling with companies in which it may be weak or where particular forceful management opposition to the union demands is encountered.

Central bargaining also creates pressure for uniformity of contracts among the plants. Those plants which are out-of-line with the others must justify this variation before those in higher authority and to their peers. It may be that any out-of-line plant or local may be able to keep its advantage in any particular negotiation. But, if either the union or management presses for elimination of the clause to the strike point, or the settlement of a strike turns on the issue, the pressure to come in line is difficult to resist. The other plant managers or local unions, as the case may be, are not likely to be willing to support such a strike.

Central negotiations also place the union in a better position to play off management's negotiation team against the top management. Where negotiations have bogged down, the union is in a better position to demand that top management enter the negotiations. The union, in its publicity to the membership and the community, can claim the negotiating committee hasn't any authority. It is a dramatic gesture and may be good tactics to get the company to move. Top officials, who haven't been publicly involved in last stand positions, may be more willing to grant additional concessions.

Finally, central negotiations enable the union to better dramatize the settlements. Maximum publicity, both for its own sake as it reflects on the union officials and because of the pattern-setting effect in other negotiations, is obtained in a central settlement. As negotiations draw to a conclusion, national officials can enter and be there as an agreement is reached. Their settlement is attributed by the public as a cause and effect relationship and the national leadership receives maximum publicity. For these and possibly other closely associated reasons the national union will strongly press for central negotiations.

It is apparent that master contract and central bargaining have separate and interrelated effects. They are important in affecting the relationship of the locals to each other and to the national union. Similarly, the relations of plant managers to each other and to the central office are affected.

Initiative, Motivation, and Morale of Management and Staff. Under centralization, the initiative and motivation of top management and staff are either maintained or increased. Their high status, involvement in decision making, and their importance to the organization support a high level of initiative and motivation. Their importance to the company results in them being well paid and well treated. On the other hand, initiative and motivation of lower level management are inhibited since lower level management are dependent, lack autonomy, and have limited potential for professional growth.

Decentralization contributes toward the opposite condition. The headquarters staff personnel are placed in an advisory relationship. Their degree of influence depends upon their ability to persuade lower level management to implement their recommendations. Top-line personnel also are placed in a different role. Their emphasis must shift to long-range planning, staffing, surveillance, and evaluation of lower level management. Their concern must be more with building the organization and development of personnel rather than making operating decisions. For most managers this is a less satisfying form of activity; they miss the immediate feedback that's associated with making decisions. Decentralization contributes toward the initiative and motivation of lower level management since they are involved in decisions and have the greater status and authority associated with being at a central point. They have a greater sense of professional development and challenge in their work.

INCREASING AUTHORITY OF LAB TECHNICIANS

A number of studies on the effects of increased delegation of authority have been done in Great Britain. One study focused upon laboratory technicians of a research unit in Imperial Chemical Industries Limited—a large chemical company.[10] The laboratory technicians were responsible for implementing experimental programs devised by scientists. They set up the equipment, recorded data, and supervised laboratory assistants who carried out routine operations. Most of the lab technicians had limited promotional opportunities, and few had the possibility of moving out of the department. Morale was low and the technicians were frustrated.

A program was implemented that sharply increased the authority of the technicians:

- They were authorized to write the final report or part of the report on developments for which they were responsible.
- They were consulted in planning projects and contributed to target setting.
- They could request time to follow up their own ideas even when this exceeded the scope of the authorized project.
- They were given authority to requisition materials, equipment, and services.
- Senior laboratory technicians were given authority to devise and implement a training program for their junior staff, interview candidates for laboratory assistant jobs and review the work of their assistants.

The changes were introduced into two sections of the department and

[10]William J. Paul, Jr., Keith B. Robertson, and Frederick Herzberg, "Job Enrichment Pays Off," *Harvard Business Review* (March-April 1969), pp. 61–78.

maintained over twelve months; a third section served as a partial control group—no changes were made for six months and then the changes were introduced. A fourth section was held as a control group and was maintained without any changes. Each of the sections was required to write monthly progress reports from which a judgment was made on the research contributions of the groups.

In the two groups with greater authority, both quantity and quality of their work rose for about three months, when it then leveled off. Both control groups improved to a lesser degree for two months and then stabilized. Apparently, the requirement to write progress reports had an impact on all the groups. When delegation was increased in the third group after six months, performance increased to a higher level than all other groups.

Although three groups in the department had participated in the changes, morale of the department remained unchanged. This reveals both some of the potential effects of increased delegation as well as its limitations. While these changes resulted in increased opportunity for professional growth and challenge, opportunities for job mobility and substantive recognition in promotion and salary increases were still limited.

DELEGATING GREATER AUTHORITY
TO SALESMEN

Another British company attempted to stimulate sales effort by greater delegation.[11] The salesmen had high morale, but the company's position in the market had declined for several years until it had finally stabilized. The management felt its products were fully competitive in price and quality and that the market position was largely determined by sales effort. The problem, then, was to motivate a group of people who were well treated and satisfied to exert extra effort. Increased authority was provided in several ways:

- Salesmen were given the authority to decide what information to pass on to higher levels about their sales contacts. The company dropped the requirement for formal reports on all customer calls.
- They were given the authority to determine the frequency of customer calls.
- Records were kept only for review purposes.
- They were authorized to make settlements up to $250 on customer complaints if in their judgment it was warranted.
- They were authorized to provide up to a 10 percent discount on prices on products the firm was pushing, as long as these were reported. Before this change, these discounts had to be cleared through headquarters.
- Arrangements were made that a supportive technical group would provide service on demand and the necessary paperwork could be completed at a later point.

[11]Ibid.

These changes were introduced into one of the sales groups of fifteen members, and the effects were observed over a nine-month period, while the rest of the sales force retained the same conditions as before. The group increased its sales by 19 percent while maintaining profit margins on sales. In the other sales group, sales declined by 5 percent. Morale of the decentralized group improved while that of the others remained the same. The increased delegation contributed substantially to the company's goal of recovering its position in the market.

INCREASING AUTHORITY OF SCIENTISTS

A study of the National Institute of Health related the degree of delegation of authority to scientists with their productivity.[12] The researchers measured the degree of freedom the scientists had to determine what problems they worked on and the follow-up steps to be taken in solving the problems. A higher percentage of scientists were high performers under decentralization. The relation was particularly strong for scientists at the medium-status level where only 47 percent of those under the centralized organization were highly productive, while 79 percent of those were highly productive under decentralization. The authority to choose problems and methods of attacking them provided the initiative, experience, and competency to be more productive.

DELEGATING AUTHORITY TO CLERKS

A well-known field experiment at the Prudential Insurance Company on the effects of delegation produced less impressive results.[13] About 500 people in four parallel units in one department were involved in the year and a half study. The employees were made up mostly of young, high school educated, unmarried women who performed clerical jobs. In two of the divisions composed of five sections each, authority was delegated to the supervisors with the understanding that they would delegate it to their clerical groups. These decisions included structuring of work methods and processes, deciding on recess periods, handling of tardiness, and other personnel matters. In effect,

[12]Donald C. Pelz, Glanding Mellinger, and Robert C. Davis, "Human Relations in a Research Organization: A Study of the National Institute of Health" (Ann Arbor, Mich.: University of Michigan, 1953), pp. 261–334.

[13]The material was drawn from three sources: Nancy C. Morse and Everett Reimer, "The Experimental Change of a Major Organization Variable," *Journal of Abnormal and Social Psychology*, 52 (1956), 120–29; Nancy C. Morse, Everett Reimer, and Arnold Tannenbaum, "Regulation and Control in Hierarchial Organizations," *Journal of Social Issues*, 3 (1951), 41–48; and Nancy C. Morse, "An Experimental Study in an Industrial Organization," in Harold Guetzkow, ed., *Groups, Leadership and Men* (New York: Russell & Russell, 1963), pp. 96–99.

a greater degree of authority was delegated to operating personnel to handle some routine work and personnel problems.

In two divisions also composed of five sections each, increased authority was given to *higher* level line and staff officials to institute changes. In effect, authority in this program was taken from the operating supervisor and reassigned to higher management and staff groups, so one division was decentralized and the other centralized. During the first six months, the staff experts studied the operations and introduced several programs to increase employee efficiency in the centralized division. One major change was that the staff ordered that the number of employees assigned to these units be reduced so that, in effect, they increased productivity standards. Little change occurred in the clerks' interest in the job or sense of development on the job under either the decentralized or centralized units. In respect to the satisfaction with the company, a slight increase occurred under decentralized program and a slight decrease under centralization.

One of the changes that accompanied the changes in delegation was imposition of higher work standards. In the centralized program, the reduction of personnel initiated by the staff personnel resulted in productivity increases from 13 to 15 percent. In the decentralized units where the method of reducing personnel was left up to the unit, productivity increased 9 to 11 percent.[14]

CENTRALIZATION IN A MENTAL HOSPITAL: VIOLATIONS OF PROFESSIONAL EXPECTATIONS

Another study indicates that either a centralized or decentralized structure may be accepted by the participants depending on expectations that management encourages. If equality of professions, teamwork, and sharing of responsibilities are emphasized, then the lower level personnel are more critical of a centralized structure.

An intensive case study of five wards in a mental hospital found that the actual decision process closely followed the traditional centralized structure, with the psychiatrists making most of the decisions on the five wards despite the ideology of the therapeutic community.[15] The idea of a therapeutic environment includes the subordination of the traditional hierarchial structure to open flexible contacts and an emphasis on teamwork and equality; the roles, duties, and obligations of each specialty are regarded as equally vital to the functioning of the organization; status and power distinctions are ideally

---

[14]This interpretation varies considerably from that of the authors. Readers would profit by a close reading of the original reports.

[15]Mark Lefton, Simon Dinizt, and Benjamin Pasamanick, "Decision-Making in a Mental Hospital: Real, Perceived and Ideal," *American Sociological Review*, 24 (1959), 822–29.

minimized, and decisions are to be made through broad participation and consensus rather than unilaterally. Despite the ideology, even general discussions were dominated by the psychiatrists; nurses and other specialists only responded to questions in their specialized areas.

The degree to which the therapeutic approach was practiced affected, in part, the influence the centralized structure had on attitudes. A therapeutic approach that emphasized personal methods of treatment, particularly the use of psychotherapy, was practiced in two wards. In the other three wards, individual therapy was combined with use of drugs and other means in a more eclectic and traditional approach to patient treatment. In these three wards, greater satisfaction existed with the authority distribution and decision-making process. Where the emphasis was on the central elements of the therapeutic environment, the entire group of professionals had higher expectations on the importance of the role they should play in treatment of patients and were more critical of the structure and decision process.

In summary, decentralization contributes to higher initiative, motivation, and satisfaction with the job and the organization. However, the degree of delegation must be of some importance to have an impact on productivity and morale. In the Prudential Insurance Company study, productivity increased more in the units with greater centralization and morale remained about unchanged in both. In this case, a major change was forced on the groups while the members were being delegated minor discretion on personnel and work matters. Other studies show substantial improvements in morale and productivity where a high degree of delegation is provided.

A study of a mental hospital indicates that a centralized organization may be accepted if this is consistent with other role definitions. Where a traditional medical approach was used in treatment of patients, the specialists were willing to accept their subordinate status and low level of participation in decisions. Traditional medical practice emphasizes that those with more extensive training have greater competency and should make decisions, which, in turn, are implemented by lesser trained specialists. But where the emphasis was on methods that required greater personal involvement, those lower in the professional hierarchy were critical of the failure to involve them in decisions.

Decentralization: A Change in the Structure of the Post Office

An article in the *Wall Street Journal* (February 18, 1971) on the postal corporation highlights many of the advantages attributed to decentralization. In 1970, the Post Office was moved from an agency of the federal government to a semi-independent corporation to improve its operation. Among other steps, the corporation decentralized a greater degree of the decisions to local post offices.

As an agency of the government, a highly structured system had developed where specifications for running the post offices were laid down in a giant manual that set forth policies, procedures, and rules for every conceivable contingency from flying the flag to the steps to take to locate missing mail. These policies were formulated at the national level and other routine decisions were referred to the regional level.

Under the decentralization, broad guidance was provided to the local postmasters along with manpower and financial resources. The postmasters were expected to operate within these policies in solving local problems. In the Baltimore post office, one of the 110 largest post offices in the country, decentralization accomplished a number of things:

- It enabled the Baltimore postmaster to adjust to the special conditions in Baltimore, such as where to expand service and otherwise adjust service.
- Considerable paperwork and time involved in securing regional approval was eliminated.
- It enabled the postmaster to deal with private truckers who carry the mail in and out of Baltimore. The postmaster could make contracts with truckers, discipline those who provided inadequate service, and otherwise deal with them on a regular basis without clearance with the regional office.
- The postmaster could pay the office's own utility bills rather than certify them to a center in Atlanta for payment.
- The postmaster could open small branch offices and make repairs and improvements up to two thousand dollars on his own initiative.
- Subordinates could be promoted.
- The postmaster was given a budget and permitted to operate within restrictions of that budget rather than having to request approval from the regional office on expenditures.
- The postmaster could negotiate with large customers to develop ways to save time and money and expedite mail services for larger users; Saturday delivery could be eliminated to firms open five days a week; arrangements could be made with big mailers to arrange local mail so that it would go directly to the letter carrier for delivery to bypass most processing steps.
- Decentralization permitted and required the regional offices to develop personnel with a general management perspective.
- The overall consequences were increased efficiency, higher morale, and greater ability to adjust to changes through time and to local conditions.

VULNERABILITY OF THE ORGANIZATION

Two factors that affect an organization's vulnerability to unanticipated developments are the degree of personnel development and the degree to which decisions depend upon the competency of top management.

Development and Recruitment of Personnel. Centralization increases the breadth of experience and development of top management and staff personnel. They make decisions, or establish policies that govern decisions, and are on the firing line. Centralization, however, adversely influences the development of lower level management and personnel. They make decisions only within the narrowly confined constraints of policies and procedures and are responsible principally for implementation. This is poor training ground for improving scope of judgment and decision skills.

In contrast, decentralization develops initiative, self-reliance, and judgment of lower level personnel. The most effective way of developing these abilities is through the day-to-day requirements of the job. Under a decentralized organization, few rules or dependable guideposts exist for the automatic solution of problems. The supervisors practice skills, exercise their capacities, and develop self-reliance as they are forced to face up to problems. If personnel are capable of development, decentralization provides visibility for their level of skill. Those who grow can be promoted and those who don't can be moved out of the organization.

Another problem is that of recruitment. Centralization adversely affects recruitment of competent individuals for positions at lower levels in the organization. Decentralization provides a better recruiting ground since the individuals are placed in positions where they are faced with responsible assignments.

Two case studies deal with the effects of increasing authority on development and recruitment of personnel.[16] In one company the production foremen were authorized to modify work schedules, make nonstandard payments, hire labor for authorized positions, and apply disciplinary action (up to dismissal), and they were given authority to evaluate, train, and develop their subordinates. In the engineering department, foremen were given authority over preventive maintenance, opportunity to participate in decisions, control over some budgets, and authority to discipline, assist, train, and develop their men.

The results were that the production foremen were able to hire a better caliber of employees. Training improved and disciplinary action was more effective. The engineering foremen improved their control and development of their personnel. Further, the foremen started working with union officers, and performance level sharply rose. The morale of the production foremen

[16]Paul, Robertson, and Herzberg, "Job Enrichment Pays Off," pp. 61–78.

remained unchanged while the morale of the engineering foremen increas ed. In summary, increased delegation of authority results in improved performance of a group. The opportunity for professional growth and exercise of independence stimulates higher commitment and assumption of responsibility. However, morale may or may not improve.

Reliance upon Top Management. The vulnerability of an organization also depends upon the methods used to centralize. The organization may be centralized in that operating decisions are made at low levels of the organization, but these decisions are governed by restrictive policies. On the other hand, the organization may be centralized in that most operating decisions are referred upward to central staff and line personnel by lower level personnel.

The loss of top management or staff personnel under a bureaucratic structure has few implications under a stable environment since the decisions continue to be made using past guidelines. The difficulty comes where new conditions or interpretations are required. If the environment is unstable, a centralized bureaucracy leads to a gradual deterioration in effectiveness since inappropriate policies and procedures govern the decisions.

Where headquarters personnel make operating decisions, the effects of centralization depend to a large extent upon the quality of the top executive and his aids. Where they are vigorous, imaginative, have great wells of energy, are flexible, and are competent judges of people, the organization can be immensely productive. With continuity of this leadership, the organization can continue to prosper. This may be one of the principal reasons why so many organizations are centralized in the light of the various dysfunctional consequences. Most organizations have a relatively small number of competent individuals, and centralization enables maximum reliance upon their abilities.

The disadvantages flow directly from the strengths. Continuity of the firm rests on relatively few people. If they become sick, decrease in ability due to age or professional obsolescence, die, or leave the organization, the functioning of the organization is sharply affected. Since the organizational form doesn't develop general management personnel, replacement of executives from within is hard.

The paradox of centralization is that the organization is dependent upon top leadership, but centralization doesn't nourish new leadership. Those on a lower level in the organization are successful if they *carry out* and *implement* decisions—not if they make decisions. The individual that exercises independence by interpreting policies or making decisions that violate policy tends to get into trouble. In contrast, the decentralized organization is less vulnerable in that a larger number of experienced managers are available, and their areas of jurisdiction are more limited when learning their jobs.

ABILITY TO MAKE CHANGES

The ability to make changes in centralized organization depends partly upon whether the organization operates as an autocracy or bureaucracy. In an autocracy, where few policies and procedures are codified and most decisions must be referred to higher levels, change can be initiated readily. Where the organization is bureaucratized in that decisions are sharply restricted by policies and procedures, changes are difficult to initiate and implement.

Changes can be rapidly initiated and a formal plan implemented under an autocracy. Top management can announce changes and order plans to be implemented. Once resources are committed, programs discontinued, major personnel shifts made, or long-term commitments determined, it is nearly impossible to unravel these decisions and go back to point zero. Centralization is an important factor determining the degree of domination the top leadership will have in these decisions.

Some changes can be initiated and implemented without consensus, such as reducing capital expenditures, establishing different priorities, or taking actions of one-point-in-time nature. However, many changes must be implemented over time. While central management can initiate changes, the changes are likely to be actively resisted or at least passively implemented where consensus is not achieved. Furthermore, where changes are achieved on *fait accompli* basis, it undermines the support for additional changes where a more positive orientation might have initially existed.

Another dimension of change is the short-term modification in decision structure to meet emergencies. Under decentralization, top management can assume authority to make decisions to adjust to emergency situations. Once the emergency has passed, authority can be returned to lower level personnel. It is less feasible, however, to decentralize a centralized organization on a temporary basis to deal with rapidly changing, or varying, conditions. Lower level supervisors don't have the decision-making experience and skills to exercise the authority.

In a centralized bureaucracy, changes are more difficult to initiate and implement. Rules, policies, and procedures normally have a high degree of cohesion and internal logic that bind the rules into a larger system. Any change in one rule has implications for others. In the area of industrial relations, for instance, the management and union objective is generally stability rather than change. Decisions are normally made in the light of the policy and practices in existence, and these place a practical limit on innovation permitted. At best, changes are delayed as information is sent up and policies and procedures are revised and communicated downward.

The degree of centralization is important in an indirect way as well as directly influencing the decision process. While the executive may seldom exercise his right to make decisions without obtaining broad consensus, centralization still creates a climate where it is easier to obtain consensus. Those consulted are normally aware that if agreement isn't arrived at, the executive can act without their input. If, on the other hand, the authority is broadly delegated, the willingness to consider the viewpoints and perspectives of the other personnel is reduced. This becomes particularly important when major differences exist among individuals and groups on the direction in which organization should move.

Wood evaluated how the degree of centralization in churches influenced basic policy adapted on integration of blacks.[17] This was a controversial policy where the majority membership sentiment was actively opposed to integrating blacks. On the other hand, the majority of clergymen were supporters of these policies. Wood found that those churches that emphasized local autonomy and were decentralized took a weaker position supporting integration; those denominations that were moderately centralized took a more vigorous stand supporting integration.

On noncontroversial issues, leaders determined policy with pro forma ratification, so the degree of autonomy wasn't relevant. The degree of centralization was important, however, in influencing positions taken on controversial issues. Leaders pressed for an integrative policy in controversial areas only when they had formal authority that insulated them from member protest. Leaders with formal authority could face controversy for two major reasons.

1. Those with the formal authority had powerful sanctions at their disposal. While they seldom used these sanctions, because of their alienating character, their availability created a climate that reinforced their persuasive efforts. A rebellious group, for instance, might have to surrender its church property if it left the church, and it was subject to possible expulsion. This tempered the extreme quality of their actions and increased their receptivity to the position of the leadership.

2. Challenges to those with formal authority were bound by the norms that the due process of questioning policy should be observed. Direct action of resorting to financial or other pressures was less likely to receive the support of the broader membership who believed in the process of church government.

SUMMARY

In summary, delegation of authority is a complex variable that includes both the level at which decisions are authorized to be made and the degree

[17]James R. Wood, "Authority and Controversial Policy: The Churches and Civil Rights," *American Sociological Review*, 35 (1970), 1057–69.

of discretion decision makers have. One usually thinks of an autocracy as representing centralized organization, where most decisions have to be referred to top management for decisions. A more subtle and pervasive form in large organizations is the centralized bureaucracy. Most operating decisions are made at lower levels, but these are sharply restricted by policies, procedures, and rules. A further complication is that the degree of delegation must be assessed at each level and within each division. Broad variations in patterns exist in the same organization.

The degree of delegation has broad implications for the strategies that will be pursued. A centralized organization means that the headquarters' perspective prevails with its focus on developing a general strategy for the common conditions facing the organization, optimizing the overall welfare even at expense of some local interest, and maintenance of order and consistency of direction. Where the organization is decentralized, attention is given to tactics to deal with local conditions and maintenance of the local division as a viable cohesive unit even if this is at the expense of other groups.

The decision process is affected by the degree of centralization. Headquarters operates away from the pressure of problems; it is concerned with collecting information and planning rationally long-term development of the organization. The local unit is physically near and emotionally involved in urgency of solutions; the thrust is to solve the problems as best as possible rather than to delay for more information, a better plan, or broader considerations. The headquarters emphasizes use of the formal structure while the local unit's thrust is upon forceful leadership.

The appropriate degree of delegation depends upon the conditions existing in an organization. As the organization becomes more complex in terms of increasing size, interdependence of work flow, complexity of tasks, and spatial-physical barriers within and among groups, a functional requisite for efficiency is to move decisions to the operating level while coordinating the parts. This is achieved, in part, by formulating policies, procedures, and rules that limit the discretion of operating personnel. Top personnel concentrate upon long-term planning and policy formulation and lower level personnel on implementation and making operational decisions within this framework.

The advantages that flow from centralization are disadvantages under decentralization and vice versa. The existing conditions determine the relative importance of the consequences of centralization or decentralization. Centralization provides greater coordination and uniformity of approach. Single direction and common policies limit variation in decisions made at the operating level. The organization as a whole receives primary attention. Communication downward is efficient where the total set of policies, procedures, rules, and supplementary instructions constitute most of the communications. The resources and information can be mobilized efficiently to meet emergency developments.

Centralization supports higher initiative, motivation, and satisfaction of top management and staff and contributes to their development. It enables an organization to capitalize on the loyalties, ability, and experience of its top management and staff personnel. Change can also be rapidly initiated under centralization.

The disadvantages of centralization—and the advantages of decentralization—are that coordination and uniformity are achieved at the expense of adapting to varying local conditions. Speed of communications *upward* and decision processes are slow. In an autocracy, central personnel are typically overloaded and adjust by delaying consideration of developing problems while giving attention to emergencies or urgent problems. Communications on developments are slow both in going up and down in the structure with the greater number of communication centers that messages pass through.

While top personnel exert high initiative, lower level personnel express lower level motivation and are more dissatisfied on their jobs. Centralization inhibits development of lower level personnel since they are trained in implementing and not making decisions. The most critical problem is that the organization is highly vulnerable to what happens to its top people. If the top personnel maintain their abilities and stay with the organization, centralization works out fine. But if they die, leave, or decrease in effectiveness as they age, become ill, or fail to grow with changing conditions, the prosperity and continuity of the organization is seriously jeopardized.

DYNAMICS OF AUTHORITY AND
DECISION MAKING

Interdependence of Structure, Process, and Behavior

One complication in sorting out the influence that formal authority has on organization processes and behavior is where prescribed relationships aren't observed. Authority may be retained centrally, but decisions may be made at lower levels. Contrarily, formal authority may be delegated but not implemented in practice. Four variations in structure and process are summarized in Table 7-4.

TABLE 7-4. Combinations of Structure and Process

| Emergent Decision Patterns | Formal Authority Relations | |
	Centralized	Decentralized
Headquarters	11 Centralized: structure and process	12 Decentralized structure, centralized process
Operating Level	21 Centralized structure, decentralized process	22 Decentralized: structure and process

Normally, the following relationships exist:

$$\text{Formal Authority} \xrightarrow{\text{(1)}} \text{Decision Process} \xrightarrow{\text{(2)}} \text{Behavior}$$

Distribution of formal authority influences the patterns of decision making (1), which, in turn, influences behavior (2). The restriction of formal authority, for example, results in lower level personnel exercising little discretion in their jobs, which, in turn, causes low initiative. In this case office holders adhere closely to the limits defined by the formal authority, i.e., cell 11 in Table 7-4. On the other hand, they may broadly deviate from those restrictions. The president, for example, may formally delegate decisions to lower level subordinates but may make the decisions in practice, or those delegated the right to make decisions may refuse to exercise those rights in an attempt to play safe (cell 12). In each of these cases, the effects of structure will be sharply moderated. The functional and dysfunctional effect summarized in the chapter can then more readily be traced to the actual process that exists. An organization may be centralized in a formal sense in that decisions are restricted by policies, procedures, and rules. But if in actual practice lower level managers ignore policies and *exercise* broad discretion, the process determines consequences rather than the formal structure, such as degrees of adaptation to local conditions, development of managers, and the like.

If prescribed decision process corresponds closely with the emergent pattern of decision making, behavior is directly influenced by both. If patterns of decision making vary from structure, the formal structure still exerts influence but in a subtle, indirect way and emerges only through time.

IMPLICATIONS OF DIFFERENCES
BETWEEN STRUCTURE AND PROCESS

Where both structure and process vary, two factors that determine the importance of formal structure are:

1. The degree that disagreement exists among groups or between higher and lower management on the decisions that should be made
2. The extent that the organization operates in a stressful environment

The formal organization is important in providing the limitations on the actual decision processes. Organizational processes may be modified by changing structure, changing processes directly, or by changing them both.

Where the formal structure has been deviated from for several years and a stable ongoing process of decision making implemented, attempts to move back to the authorized decision process generate resistance and conflict. The effects of formal structure may be revealed only when critical issues arise and where there are differences in opinion between higher level personnel and operating managers on the decisions that should be made. While a structure may be deviated from in terms of the patterns of decision making, the formal specifications become important during periods of confrontation.

When disputes arise, the parties fall back upon their legitimacy or right to make the decisions. Lower level managers may regularly hire personnel, for instance, but may never be given the authority to do so. The assumed authority in this instance has greater impact on behavior than the formal structure. However, if a major issue arises on staffing where the lower and higher level managers have different views, then the issue rapidly becomes one of who has a legitimate right to make such decisions. At that point, the formal authority is important since structure is likely to determine the outcome.

The importance of the formal authority structure also emerges when the executive tries to increase his control and influence over the decision process. In a university, for instance, the president may permit the faculty or deans the authority to hire personnel, and he approves this decision with only pro forma consideration. At some future time, he or another president may wish to exercise this authority. The attempt to change the organization normally will be associated with conflict if the decision process has been exercised over a number of years. The faculty members rely upon past actions to legitimize the correctness of the ongoing process. If the president, however, holds that the authority lies with him and reasserts his right to make these decisions, a major conflict may result. He is likely to win this struggle, though, if he persists, since he has the legitimatized right. In contrast, if the decision had been formally delegated to the deans, or faculty, the president is in a vulnerable position if he tries to appoint personnel. His right to make these decisions can be challenged. He would have to achieve a redefinition of the structural relation between his office and colleges to be on safe ground.

STRUCTURE AND PROCESS UNDER INCREASING STRESS

A study by Melcher and Kayser supports the thesis that the formal structure becomes important in dealing with controversial issues, particularly as pressure on the organization increases.[18] A "new products department" in a large industrial firm was assigned the responsibility for developing new products. Initially, the department concentrated on a new synthetic material. While this required input and cooperation from specialist groups at headquarters level and the independent operating divisions, the project manager had no formal authority over these units. He reported to a vice-president, and the authority to order cooperation among areas was retained at that level. The cooperation of divisional groups and specialists at the headquarters level could be obtained either by persuasion or by appealing decisions to the vice-presidential level.

[18]Arlyn Melcher and Thomas Kayser, "Leadership Without Formal Authority: The Project Department," *California Management Review*, 18 (Winter 1970), 57–64.

In the early years of development, the project manager was successful in interesting top executives in the project and in eliciting the support of the various units to contribute to the project. These were the golden years where all who were involved in the project developed an intensive team relationship and found broad satisfaction and fulfillment in their work. These early years support the thesis that the formal relationships are unimportant, or at least can be easily compensated for by agressive leadership.

As the product neared the point of being introduced in the market, several changes occurred that had broad repercussions on the relationships with other departments. Other competitors were nearing the completion of similar products, and one major firm aggressively introduced its product. Further, the development and manufacturing of the product stretched out into a longer period than was initially visualized. In the early stages, only modest resources were required to support the product development. At later stages, the resource commitment for both the preceding years and the future was running into several millions of dollars. The increased length of time, the amount of resources required, the introduction of a product by a major competitor, and the emergence of several other competitors translated into high pressure to complete the development of the project and get it into the market. Another change was equally important. The top administration of the company changed, and his immediate superior was also replaced. The new executives had many responsibilities and pressures; the product manager, while trying to coordinate the further development of the project, tried to educate them on the nature and promise of the product and elicit their support. It was a difficult environment to operate within, and he was unsuccessful in cooptating them. The cooperation with key units deteriorated simultaneously as they responded to other pressures and made independent judgments on the direction and amount of support they would provide. For instance, in the early years the product manager had built up a good relationship with the technical director of the research laboratory. When the director moved to another position, the new director felt that "outsiders" had unduly influenced past policy, and he set about correcting this. He demonstrated his independence by rejecting requests and initiatives from the product manager.

The product manager was faced with appealing decisions to higher levels to obtain the cooperation of other departments. However, his immediate superior was unresponsive to his view of what should be done and the need for further developmental work before going to market with the product. While the product manager was willing to go topside "to fight the good fight," he had less opportunity to do so and was less effective when he did.

While all his problems wouldn't have been solved by authority over other units, having authority would have created a better position for him to exercise his naturally persuasive style. He wouldn't have been completely dependent upon sponsorship and support from higher level executives. As the pressures increased, he would have been able to exert some pressure for cooperation rather than having to rely solely upon persuasion. When the climate was permissive, his lack of authority had little relevance; when the climate was oppressive and pressures high, the lack of authority was critical in undermining his position and ultimately destroyed his effectiveness.

IMPACT OF FORMAL STRUCTURE
IN MODIFYING DECISIONS

The formal authority may be important in another subtle way. The formal structure influences the decision process by providing limitations on decisions that can be made. A university senate or other body may not have the formal authority to make final decisions. However, the ongoing pattern may be that it makes various types of recommendations and these are normally implemented by the president. However, if these decisions are made with the knowledge that the president has veto power, recommendations are made within the perspective of what is probably acceptable to the president. Even though the patterns of decision making vary from the formal structure, the formal distribution of authority affects the decision processes.

A case study illustrates how the level at which decisions are to be made and the limitations imposed by the policies influence the decision process and behavior.[19] Under Ralph Cordner, General Electric organized twenty-seven product divisions and decentralized extensively down to the division level. However, one decision on which the divisions were restricted was in the area of pricing. Previous presidents had issued a broad policy that actions couldn't be taken in collusion with competitors that were in violation of antitrust laws. Ralph Cordner replaced this directive with one that was more explicit and went beyond the requirements of the law by blanketing the subject with every conceivable admonition. While the divisions were relatively decentralized, the detailed policy formally restricted the decisions that could be made in respect to colluding or communicating with competitors.

Despite this directive, a number of the divisions colluded anyway with competitors to establish prices. This came to a temporary end in 1954—a recession period. Faced with a sharp dropoff in orders, the firms started to covertly compete for orders by price cutting while still maintaining the pretence of price fixing. The issue came to a head when G. E. was beaten out of a large contract by Westinghouse, who had deviated from its agreement—illegal as it was—to maintain the price level. Paxton, G. E.'s executive vice-president (who apparently was unaware of the price collusion), decided that

---

[19]Richard Austin Smith, "The Incredible Electric Conspiracy," *Fortune* (April 1961), pp. 132–37, 170–80.

the firm was losing business because its prices weren't competitive. He relieved the general sales manager of authority to make pricing decisions and centralized pricing at his level. This meant that decisions on pricing had now to be approved by executive management.

Since the general sales manager and his sales staff, who were responsible for sales and profits, could no longer make covert, illegal agreements with competitors on prices and division of the market, the cartel broke. As G. E. aggressively moved to increase its share of the market, prices declined sharply to where discounts of 40–45 percent were given on contracts up to five years ahead. This played havoc with G. E.'s profits. Paxton, faced with declining profits, returned the sales responsibility to the general managers.

With their authority restored over pricing, the sales personnel proceeded to stabilize the shares of market and to increase prices. They did so by reestablishing the cartel arrangement with competitors. Although company policy formally prohibited these acts, they still could make them now that decisions were back at the operating level.

The policies provided some restraint on the decision process since some supervisors resigned from their jobs because they felt they couldn't accept the deviations from policy. The agreements had to be undertaken in secret, and decisions had to be made within the perspective that the actions were illegal. Ultimately, when the government uncovered the price conspiracy, both the corporations and individuals involved were fined, and individuals at the operating level who had violated company policy and the law were sent to jail.

EFFECTS OF STRUCTURE AND PROCESS ON BEHAVIOR: A STUDY IN CONFLICT RESOLUTION

Where formal structure and emerging decision process diverge, behavior may be influenced by changes in structure, process, or both, or the emergent behavior may bring about changes in structure in an attempt to modify the decision process and behavior. These changes and their implications are illustrated by a study of International Harvester. McKersie and Shropshire studied the operation of the grievance system and the effects of changes in decision process on the settlement of grievances and other relationships of the parties.[20] Various conditions contributed to the filing of numerous grievances including rival relationships between two unions, the radical nature of the leadership of one of the unions, a poorly rationalized piecework system, diversity of conditions among plants, and an attempt to tighten up on stan-

[20]Robert B. McKersie and William H. Shropshire, Jr., "Avoiding Written Grievances: A Successful Program," *Journal of Business*, 35 (April 1962), 135–52.

dards during the postwar period to meet competitive conditions. These and other factors generated a high rate of grievances.

Initially, the structure of the grievance system was changed by eliminating the middle steps between arbitration and the first level where they were generated. Over a period of time, the firm reduced six steps in the system to three steps. This meant that if the issue wasn't settled at the employee level, it moved to the plant level and was then appealed to arbitration.

Aside from the reduction in steps, which made it quicker to move the decision to the headquarters level, the degree of discretion in handling decisions at all levels was substantially reduced. The master contract expanded from 50 to 60 pages to over 300 pages; this was further supplemented by local contracts. An extensive system of rules and regulation was codified into the contract. Further, as the arbitrators ruled on grievances, they laid down rules for similar decisions; these decisions became a body of rules further restricting discretion. Up to 1959, grievances filed at local level were nearly automatically referred to the plant level; about 30 percent of these were appealed to the arbitration step between 1954 and 1959. The grievances accumulated, since it wasn't feasible to arbitrate more than ten or twenty grievances each year.

This failure to settle grievances at the first step occurred partly because the foremen had difficulty interpreting the complex contract. In part, it was a play-safe position on the part of the foremen, who felt that it was better to err in refusing to settle a legitimate grievance than to pay off an illegitimate one. Grievances referred to the central level overloaded both the union and management personnel at headquarters level. Both the structure and decision process resulted in a rapid accumulation of unresolved grievances. This, in turn, contributed to poor behavior patterns, frustration of employees, generation of anger, and submission of additional grievances.

The grievances became a major issue in the contract negotiations. The union took the position that until the grievances were resolved, the contract wouldn't be settled. Therefore, the parties developed ad hoc arrangements to deal with the grievances at the central level. This wholesale approach to grievance settlement, in turn, encouraged multiple submission of grievances since at least some of those were settled at the central negotiations.

To resolve the issue of continuing conflict during the contract administration and at negotiations, the union and company moved the settlement of the issues back to the local level. The same structural arrangements were maintained in terms of the number of steps and in terms of complexity of the issue of rules and regulations governing the settlement. However, the emphasis was placed on settling the issues at the first level by the local parties or by bringing in central personnel as advisors to the local level to assist in the settlement. This was to be done *prior* to the grievance being written. While the structural features remained the same, the process of settling the issues moved back to the local level. The settlement of issues sharply increased along with basic changes in the attitude of local union and company personnel. According to McKersie and Shropshire, this wasn't at the expense of being more liberal in settling the issues. The practical elimination of written grievances and of the appeal to the arbitration stage was achieved by focusing upon the settlement at the point where they arose.

In summary, this complex case illustrates the intricate relationship between structure and process of decision making. The reduction of steps in the grievance process and enormous expansion of rules and regulations governing local relationships sharply reduced the discretion of local union and supervisory personnel. The rivalry among unions, coupled with a poorly rationalized piecework system, diversity of conditions, and other stressful factors, meant that many disputes were generated. The complexity of the contract and play-safe position on part of foremen resulted in their refusing to make decisions even where they had the authority. The result was extensive appealing of grievances to the central level for resolution.

Overloading the system at that level resulted in accumulation of thousands of grievances, where they became part of the issues to be negotiated at the contract time. The breakdown of the process of settlement during the contract period meant that the grievances became issues to be resolved by pressure tactics at negotiations. Attempts to solve the problems by adding further provisions to the contracts and by arbitration decisions perpetuated the impass.

The issue was resolved by a concentrated attempt on the part of national union and headquarters management to move the decisions back to the local level. They achieved this by a structural change—grievances were *not* written up except as a last resort—and by a change in process—local personnel were pressured to resolve the issues by oral agreements at the point where the problems arose. These agreements, in turn, resulted in improvements in attitudes on part of all concerned and reduction in the number of issues in dispute.

SUMMARY OF DYNAMICS OF FORMAL AUTHORITY AND DECISION PROCESS

Where the structure and process are closely parallel, the two work in similar directions; where they vary, the influences of both are more indirect and may develop over time. Formal structure assumes an important role when conflict exists among power groups or managers at different levels on the appropriate action to take and when environmental or internal stresses build up on the units. Conflicts force parties to fall back on their legitimacy to make decisions when normal accommodation and compromise break down. Organization stress exerts severe strain on informal relationships and understanding. The pressure causes the parties to reevaluate their own positions and stakes in past commitments. Where formal patterns are specified, these provide a minimal commitment that must be maintained.

Formal patterns also exert a restraining influence on the decision process. Where policies are deviated from, individuals assume risks if decisions are challenged or errors are made. Potential veto power of higher level executives must be considered where the ongoing process is to make decisions but decisions are posed in terms of recommendations.

In changing patterns of behavior, the focus may be on either the structure or the process, or both simultaneously. The detailed case describing attempts to reduce the level of conflict at International Harvester illustrates the combined approach. Structural changes were made in the appeal procedure that enabled grievances to move easily to the central level. The refusal or inability of lower level personnel to make decisions resulted in an overloading of central personnel. Both the structure and process contributed to additional conflict. Ad hoc attempts at modifying the process by trying to settle issues in a wholesale manner solved the immediate problem of getting agreement on contracts but perpetuated the process generating high conflict. When both the structure and process were simultaneously changed by requiring that grievances be processed on an oral rather than a written basis and when pressure was exerted on local personnel to make decisions, the problem was solved.

8

DEPARTMENTATION:
Specialization and Grouping
at the Supervisory Level

INTRODUCTION

Nature of Departmentation

In designing positions at the first supervisory or higher level, the work can be grouped along a specialized basis where the supervisor is responsible for a narrow aspect of the total operation. Contrarily, a project form of departmentation can be used so that the supervisory responsibilities extend over a complete unit of work. Typical project departments in industrial firms are product, geographic, and customer groupings. In each, all specialists who contribute to that product, geographic area, or type of customer are grouped into separate units.

With the project approach, it is possible to break down large firms into independent units. Theodore Vail, who designed the structure of the Bell Telephone system in the 1880s, laid the basis for one of the largest corporations in the world.[1] Except for research subsidiaries, Bell Telephone laboratories, and their manufacturing arm, Western Electric, AT&T is essentially a conglomeration of twenty-three separate phone companies. These units are largely independent with their own presidents and directors, who plan their own construction, decide what services to offer, when to expand, and how to deal with their state and regulatory agencies.

A different approach is to group together the specialists who perform the same activities. Common forms of such units in industrial firms are time, process, and function. In a time grouping, those on different shifts are designated into separate units; under functional form, all those with specialized skills are placed in the same unit; and under process form, those at designated stages of the process are grouped together. Various combinations

[1]Jerry E. Bishop, "FCC Investigation of AT&T Puts Spotlight on Art of Running Giant Bell," *Wall Street Journal,* December 16, 1965.

© DATAMATION ® May 15, 1971, p. 45.

of specialized or project grouping in the organization can be used, such as typically exist in large industrial firms with both divisions organized on a project basis with divisions or staff specialists at the headquarters level serving and issuing policies for the divisions.

Illustration of Simple Society of Substantial Size

The brief excerpt provides an example of a religious group that has been able to maintain a simple society by subgrouping as it has increased in size.

The growth of the Hutterites, a religious group practicing a communal form of society, illustrates the way an organization may increase without greater specialization. They have distinctive dress, hairstyles, customs and religious beliefs that set them off from the larger society. They are an agricultural society that practices strict communism in that their property is owned by the commune and the entire community work the land. The people have a high birth rate with parents averaging twelve children. The 17,000 Hutterites solve the problem of a large number owning common property and working the land together by breaking into subunits to form bruderhods or colonies. When a colony reaches 130 members, a new unit is established.

Each colony in turn is broken down into communal households with three families normally living in the same house and eating together. Since the average colony is 100 members, this averages out to three households and nine families to a bruderhod. This religious group is able to grow without much increase in the complexity of the society since each bruderhod largely operates independently of the others except in adherence to a common ideology.[2]

ADVANTAGES AND DISADVANTAGES OF ALTERNATIVE FORMS OF GROUPING

Nearly all management textbooks have a section where they outline the alternative forms of organizing and the advantages that are supposed to flow from each. Koontz and O'Donnell, for instance, contend that organizing into functional units has several advantages.[3] It is "logical and time proven," uses manpower resources efficiently by utilizing specialized skills and training, and ensures that basic functions will be coordinated and defended by top managers. They quote Henri Fayol, an early writer on organization theory, in saying that this is the way to implement "the principle of specialization"; that is, to divide "work to produce more and better work with the same effort." Filley and House add that bringing specialists together provides professional reinforcement of skills, reduces duplication of skilled resources, and provides advancement opportunity within the skill hierarchy rather than necessitating movement to general administrative posts.[4]

Koontz and O'Donnell contend that the disadvantages are that functional areas may be emphasized at the expense of enterprise objectives, managers are trained in a functional specialty but not with an overall perspective necessary for developing into general managers, and it is difficult to fix accountability on anyone except the chief executive for achieving the organization's goals. Communication and cooperation among functional units are usually lower.

Filley and House state that the advantages of project departmentation such as product or customer grouping include: bringing together all the activities for a single project or purpose under a single manager, reducing dependence among units, creating greater autonomy, and providing the basis for greater service and identity with the customer. Project grouping also enables systems and procedures in each unit to be highly standardized. Koontz and O'Donnell add that substantial authority can be delegated and responsibility for total organizational effectiveness fixed at the departmental manager's level; it provides good training for general management positions and aids coordination within the departmental unit.

[2]Charles Hillinge, "Prolific Sect Grows," *Akron Beacon Journal*, December 2, 1968.

[3]Harold Koontz and Cyril O'Donnell, *Principles of Management*, 4th ed. (New York: McGraw-Hill Book Co., 1968), pp. 260–63, 277–78.

[4]Alan C. Filley and Robert J. House, *Managerial Process and Organizational Behavior* (New York: Scott, Foresman & Co., 1969), pp. 218–19.

The disadvantages are developed as possible subordination of company goals for departmental ends, duplication and lower utilization of specialized equipment and services, and lowering the quality of specialized skills. Koontz and O'Donnell add that project departmentalization also contributes to greater rivalry among ambitious department managers and may enable them to build empires that challenge the president's power.

Behavior Implications of Alternative Groupings

In the following excerpt, James Worthy develops some of the effects of functional and project grouping at the supervisory level.[5] His point of reference is the store units at Sears and Roebuck, but his discussion has general applicability.

The breaking down of larger organizations into smaller units must be done in such a manner as to permit these smaller units to function as integrated and meaningful entities. The change, in Peter Drucker's phrase, must be constitutional, not mechanical; it must be in the structure of the enterprise, not merely in its procedures. Specifically, this will require the scrapping of the concept of "functional organization," one of the central concepts of Frederick Taylor's theory of management and the basic idea on which much of modern management practice rests.

Essentially, functionalization is an extension of the principle of specialization. Just as particular activities have been broken down into their simplest possible components and each component assigned to a different person, so many operations (often after having been highly "simplified") have been separated out of the broader complex of activities of which they are a part and set up as specialized and semi-independent organizational entities. This procedure is justified as a means of speeding output through specialization, providing better supervision and control, and permitting the use of persons of lesser skill (either to achieve lower costs or to overcome shortages in the supply of skilled workers).

There may be a certain spurious efficiency in this kind of organization, but it is likely to have many off-setting liabilities. We are here concerned with one of the consequences of functionalization which has been almost entirely overlooked and one which has particularly serious consequences, namely, the fact that *it has the inevitable effect of increasing*

[5]James C. Worthy, "Some Aspects of Organizational Structure in Relation to Pressures on Company Decision Making," L. Reed Tripp, ed., *Industrial Relations Research Proceedings* (New York: Harper & Brothers, 1953), pp. 71–76.

*the size of the administrative unit and making effective managerial decentraliza-
tion impossible beyond the point in the organization hierarchy at which the functional divisions begin.*

This fact can be illustrated by a hypothetical example. Assume an
organization which performs three primary functions or operations,
A, B, and C. (These might be punch press, welding, and assembly, or
any other three processes likely to be found in a producing unit; their
actual nature is not important for purpose of this illustration.) Assume
further that the volume of output requires three units each of A, B, and
C. Under these circumstances, the organization could be set up in
either of two ways:

1. It could be set up in three divisions, each function (A, B, and C)
being represented in each division. Such an organization, to which we
will apply the term "integrated," might be diagrammed as follows ("S"
representing first-line supervision and "M" representing general plant
management):

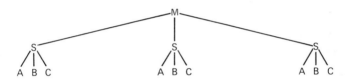

FIGURE 8-1.   Integrated organization

2. On the other hand, the organization could be set up in three *functional* divisions, one division having all three A units, another all three
B units, and the third all three C units. Such an organization could be
represented in this manner (again using "S" and "M" to designate the
two levels of supervision and management):

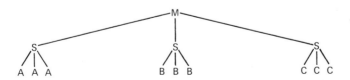

FIGURE 8-2.   Functional organization

This second alternative illustrates the functional type of organization. It is the norm of scientific management theory and typical of much
modern organization practice in industry, government, and elsewhere.

Whatever its advantages, real or apparent, it unquestionably has the effect of greatly expanding the size of the administrative unit.

In the integrated type of organization, illustrated by the first example given, the administrative unit is the division, because each division (comprising as it does all operations essential to the turning out of a completed product) can operate with a high degree of autonomy. The total organization is composed of three relatively independent divisions, any one of which could continue to function even if the others shut down (Figure 8-3).

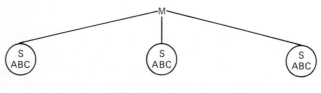

FIGURE 8-3

The situation is quite otherwise, however, in the functional type of organization. Here no division can operate except in the closest coordination with both the others; any difficulty in one will have immediate repercussions in the others, and if one breaks down, the others must very soon come to a halt. In this case, *the administrative unit is no longer the division but must of necessity be the organization as a whole* (Figure 8-4).

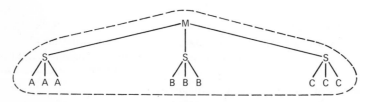

FIGURE 8-4

In the current example, this unit is by definition three times as large as that represented in Figure 8-3 and to that extent far more subject to the difficulties inherent in larger size per se.

This point can be further illustrated by reference to the problem of delegation. In the integrative type of organization represented by Figures 8-1 and 8-3, M, the plant manager, can delegate a very substantial measure of authority and responsibility to each of his three S's, because each S has under his direct supervision and control all the functions necessary to turn out a completed product. In the functional type of organization represented by Figures 8-2 and 8-4, however, M can delegate only a limited amount of authority and responsibility. Each S supervises a single function and therefore controls only part of the total process. All significant decisions must be made by M for only he holds within his hands all the elements which must be kept in proper balance. All that he can delegate effectively are matters pertaining immediately and more or less exclusively to each of the individual functions, and in practice these are likely to be largely routine.

People in management talk a great deal about the importance of delegation and are often critical of their subordinates for failing to exercise the responsibility supposedly delegated to them. But if an organization is set up along strictly functional lines, no amount of "supervisory training" can make it possible for people in the S position to exercise anything approaching real responsibility. Failure to assume delegated responsibility is no doubt often a matter of individual temperament, but in a very great many cases the structure of the organization makes significant delegation impossible regardless of how much management may wish to delegate and regardless of how willing and even anxious subordinates may be to accept larger measures of responsibility.

Such an organization, in fact, puts a premium on people in the S position who do not have too strong a drive in the direction of independent authority and responsibility, for any marked effort along these lines is likely to lead to serious conflict with the other S's and to create a critical situation which will require the intervention of M to restore the necessary balance and harmony within the organization. This suggests another serious weakness of this particular type of organization structure. Individuals with the capacity for independent action necessary to function properly in the M position are not likely to survive too long in the S position; they either learn to adapt themselves (and perhaps lose permanently the special capacities of independence which the M position requires), or they are likely to be forced out by the conflicts they create.

The difficulty which the functional type of organization has in developing men for higher levels of responsibility is increased further by the kind and quality of experience men in the S position acquire. In the integrated type of organization represented in Figures 8-1 and 8-3, each S performs many of the same functions and exercises much the same kind of responsibility and authority as M; each division, in fact, is a smaller version of the organization as a whole. Each S, therefore, acquires a kind of experience that will help prepare him for eventual advancement to the M position; as S, in fact, he has an opportunity to practice at and gain skill in the M role. His *level* of responsibility is less than that of M but is not greatly different in *kind*. He can practice the M role, therefore, without exposing the organization as a whole to unduly serious consequences in the case of mistakes made in the process of learning.

The situation is quite different in the case of the S's in the functional type of organization represented in Figures 8-2 and 8-4. Here the S in charge of AAA becomes more and more skilled in the A function. He may know something about B and C. In fact, he may have had experience in running B and C (perhaps in the course of a "job rotation" program to "train" him for further advancement), but he does not see the organization as a whole and he does not gain the experience in coordination or the skill in *management* which his counterpart in the integrated organization acquires as a natural (and perhaps unintended) by-product of supervising ABC. Above all, each S in the integrated type of organization is likely to have delegated to him a much larger measure of real responsibility and authority than is possible in the functional type of organization. The opportunities for personal growth and development are therefore likely to be far greater in the former than in the latter.

Chapple and Sayles contend that grouping along specialized lines contributes to greater problems among managers.[6] Breaking the activities in an interdependent work flow so they are under the control of several departments sharply increases the level of stress and conflict among departments. Reorganization into a unit grouping where a supervisor has the complete set of steps under his jurisdiction aids coordination, increases efficiency, and reduces stress and conflict among managers.

Chapple and Sayles give several examples. In one case, sales orders went through a series of steps: (1) after the orders were received, they were reviewed by salesclerks for any special problems; (2) next, order-editing checked the form for accuracy and to determine if goods were in stock; (3) next, the credit department then checked credit ratings and approved or disapproved the order; (4) last, the orders were filled and proper records made of the transactions. The supervisor of the sales office, production control manager, credit manager, IBM operations manager, and warehouse manager were each involved and had jurisdiction over handling the order at different points in the process. Intense conflict developed between the credit manager and sales manager; among other incidents, the credit manager sometimes

[6]Eliot D. Chapple and Leonard R. Sayles, *The Measure of Management* (New York: Macmillan Co., 1961), pp. 18–45.

canceled orders after the sales manager had contacted the customer to thank him for his business. It was difficult also to coordinate operations so that orders were processed in the expected time or to settle disputes short of appeal to the vice-presidential level.

These problems were partially solved by placing the critical steps of crediting orders, corresponding with customers, and credit analysis under one unit supervisor. Changing the sequence of steps so that credit analysis was made first also eliminated some conflict between the credit and sales sections. This placed the supervisor in a better position to coordinate the steps. A good part of the stress was thus removed from the credit and sales managers' relationship, and a basis was established for greater efficiency.

Measuring Departmentation

The scale used in chapter 4 to measure specialization at the worker level also can be used at the supervisory level. The only change is that the focus moves from interdependence among positions in a formal unit to interdependence among formal units.

	Interdependence Among Units								
	1	*2*	*3*	*4*	*5*	*6*	*7*	*8*	*9*
1. Degree of Specialization	Low							High	
2. Interdependence Complexity	Low							High	
3. Buffers	Extensive							Few	

RESEARCH STUDIES

Several intensive case studies provide further understanding of the effects of grouping.

FORM OF GROUPING AND FOCUS OF CONFLICT

Melville Dalton's investigation of relationship of maintenance personnel to line departments indicates how groupings of specialists determine the focus and degree of conflict in an organization.[7] In a large manufacturing plant of several thousand employees, management reorganized the maintenance section several times to try to solve problems of intergroup conflict.

---

[7]Melville Dalton, *Men Who Manage* (New York: John Wiley & Sons, 1964), pp. 18–70.

These changes are outlined below:

1. Functional Department—Maintenance departments were organized as separate units under the jurisdiction of a maintenance supervisor, who reported to the plant manager.
2. Functional Modification—A control unit was established where requests for service were transmitted. These were sent to the maintenance unit that did the actual work.
3. Project Departmentation—The total maintenance group was broken into smaller units and assigned to various production departments.
4. Headquarters Control—The previous organization was maintained, but controls were set up over purchase of new parts—a substantial element of maintenance costs.

Under the functional organization, continuous conflict occurred between the maintenance units and the production lines that they serviced. The production departments were under intensive pressure to keep costs down and meet their schedules. When breakdowns occurred, the departments put in service requests to have equipment fixed or whatever else was required. The aggressive foreman pressed the maintenance units to have his work done immediately and was successful in obtaining priority treatment. This meant that service requests from less aggressive production units were delayed. This service was reflected in the relative level of costs of the production units, with aggressive foremen consistently having lower costs than those foremen who assumed they were getting equal treatment. While the maintenance units responded to this pressure, they developed a strong hostility toward aggressive line units.

Management became aware that something was wrong with the system when an investigation of complaints about slow service revealed that some line departments had no backlog of maintenance requests and others had a long list of unfilled orders. They reorganized to better control the processing of the orders by setting up a "Field Work Department" (FWD). The production units now sent their orders to the FWD, which, in turn, sent them to the maintenance units for actual work. In effect, the FWD was a buffer between the line units and maintenance sections. The line units had no leverage over the new control unit so they could not demand special treatment in processing of their service requests. Under the system the FWD estimated the costs of the service request and, if this cost was acceptable to the line unit, forwarded the order to the maintenance unit that actually did the work. The maintenance unit then allocated costs incurred in processing the order and notified FWD, the line unit, and the accounting department.

Even under this system, the conflict continued between maintenance and line departments. While the FWD controlled the paper work that set up priorities, the maintenance units still actually did the work and recorded costs. They now took the opportunity to discredit the line foremen who had previously pressured them. While formally observing the system of paper flow, they actually gave priorities to work of line departments whose foremen had treated them better in the past. Further, they arbitrarily allocated costs that belonged to favored departments to those departments they were intent on discrediting. This resulted in embarrassing the FWD and *both* the favored line departments and those in disfavor with maintenance. Cost estimates were way off and this reflected on FWD. Favored departments showed such remarkable gains in cost reduction and efficiency that it wasn't credible; those departments who had been aggressive in the past and had had outstanding records now faltered and had poor showings. This resulted in sharp conflict between the aggressive foremen, who were showing sharp declines in efficiency and increased costs, and the FWD, which was caught in the middle. In time the control unit was discredited and management again reorganized.

The FWD was eliminated and the central maintenance unit was broken up and maintenance groups assigned to the production units. Conflicts between maintenance and production sharply declined. Since each maintenance unit now was assigned to work directly with a production department, the production foreman was in a better position to coordinate and control maintenance work and balance these activities with short- and long-term strategies in keeping production flowing. But part of the change was that maintenance costs weren't charged to the production departments. Cost of maintenance rose sharply.

Management sought to control these costs by instituting central controls over purchase of parts—a substantial part of maintenance costs. This quickly shifted the focus of conflict to headquarters vis-à-vis the plant relationship. The production departments in cooperation with maintenance sections developed clever strategies to undermine the effectiveness of headquarters control. Groups that had sharply divisive relationships formed together in a common clique to minimize headquarters control.

In summary, in a detailed study of line and maintenance units, Dalton found that the focus of conflict changed as the firm regrouped the maintenance unit from a functional to project grouping. Functional grouping resulted in sharp conflict between the maintenance and production departments. Even when a buffer unit was formed—a control center that determined the sequence orders that were to be processed—high conflict still existed between maintenance and production units. When the firm was reorganized and maintenance units were placed under the direction of production departments, the conflict sharply declined.

Effects of Grouping on Managerial Perspective. Walker and Lorsch explored the effects of contrasting approaches to organizing two similar manufacturing units.[8] The plants made the same product, served the same markets, had similar technology, and were subunits of a large corporation. They differed principally in the way in which specialists were grouped, with one based on product grouping and the other on a functional basis. In product grouping, specialists, except those in engineering, reported to the plant manager. Under the functional approach, all specialists, except those in manufacturing departments and scheduling, reported to parallel specialists at divisional headquarters.

The functional grouping contributed to a narrow focus: quality control specialists were concerned almost exclusively with quality standards, industrial engineering with methods improvement and cost reduction, and scheduling with production standards. There was little appreciation of a need to balance their activities to achieve overall plant operation. In contrast, under product organization, the specialists were concerned both with their own goals and the need to balance these with others in the plant.

The functional organization also contributed to a short-term perspective on the part of specialists. Each specialist was concerned with dealing with immediate rather than longer term problems. In contrast, the product organization contributed to a longer term perspective, with 30 percent of their time spent on daily problems; in the functional organization, 49 percent of the time was spent on immediate problems. This difference was reflected by plant performance. Both had short-term goals of low costs and longer term goals of improving plant capabilities. The functionally organized plant, however, had higher productivity and lower costs but a lower rate of improving plant capabilities. The product-organized plant had improved productivity to a greater degree—23 percent, in three years compared with 3 percent for the functional plant.

Both plants had coordination problems, but they were somewhat greater at the functionally organized plant. Here communication among specialists was more of a problem along with a greater tendency to smooth over conflict rather than solving it directly by dealing with the issues; also, issues were referred to higher level supervision for resolution more often.

The personnel in the product organization had greater involvement but felt greater stress and pressure and had less satisfaction with their work and the company. The focus upon both daily and long-range problems, balancing their own viewpoints with those of other specialists, and direct contact and confrontation of differences rather than smoothing over of problems created the greater stress and less satisfaction in the product organization.

In summary, the form of grouping was associated with different perspectives on importance of short-term and long-term goals and the need to

[8]Arthur H. Walker and Jay W. Lorsch, "Organizational Choice: Product vs. Function," *Harvard Business Review*, 46 (1968), 129–38; Arthur H. Walker, "Behavioral Consequences of Contrasting Patterns of Organization" (Ph.D. diss., Harvard Business School, 1967).

suboptimize in specialized areas to achieve overall plant goals. It also affected problems of coordination, job involvement, and satisfaction with the work and the company.

Effects on Interaction Within and Among Groups. Price explored the effects that the form of grouping had on interaction and cooperation within two state agencies in Oregon, The Fish and Game Commissions.[9] The Fish Commision was organized along functional lines with its activities grouped into four units: research, fish culture, engineering, and administration. Research made recommendations on wildlife management; the fish division raised and placed fish in streams; engineering planned, constructed, and maintained roads and other projects; administration undertook service activities for the other three units. The Game Commission was organized along geographic lines into five units—Northwest, Southwest, Central, Northeast, and Southeast regions. Each region carried on the multiple activities involved in wildlife management rather than specializing.

In the Fish Commission, about 55 percent of employees had friends in another specialty, compared with 68 percent in the Game Commission. Other data supported the idea that greater cohesion and working relationships developed among specialists in the Game Commission. Biologists in the Game Commission obtained the cooperation of hatcherymen in building a fish program based on the latest research. In the Fish Commission, the hatcherymen more often ignored the biologists' recommendations. The specialists in the Game Commission interacted more in both formal divisional meetings, which included all the specialists in the Game Commission, and in social activities. In contrast, in the Fish Commission, meetings and social activities were attended only by specialists. Only biologists, for instance, attended the research division picnic; in the Game Commission both hatcherymen and biologists assigned to that region attended.

Effects on Internal and External Interaction and Professional Satisfaction. Some of the subtleties of the effects of grouping are apparent in Kover's study of an advertising agency.[10] The firm was reorganized from a combination functional-client grouping to a simpler client departmentation. Under the original organization, specialists were grouped into three functional departments: account management, creative, and marketing. A client-centered department overlapped these units: specialists were assigned to work with particular clients, and an account executive was responsible for coordinating their work; account supervisors coordinated the work of two or more account executives.

[9]James L. Price, "The Impact of Departmentalization on Interoccupational Cooperation," *Human Organization,* 27 (Winter 1968), 362–67.

[10]Arthur J. Kover, "Reorganization in an Advertising Agency: A Case Study of a Decrease in Integration," *Human Organization,* 22, No. 4 (Winter 1963–64), 252–59.

The creative branch designed and produced the advertisements and commercials; copy specialists drafted the scripts while the media section determined the form of media to use—newspapers, television, etc. Merchandising organized exhibits and recommended packaging and channels of distribution. Research surveyed market potential and evaluated advertising effectiveness. These aspects of the organization are summarized in Table 8-1.

TABLE 8-1. Functional-Client Departmentation of Paragon Advertising Agency (Before Reorganization)

	Client Departments				
Functional Departments	A	B	C	D	—
Account Management					
—Account Supervisors					
—Account Executives					
Creative					
—Copy					
—Art					
—Production: Newspapers/ Magazines					
—Production: TV and Radio					
Marketing					
—Media					
—Merchandising					
—Research					

Both the functional and client departmentation influenced the internal and external interaction patterns. Account supervisors and executives were formally charged with maintaining liaison between the agency and client. In reality, the specialists in the agency often dealt directly with their counterparts in the client's organization. Agency research personnel worked with the client's research department: copywriters were often called directly by the client's advertising managers; creative workers often presented and defended their work directly to the client in meetings. The account executive had various specialists working on each account but lacked formal authority to regulate them. It was difficult to coordinate a unified approach to clients. The relation between the agency and client usually was open with close working relations between agency and client personnel.

The client department often contributed to communications among functional departments. Since each account was served by specialists from the three departments, each small group worked on an intensive basis. Personnel were often transferred from one account to another, so many different contacts and working relationships developed among the specialists. At the same time, each specialist was assigned and maintained his base in a functional department—copy, research, art, etc. Widespread communications developed of a professional-technical nature among similar specialists, with advice exchanged and professional information and problems communicated and discussed in seminars.

Authority over promotions within the department and supervision of the work enabled functional departmental control. Copy on an important account, for instance, typically was closely evaluated before being released for presentation outside the copy unit. Work had to meet the standards of the professionals in the unit before nonprofessionals saw it.

As often happens in the industry, the firm ran into problems when it had a major turnover in its accounts. Management reorganized the agency to adjust to the changed situation. It disbanded the functional departments: market and creative specialists were assigned to new client-centered groups. In effect, several partially autonomous agencies were formed and coordinated at higher management levels. Group supervisors were given authority to coordinate both internal communication among specialists and external contacts with other groups and the clients. In addition, the service groups were shifted to offices that were located together and client groups were physically separated.

The change sharply controlled contacts of agency personnel with the clients, reduced the amount of communication among like specialists, and restricted the degree of interaction among the groups. In dealing with clients, fewer people represented the agency, and their positions were coordinated. The direct contact with clients below the supervision level was sharply reduced. Communication among the service groups fell sharply. Initially, news and gossip that had previously flowed among groups now largely dried up. Greater reliance was given to using formal communication channels upward and downward. After several months, limited informal, semicovert channels developed that conveyed gossip and professional news. These partially supplemented formal channels; previously, these exchanged had been open and pervasive. One of the most marked effects of dropping the functional grouping was to decrease the sense of professional worth. The change eliminated the dual system of evaluation whereby one's work was evaluated by both his fellow professionals and by others. Under the functional department, the evaluation of one's work by his fellow professionals was accepted since they had technical competence to make a fair judgment and promotions were controlled by professionals. Under the new system, general management rather than professional specialists judged the work and controlled promotions.

The opportunity to interact now was principally with different specialists within the group rather than like specialists. Less opportunity existed to talk about a particular specialty. One researcher expressed feelings of loneliness, saying that now he could only talk to others about business. He contrasted this with the previous organization when he had had other research people look over his work and they used to talk about all sorts of other things. "I don't know why it is but I can't seem to warm up to other people in this group . . . what do these people know about research? I can't talk to them about what I do. So what *do* I talk about—sales figures?"[11]

The changes exerted different effects depending upon the career orientation of individuals. The "careerists" saw their work in terms of organizational relationships and status, with instrumental friendships developed with those who could help to get the job done. The "craftsmen," on the other hand, thought principally in terms of their specialized skills and creative production; acquaintances and friendships were mainly with those who had similar values. The careerists looked to their superiors to judge the value of their work and the craftsmen to their fellow professionals.

The new organization provided different supervisors but did not change the basis for validating the workers' sense of worth. The careerists readily adjusted to the new arrangement. New contacts were made and communication with key people arranged. The craftsmen, however, after several months became increasingly dissatisfied with their work. Many left within a year after the reorganization. The separation from fellow professionals and evaluation of their work by nonprofessionals created a sense of alienation. They needed the support and validation from other professionals to give them a feeling that their work was good and important to the agency and client.

In summary, a modest change in regrouping occurred in this advertising agency. Essentially, an overlapping functional-client form was replaced by a semiautonomous client department. The short-term effectiveness of the agency increased. There were fewer mistakes, greater coordination, and presentation of unified positions when dealing with clients. The interaction of agency personnel with client personnel was controlled and largely limited to upper level coordinators. A sharp reduction in intergroup communications and increase in intragroup interaction occurred. On the other hand, the movement of control from professional to client departments alienated the craft-oriented workers. They found less satisfaction in their work and were frustrated in not being able to interact regularly with fellow professionals. Careerist types who viewed the work instrumentally and obtained their satisfaction from organizational success and achievement quickly accommodated themselves to the new organization.

Effects of Grouping on Stability and Cohesion of Work Groups. A couple of field studies of production groups provide further insights into the effects of grouping at the supervisory level. Rice's study of reorganization of a small textile mill in India has won wide attention.[12] The firm moved from

---

[11]Ibid., p. 257.

[12]A. K. Rice, "Productivity and Social Organization in an Indian Weaving Shed," *Human Relations*, 6 (November 1953), 297–330.

a functional to project grouping of workers in a small experimental unit where automatic looms were being introduced. Under the functional setup, weaving was subdivided into twelve specialized operations and assigned to twenty-nine workers. This is summarized in Table 8-2.[13]

TABLE 8-2. The Number of Looms per Worker and the Number of Workers in Each Occupational Role in the Experimental Automatic Loom Shed

Activity	Task	Occupational Role	Number of Looms Per Worker	Number of Workers
Weaving	Knotting broken yarn	Weaver	24–32	8
	Battery filling	Battery filler	40–50	5
	Removing empty bobbins	Bobbin carrier	224	1
	Knotting broken yarn	Smash-hand	60–80	3
Loading and	Replacing empty beams	Gater	112	2
Unloading	Removing woven cloth	Cloth carrier	112	2
Loom	Fitting and tuning	Jobber	112	2
Maintenance	Fitting	Assistant jobber	112	2
	Specialized fitting	Feeler-motion fitter	224	1
	Oiling	Oiler	224	1
Cleaning	Sweeping and cleaning	Sweeper	224	1
Humidifying	Specialized fitting	Humidification fitter	224	1
Totals	12	12	–	29

Under this organization, all activities had to be performed in close co-ordination to maintain continuous production. The number of looms assigned each worker depended on his specialty, with 24 to 32 looms assigned to weavers, 40 to 50 looms to battery fillers, and the entire set of 224 looms assigned to those performing narrow activities, such as the oiler who serviced the machines and the sweeper who cleaned the area. One consequence was that workers could not conveniently be subgrouped; the supervisor had twenty-six individuals directly reporting to him. Thus, each weaver—varying somewhat with the cloth being woven—depended upon a jobber and an assistant jobber for one-quarter of their time; a battery filler for five-eighths of his time, a smash-hand for three-eighths of his time, and so on.

One difficulty was that a change in the kind of cloth woven often changed the workload of the workers. Each change altered the need for assistance, contributed to confusion of task and worker relationships, and resulted in an unstable group structure. The tasks and varying workloads worked against formation of small, stable, structured work groups.

[13]Ibid., p. 303.

The groups were reorganized into two seven-member semiautonomous units on each shift. Several other changes were also made: one of the specialized jobs was eliminated, pay grades were reduced to three categories, and titles that described the jobs were eliminated and A, B, and, C grades substituted; piece rates were expanded from two of the categories to the entire crew. The first-level supervisors and workers determined the composition of each work group in two days of discussion. A last factor that both was a result and probably affected the results was a reduction in supervision and inspection by management once the group was operating. As a consequence, within two months efficiency increased about 15 percent and quality of the work—the percentage of work that was accepted as meeting standards—increased 10 percent; the groups also developed greater stability in their membership, structure, and functioning.

In summary, the group was reorganized from one interdependent unit to four semiautonomous groups. Several factors contributing to group cohesion were slightly less specialization, reduced number of job distinctions, common rate of paying all members, and involvement of workers in the changes. It isn't possible to sort out the contribution of each of these factors to increases in productivity and quality and stable relations, but it is evident that the regrouping from a functional to semiproject group was helpful.

Effects of Grouping on Multiple Aspects of Behavior. A study where the grouping of departments was systematically varied was done by Valfer under the supervision of Davis and Pool.[14] They explored how changes in functions grouped under supervision affected costs, quality, and various aspects of behavior. Eleven shops ranging from twelve to thirty employees in a large military installation overhauled, repaired, and tested complex aircraft and the components. Items to be repaired arrived in batches of from one to several dozen units.

Two changes were planned in the supervisor's job from the initial period whereby the supervisor's control over the complete repair was enlarged. This is outlined below:

t_1—Functional/Process Grouping—Each shop was assigned a part of the total process required to repair an item. The item to be repaired moved through two shops with the first shop making repairs and the next shop making final adjustments; the items then moved to an external group for inspection.

t_2—Modified Project Grouping—Repair and final adjustments were combined

---

[14]E. S. Valfer, "Performance and Intervening Effects of Two Supervisory Job Design Treatments" (Ph.D. diss., University of California, Berkeley, 1964); L. E. Davis, E. S. Valfer, and K. Pool, *Supervisory Job Design* (Berkeley, Calif.: Institute of Engineering Research 1964); L. E. Davis and E. S. Valfer, "Supervisory Job Design," in *Proceedings of Second International Congress, Ergonomics* (1965); L. E. Davis and E. S. Valfer, "Intervening Responses to Changes in Supervisor Job Designs," *Occupational Psychology*, 39 (July 1965), 171–89.

under one supervisor. Two shops made this change and two that had previously changed were used as control groups.

t₃—Project Grouping—Repair, final adjustment, and *inspection* were placed under one supervisor. Increases in quality standards also were imposed by management, who feared that quality might decline with internal control. Four groups were changed; three other groups were used as controls. In effect, quality standards were increased in all seven groups with the four experimental groups also moving from external to internal quality control.

The behavioral changes highlight some of the effects of regrouping at both the supervisory and worker level. Table 8-3 summarizes the changes as

TABLE 8-3. Changes in Attitudes and Perceptions Associated with Increased Scope of Supervisor's Task

	Modified Project Grouping		Project Grouping	
	Perceived by Supervisor	Perceived by Worker	Perceived by Supervisor	Perceived by Worker
Supervisor and Workers Reactions				
Information flow: Across departments	—			
Information flow: Up			+	
Information flow: Down	+		+	+
Time and emphasis on technical activities	+		+	
Authority	+	N/C	N/C	N/C
Satisfaction	N/C	—	+	N/C
Responsibility	—		N/C	
Consideration	N/C	—	N/C	+
Initiation of structure	—	—	N/C	+
Delegation	—		—	
Independence			N/C	
Workers Reactions				
Job interest and responsibility		N/C		
Pressure for reduced costs		+		
Pressure for quality		N/C		N/C
Pressure for quantity		N/C		
Pressure to meet scheduling		N/C		—
Functional responsibilities		N/C		+
Involvement in shop planning		+		N/C

Legend:
  — decreased
  + increased
  N/C no change

perceived by both the workers and supervisors.[15] Under the first change where the supervisor job was expanded to include both repairing and adjusting the equipment, the supervisor perceived less information flow across departments but more flow downward, more attention to technical activities, increased authority but less responsibility, and less delegation of authority. Workers perceived greater pressure to reduce costs but no change in quality or quantity standards or changes in their jobs other than increased involvement in shop planning.

When inspection was also added to the supervisor's job, the supervisors perceived increased information up and down, greater emphasis on technical activities, decreased delegation, and increased satisfaction. The workers saw less pressure for reduced costs and meeting schedules and greater responsibility in their jobs.

Valfer also asked the supervisors to estimate the amount of time they spent on various aspects of their jobs. Table 8-4 provides a rough reflection of time spent under the two forms of organization.[16] Under the arrangement where repairing and adjustment were combined, supervisors' estimated time in working with shop personnel on production problems was 17 percent greater than in the control group. Other changes were relatively small. In those shops where inspection was added to the supervisor's responsibilities, supervisors spent 16 percent less time with shop personnel on production problems and 23 percent more time on quality control.

TABLE 8-4. Estimation by Supervisors of their Activities as a Percentage of Total Day*

	Modified Project Shops			Project Shops		
	Exptl.	Control	Difference	Exptl.	Control	Difference
Production involvement with shop personnel	34.4%	17.4%	17.0%	29.6%	46.2%	−16.6%
Control center, planners	21.3	12.0	9.3	12.2	16.5	−4.3
Personnel work: Attend. manning	6.9	13.55	−6.65	10.2	6.5	3.7
Quality control	8.75	1.9	6.85	26.2	3.0	23.2
Review tech.— Material	0	6.35	−6.35	5.2	9.6	−4.4
Gen. admin.	19.95	20.85	−0.9	4.5	5.7	−1.2

Legend:
*Minor categories have been dropped to simplify the presentation
Exptl. —Experimental groups
Control—Control groups

[15]Davis, Valfer, and Pool, *Supervisory Job Design*, p. 206.
[16]Ibid., p. 121.

In summary, regrouping of a unit to include a broader set of activities under a supervisor sets into motion a number of adjustments that affect his activities and those under him. Factors that change include his approach to the job, pressures he exerts on subordinates and others, the way he relates to supervisors, and the extent to which standards are shifted up or down.

SUMMARY AND CONCLUSION

In summary, the alternatives in specialization and grouping that are available at the employee level exist also at the supervisory level. The grouping may be of a project form where, in effect, little specialization at the supervisory level is used, or, in contrast, a functional grouping where the scope of the supervisor's job is narrowed. Formal grouping has implications for the degree of organizational complexity by determining the size and number of units and their interdependency. The typical organization utilizes some combination of project and functional groupings, and considerable variability among departments may be used.

The functional form of organization has long had its adherents. Koontz and O'Donnell state that it is "logical and time proven, utilizes manpower sources efficiently by drawing upon specialized skills and training, and it insures coordination within each specialized area." Other advantages are that it provides professional reinforcement of skills and provides advancement opportunities for specialists within their specialized area. It achieves these advantages by incurring a number of disadvantages including subordination of departmental goals at the expense of functional goals, impediment of communication among specialized units, training of managers in functional competence but not in the overall perspective necessary to move into general management, and diffusion of accountability at lower levels of organization. The project organization, in turn, reverses the advantages and disadvantages.

Some additional consequences of alternative groupings have been developed in several intensive case studies. Dalton, in a study of a complex manufacturing plant, found that the form of grouping affected both the focus and degree of conflict among units. With functional departmentation, sharp conflict developed between the service unit and line departments. The case was complicated by some of the effects created by changing the control system along with form of grouping, but the two factors largely defined the focus of conflict among groups.

Walker and Lorsch studied the contrasting perspectives that supervisors had under the two methods of organizing. Functional grouping contributed to a narrow focus and short-term orientation. Specialists were concerned with their immediate goals and responsibilities and had little appreciation of the need to balance these ends with the larger purposes of the plant. They focused upon immediate problems and dealt with them, creating a better record in terms of short-term costs and productivity measures.

Under the project organization, aside from having a broader departmental focus and an orientation toward balancing their viewpoints with others and giving greater attention to long-term goals, supervisors felt greater stress and less satisfaction with their work and the company. The problems of short-term pressures, direct confrontation of differences, and multiple perspectives led to a more complicated and less satisfying existence.

Price's study found that functional grouping elicited fewer contacts between different kinds of specialists and greater contact among like specialists. Krover's study of a change from one form of specialization to another highlights some additional subtleties of organization. The form of departmentation affected both internal and external communication. Under the functional grouping, the specialists had more contacts and a less coordinated approach to clients. Considerable communication among functional departments developed, but this probably was due to the overlapping client departmentation. Considerable shifting of specialists from one client to another occurred so that it provided different working relationships. At the same time the specialists maintained a consistent base in the functional department, so the overlapping organization created good communication both within each professional unit and among units. Professional status was reinforced by the functional departmentation since the specialists judged their work, and raises and promotions were based largely on professional achievements.

When the firm was reorganized into semiautonomous groupings and the functional departmentation was largely abandoned, the change reduced contacts of agency personnel with clients. It increased the amount of communications within the unit but reduced the amount among departments. The grouping of similar specialists together to serve a client enabled close coordination to be achieved on that client's work. It also sharply changed the control system the specialists operated under. In effect, nonspecialists now evaluated their work, and they were promoted on the basis of their ability to work with other specialists, as evaluated by nonspecialists. This was acceptable to a careerist type of individual but unacceptable to craft-oriented specialists.

Rice's study develops the implications of functional organization to span of control and creation of stable work groups. The effect of the combination of a varying work load and specialized positions sharply reduced the possibility of subgrouping of workers and required the supervisor to directly deal with each of the twenty-six individuals reporting to him. The reorganization that created partially independent units established autonomous informal work groups and reduced the effective span of control. While the changes were also confounded by other variables, the case is illustrative of some of the problems associated with functional grouping under unstable working conditions.

This summary of functional and dysfunctional consequences of alternative groupings reveals that the form of departmentation has important implications for organizational processes. The form of grouping that is most useful in each department and at each level in the department depends upon the conditions. Generally, the greater the complexity of conditions, the more appropriate an autonomous grouping is. This enables the organization to grow by increasing numbers of units with minimal impact upon coordination and control problems. The burden of coordination and control is placed on subunits and lower level managers and supervisors. The separate units can be coordinated by appropriate centralization by setting broad policy and procedural guidelines.

Either form of departmentalization can be combined with centralization, but only autonomous groupings can be combined with decentralization. Interdependent grouping complements an autocracy (centralized decision making with few policies specified that enables lower level supervisors to make operating decisions) and a centralized bureaucracy (extensive policies are specified; operating decisions that aren't covered must be referred to higher levels for decisions). No formal means exist for resolving decisions at lower levels under interdependent departmentation. Differences among specialists move up to top management for resolution.

Autonomous departmentation can be combined with decentralization or a centralized bureaucracy. In the case of decentralization, operating decisions are delegated to the department level and few policies are prescribed that restrict action. In a centralized bureaucracy—the common organizational form in large industrial corporations—operational decisions are delegated to the department level, but the degree of discretion is restricted by the policies, procedures, and rules established centrally. Thus, the form of departmentation used may turn on whether it is beneficial to decentralize the organization.

SECTION III

DISCUSSION QUESTIONS

A. Delegation
1. Develop what relevance, if any, (a) the level at which decisions are authorized to be made and (b) the breadth of policies, procedures, and rules for the degree an organization is centralized. Illustrate your point.
2. Explain why the formulation of policies, procedures, and rules enable decisions to be moved down to the operating level while still maintaining coordination.

3. In the industrial relations area, develop how the following factors determine the degree industrial relations activities are centralized or decentralized:
—The use of master contract or local contracts.
—Bargaining at local level or at headquarters level.
—Having few or many steps in the grievance procedure when grievances aren't settled at the operating level.
—Covering relatively few or many contract provisions between the company and the union.
—Establishing a policy that grievances must be written up before they are considered, or that all grievances should be considered when they are verbally submitted.

4. It is often said in management books that as an organization increases in size, it is necessary to decentralize. Melcher takes the opposite position. Can these two views be reconciled?

5. In many large·organizations, many specialists are employed at the headquarters level and the organization is divided into a number of product divisions as indicated below:

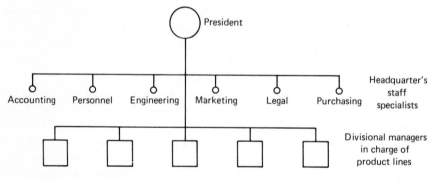

Given this form of departmentation, how would you decentralize to the divisional level? How would you centralize at the headquarters level, but move the operating decisions to the divisional level? In these two questions, be specific on the formal relationship between the specialists at headquarters level and divisional managers.

6. Develop the ways in which the perspective of a department head differs from those of top administration. Illustrate your position using examples from organizations with which you are familiar.

7. Develop key advantages and disadvantages of centralizing an organization. Develop key advantages and disadvantages of decentralizing an organization.

8. By drawing upon your analysis in questions 6 and 7, develop what implications, if any, each of the following conditions has for the degree that an organization would be centralized or decentralized to improve its functioning:

a. Size of an organization, and size of plants.

b. High degree of specialization among plants (i.e., the manufacturing plants produce parts for each other and for final assembly plants).

   c. Physical dispersion of plants into several parts of the country.

   d. The degree that problems at the plant level are resolvable with existing knowledge.

9. Given the following set of conditions, to what degree would you centralize a firm in the areas of personnel and production?

   a. Size: twenty plants varying from 200 to 2000 employees for a total of 15,000 employees.

   b. Fifteen manufacturing plants each concentrates on producing parts or components for the final product. The five assembly plants each assembles the final product.

   c. The twenty plants are geographically dispersed around the country with one or more plants in all regions of the country.

   d. The product is standardized; while difficult engineering problems are encountered in designing a competitive product, the manufacturing and assembly are done using standardized equipment and processes.

10. What distinction is there between the authority to make decisions and the amount of discretion exercised in decision making?

11. If—as commonly occurs—the actual decision process varies from the formal authority assigned to an office, what value is there in trying to relate the degree of delegation of authority to behavior and organizational processes?

12. Suppose that an organization is highly centralized in that policies sharply limit the discretion of lower personnel; but in the ongoing decision process, broad discretion is exercised. Does the formal structure have any meaning? What does General Electric's experience with the illegal price collusion indicate? If errors are made, what implication does this have for the risks assumed by the supervisor who exceeds the limits of his formal authority? Does it have any meaning when conflicts develop on the nature of decisions to be made?

13. In what way do limits on formal authority affect the scope of discretion exercised? In what way does the scope of discretion exercised influence the degree of formal delegation? In what way does International Harvester's experience with its grievance plan indicate that structure and process influence each other through time?

14. Examine situations at home, at work, or in social activities where structure influences process and process influences structure. Be prepared to relate this experience in class.

IV

SECONDARY
STRUCTURAL VARIABLES:
Formal Control System

CONTROL SYSTEMS:
Institutional to Individual

THE NATURE OF A FORMAL CONTROL SYSTEM

The formal control system includes (1) standards that are established, (2) formal measuring instruments to determine if these standards have been achieved, and (3) formal systems for allocating rewards and penalties. The control system ranges along a continuum from institutional to individual system.

CONTROL SYSTEM CONTINUUM

Institutional								Individual
1	2	3	4	5	6	7	8	9

The institutional system exists when formal standards, measuring instruments, and procedures for allocating rewards-penalties are based upon membership in the group; an example is where rewards are based on seniority. The individual system exists when formal standards are set for individuals, formal measuring instruments are designed to monitor individual performance, and the formal reward-penalty system is designed to reward or apply penalties on the basis of differential individual performance levels.

MAJOR INFLUENCE OF A CONTROL SYSTEM

Mace makes several useful distinctions in evaluating the effects of control systems.[1] A control system affects the direction, intensity, and duration of motivation; the resulting efficiency of the worker is largely a product of these

[1]C. A. Mace, *Incentives: Some Experimental Studies*, Medical Research Council, Industrial Health Research Board, Report no. 72 (London: Her Britannic Majesty's Stationery Office, 1935).

three factors. The direction is how the worker conceives his task in terms of standards and important dimensions to emphasize. The intensity is how strongly he is motivated to perform his tasks. The duration is the time that he maintains concentrated attention.

One aspect of direction is level of achievement. The worker may set a vague norm of "a fair day's work" or a specific standard such as a given number of units per day or week. These standards, whether they are implicitly or explicitly adopted, vary considerably with inexperienced workers. But as employees develop experience on the job, stable norms develop. This standard, in turn, is influenced by external conditions including the employment of incentives.

In respect to the activities that the worker emphasizes, typical choices are whether accuracy and quality are important, or speed and quantity. The worker's interpretation of the primary objective influences his emphasis. The activities may be influenced by a number of external factors including instructions and formal standards.

The intensity and duration of application are important determinants of efficiency and productivity. The intensity varies from complete indifference to the high application attained in emergencies or under the stress of powerful emotions. Ordinary industrial conditions typically draw upon a narrow range of values between these extremes. The importance of the intensification of the will to work is often overstated. Higher efficiency and productivity may be due to willingness to apply oneself. However, efficiency is a result of the *combined* influence of direction of activity, intensity of application, and duration of commitment.

Generally, productivity increases with greater intensity of application. Limitations on this process are that while moderate commitment increases efficiency, at one point greater intensity impairs efficiency and productivity. This is the case when the application is associated with a high degree of emotionality. Emotionality interferes with precision of movement and acts against the maintenance of a steady level of performance. High application may result in increased anxiety and diffused activity. Both laboratory and factory experiments show this, and it is supported by casual observation when watching those working under emotional stress. The most efficient workers typically perform their task in a cool, effortless manner and are free of emotion and anxieties. This may be the reason why the incentives systems sometimes are detrimental to the performance of new workers learning a skilled task. For a normal working period, a point is reached beyond which increased intensity of effort results in reduced efficiency because of fatigue. For a short period, intense application results in high performance. The athelete running a 100-yard dash can go all out for the distance. Where the activity must be carried on, a controlled approach is more appropriate. The long-distance runner must pace himself so that the first part of the race is run approximately as the last part; otherwise he falls from exhaustion.

In industrial work, the problem is to intensify effort consistent with the maintenance of activity throughout the day and the days of each week. This may require that the initial effort be dampened and special inducements be provided to prolong the will to work over a period of time. Incentives that stimulate initial application may be inadequate to maintain it. Absolute standards may induce the same output initially, but competitive-based standards stimulate more sustained effort and reduce the sense of fatigue. To prolong the will to work, the individual may have to be periodically reinforced. An incentive system would need to be designed to regularly reinforce the desired activity.

The system of reward-penalities can be a powerful instrument for influencing the worker's efficiency. It operates both directly and indirectly. An incentive system exerts its influence directly by providing an incentive, but its influence depends partly upon what appears to be incidental features of the system. Incentive systems include special features for measuring units of production and more or less frequent measures of output. The measurement itself acts as an incentive value apart from the uses made in calculating the level of reward. Further, every system has either implicitly or explicitly some level of standard to attain. This too constitutes an incentive.

Interface of Internal and External Motivators

Mace, nearly four decades ago, examined the way in which behavior emerges as a product of both an individual's predispositions and the nature of the context within which he operates.[2] His focus here is upon the way in which formal controls channel behavior.

The output of an industrial worker depends partly upon conditions which are external to himself and partly upon internal conditions. It depends upon such well-known external conditions as temperature, lighting, and ventilation; upon the rate at which, and the form in which, raw material is supplied; and upon the construction and the speed of the machinery employed. Among the internal conditions two sets of factors may be distinguished. In the first place there is a complex set of conditions which determines the worker's abilities, his motor abilities, his powers of discrimination, his general intelligence, and such

[2]Ibid., pp. 1–2. Reprinted with permission of the Controller of Her Britannic Majesty's Stationery Office.

other special abilities as the particular task may demand. The possession of ability, however, does not in itself ensure that it will be employed. A second set of internal conditions relates to the will as opposed to the capacity of work.

The extent to which a worker performs his allotted task up to the limit of his powers depends upon inborn traits of character, upon interests, and temperamental disposition; and it depends upon the extent to which the conditions under which he works stimulate him to release the energies with which he is endowed.

The will, or at least the willingness, to work occurs, no doubt, in a more or less generalized form. A man of normal constitution and in normal health will prefer almost any form of activity to total idleness. But industrial efficiency depends less upon any general will to work than upon an effective will to perform the particular task assigned. A fairly generalized disposition towards activity may be accompanied by a positive disinclination to perform some particular kind of work which requires to be done. Conversely, a worker not conspicuously of an energetic or active disposition may often be induced to concentrate will and efficiency upon a highly specialized operation. In consequence the practical problem is not so much that of stimulating a generalized will to work as one of directing available energy into specified channels.

The normal procedure in so directing human energy consists in the employment of incentives, commonly the incentive of a reward. The worker who has no desire to perform a given industrial operation for its own sake is induced to do so by an arrangement of conditions which enables him to see that the performance of the task procures for him something which he does actually desire. Under the most favorable conditions the interest and energy available in the desire for the reward is transferred without serious loss to the performance of the required industrial operation. The desire for the reward engenders a more specific intention to perform the industrial operation. The performance of any task is throughout controlled by some *specific intention*, commonly, the intention to perform a determinate set of movements resulting in some industrial product conforming to certain standards. Special incentives, the desire for a reward, the fear of penalties, self-esteem, group loyalty, and so on, are of value and importance in proportion to the measure of their incidence upon this specific intention. One incentive may be of less value than another, not because it is intrinsically weaker, but because under the particular industrial conditions it fails to direct the worker's attention to the specific task in hand. Similar considerations apply to external incentive conditions. Supervision, verbal encouragement or reproof, the prescription of standards, and so forth are of value just in so far as, directly or indirectly, they control the specific intention which is operative in the performance of the given task. They may be useless or even harmful in releasing energy in ways which do not contribute to the performance of the particular task.

This section is broken into two chapters. Chapter 9 discusses the research on the influence that standards exert over behavior, and chapter 10 reviews the research on the influence of rewards.

9

STANDARDS:
Level of Formal
Work Demands

PART 1

INTRODUCTION

Relevance of Formal Standards. The level of standards is one of the more powerful variables that has been discussed, particularly when combined with an individual reward system, participation, or motivating by use of rewards and penalties. High participation contributes to acceptance of the standards, and standards exert a powerful influence over behavior. Individual rewards direct one's attention and energies to achievement, and the standards influence the level of achievement. Standards influence the internalization of goals and level of aspiration and leadership; expression of support or criticism influences the confidence and direction of energies to that goal.

Drawing by Brickman; copyright © 1973, by Washington Star Syndicate, Inc.

Illustration of the Impact of
Standards and Rewards

In his book, Peter has related the experiences of an extraordinary teacher who drama-
tized the dynamics of discrimination.[1]

Jane Elliott, a third grade teacher, has repeatedly conducted a series
of episodes where she sets up implicit standards of performance for her
students and provides positive feedback to those with high standards
and negative feedback to those with low standards. She separates her
students into brown-eyed and blue-eyed students, then asserts that
brown-eyed people are cleaner, more civilized, and smarter than blue-
eyed people. She then relates many examples of achievements of brown-
eyed people to support her position and relates weaknesses that are a
part of the heritage of blue-eyed people. To further reinforce the point,
she provides special privileges to the brown-eyed students on the
grounds that they have earned their right to better treatment by superior performance.

After one day she reverses her position and asserts that she was
wrong—that blue-eyed people are superior, and she supports the position with numerous examples and then gives the blue-eyed students
special privileges. The self-esteem, respect of other children, and performance in each case are sharply superior in the group that is attributed
to have superior qualities. The experiment has been replayed in many
contexts with both children and adults with similar results. While the
experiment is intended to dramatize the dynamics of discrimination, it
illustrates the power of standards and support of those standards by rewards and penalties.

Definition of Standards. Standards such as time, cost, quality, and
quantity goals, or other measures of performance, may be specified at relatively low levels to high levels. Where the standards are low, they are easily
met. This is often the case when standards aren't explicitly defined by management—either in formal policy statements or otherwise—before the activities or assigned duties are carried out. Individuals or groups establish their
own performance norms. Low standards also typically exist where the supervisor uses past levels of average production as the benchmark. In the other
extreme, standards such as time, cost, quality, quantity, or other ends are

[1]Bill Peter, *A Class Divided* (New York: Doubleday, 1971).

specifically defined and set at 100 percent or higher than historical performance levels. Further, as these standards are achieved, higher standards again are set.

Standards and measurements directly complement each other. Standards provide the basis for evaluation, and the measures of performance operationalize the standards that are implemented in practice. In universities, for instance, standards are often established that faculty members are expected to teach, do research, and provide service to the university and community. In many universities, however, only research is systematically measured. So operationally, this is the principal standard that the faculty members need to be concerned with as long as they aren't so poor in the other areas that crises are created or dramatic incidents of negligence occur.

Operational Measures of Standards

The following brief excerpt provides an operational measure of standards and measuring instruments.

Clarity of Standards. Standards such as time, cost, quantity, quality, or other aspects of performance expected of each individual may be specified in varying degrees. These may range from diffuse statements on what is expected to precise statements of expected performance levels. What best describes the situation of your work group?

1	2	3	4	5	6	7	8	9
Vague: Standards are nearly all vague		Mostly vague with some that are clear.		Moderately clear		Usually clear but some that are vague		Clear: Standards are clear.

Level of Standards. What percentage of work demands are relatively high and difficult to meet?

1	2	3	4	5	6	7	8	9
Low: Standards are low and easily met by nearly anyone with little effort		Standards are modest and can be met with some applications by nearly all		Standards are moderate and can usually be met by nearly every- one by aver- age effort		Standards are above average but can be met with extra effort		High: Standards are high and difficult to achieve by any but the best workers

Measuring Instruments. Measuring instruments are used to measure the degree that time, cost, quantity, quality, and other standards are achieved. Few elements of a formal system may exist to measure performance level, and reliance is on informal methods to measure individual performance. Contrarily, there may be a well-designed system for continual measurement of performance, and little reliance on informal methods. What best describes the situation in your work group?

1	2	3	4	5	6	7	8	9
Little: Poor measures of degree individual standards are achieved		Some measures of individual performance		Moderate: Measures about half the time the degree individual standards are achieved		Considerable: Good measure of individual performance		Excellent: Measures accurately degree indi- vidual stan- dards are achieved

PART 2

LABORATORY STUDIES

Level of Standards. One question researchers have directed their attention to is: what effects does establishing standards at a low, medium, or high level have on behavior and performance? Does the level of standards matter? In 1915, Myers found that girls learned more quickly and as accurately when they were given a time limit rather than being urged to do work as quickly as possible.[2] McKinley found, however, that in four tasks the number of errors increased as tighter time standards were imposed.[3] Similar findings have been reported by other investigators. Zander and Newcomb studied goal setting by the United Fund campaigns in 149 communities over a period of four years. They found that communities who set goals higher than the previous year's performance raised more money in dollars per capita than communities who set lower goals; however, in those communities that had failed to reach their goals, higher standards had little effect on the money

[2]G. C. Myers, "Learning Against Time," *Journal of Educational Psychology*, 6 (1915), 115–16.

[3]Fred McKinley, "Certain Emotional Factors in Learning and Efficiency," *Journal of General Psychology*, 9 (1933), 101–16.

raised.[4] Locke and a couple of colleagues, in a series of studies in 1966 through 1970,[5] also found that when individuals were given easy, medium, and hard standards, their productivity was directly related to the rigor of standards— the higher the standards, the higher the output.[6]

Several Types of Standards. Locke has also compared the effects of several types of standards. Four situations were compared: (1) where the standard was low, (2) where individuals set their own standards under the instructions to "do your best," (3) where individuals were given high standards, and (4) where the standards increased as they were achieved.[7] In the latter case, the standards were set at the level of the easy group but gradually were raised until the last trial, when the standards were slightly higher than the standards of the hard group. Those with the easiest standards achieved the lowest level of productivity; the hardest standards elicited the highest productivity. Those with self-set standards were in the medium range. Productivity of those under an increasing standard rose through time but not to the level of the group with hard standards.

Level of Standards and Reference Base Used. Day and Kaur provide some insights into the way in which the level of standards and the reference base used influence performance.[8] After a trial period where the level of performance and abilities were determined, the experimenter set targets at five different levels: 20, 40, 60, 80, and 100 percent higher than what was achieved in the trial period. These standards were couched in terms of two reference bases. One was the norm for the performance of the subjects' college class and the other was for the general community of college students. One-half of the subjects were told that these levels of standards had been achieved in their class; the other half were told that the standards were derived from the general level achieved by college students.

The performance level increased with each higher standard up to the point where standards were 80 percent higher than in the trial period. Productivity

[4]A. Zander and T. Newcomb, "Group Levels of Aspiration in United Fund Campaigns," *Journal of Personality and Social Psychology*, 6 (1967), 157–62.

[5]For a summary of Locke and Bryan studies up to 1968, see Edwin A. Locke, "Toward a Theory of Task Motivation and Incentive," *Organizational Behavior and Human Performance*, 3 (1968), 168–71; Judith F. Bryan and Edwin A. Locke, "Parkinson's Law as a Goal-Setting Phenomenon," *Organizational Behavior and Human Performance*, 2 (1967), 258–75; Edwin A. Locke and Judith F. Bryan, "Knowledge of Score and Goal Level as Determinants of Work Rate," *Journal of Applied Psychology*, 53 (1969), 59–65; Edwin A. Locke, Norman Cartledge, and Claramanes Knerr, "Studies of the Relationship Between Satisfaction, Goal-Setting, and Performance," *Organizational Behavior and Human Performance*, 5 (1970), 135–58.

[6]Locke, "Toward a Theory of Task Motivation and Incentives."

[7]Edwin A. Locke, "The Relationship of Intentions to Level of Performance," *Journal of Applied Psychology*, 50 (1966), 60–66.

[8]Mukul K. Day and Gurmindd Kaur, "Facilitation of Performance by Experimentally Induced Ego Motivation," *Journal of General Psychology*, 73 (1965), 237–47.

improved 25 percent when standards were set at the 20 percent level, and an additional 12 percent improvement was achieved by setting standards at the 80 percent level; however, performance declined with the 100 percent increase in standards. Standards that were related to the subjects' class motivated slightly higher performance compared with standards based on the general college group. In summary, increasing standards improved performance up to a certain point. The largest improvement occurred when 20 percent higher standards were set over the trial period. Performance improved when higher standards were set, but improvements were at a lower rate until the 80 percent higher level was set.

Other factors may moderate or amplify the influence of the level of standards. Several factors are closely associated with the implementation of standards, including the effects of feedback to the individual on how he is doing in respect to standards, the effects of providing standards and feedback on either quality, quantity, or both, the influence standards have under hot and humid conditions, and interaction of standards with the nature of the task and incentives used.

Level of Standards and Knowledge of Results.

Several studies have demonstrated that having knowledge of how one is doing is related to performance.[9] Those provided *feedback* on their achievements have a greater sense of satisfaction and perform at a higher level. The research also has shown that those who are provided high but attainable *standards* have a more positive attitude and perform at a higher level than those given lower standards. The question then is: what influence do these two factors separately exert on behavior and performance?

Knowledge of results may influence behavior in two ways—by providing clues that enable one to correct errors or by motivating performance. Knowledge of results may motivate performance by influencing the degree to which one accepts external standards and internalizes them as a goal. When one is provided feedback on the degree to which he has exceeded, met, or is short of the established goals, this should directly motivate him, positively or negatively. If one's performance is sharply below the standard, the individual is likely to be discouraged and not try to achieve. If one learns that he is approaching the standard, this may result in renewed effort. If one receives feedback that the standards have been achieved or exceeded, then a renewed

[9]R. B. Ammons, "Effects of Knowledge of Performance: A Survey and Tentative Theoretical Formulation," *Journal of General Psychology*, 54 (1956), 279–99; J. Annett, "The Role of Knowledge of Results of Learning: A Survey," United States Naval Training Device Center, *Technical Report* 342–3; G. F. Arps, "Work with Knowledge of Results versus Work without Knowledge of Results," *Psychological Review Monograph Supplement*, 28 (1921) (3, whole no. 125); E. A. Locke, N. Cartledge, and J. Koeppel, "The Motivational Effects of Knowledge of Results: A Goal-Setting Phenomenon?" *Psychological Bulletin*, 70 (1968), 474–85; R. B. Payne and G. T. Hauty, "Effect of Psychological Feedback Upon Work Decrement," *Journal of Experimental Psychology*, 50 (1955), 343–51.

effort may occur with a new norm set at the standard or somewhat above the standard.

Locke and Bryan designed several experiments to explore these issues.[10] In one experiment, both feedback and knowledge of results were manipulated. Setting higher standards resulted in greater performance. The individuals, however, did not need explicit feedback or knowledge of results to pace themselves to meet these standards. Those at low standards with or without knowledge of results performed at the same level; those with high standards with or without knowledge of results performed at a higher level. While knowledge of results wasn't important in these brief nine- to fifteen-minute sessions, it may be necessary over a longer period of time for the standards to remain influential.

In another experiment by Locke, the level of standards and feedback on results interacted to influence performance level after several sessions.[11] A simple computational task was assigned; the tasks were broken up into five trials of ten to fifteen minutes in length. One-half of the subjects were provided knowledge of their results at the end of each period and one-half were given no feedback. Further, one-half of the subjects were given the goal "do your best" and one-half were given standards that were 10 percent higher than the subjects had achieved on the previous trial. Figure 9-1 summarizes results.[12]

The level of standards substantially influenced the performance patterns of the groups, while feedback on results initially had little influence. Performance of all groups dropped during the pretest period until standards were set. Then those with high standards improved their performance while the "do your best" group maintained theirs. Knowledge of results didn't influence any group's performance until the last period, when the combination of standards and knowledge of results resulted in greater production.

Level of Standards and Feedback: Impact on Speed and Accuracy. Either accuracy or speed may be emphasized, whichever is selected as the main objective. Generally, standards and feedback on performance should direct attention to both. When standards and feedback are provided on speed but not accuracy, speed should be emphasized; when standards and feedback are provided on errors but not speed, accuracy should be emphasized, and when standards are provided on both, some combination of speed and accuracy should be emphasized.

[10]Locke and Bryan, "Knowledge of Score and Goal Level as Determinants of Work Rate," pp. 59–65.
[11]Edwin Locke, "Motivational Effects of Knowledge and Results: Knowledge or Goal-Setting?" *Journal of Applied Psychology*, 51 (1967), 324–29.
[12]Ibid., p. 327.

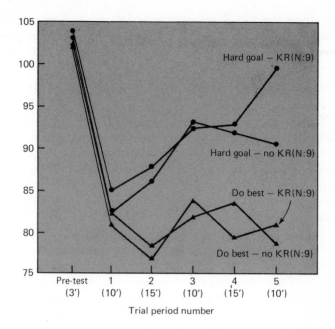

FIGURE 9-1. Effects of standards and knowledge of results on productivity of groups

Mace designed a set of theoretically significant experiments in the early 1930s to explore these issues. In one experiment, he compared the influence of relative, absolute, and vague standards. Group B, with relative standards, was instructed to surpass its past performance level (which was the average of the previous week). Group A, with absolute standards, was given a goal that was about 17 percent over levels obtained during the practice period. Both groups were informed on the performance of the previous day including the number of errors and the degree to which they were short of meeting the standard. Group C, which was under diffuse standards, was simply told, "do your best," but wasn't provided any feedback on the amount or accuracy of its work.

The task was to perform simple computations, with the output being the number of correct answers. In effect, the first two groups were given explicitly the standard of obtaining *correct* computations and were provided immediate feedback on the previous day's performance. The third group only implicitly had the standard to produce correct answers and wasn't given feedback. The experiment lasted six weeks, with the subjects working four days a week. All three groups improved with practice: group B, with relative standards, improved 7.7 percent more than group A, which was operating under the "absolute" standards.[13] Group C, with "do your best" standards, had *the highest level of performance* consistently throughout the period: production was 22.5 percent greater than in group A and 15 percent higher than in group B. However, group C's error levels rose 9.3 percent during the twenty days; in comparison, group A's errors fell 20.2 percent and group B's fell 37.8 percent. In effect, the more diffuse standards caused group C to emphasize speed at the expense of accuracy.

Standards Under Hot and Humid Conditions. The effects of standards have been explored under hot and humid conditions by Mackworth.[14] The members were given a simple physical task: they each had to raise and lower a fifteen-pound weight by bending and straightening their arm when paced by a timing mechanism. After a trial period where the base level of ability was established, one group was given the standard to do 25 percent more than the previous highest score and asked to work until exhausted. In turn, the experimenter provided continuous information on how well each person was doing and encouragement for greater effort. The other group was told "to do the best that they could"; the experimenter made no comments on how they were doing. Both groups worked under temperature conditions ranging in six steps from 65 degrees humidity, 60 degrees Farenheit to 100 degrees humidity, 90 degrees Farenheit. Those with high standards performed at a 58 percent higher level than those with low standards. Performance deteriorated as the temperature and humidity rose, with the productivity of the high-standards group dropping 36 percent compared with a drop of 40 percent for the low-standards group. In summary, those working under high standards produced at a higher rate than those under lower standards of "do your best." They were able to sustain their *relatively* higher productivity level as temperature and humidity rose even though both groups' absolute level of performance fell under the more stressful temperature-humidity conditions.

Standards: Effects on Group Processes. Lanzetta explored the effects of standards, rewards, and the nature of tasks on various aspects of behavior.[15] While the research design is not as clean as some of the simpler laboratory studies, the results provide a multiple perspective of the influence of these factors on behavior. Four-man groups were assigned a reasoning and a mechanical assembly task. They worked under two types of reward systems and three levels of standards. In one set of groups, no standards were estab-

[13]C. A. Mace, *Incentives: Some Experimental Studies*, Medical Research Council, Industrial Health Research Board Report no. 72 (London: Her Britannic Majesty's Stationery Office, 1935).

[14]N. H. Mackworth, "High Incentives vs. Hot and Humid Atmospheres in a Physical Effort Task," *British Journal of Psychology*, 38 (1947), 90–102.

[15]John T. Lanzetta, "Group Behavior Under Stress," *Human Relations*, 8 (1955), 29–52.

lished. In the second set of groups, a time standard was set and the experimenter announced every five minutes the remaining time to complete the task; during the last five minutes, the groups were informed every minute the amount of time left.

In the third set of groups, initially the subjects were given twenty minutes to perform the task, but after ten minutes they were told that only five minutes remained. Members also were publicly reprimanded when they made errors and were falling short of the standards. In addition, on the mechanical assignment, a barrier was imposed that thwarted completion of the task, and the work space was so sharply confined that it was difficult to work. Thus, in the third situation, a number of methods were used to create high stress including time standards, punitive leadership style, and an unprogrammed task.

Standards affected (1) changes that reduced tension, friction, and disequilibrium in the groups, (2) changes that reduced tension and increased integration of the groups, and (3) changes in problem-solving activity. As the standards rose, internal friction in the groups fell, with fewer disagreements, arguments, aggressions, deflations, and other negative behavioral patterns as well as less self-oriented behavior. As pressures sharply rose, integration increased with more collaborating, mediating, and cooperating-type behavior. Apparently, as stress increases, individuals try to keep interpersonal tensions at a low level and substitute positive, group-oriented actions for negative, individually oriented behavior. Groups become less competitive, more cooperative, and more friendly. In the face of high stress with the associated increased anxiety, members look to a group as a source of security and try to stabilize their position in it and minimize uncooperative and competitive behavior.

The group members sublimated their stress and anxiety and channeled it externally. Since the groups were randomly varied in terms of their exposure to standards, some groups received high stress and some groups low stress in the first session. Those receiving high stress initially were reluctant to return for further sessions and were more likely to delay, cancel their participation, and be more sullen and irritable with the experimenter. They directed their tension toward the experimenter rather than toward one another.

In respect to problem-solving behavior, higher stress reduces behavior that contributes to diagnosing the situation and making interpretations that aid task achievement; at the same time, discussion of the task increases. These changes reflect a more democratically, less individually oriented approach to solutions; it is, however, a more disorganized and less efficient approach. Problem-solving performance in groups was best under moderate standards and lowest but about equal for the low- and high-stress situations.

Summary of Laboratory Studies. In summary, the level of standards influences the direction, intensity, and sustaining power of effort. The experimental work goes back to 1945 when Myers found that girls learned more quickly and accurately when given a time limit. Greater money was raised in communities that set higher standards, except in those communities that had failed to meet their goals in the past. High standards are effective in improving performance as long as they are potentially within reach. They elicit the greatest improvement when they are about 20 percent higher than past achievements. When they are set at 100 percent over past levels, performance declines.

Higher standards have a positive influence on performance under a wide variety of situations. While hot and humid conditions cause performance to decline, high standards reduce the level of performance deterioration. Standards exert their influence over behavior even though individuals aren't provided feedback on their performance levels, at least for short periods. When multiple measures of performance exist, it is necessary to establish standards on each element of desired performance. Unless this is done, trade-offs are made among the different goals. If standards are set on quantity but nothing is said about quality, greater quantity will be achieved at the expense of quality and vice versa. "Do your best" standards have less effect than moderately high standards that are formally set.

Lanzetta demonstrated that increased standards and stress on a group contributed to improved group relationships. There was a pulling together in the face of the increased stress. This, however, is inconsistent with the findings of Torrance in his field studies of men placed in high-stress positions (see chapter 5 on task complexity). Probably only moderate stress was achieved in the laboratory setting and more intense stress observed by Torrance. A fragmentation and breaking up of the group would probably occur with the associated breakdown in communication, cooperation, and feeling of good will among the members if greater stress were created in the laboratory.

PART 3

DYNAMICS OF STANDARDS AND BEHAVIOR

A number of studies have explored some of the dynamics of standards on behavior and performance. These include what happens when a high-achieving group is given diffuse standards and a low-achieving group high standards, the effects of a fixed standard compared with an increasing level of standards, and the special case of increasing standards that are based upon competitive performance levels of other groups.

Increasing Standards with a Low-Motivated Group. An experiment by Bryan and Locke dramatizes the influence that standards exert on interest, commitment, and performance of low- and high-motivated groups.[16] Two groups with similar abilities but different levels of motivation were given three tests on a simple addition task. After test 1, twelve of the twenty-seven participants who had achieved similar scores were selected for tests 2 and 3. The six individual with the poorest commitment were assigned the goal to exceed their previous level of performance. The six who had the highest scores on commitment were assigned a standard to do their best. Three weeks later, they were given the third test. The same task and instructions were provided, with the high-motivated group again given a standard to do their best. The low-motivated group, however, was assigned specific standards that were 10 percent above the group's previous performance for tests 1 and 2.

The highly motivated group initially had a high level of performance, and this was maintained through the three tests. Those from the lower motivated group started out at a low level and moved up each period for a sharp improvement to nearly the performance level of the high-motivated group. In respect to interest in the task, the high-motivated group started out with a higher level of interest, but this fell sharply by the third period. The lower motivated group started with lesser interest; this rose slightly in the second period and then leveled off to the same level as the high-motivated group. The level of effort declined sharply over the three trials for the high-motivated group and increased for each trial for the low-motivated group.

In summary, the experiment indicates that specific performance standards can increase commitment and performance of those who initially have a low level of motivation. Performance is increased and more positive attitudes develop toward the task. On the other hand, if individuals start out with a high level of motivation, their performance remains about the same but the attitudes toward the task decline if only general standards of "do your best" are provided. Other experiments indicate that these trends continue the longer a task lasts.

Rising Standards Reinforced by a Bonus. Mace also explored whether a shifting set of higher standards increased effort.[17] Groups of children, averaging eleven years old, were assigned a simple arithmetic task. Group A was given the standard "do your best to improve each day;" and group B

[16]Judith F. Bryan and Edwin F. Locke, "Goal-Setting as a Means of Increasing Motivation," *Journal of Applied Psychology*, 51 (1967), 274–77.

[17]Mace, *Incentives*.

was given a standard somewhat above previous performance level. The children were given a small bonus for surpassing their previous performance; this was slightly increased each week to compensate for loss of interest and difficulty of improving in later stages.

Group A started out at a high level and increased output 35 percent by the tenth day. In contrast, group B, which was given specific standards at a steadily higher level, started out 25.7 percent lower level but caught up with group A by the fourth day. By the tenth day group B had increased productivity 149 percent over its starting point, or 40 percent higher than group A. This gain is even more impressive since group A had improved at a rate that was only obtained under favorable conditions and under the influence of strong incentives.

The superiority of the shifting level of standards is further exhibited by the individual productivity curves. They were uniformly steep and continuously increased. In group A, 52 percent of the subjects had reversals— that is, occasions on which an individual's score fell below his previous best performance; in group B, only 10 percent of the subjects had such reversals.[18] The shifting standards induced a steeper level of improvement by reducing the level of retrogression to previous performance levels.

The standards exerted the most incentive as they came within reach. Those people given an absolute standard were told to strive for seventy correct computations. Figure 9-2 compares the performance five days before the subjects obtained a score of 70 and five days after for the group under the fixed standards compared with the group under changing standards.[19]

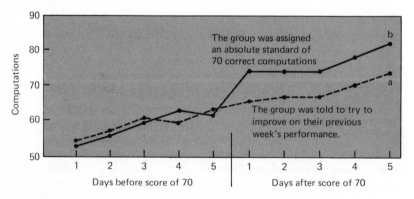

FIGURE 9-2. Average number of computations made by a group with specific standards of 70 units compared with a group with a standard to "do better than the previous day"

18Ibid., p. 22.

19Ibid., p. 21. Reprinted with permission of the Controller of Her Britannic Majesty's Stationery Office.

Figure 9-2 shows the striking improvement that occurred when the standard was within reach. Once the score of 70 was obtained, those under the absolute standards considered that score a minimum, while those who were using past performance as their standards were not as influenced. Performance of those under absolute standards rose 16 percent over the trend line of improvement from the practice period. The absolute standards directed the attention of the subjects to a precise objective and stimulated their desire to obtain it and then to improve upon it. The standard was most effective just at the point at which it was within reach, but the increased skill that occurred under this incentive persisted for the rest of the experiment. This study suggests that an optimum ratio exists between standards and the previous level of performance.

The form of standards also influenced the continuity of the work rate during each twenty-minute session.[20] Group A's work rate rapidly declined until the middle of the period when a steady level of performance was obtained. In group B, performance also fell until midperiod, but then a distinct and continuous improvement occurred that brought the level of performance up to the level of the initial spurt by the end of the work period.

Impact of Competitively Based Standards.   Absolute team standard exists where performance is evaluated against a fixed standard; the reference base is usually implicit. Another type of standard is where the level of achievement of competitors is used as the base for comparison. In this case, the difficulty of the standard is determined by the caliber of the competition. Myers explored the influence of these two types of standards on intragroup relationships.[21] ROTC students were organized into sixty 3-man rifle teams. One-half of the teams competed against one another and the other half against low, medium, and high standards. The competitive standards resulted in a higher degree of esteem and acceptance of other team members. Those under competitive conditions were less likely to blame other members for the poor performance (21 percent under competitive standards compared with 35 percent under absolute standards) or to blame their lack of achievement on poor equipment (0 versus 5 percent) and more often assumed the responsibility themselves for poor performances (34 versus 25 percent). Competition had the property of drawing teammates together; the comparison with an external group created a sense of unity.

Imposed and Self-Set Standards Combined.   Locke explored further the implications of setting easy standards, them following these up by allowing the group to set its own standards, and then imposing hard standards put

[20]Ibid., p. 25.

[21]Albert Myers, "Team Competition, Success, and the Adjustment of Group Members," *Journal of Applied and Social Psychology*, 65 (1962), 325–32.

in a coercive context.[22] The individuals were given a task that was introduced as a test of their creativity where they had to create as many words with a set of letters as they could. On the first six trials, they were given an easy standard of developing four uses in one minute on each trial; on the next six trials they were told to choose their own standard but to do their best. For the third set of six trials, they were given a high standard of fourteen uses on each trial; this was explained as being equivalent to the 80th percentile for Ivy League graduate students. Where the individuals set their own standards after having been given relatively low standards, they performed at an 18 percent higher level. When this was followed by an even higher set of standards, the performance level rose 12 percent further.

Nature and Effects of Competitive Standards

In this brief excerpt, Locke develops some of the characteristics of competitive standards and why they exert a strong influence over behavior.[23]

Competition. It is well known, both from experimental studies and from everyday experience, that competition can serve as an incentive to increase one's effort on a task. This phenomenon is an intrinsic part of athletics and business and is not unknown in academia. In the paradigm case of competition, another person's or group's performance is the standard by which goals are set and success and failure judged. One reason competition in athletics is so effective is that winning requires that one surpass the performance of the best existing competitor. This typically results in the standard of success becoming progressively more difficult with time. Each time a record is broken, the level of performance required to win (against the record holder) is raised. Each competitor must then readjust his goal and his level of effort to the difficulty of the task. The result is progressively better performance. (Of course cognitive factors can facilitate performance improvement, i.e., discovering better methods of performing the task. But it is the individual's goal to win or improve that generally motivates the search for such innovations.)

The case is similar though not identical in business (unlike athletics, business is not a "zero-sum game," where one man's gain necessarily means another man's loss. In business, wealth is created and therefore

---

[22]Edwin A. Locke, "Relationship of Intentions to Level of Performance," pp. 60–66.

[23]Edwin A. Locke, "Toward a Theory of Task Motivation and Incentives," *Organizational Behavior and Human Performance*, 3 (1968), 179–80.

everyone benefits in the long run.) Competition will encourage the development of better and better products as long as there are firms who wish to increase their share of the market. Competition may also spur firms to increase their quality or lower prices in order not to lose businesses.

The effect of competition, both between individuals and between groups, depends upon the particular person or persons one is competing with and one's own values. In athletics, the goal is typically to beat the best other competitor. In business this is not always the case; typically, business firms are satisfied to surpass their own best previous performances. Students if they are competing will ordinarily pick other students with grades or abilities similar to their own to compete with, or else will try to surpass their own best previous grade-point average.

The case of an individual trying to improve over his own previous performance on a task can be considered a special case of competition: self-competition.

As with participation, competition may have other effects besides inducing goal-setting. Above all, competition probably encourages individuals to remain committed to goals that they might otherwise abandon in the face of fatigue and difficulty. For instance, if mile runners only ran against themselves or against a stop watch, the 4-minute mile might never have been broken.

In addition, competition encourages the setting of goals that might not have been set at all in the absence of the other party. For example, if the Ford Motor Company had not developed a mass-produced low-priced automobile, General Motors might not have thought of developing a similar (competing) model (at that particular time).

Work Group Adjustment to Higher Standards. Higher demands may be imposed on a group or on an organization as a whole. While this means that ultimately the work load of each individual rises, the pressure is upon the group or organization to make an adjustment.

One of the more ambitious programs for studying the effects of the demands on a work group and the adaptation patterns was done in the early 1950s. Three psychologists and a mathematician studied an air defense direction center in the research laboratory of the Rand Corporation from 1952 to 1954.[24] A direction center was composed of about fourteen air force officers and enlisted men. Its job was to defend against enemy air attack, and it did so by maintaining radar surveillance over its area of responsi-

---

[24]Robert L. Chapman et al, "The Systems Research Laboratory's Air Defence Experiments," *Management Science*, 5 (1959), 250–69.

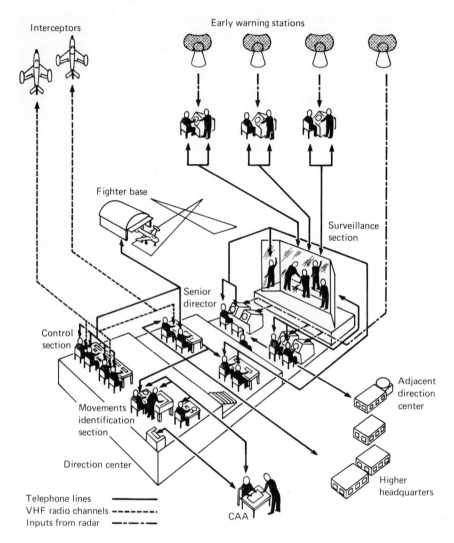

Interceptors

Early warning stations

Fighter base

Surveillance
section

Senior
director

Control
section

Adjacent
direction
center

Movements
identification
section

Direction center

Higher
headquarters

Telephone lines ————————
VHF radio channels ----------.
Inputs from radar —-—-—-—

CAA

FIGURE 9-3.[25]   Simplified model of direction center*

*This simplified model profiles the direction center's operation: the physical arrangements within
the center and the complex communication net (consisting of telephone lines, VHF radio channels,
and radar inputs) that linked crew members to each other and to the external embedding organizations. Much of the communication within the center itself is either visual or by face-to-face conversa-
tions.

bility, identifying aircraft as friendly or hostile, and directing aircraft to
intercept hostile planes. The degree of failure was determined by the number
of bombs dropped by hostile aircraft on targets in the area.

[25]Ibid., p. 255.

Personnel watched radar scopes. When an aircraft was spotted, they phoned the position of the plane to central display where the plane's path was plotted. Friendly aircraft were identified from flight plans filed with the civil aeronautics authority. Positions predicted by flight plans were compared with the paths followed by aircraft observed in the sector. When a plane could not be identified, it was tagged as unknown, and interceptors were ordered to take off and were directed toward the unknown aircraft. The aircraft was then identified as friendly, hostile, or unknown. If an unknown aircraft acted suspiciously, or committed a hostile act, the interceptor might be ordered to open fire and the whole defense system alerted. A simplified model emphasizing the elements of the direction center's operations is outlined in Figure 9-3.

The information received from the direction center's radar scopes and the Civil Aeronautics Authority partially identified the aircraft in action; personnel needed to match these data with the information on the presence of enemy planes within limited time constraints. Personnel had to work closely together and efficiently to adequately defend an area.

In the experiment, a directional center was simulated. The physical layout, communication nets, central displays, and the general atmosphere of the center were created. Four sets of experiments were designed. In each the task load was increased by changing the number and kind of known and unknown aircraft in a series of steps over the sixty-four 100-minute periods. By the end of the experiment, the task load was three times as great as in the beginning, i.e., each of the four crews had to defend an area with three times as much data on the aircraft.

The traffic increased in the last part of the experiment to the level where it was heavier than normal air traffic in any part of the United States. Yet each crew's defense against hostile attacks continued at an effective level. Each time the workload increased, the work limits of the crew were approached. But each time the saturation seemed about to occur, a method was found to simplify the job. The coordination and skill development of the group was characterized by three periods: the basal period, consolidation period, and organization period.[26]

The Basal Period. This period began as the group members became acquainted with each other and ended as the group structured itself and accepted the organization's goal. The period was marked by habitual ways of perceiving the organization and the task and directly transferring past experience to this task.

The Consolidation Period. As the members were faced with a stressful task environment, they found that habitual ways of behaving were inade-

[26]John L. Kennedy, "A Transition Model Laboratory for Research on Cultural Change," *Human Organization*, 14 (fall, 1955), 17–18.

quate and they made one or more adaptations: (1) individuals tried to work harder or with greater skill; (2) methods were borrowed that had worked in some previous context; or (3) the task or goal was rejected and failure was blamed on equipment; that is, individuals adjusted to failure rather than developing new forms of interaction and coordination.

The Organization Period. In the organization period, new concepts developed that helped members as a unit meet the challenge of the environment. Adjustment patterns that developed for coordinating the members were: (1) priority rules were established that determined the problems that would receive attention and in what order; (2) storage rules for information were developed for determining which events had implications for future use; (3) rules of action were developed for dealing with uncertainty; (4) rules were formulated for balancing workload among the members in emergencies; and (5) rules were developed for assessing other organizations' adaptations to their environment.

A number of methods used by the experimenters contributed to organizational efficiency. (1) Organizational rather than individual goals were defined and reinforced. (2) Immediate feedback was provided on the degree of success and failure in adjusting to the environment. (3) A formal method was instituted for self-evaluation of the group. In a briefing after each operation, the members had the opportunity to assess and evaluate their performance. (4) The level of demands on the organization were increased only as adaptation patterns developed.

We have a complex experiment where the members of the organization achieved a high level of effectiveness in terms of adjusting to an increasing level of demands. The members adapted rather than falling apart because the methods of learning were reinforced by continued focus on organizational goals and feedback, and opportunity was provided for objective self-evaluation. Some of the dynamics of group adjustment to higher standards that result in a high level of performance are illustrated by the above set of experiments.

In summary, several studies provide insights on the dynamic effects that standards exert over behavior. While some individuals have a drive to produce more than others, the level of production of a low-achieving group can be increased by raising standards. Generally, shifting standards to a higher level after performance rises stimulates continued improvements in production. The standards exert their greatest influence over performance just as they are about to be achieved. Once achieved, the higher rate is then maintained. The standards exert this influence by increasing both the intensity of application and continuity of effort. A special case of increasing standards is when the standards are established by competitive groups. In this case, as group performance increases, standards move upward. The competitive standards contribute to greater group unity, better task orientation, and greater willingness on the part of individuals to accept that poor performance is their own fault rather than the result of poor equipment or because of incompetency of others in the group. Where standards are set for a group, then followed by self-set standards, and then set for the group again, each action causes group performance to rise.

The dynamics of a work group making an adjustment to higher standards are developed in the Rand study. After the initial attempts to solve problems in the old ways, the group initiates new rules for giving priority to problems, develops new rules for sorting information to be stored for future use, and generates methods for balancing the workload among the group members to handle emergencies.

Copyright, 1971, G. B. Trudeau/distributed by Universal Press Syndicate.

PART 4

FIELD STUDIES

Effects of Standards on the Social System. The field studies reveal some of the broader effects standards exert in a complex social system. The establishment of formal standards—with an individual incentive system—affects the relationships of the workers to the staff group that sets the standards, to one another, and to their immediate supervisor. Roy has summarized some of the satisfactions that accrue from standards that are a part of a piecework system.[27] He worked in a machine shop where he kept a systematic diary on his experience. He observed that the standards created a situation that (1) enabled workers to approach their work in a game spirit, (2) enabled workers to control to a greater degree the way in which they spent their time, (3) enabled workers to express aggression against lower level manage-

---

[27]Donald F. Roy, "Work Satisfaction and Social Reward in Quota Achievement: An Analysis of Piecework Incentive," *American Sociological Review,* 18 (1953), 507–14.

ment and staff groups in a nondestructive way, and (4) generated support from members of the work group. The standards contributed to a work experience that was largely self-governed with the accompanying satisfaction of completing self-imposed goals. When the pieceworker accepted the standard, he organized his activities to control the outcome. If the quota was attainable, but attainment was still uncertain because other factors might affect the output, quota attainment became an exciting make-out game played against the clock where the individual applied his knowledge, ingenuity, and speed to achieve the standard. This heightened his interest and contributed to feelings of accomplishment.

In what became known as the make-out game broke the monotony of repetitive work and made the long day pass. Under day work, the operator had only the normal breaks at lunch time and rest periods to break up the flow of time; under piecework, he often established hourly series of completion points that served to mark his position in completing the day's work. This interest only existed where the standard was at a level that was neither too easy nor too difficult to achieve and where the central elements of achieving were under the worker's control. If the standards became excessively high or were so low that they were easy to achieve, or if other factors outside of the worker's control were principal elements affecting his work rate, standards exerted little motivating influence.

Another aspect of standards was that they set the ground rules for interaction with supervisors. When an operator was able to work at a pace that met standards, the supervisor left him alone; a foreman only applied pressures when one fell short of the standard. Furthermore, once the standard was achieved, the individual's time was largely his own. Thus, if the standard could be achieved in six hours, the worker could use the last two hours in a manner largely as he saw fit.

Standards shaped the development of antagonistic relations between line personnel and the methods department. The achievement of quotas—and the more rapidly a quota is achieved, the better one's standing—was interpreted as a victory over the methods department. While the worker could not flaunt his success before the methods group, he was able to demonstrate to his fellow workers the ability to win over their perennial antagonist.

The standards also established the basis for intergroup norms and intragroup status. The achievement of the standard elicited the approval of fellow workers and secured one's position in the group as a good worker. If one could beat a difficult standard or cut down the time required, this provided a measure of achievement and earned admiration from fellow workers. On the other hand, if a worker was unable to achieve this level, it meant a loss of prestige unless it could be explained by factors outside the control of the operator. While the group norms discouraged overachievement of standards, they exerted pressure to achieve up to a reasonable level.

Standards and Their Perceived Possibility of Attainment. Stedry and Kay, in a field experiment, explored the way in which the level of standards influenced attention to errors and quantity of output.[28] Nineteen foremen working in a department in a General Electric manufacturing plant were studied. The management set standards on productivity and on the amount of rework done. The foremen were divided under four conditions: (1) easy standards—meet the standard of average productivity and rework achieved during the previous six months; (2) difficult standards—"significantly" improve performance on both productivity and rework; (3) difficult standards on rework—improve "significantly" performance on *rework* while maintaining performance level on productivity; (4) difficult standards on productivity—improve "significantly" *productivity* while maintaining performance level on rework. The foremen were interviewed two weeks after the standards were set to assess their perception of the standards as easy (80 percent or greater possibility of attainment), challenging (30–70 percent probability of attainment), or impossible (0–20 percent chance of attaining standards).[29]

Table 9-1 summarizes the results. The extreme cases are easy to interpret. Where the standards were to meet the performance level of the last six months, productivity and rework were either increased or maintained (cell 11). Where the standards were to improve performance significantly, but this was perceived as only 0 to 20 percent possible, productivity and quality declined (cell 33). When standards were to increase performance significantly on quality *or* productivity, both productivity and quality improved or, at the minimum, were maintained when the goal was viewed as having a 30 to 70 percent possibility of being obtained (cells 12 and 21). Where standards were to improve *both* quality and productivity, and goals were viewed as 30 to 70 percent attainable, both increased (cell 22), but where one of the standards was viewed as unattainable, both declined (cell 23).

These findings must be viewed with caution since other experiments have consistently found that quality and productivity are tradeoffs. In this case, they apparently were joint products so that the foremen could not improve one without giving attention to the other. The experiment emphasizes the importance of the acceptance of goals. What is unknown is whether the goals were viewed as impossible by three of the foremen because this was a realistic reading of the particular difficulties they were facing at that time.

[28]Andrew C. Stedry and Emanuel Kay, "The Effects of Goal Difficulty on Performance: A Field Experiment," *Behavioral Science*, 2 (November 1966), 459–70.

[29]Two foremen were dropped from the analysis at this point because their perception of the goal difficulty contradicted the manipulation of the standards; the other foremen who were given the goal to maintain standards at the level of the previous six months saw this as easy; those other foremen who were given the goal to significantly improve their performance saw this as either challenging or impossible.

TABLE 9-1. Relation of Standards (Actual and Perceived) to Percentage Changes in Performance on Productivity (1st Item in Each Cell) and Rework (2nd Item in Each Cell)

	Rework Standards		
		Foreman Perception of Rework Standards	
Foreman Perception of Productivity Standards	Maintain Performance of Last 6 Months Easy*	"Significantly" Improve Performance in 13 Weeks Challenging**	Impossible***
Productivity Standards			
Maintain performance of last 6 months — Easy	11 36.5/4.3% 14.1/3.9 4.1/0.2	12 50.8/6.7% 49.7/6.7 13.4/2.3 9.1/1.5 1.8/−1.1	13
"Significantly" improve in next 13 weeks — Challenging	21 42.0/4.7% 16.9/3.9 1.0/−2.8 −2.9/−4.4	22 44.9/6.0% 17.7/4.1	23 −5.1/−4.9%
Impossible	31	32	33 −6.9/−6.4% −153.6/−9.4

*Easy standards: Foreman perceived that he could attain the level of performance with 80 percent or higher probability.

**Challenging standards: Foreman thought that there was a 30 to 70 percent probability of achieving standards, i.e., of making a "significant" improvement over performance of last six months.

***Impossible standards: Foreman thought there was a 0 to 20 percent probability of achieving these standards, i.e., of making a "significant" improvement over performance of last six months.

If so, the decline in productivity and quality might have been minimized with the establishment of standards—which is a conclusion that would be consistent with the other studies. These findings are consistent with the laboratory study reported earlier in the chapter. When standards in the laboratory were increased 80 percent or more, productivity declined.

Budgets as Formal Standards: Response of Production Employees. A couple of studies focus upon some of the adverse effects of high standards incorporated into budgets, particularly where the standards are reinforced by incentive systems. Argyris studied two manufacturing plants: plant X had loose standards and low pressure from management to meet standards. Plant Y had moved from relatively low to relatively high standards. Argyris examined various dimensions of behavior and contrasted the relationships that existed in an unskilled and skilled department in each plant.[30] The results of Argyris's work on the effects of higher standards in both skilled and unskilled departments are summarized in Table 9-2.

TABLE 9-2[31] Effects of Standards and Management Pressure on Percentage of Employees with Particular Attitudes in Two Plants

| | Skilled Department | | Unskilled Department | |
	*Plant X**	*Plant Y***	*Plant X**	*Plant Y***
Employee desire for understanding foreman	69%	100%	67%	100%
Sense of high pressure	0	27	10	13
Least liked condition in the company was pressure	0	50	0	10
Instrumental commitment to their work	39	73	43	87
Sense quality is sacrificed for quantity	71	90	10	80
Absenteeism	3.6	3.9	3	3.2
Turnover	7.3	21.7	15.7	16.4
People are friendly	90	30	90	71

*Plant X had loose standards and low management pressure for efficiency.
**Plant Y had tightened standards and increased management pressure for efficiency.

[30]Chris Argyris, *Understanding Organizational Behavior* (Homewood, Ill.: Dorsey Press, 1960).

[31]Abstracted from Argyris, *Understanding Organizational Behavior*, pp. 120–54. Only part of the data is used because the author did not maintain a consistent focus in comparing the departments in plants X and Y. Further, Argyris's analytical orientation was to translate structural variables into "employee needs," while I have been concerned exclusively with the effects that the structural variable exerts over behavior.

In plant X, 69 percent of the employees reported that they desired a foreman who was understanding compared with 100 percent in plant Y. The higher stress in plant Y placed an emphasis upon the foreman to act as a mediating figure. In the high-skilled departments, 27 percent of the employees reported that they felt high pressure in plant Y, while no one reported pressure in plant X. The employees in the unskilled department noted little difference in degrees of pressure in the two plants.

The employees were also asked what they least liked about the company. No one in plant X, in either low- or high-skilled departments, reported that they least liked pressure; however, in plant Y, 50 percent of the skilled employees and 10 percent of the unskilled reported that this was the worst feature. More employees in plant X reported a lower level of commitment to work hard to earn a day's pay, i.e., to "make out," than in plant Y. In plant Y, the standards were higher, so employees had to work harder to achieve the same level of earnings, and the employees applied themselves to do so. The employees' sense that quantity was sacrificed for quality was moderately higher in the skilled departments in plant Y compared to plant X and sharply higher in the unskilled departments in plant Y. The goal of earning a fair day's wages took priority over an emphasis on quality as standards rose.

Turnover and absenteeism are one adaptive mechanism for dealing with pressure. Absenteeism was slightly higher in plant Y compared with plant X. Turnover was substantially higher in skilled departments in plant Y, because apprentices transferred to other departments or factories. Apparently, apprentices made an assessment of whether they would be able to cope with the piecework, and when they found they could not, or that it would take more effort than they were willing to put into it, they transferred out. Among the regular employees in the skilled departments, the turnover was less in plant Y than in plant X. In the skilled departments of plant X, a substantially higher percentage of employees reported that people were friendly. The emphasis upon making a fair day's pay in plant Y increased rivalry among the employees and reduced the cohesion and friendliness among them.

In summary, the higher pressure in plant Y had a greater effect in the skilled than unskilled departments: personnel felt the pressure, reacted negatively to it, and judged their fellow workers as less friendly. In the unskilled departments, more workers felt that quality was sacrificed to achieve quantity. Overall, regular employees in plant Y also had a greater need for an understanding foreman and a higher instrumental commitment to their work, but this had little effect on absenteeism and turnover; new employees transferred out at a higher rate.

Response of Management to Budget Pressure. Budgets have built-in standards for expenditures. A manager is provided with a resource restriction that is typically difficult to remain within where pressures for efficiency exist. If expenditures exceed those authorized, the manager falls short of the standards. The study of management reaction to budgets provides some insight into both the effects of standards and some of the dynamics as high standards are imposed in a complex social situation of a production plant. Argyris, in a comparative field study of three medium-sized plants, evaluated the effects of budgets by interviewing supervisors and observing them in action.[32] The management methods used to enforce the level of standards were giving budget talks to foremen, red circling the poor showing of departments, production drives, and reprimanding or threatening to discipline if budgets were not met.

Argyris saw this as causing tension, intergroup suspicion, and counteractions to resist management; production was maintained only if management paid for it (such as with greater pay or negative actions such as slowdown strikes). Argyris contends that high standards create a situation where management has to work increasingly harder to overcome the forces for reduced production; any decrease in pressure results in an immediate drop in production. The groups become more resistant to management initiative, more rigid, harder to get along with, and they pursue issues that otherwise would not be important. Further, budgets develop major differences in orientation and cleavages between employees and management. Interdepartmental strife, and conflict between staff and line personnel are generated; also, pressures are internalized that adversely affect the emotional stability of individuals.

Interdepartmental strife develops as foremen explain their failure to meet the standards by blaming other supervisors, or as one foreman put it, they try ". . . to throw the cat in each other's back yards."[33] The production line personnel try to diminish pressure by blaming staff people, or sales people, for their problems. Those who internalize the pressure work excessively and unproductively; others get nervous and express their anxieties in terms of checking up on others; their actions became random and erratic in carrying out their jobs.

The pressure to meet the budget becomes a central focus. It presses supervisors to become department rather than plant centered. Since the budgets measure the effectiveness of the supervisor, the supervisor becomes principally concerned with operating within his budget rather than contributing to plant efficiency and productivity. The difficulty is that for most plants, departments are interdependent, so it is necessary to suboptimize in each department to obtain optimal productivity in the plant.

In summary, Argyris concentrates on some of the dysfunctional conse-

[32]Chris Argyris, "Human Problems with Budgets," *Harvard Business Review,* 31 (January 1953), 97–110.

[33]Ibid., p. 111.

quences of imposing high standards. He emphasizes that an alternative to responding to the standards is to scapegoat others as being at fault when performance doesn't measure up, such as line personnel blaming staff and production faulting sales. Another response is that while the standards are accepted and internalized, the pressure causes erratic behavioral and emotional tension that incapacitates those involved; a third response is that the supervisors direct attention to their immediate problems of meeting the pressures regardless of whether their actions contribute to problems of other departments; and last, the increased standards may be met by either passive resistance and/or overt sabotage of management's actions.

These findings are consistent with Dalton's analysis of and conclusions on behavior in several large manufacturing plants.[34] Dalton's study, however, emphasizes that while these are side effects of increased standards, they also caused most managers to commit themselves at a high level. Supervisors tried to protect themselves through the devices summarized by Argyris only when they didn't measure up.

Implications of Rising Standards: "Storming." Other dysfunctional factors associated with standards have been summarized in a field study by Berliner.[35] Standards that increase as performance levels rise motivate managers to a high degree in Soviet enterprises but also contribute to the disruptive practice of "storming." Storming occurs when the largest percentage of production is made as an accounting period ends. One example of a plant in Russia illustrates this type of behavior. This plant produced 3.4 percent of its month's output in the first ten days, 27.5 percent in the second ten days, and 69.1 percent in the last ten days.[36] This practice is widespread in Soviet industrial firms and leads to a number of adverse economic consequences. It generates states of emergency: men and equipment are subject to a wide range of demands varying from idleness to excessive overtime and intensive pressure. Storming upsets the maintenance cycle for machinery and uneconomic use of equipment; it creates a high degree of fluctuation in supplies among industrial firms and to customers.

The factors contributing to storming are principally the way in which standards are established and the enforcement of these standards through the incentive system. Each plant manager is provided a monthly output standard. If these benchmarks are achieved, the manager earns a bonus of 30 to 100 percent of his base salary. For each percentage over fulfillment, he earns additional bonuses of 2 to 10 percent of his base salary. He may

---

[34]Melville Dalton, *Men Who Manage* (New York: John Wiley & Sons, 1959).

[35]Joseph F. Berliner, "A Problem in Soviet Business Administration," *Administrative Science Quarterly*, 1 (1956), 86–101.

[36]Ibid., p. 88.

earn two and a half times his salary by exceeding the standard by 5 percent. On the other side, if he fails to meet his standards, he is likely to be demoted. When standards are achieved or when an enterprise exceeds its target, the standards for the following period are placed at successively higher levels based on the "ratchet" method, which provides an ever-rising floor for standards. The bonuses induce managers to meet their plans; the ratchet then snaps the catch beneath the new level of output and the manager is faced with exerting even greater effort to meet the standard for the next period.

Managers adapt to this in a number of ways. The prudent manager provides a safety factor in the targets he tries to achieve so that he doesn't exhaust the complete production potential of the plant. A second major adjustment to meeting the standards is storming behavior. As the end of the month arrives, all resources are mobilized to meet the standards. Maintenance is delayed, overtime weekends are scheduled, and high pressures are exerted on the workers to meet the standards; all factors that contribute to meeting the standards at the end of the month are mobilized, and those factors that affect the longer term productivity of the organization are subordinated to the immediate goal. Managers may borrow from the production in the next period and allocate it to the current period, making the necessary accounting adjustments. This increases the sharpness of storming behavior until the enterprise is unable to meet its targets and the manager is fired and a new one appointed. The problem is severe, and managers turn over in their positions at a rapid rate, ranging up to 40 to 50 percent annually in some industrial sectors.

The bonus system aggravates the problem in the Soviet firms, but a similar pattern of "storming" probably takes place in any organization at the time that a manager is evaluated. The laboratory studies and the field studies show that increasing standards sharply improve performance. The ratchet idea is an effective device for increasing the level of standards with the resulting pressure on improved performance. It is evident, though, that when combined with an incentive system that exerts high pressure for performance the combined effect has serious adverse side effects in complex social systems.

Summary. The field studies reveal the complex impact that standards have on both groups and organizations. Where standards and piecework are combined, it affects the entire social system in a shop. It shifts the responsibility to the individual to organize his time, provides greater independence of supervision, provides a way of channeling aggression against supervision and staff groups in a nondestructive way, and creates a game context for the workers in approaching their work. Standards also influence the norms for minimum and maximum performance and affect the status members have in the work group. The field studies also support the idea that standards that are considered achievable positively influence behavior, while standards that are unlikely to be reached adversely affect performance.

While standards exert pressure for higher performance, they may also result in various adverse effects. The higher standards apply stress to workers, exert pressure to sacrifice quality for quantity (where only speed is emphasized), reduce friendliness, and develop a greater sense in employees that supervision doesn't understand their problems. Increased standards build counterpressure from employees to resist management's actions and contribute to intergroup suspicion, particularly where individuals and groups find it difficult to meet the standards. The activities of building an efficient organization over a long period of time become subordinated to the immediate problems of meeting standards at the end of the month or accounting period. If the standards are coupled with individual incentives, or group bonus systems, the short-term perspective dominates at the expense of longer term; a departmental focus predominates as supervisors and workers concentrate upon solving their problems regardless of the difficulties created for other units.

In review, aspects of standards that determine their impact include:

—*The level at which they are set.* Performance increases up to a point where standards are 80 percent over past performance. Greatest incentive is provided when standards are 20 percent over past levels of achievement.

—*Setting specific versus "do your best" standards.* Specific standards elicit higher productivity by motivating greater continuity of effort. The field studies reveal that specific standards set at attainable levels when combined with piecework generate greater interest in the work, cause the worker to pace himself better to maintain high productivity, permit expression of nondestructive aggression against lower level supervision and staff groups, and enable the worker to elicit support from fellow workers when the standards are achieved. At the supervisory level, if standards are set at a level where the supervisor believes their achievement is less than 20 percent possible, performance declines. Where they are set at a level where a reasonable possibility exists for their attainment (30 to 70 percent), performance rises.

—*The reference base used.* Standards based upon an identifiable group elicit greater motivation than those based on a general group. Competitively based standards generate higher application than those based upon past performance of the group. Competitively based standards elicit higher esteem and acceptance of other team members, a greater sense of responsibility, and less scapegoating when individuals are faced with failure.

—*The degree standards are set on all trade-off factors.* Standards channelize the direction of application. If they are set only on quantity, productivity will increase but quality will fall, and vice versa. Standards must be set on all trade-off factors to focus attention on joint goals.

—*Whether feedback is provided on degree of achievement.* In the short term, standards exert their influence even if individuals aren't appraised of results. Over a longer period, standards and information on degree of achievement are both important in eliciting higher application. The greatest improvements are elicited at the point where standards are just about to be met. Once standards are achieved, performance is stabilized at the higher level.

—*Degree standards are self-set or formally assigned.* Assigned standards elicit higher application than self-set standards. Performance declines under hot and humid conditions, but higher standards reduce the fall in productivity to a greater degree than self-set standards.

—*Degree standards increase as performance rises.* Increasing standards as performance rises elicits greater continual application and productivity. The productivity and interest of a low-motivated group can be increased to the level of a high-motivated group by raising standards as productivity is stimulated. If higher standards are reinforced through an incentive bonus, striking improvements in productivity are elicited. Where standards are initially imposed, then self-set, than imposed at a higher level, performance rises each time.

—*Degree group processes that aid adaptation to higher standards are supported.* Interdependent members of a group can adjust to increasingly higher work demands, if group processes are modified to adjust to higher demands. Setting priority rules on handling problems, adapting rules for accumulating revelant information, and formulating rules for distributing work among members for overloads and emergencies are some methods that can be used. Increasing standards have a pervasive effect on the nature of the social system. At the supervisory level, adaptations to high pressure may include hostility toward higher management, intergroup scapegoating when standards aren't met, high anxiety, diffuse and unproductive behavior, departmental focus rather plant-wide consideration, and greater resistance to management's initiatives. In the extreme, attempts to meet rising standards lead to "storming" behavior: a completely short-term orientation is taken to meet the standards regardless of the longer term implications.

Maximum efficiency is attained where standards are set at a level that challenges greater application and productivity without disrupting organizational processes. A fine line exists between standards that are set at a level that *discourages* application and generates a wide variety of adverse behavioral patterns rather than encouraging individual and group innovation to meet the challenge. The impact of standards depends on how fast they are increased and the degree to which group processes are constructively modified to meet the higher demands.

10

REWARDS-PENALTIES: The Focus of the Formal Incentive System

PART 1

INTRODUCTION

The Nature of Formal Systems. The formal system in an organization may directly reward good performance and penalize poor performance. In this case, the level of individual performance is directly rewarded so that earnings rise and fall in a direct ratio to performance levels. Typical examples are piece-rate systems, promotion for outstanding performance, or when other special recognition is given because of exceptional contributions. On the other hand, rewards and penalties may be allocated on an institutional basis. That is, everyone by virtue of membership in the organization receives the same benefits such as pensions, hospital insurance plans, recreational facilities, cost-of-living increases, across-the-board upgrading, or identical hourly rates and salaries. These benefits go to all members of the organization regardless of their level of contribution and stop only when membership in the organization is terminated.

©King Features Syndicate 1973.

An intermediate system of rewarding is where the level of group performance is evaluated and rewards and penalties are based upon achievement. All those in a group receive the same rewards or penalties, but there are differences among groups. A group incentive plan where subgroups in an organization are rewarded or penalized would be of this nature.

An institutional, group, or individual focus is implemented by the way in which instructions are communicated, by the way in which supervisors evaluate performance—whether attention is on how well the organization, subgroups, or the individuals are doing—the awarding of status symbols such as special privileges, and probably most important, the basis used for allocating money and promotions. Penalties may be allocated on these various bases also.

Operationalizing the Reward-Penalty System

The measure of a reward-penalty system is set forth in the excerpt. The following questions may be asked to gain an operational measure of a reward-penalty system.

REWARD-PENALTY SCALE

Degree rewards are	Little			Partial			Extensive		
related to performance	1	2	3	4	5	6	7	8	9

Relation of penalties to performance	10%	20%	30%	40%	50%	60%	70%	80%	90%

1. Rewards (salary increase, promotions, special recognition, and privileges) may be granted on a basis that is *largely unrelated* or *directly related* to performance levels. Which of the following best describes the relationship of rewards and different performance levels in your work group?

REWARD SCALE

10%	20%	30%	40%	50%	60%	70%	80%	90%
Little				Partial			Extensive	

1. *Little Relationship*—There seems to be little relationship between how good a job one does and the reward. Only 10 percent or less of time are rewards, raises, promotions, or special recognition related to actual performance.

5. *Partial Relationship*—There is a mixed picture; 50 percent of those who do an outstanding job usually receive recognition, raises, and a chance for a pro-

motion; however, 50 percent of those who do a relatively poor job are still rewarded because of their seniority, friendship, or special ties with key people.

9. *Extensive Relationship*—If one does a good job, 90 percent or more of the time one receives recognition, rewards, and a chance for promotions. Seniority or special connections are important only when decisions could go either way.

2. Penalties such as taking away of special privileges, salary reductions, demotions, and firing may be largely unrelated to poor performance levels over which individuals have control. What best describes the situation in your work group?

PENALTY SCALE

Little				Partial				Extensive
1	2	3	4	5	6	7	8	9
10%	20%	30%	40%	50%	60%	70%	80%	90%

1. *Little Relationship*—Ten percent or fewer of the penalties are actually related to poor performance; in 90 percent of the cases, individuals are penalized for things over which they have little control.

5. *Partial Relationship*—About 50 percent of penalties are related to poor performance and 50 percent to things over which individuals don't have control.

9. *Extensive Relationship*—Ninety percent or more of penalties are related to poor performance over which individuals have control.

Perspectives on Individual Reward Systems. A high degree of controversy exists on the influence of different reward systems. On the one hand, it is contended that individual reward systems are a powerful influence over behavior. Adam Smith, in *The Wealth of Nations*, observed, "Workmen, when they are liberally paid by the piece, are very apt to overwork themselves, and to ruin their health and constitution in a few years."[1] This view of potency of individual incentive systems in subscribed to by a wide variety of management writers, personnel textbooks, and practicing industrialists. Arthur Rath, chairman of a large firm in Boston, observed that in the hundreds of plants in every type of industry that he had observed where various incentives were in operation, "nothing will stimulate an employee to perform his top capacity as well as individual incentives—a system of compensation

[1] Adam Smith, *The Wealth of Nations* (London: J. M. Dent and Sons; New York: E. P. Dutton & Co., 1934).

which links its reward as directly as possible with his own efforts."[2] A survey in 1959 found that over 50 percent of manufacturing plants were operating under some form of incentive system.[3] As one industrialist put it,

> With twenty years' experience to temper my judgment, I am certain that almost without exception an individual incentive plan properly installed and administered will result in decreased costs, increased wages, and increased profits. An individual incentive plan puts every incentive operator in business for himself, with no capital investment on his part.[4]

A plant manager of another manufacturing company commented on his experience with an incentive plan stating that real savings in direct labor amounted to about 40 percent, with the cost of maintaining the incentive system reducing this to 35 percent.[5]

These views on the usefulness and positive impact of individual incentives are challenged directly by others. Wilfred Brown, the chief executive of the Glacier Metal Company in Great Britain, a firm that has been intensively studied by Jacques and others from the Tavistock Institute, cogently presents the viewpoints of those critical of the incentive systems.[6] He contends that the benefits claimed for wage incentives are due to changes on a wide front. He criticizes incentive systems as contributing toward widespread restrictive practices where workers set themselves a norm and then don't work beyond that. Incentive systems contribute to the practice of "banking," where workers only partially report the work they have done in a particular day and put the rest in a "bank" to be reported another day. Individual incentives adversely influence the willingness of management and workers to invest in new machinery and improve working methods since "experiences have taught managers that innovation in methods means trouble, conflicts, and even strikes ... due largely to the workers' doubts and uncertainties about the effects of changes on their earnings."[7] Many jobs don't lend themselves to payment by result since output is determined by machines or

---

[2]Arthur A. Rath, "The Case for Individual Incentives: Management's Most Potent Motivational Tool," *Personnel Journal*, 39 (1960), 172–75.

[3]Ibid., p. 173.

[4]Ibid., p. 174.

[5]Ibid.

[6]Wilfred Brown, *Piecework Abandoned* (London: Heinemann, 1962).

[7]Ibid., p. 24.

other factors outside of the control of the worker. Pressure is exerted on time study personnel to loosen rates and increase bonus earnings as time goes on, thus increasing labor costs. Further, he contends that the systems contribute toward reduced quality of work.

Some behavioral scientists have attacked incentive systems not so much on the basis of their results but on theoretical grounds. Maslow's thesis is that all workers respond to a hierarchy of needs with safety and security, i.e., money, as some of their lower level needs and self-esteem and self-actualization needs as their higher level needs.[8] He contends that the higher level needs are greater motivators then the lower level needs once some minimal level of satisfaction is achieved of these lower level needs. Thus, Maslow contends that incentive systems attempt to capitalize on the weakest needs of workers.

Herzberg, another behavioralist, develops the Maslow thesis further. He believes there are sets of factors that are "hygenic" in character—which include pay, job security, fringe benefits, and working conditions—that are *not* motivators under normal conditions. Once these are achieved at some minimal level, they cease to exert a motivating influence on the workers or management. He believes that factors that motivate are those that appeal to higher level needs. Principal motivators are believed to be those contributing to achievement needs, such as the opportunity to be creative, to be more expert in one's job, to be trusted, to have autonomy and freedom to solve problems in one's own way, and to be assigned responsibility.[9]

There is an extensive literature on incentive systems. Nearly forty years ago, Bloomfield was able to cite over 130 references;[10] an annotated bibliography by Aronson in 1949 refers to over 90 sources;[11] the British Institute of Management, drawing heavily upon British sources, quoted over 90 in 1950;[12] the American Management Association noted over 160 references in their bibliographical listing in 1953 and 1954.[13] Viteles in 1953 provided 300 sources dealing directly with incentive systems.[14] Broad reviews and syntheses of many of the older sources in the area, particularly factory

[8]A. H. Maslow, "A Theory of Human Motivation," *Psychological Review*, 50 (July 1943), 370–96.

[9]Frederick Herzberg, Bernard Mausner, and Barbara B. Snyderman, *The Motivation to Work* (New York: John Wiley & Sons, 1959); Frederick Herzberg, *Work and the Nature of Man* (New York: World Publishing Co., 1966).

[10]Reported in R. Marriott, *Incentive Payment Systems: A Review of Research and Opinion* (London: Staples, 1957), p. 13.

[11]Ibid.

[12]Ibid.

[13]Ibid.

[14]Morris S. Viteles, *Motivation and Morale in Industry* (New York: W. W. Norton & Co., 1953).

studies, have been made by Marriott,[15] Wolf,[16] Pym,[17] Mangum,[18] McKersie,[19] and Opsahl and Dunnette.[20]

The evaluation of the effects of different forms of reward systems is confounded by the interaction with the level of standards that are imposed, the degree of interdependence of work flow, and size of group. The degree of cohesion in the group that exists when the reward-sanction system is introduced also mediates the influence that reward systems exert. In practice, a dynamic relation exists among these variables with each being affected and affecting the other.

Organization of the Chapter. The laboratory studies have greater reliability and are simpler to interpret. Parts 2 and 3 review the laboratory studies. Part 4 moves on to the field work and develops some of the factors that contribute to the diverse results of reward systems. Part 5 summarizes the conditions that determine the prospects for success or failure of incentive systems. Part 6 summarizes some key points developed in the chapter.

Problems of Research Design that Confound Results of Research

A particular knotty problem in evaluating reward systems is that the rewards interact with the standards that are set. The following variations in research design are common to these studies:

1. *Rewards are contrasted, with standards constant.* In these studies, institutional (no differentiated rewards) are contrasted with individual or group reward systems. The institutional rewards are usually assigned to a control group. Standards are either undefined or specified in absolute terms so they are constant among units.

2. *Rewards and standards both are varied.* Another approach is to contrast the cases where individuals are rewarded based *on their relative standing in a group* with the cases where individuals receive equal rewards in a

---

[15]R. Marriott, *Incentive Payment Systems*, pp. 13–206.

[16]William Wolf, *Wage Incentives as a Managerial Tool* (New York: Columbia University Press, 1957).

[17]Dennis Pym, "Is There a Future for Wage Incentives?" *British Journal of Industrial Relations*, 11 (1964), 379–97.

[18]Garth Mangum, "Are Wage Incentives Becoming Obsolete?" *Industrial Relations*, 2 (1972), 73–96.

[19]Robert B. McKersie, "Wage Payment Methods of the Future," *British Journal of Industrial Relations*, 1 (1963), 191–212.

[20]Robert L. Opsahl and Marvin D. Dunnette, "The Role of Financial Compensation," *Psychological Bulletin*, 66 (1966), 94–118.

group but the size of rewards depends upon *relative standing of the groups.* Typically, there also is a "control group" where there are no incentives and no comparison among individuals or groups on their relative performance. In this case, results are usually inconclusive since the design usually explores only blocks indicated by X's in Table 10-1 and control groups so that both the reward system and the standards are changed.

TABLE 10-1. Typical Experimental Design

| | Reward System | | |
Standards	Individual	Group	Institutional
Individual: Relative standing of each individual in the group	X		
Group: Relative standing of each group		X	
None specified			Control group

3. *Different levels of individual or group rewards are contrasted with each other and with an institutional reward system.* Typically, standards are also manipulated so that the experimental results confound rewards and standards. We will highlight these features of the design as each study is reviewed.

PART 2

LABORATORY STUDIES

Table 10-2 summarizes the research design and results of ten studies. The projects comparing group with individual systems are first summarized. Next, the studies are reviewed where institutional systems are contrasted with individual systems.

Group and Individual Systems: Intragroup Relations

Grossack examined some of the detailed behavioral patterns that emerge under individual and group reward systems.[21] Nine 5-member groups of

[21]Martin M. Grossack, "Some Effects of Cooperation and Competition Upon Small Group Behavior," *Journal of Abnormal and Social Psychology,* 49, no. 3 (July 1954), 341–48.

TABLE 10-2. Selected Laboratory Studies on Reward Systems

Author/Year	Independent Variables	Dependent Variables	Relationship
GROSSACK (1954)	Individual-group evaluation	Intragroup behavior	Group evaluation resulted in greater interaction and cooperation
DEUTSCH (1960)	Group vs. individual grade	Individual competitiveness	Group grade reduced intragroup competition and increased intragroup cohesion
HAMMOND & GOLDMAN (1961)	Group vs. individual grade and absolute vs. relative stds.	Intragroup activity: task-directed acts, non-task-directed acts	Group grade reduced both task- and non-task-directed activities
ZANDER & WOLFE (1964)	Indiv/group/combined indiv-group system	Interaction acts	Different evaluation systems had little effect on behavior except group rating increased exchange of data
THOMAS (1957)	Individual-group evaluation	Productivity & intragroup behavior	Interaction between evaluation and specialization with group evaluation under non-specialization created more positive effects
DE CHARMS (1957)	Individual-group evaluation	Productivity	Higher productivity under individual rating system; some interaction with personality
TOPPEN (1965)	Hourly vs. piecework	Productivity	Piecework related to higher productivity
SMITH et al. (1967)	Individual incentives and penalties vs. no incentives/penalties	Productivity	Incentives increased qualtity; penalties for errors reduced productivity but increased quality

(TABLE 10-2 continued on page 262.)

TABLE 10-2 (Cont.)

Author/Year	Independent Variables	Dependent Variables	Relationship
TSENG (1952)	Individual incentives at various levels vs. institutional (equal rewards & no rewards)	Productivity quality intragroup relations	Moderate incentives created highest productivity. Institutional systems had highest quality.
MINTZ (1951)	Group & individual incentives	Coordination among group members	Individual incentives disrupted cooperation and coordination

Task/Work Flow	Standards	Group Size	Subjects and Cohesion of Group
Independent W.F.: Solutions to human relations problems	Relative: Forced rating of individual vs. forced rating of groups	5	Low—(female college students)
Interdependent W.F: Discussion of human relations problem w/one solution and solution of a puzzle problem	Relative: Forced rank of individuals vs. forced rank of groups	5	Probably low— strangers (college students in psychology class)
Interdependent W.F: Discussion and group solution of human relations problems	Relative (forced rank within group & forced rank among groups) vs. absolute (indiv. and groups evaluated w/fixed standards)	5	Low—strangers (college students)
Independent W.F.: Predicting w/limited information	Absolute (but implicit standards)	7	High—probably colleagues (business executives)
Independent and interdependent W.F.	Absolute: Do as well as possible	5	Low—strangers (telephone operators)
Independent W.F.: Arithmetic task	Relative: Forced ranking of group members vs. no ranking	6	Low—(male college students)

TABLE 10-2 (Cont.)

Task/Work Flow	Standards	Group Size	Subjects and Cohesion of Group
Independent W.F.: Repetitive short pulls on a device	Absolute: Low (50 pulls where it is possible to do 3,000 hourly) vs. past performance level for piecework	1	Low—stranger (college students)
Independent W.F.: Identify targets	Relative	4–6	Low—stranger (college students)
Partly interdependent: Building a house with play bricks	Varying: Relative standing compared to no standards	4	High—peers (Chinese children, classmates)
Interdependent: Pull objects out of a bottle	Absolute: Trial period achievement taken as the base	20	Low—strangers (college students)

women were told that they would be evaluated as a group. The other members of nine groups were individually evaluated on the assigned task. The groups were placed in a room where they could only communicate through written notes. The group evaluation generated a greater degree of cohesiveness, more pressure for uniformity, more initiatives to solve problems and responses to initatives, and more attempts to influence one another; members also sent fewer communications that expressed tension and antagonism. Greater use was made of nondirective methods of exerting influence.

The group evaluation provides a common perspective for each group member that contributes to greater cohesiveness and supports processes leading to cohesion. These include attempts to influence, exerting pressure for consensus and uniformity, and sending and receiving communication—proposed solutions to problems, opinions, and questions. The communication of tension is inhibited because members don't want to be thought of as disrupting working relationships. The greater use of nondirective methods under group evaluation is possible since more members have a common orientation. In total, Grossack's experiment suggests that group evaluation contributes to processes that enable a group to more effectively work together.

Evaluation Systems and Standards.   Deutsch[22] assigned five-man groups two tasks—to solve a puzzle and a human relations problem. Two forms of rewards were set up: under a group system, groups were ranked relative to each other, based on their performance, and each member received the group grade; this was contrasted with a system where individuals within each group were ranked relative to each other with the highest ranked member obtaining the best grade. In this design, both standards and rewards are manipulated.

On most measures, those with competitive group standards who were evaluated on a group basis had a greater degree of group cohesion, coordination, greater acceptance of ideas, and fewer communication difficulties. The two variables influenced most aspects of individual behavior, with members feeling greater pressure to achieve, being more attentive to the task, being more problem oriented, and having greater insights in the problems. They also had a greater sense that the discussion proceeded in an orderly way and that the group was productive.

The results of a questionnaire showed that the group evaluation resulted in less desire to excel over others but about the same level of motivation to achieve; while the orientation was less competitive, motivation was still high. The individuals under the group system also felt obligation to others and a desire to win their respect.

In summary, Deutsch's results support that a group evaluation with forced ranking among groups contributes to better group relationships than individual evaluations with forced ranking within a group. It makes little difference whether the problem is of a structured or unstructured nature, since so little interaction exists between task complexity and combination of reward-standards used.

Hammond and Goldman followed up the Deutsch study to explore whether the group-individual reward or the competitive standards resulted in differences in behavior.[23] Five-member groups were assigned the task of discussing four types of human relations problems and writing up recommendations in a group report. Four types of rewards were established. One set of groups was informed that the members would receive credit depending upon their *individual* contributions; a second set of groups was told all members in their groups would receive the *same credit* depending upon the total participation of members and quality of the written reports. A third set was told their credit depended upon *their relative rank in the group*; and the last set was told all members would receive the points dependent upon *the relative rank of their group* with the other three groups. In effect, the first two sets of

[22]Morton Deutsch, "The Effects of Cooperation and Competition Upon Group Process," in Alvin Zander and Dorwin Cartwright, eds., *Group Dynamics*, 2nd ed. (Evanston, Ill.: Row, Peterson & Co., 1960), pp. 414–48.

[23]Leo K. Hammond and Morton Goldman, "Competition and Non-Competition and Its Relationship to Individual Group Productivity," *Sociometry*, 24 (1961), 46–60.

groups had an individual and group reward system with implicit, fixed standards by which they were judged; the second two groups were evaluated on an individual or group basis with competitively based standards (relative performance of individuals in a group or relative performance of the three groups).

The individual evaluation system contributed to higher participation of group members in task-directed activities and personal and social expressions. Individual systems contributed toward a higher level of social interaction, probably because of the greater need for group maintenance and tension reduction. The nature of the standards also influenced group interaction.

Competitive standards—whether forced ranking of individuals or groups —reduced the communication exchange related to the task and increased social and personal exchanges. In respect to coordination of effort, orientation to the task, communication, involvement, and recognition of relevant factors, the highest ranked groups operated under the fixed standards and individual evaluation; the next ranked had a group evaluation and fixed standards. However, with competitive standards, no consistent behavior developed under group or individual evaluation systems.

In summary, Hammond and Goldman found that both the nature of standards and the evaluation system influenced group processes. Individual evaluation systems were superior to group systems in encouraging task-related activity. Competitively based standards discouraged group processes related to task activities. Fixed standards with individual evaluations were the best combination for supporting group processes in these small groups.

Individual Versus Group Evaluation and Publicity Effects. Zander and Wolfe sought to determine the effects that individual, group, and combination individual-group evaluation have upon functioning of small groups.[24] They also partially explored the effects of publicly posting and reporting results to their superiors. Department heads from geographic districts of large cities were given a simple task that required cooperation for maximum effectiveness. Seven-man groups sat on one side of a large table and were assigned a simple prediction task. They had little or no information to make an appropriate judgment. They could obtain the correct information from the experimenter by giving up some prespecified number of points, or they could obtain it from other group members for a negotiated number of points, or they could guess. They could also sell information to the other group members or provide it to them free. Communication to others was limited to requesting or giving information by written notes.

Four experimental conditions were established. All groups were taught the basic task and worked on it for six trials—called test 1. Their individual

[24]Alvin Zander and Donald Wolfe, "Administrative Rewards and Coordination Among Committee Members," *Administrative Science Quarterly*, 9 (June 1964), 50–69.

scores were reported to them privately after each trial. The situation was then changed to public reporting of individual scores, public reporting of group scores, and public reporting of both group and individual scores.

When individuals were told their scores would be reported to their superior and posted after each trial, cooperative acts declined. Less information was offered for sale or given to other members, and fewer negotiations on procedures for obtaining information were made. Under the group evaluation system, cooperative acts increased, with more information sold or given and fewer guesses made without information. Under the combined group and individual system, greater attention was given to negotiating rather than cooperating with other members. Offers of information for sale declined, but negotiations on procedures for obtaining information increased.

In summary, few changes took place when an individual evaluation with private reports on results was replaced with a system where information was given to superiors and publicly posted. Cooperative acts were greater under a group system compared with an individual system. Under the combined group and individual system, increased attention was given to negotiating the procedures for obtaining or giving information but fewer offers were made for selling information.

Reward Systems and Specialization: Effects on Group Processes.
Thomas has explored the effects of individual and group evaluations under conditions of no specialization and a moderate degree of specialization in small groups.[25] Women telephone operators were formed into five-member groups and assigned a task of building miniature houses. One-half of the women were assigned the task of building a total house, and the other half specialized so that each of the five women performed one part of the building activity. Some of the women were evaluated on an individual basis and the rest on a group basis.

Productivity was substantially higher for groups that specialized. The rate was 42 percent higher under the individual system and 12 percent higher under the group system. The evaluation method increased productivity *only* in the nonspecialized groups. The group system resulted in 21 percent higher productivity compared with no difference in the specialized groups. In effect, the degree of specialization had a strong effect on productivity and the evaluation system a weak effect. The sense of responsibility was increased by the group system and by specialization, with specialization exerting the stronger influence. Few contrasts existed on other group measures: helpfulness, tension, and sense of anger were unaffected by the evaluation method, while the attraction to the group increased slightly under the group method.[26]

[25]Edwin J. Thomas, "Effects of Facilitative Role Interdependence on Group Functioning," *Human Relations*, 10 (1957), 347–66.

[26]Ibid., summarized from Tables 2–9, pp. 356–61.

Interaction of Evaluation System, Personality, and Competitively Based Standards. DeCharms designed a complex experiment to determine the influence of personality (as measured by affiliation), group and individual evaluation systems, and the effects of a peer ranking on productivity.[27] Males were divided up based upon their scores on their measure of affiliation. This personality characteristic provided a measure of desire to be accepted. One could be low or high in positively eliciting acceptance or low or high in actions that interfered with acceptance. The men were given an exercise to discuss undesirable traits in individuals. One-half of them publicly evaluated one another in terms of these traits and chose work partners, while the other half chose work partners without the public evaluation. In effect, this procedure operationalized competitively based standards for one set of groups on a dimension unrelated to the task and implicit, fixed standards for the other set. One-half the groups were then evaluated on the basis of their individual productivity scales and the other half based on group scores. All members worked on a simple arithmetic exercise. Table 10-3 summarizes the relationship of the three variables to the subjects' productivity in doing the problems.

TABLE 10-3[28]   Effects of Evaluation Method, Personality, and Peer Rating on Productivity

Rating Prior to Task		Evaluation Method	
	Personality- Affiliation	Individual	Group
	Negative		
Peer	High—	134	101
rating	Low—	115	110
(competitively			
based	Positive		
standards)	High+	126	102
	Low+	124	110
	Negative		
No	High—	126	88
rating	Low—	115	85
(implicit			
fixed	Positive		
standards)	High+	118	93
	Low+	121	77

[27]Richard DeCharms, "Affiliation, Motivation and Productivity in Small Groups," *Journal of Abnormal and Social Psychology*, 55 (1957), 222–26.

[28]Ibid., abstracted from Tables 1 and 2, p. 224. Copyright 1957 by the American Psychological Association. Reprinted by permission.

The individual evaluation system consistently contributed to a higher level of productivity than did the group evaluation. The peer rating also elicited higher productivity compared with where peers weren't evaluated. The nature of affliation didn't have a consistent effect on productivity. The highest productivity, however, was achieved by a combination of individual evaluation, peer rating (competitively based standards), and high negative affiliation; productivity was 57 percent lower under opposite conditions (group evaluation, no peer rating on traits, and low negative affiliation). The evaluation method had greatest impact, competitively based standards on an item unrelated to the task the second strongest effect, and nature of personality the least.

Summary. The laboratory studies contrasted the effects of group and individual evaluation systems, which are regarded as equivalent to group and individual reward systems. The studies show that group systems positively influence task orientation and productivity. A number of factors may overweigh the influence of the nature of evaluation used or may interact with the evaluation system in their impact on group processes and productivity. Where both standards and evaluation methods are changed together, individual systems focus group processes on task-directed activities to a greater degree than group systems. Competitive-based standards reduces communication on both task-directed and non-task-directed activities. Individual systems combined with fixed standards generate the most attention to task, communication, involvement, and focus on relevant factors in the problems.

Group evaluations combined with fixed standards exert the greatest effect on coordination; competitively based standards adversely affect these processes.

Individual evaluation combined with public posting of scores reduces intragroup cooperation compared with a group system. When individual and group evaluations are combined, greater attention is given to negotiating the terms of cooperation while actual cooperation declines. A group system when combined with low specialization creates higher productivity than a combined individual evaluation–low-specialized combination. The nature of evaluation has no effect under specialization except to increase sense of responsibility.

Evaluation systems also interact with personality and competitively based standards. The highest productivity is achieved by a combination of individual evaluation, competitive standards, and a personality type that aggressively seeks to be accepted.

In conclusion, individual and group evaluation systems influence group processes and productivity. Their influence may be overweighted by powerful variables such as standards and specialization or confounded by factors such as publicly reporting results and personality.

"Earn, Jim, earn! Earn, Jim, earn! Compromise; Free Enterprise and earn, Jim earn!"

PART 3

Institutional Reward System Versus Individual Rewards. Another dimension of reward systems is the effects that institutional systems (none or equal rewards) compared with individual reward systems have on behavior and productivity. Topen set up a simple design to determine the short-term effects on productivity of paying by straight piecework or on an hourly rate.[29] One set of subjects was given a low standard, and payment was fixed at $1.50 per hour. They were not required to work further but were required to stay for the complete hour. Those under the piecework system were implicitly given the standard of producing at the same pace as achieved on two trial periods and were paid a straight incentive based on $1.50 an hour. The different payment systems had substantial effects on production of the two groups, with those paid the hourly rate producing one-half the amount of those paid by piecework.

Dynamics of Institutional and Individual Rewards. Tseng explored the effects of two interrelated factors: (1) the absolute size of individual incentives

---

[29]J. T. Toppen, "Money Reinforcement and Human Operant (Work) Behavior: III. Piecework—Payment and Time—Payment Comparisons," *Perceptual and Motor Skills,* 21 (1965), 907–13.

and (2) the effects of providing a given incentive from one period to another.[30] His thesis was that when an individual is presented with an incentive, he considers both absolute size and its relative value, e.g., those incentives he has received in the past and those received by his peers. If the incentive given is larger than those he received in the past or greater than those given to his fellows, he will be satisfied and feel rewarded. If it is smaller, he will be dissatisfied and feel punished. Thus, in considering a reward, one uses a double frame of reference—one's past experience and the reward's relative position among those of one's fellows.

Tseng designed an experiment to study the effect of these factors on productivity of a small group, their quality of work, intragroup relationships, and the preferences for reward systems. Forty-eight children, ages eight to eleven, from a Chinese evening school in New York City were divided into four-member groups. The children were assigned a group project building a house with small bricks. Four children worked together with each being responsible for one side. However, they needed to cooperate on corners to erect the house.

Four different reward systems were used to reward the productivity of the children. One system was highly differentiated (with 150 pieces of candy going to the first child, 40 to the second, 9 to the third, and 1 to the fourth); the second method was less differentiated (100 to the first child, 60 to the second, 30 to the third, 10 to the fourth); the third method gave equal amounts to each child (50 pieces); the fourth system gave no rewards for performance (0 going to each child). After the first day's practice, each group worked for five days, and then the groups were rotated around the different reward systems.

Table 10-4 summarizes the level of productivity of each group during the first and second period. During the first period, the individual systems,

TABLE 10-4[31]   Average Scores Under Four Reward Systems For Two Work Periods

| | Reward Systems | | | | | |
| | Individual | | | Institutional | | |
Time Periods	Highly Unequal Rewards	Unequal Rewards	Percent Change	Equal Rewards	No Reward	Percent Change
First	196	194	−1%	179	176	−2%
Second	194	226	+14%	199	158	−21%
Percent change	−1%	+14%		+11%	−11%	

[30]Sing-Chu Tseng, "An Experimental Study of Three Types of Distribution of Reward Upon Work Efficiency and Group Dynamics," (Ph.D. diss., Teachers College, Columbia University, 1952).

[31]Ibid., abstracted from Table 4, p. 27.

whether highly unequal or moderately unequal, exerted the same influence over productivity; similarly, it made no difference on productivity whether equal or no rewards were distributed. However, the individual systems increased productivity 12 percent more than the institutional systems. During the second period, a substantial change in the effort of the members occurred under the different systems.

Under the highly unequal system, productivity remained the same; but where rewards were moderately unequal, a 14 percent improvement occurred; under equal rewards, productivity rose 11 percent; with no rewards, productivity *declined* 11 percent. In summary, the highly unequal system contributed to relatively high production with no change through time; the moderately unequal system started out relatively high and then increased further; the equal system started out moderately low but increased with time. The no-reward system resulted in moving from a moderately low base to an even lower base.

The effects of the reward system on the quality, group cooperation, and individual reactions are summarized in Table 10-5. There was some differ-

TABLE 10-5[32] Relation of Reward System to Measures of Work Quality and Group Relationships

	Reward Systems			
	Individual		Institutional	
	Highly Unequal (150 to 1)	Unequal (100 to 10)	Equal (50 each)	No Reward (0)
Quality Measures				
1. Mistakes in pattern	184	149	52	44
2. Neatness	14	28	43	35
3. Wall falling	16	12	4	3
Indices of Group Cooperation				
4. Gaps on corner	48	39	15	16
5. Superficially joined corners	9	8	3	3
6. Number of bricks put on others' side	15	19	44	49
7. "Cheating"	21	18	7	9
Individual Reactions				
8. Tension	Highest	High	Low	Low
9. Frustration	Highest	High	Moderate	Lowest
10. Systems preferred	16%	31%	48%	5%

[32]Ibid., abstracted from text and Table 12, p. 48.

ence between the highly unequal and relatively unequal systems, with the first resulting in more mistakes, less neatness, and more major accidents; where coordination was required, as in the construction of corners, there was less cooperation, greater tension, and more frustration.

The biggest differences, though, were between the individual and institutional systems. In nearly all categories, quality, group cooperation, and individual reactions, the individual systems were more dysfunctional. When the children were interviewed on the systems they preferred, 48 percent preferred the system where each received the same reward, 31 percent liked the moderately unequal system, and 16 percent preferred the highly unequal system, with only 5 percent choosing the no-reward system. Those who chose the highly unequal system were all first or second winners. But even here, only one-third of the second winners preferred highly unequal rewards.

Changing from One Payment System to Another. A couple of experimental studies show that the effects achieved under one payment system partly carry over to the succeeding method. Piecework stimulates greater productivity than daywork, but the norms developed under daywork restrict the level at which productivity stabilizes; further, while productivity falls when daywork replaces piecework, it doesn't fall to the same level as existed under a previous daywork plan.

One of the earliest and perhaps the best field experiments was undertaken in Great Britain.[33] Ten girls, fifteen to sixteen years old, were hired to perform a simple repetitive task. It involved (1) unwrapping taffy that had been improperly wrapped by machines, (2) wrapping the taffy, (3) packing the candy, (4) weighing and adjusting containers so that each weighed the same. A separate operation involved filling, weighing, and wrapping a four-pound can, weighing and adjusting the contents to proper weight, and then wrapping the tin with paper and labeling it. The length of operations varied considerably, with the average number of units output completed in the same time period for each step as follows:

Operations	Pieces Processed in Unit of Time
1. Unwrapping	40
2. Wrapping	20
3. Packing	12
4. Weighing	6
5. Packing, weighing, and wrapping	1

[33]S. Wyatt, L. Frost, and F. G. L. Stock, *Incentive in Repetitive Work: A Practical Experiment in a Factory*, Medical Research Board, Industrial Research Board Report no. 69 (London: Her Britannic Majesty's Stationery Office, 1934), pp. 1–54.

The work was done on a specialized basis with each girl doing only one step in the process. The girls were rotated to the next step each five days so they had the same experience on all operations. Three methods of payment were introduced in sequence: 1) a time rate for the first nine weeks, 2) a bonus system where individuals were ranked according to their productivity and given a small bonus for the fastest and zero for the slowest, 3) piecework for the last twelve weeks. The level of productivity compared with output of the first week is shown in Figure 10-1.

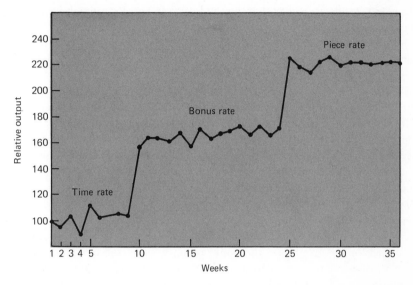

FIGURE 10-1[34] Effect of different systems of payment on rate of improvement

Since the girls were learning a new job, some increase could be expected during their early weeks. In fact, there was a 12 percent improvement under a day-wage method. The introduction of the bonus system resulted in a 46 percent increase in productivity. Since the bonus was paid on the basis of the girls' relative level of productivity, this method, in effect, ranked the workers and apparently resulted in the establishment of standards of the fastest worker. The introduction of piecework resulted in another 30 percent increase in productivity.

In a subsequent variation of the experiment, three different payment methods were used at the same time for a six-week period. The piecework was retained on wrapping and packing; the bonus system was introduced

[34]Ibid., p. 7.

again on weighing and wrapping; the time-rate system was reintroduced on the unwrapping operation.

No change in production occurred where the piecework was retained. However, the introduction of the bonus system again increased productivity nearly 10 percent on the weighing operation and nearly 15 percent on the weighing-wrapping step. In contrast, productivity on unwrapping where the time rate now was used dropped 25 percent. The movement from a bonus to piecework rate increased productivity by 30 percent; subsequently, the change from piecework to bonus rate on two steps of the operation resulted in a further 15 percent rise. This anomaly may be explained in terms of changing standards rather than method of payment. By ranking individuals, the pace of the fastest apparently is established as the standard; this is reinforced by the slight bonus. Thus, in moving from time rate to bonus rate to piece rate and back to bonus rate, standards increased with each change.[35]

Under time rate, standards evolve in the group, but the pressure within the group is to set low or moderate standards that all can readily achieve. The bonus system upsets this system by rank ordering individuals and paying the faster members more money. Under this system a new set of standards evolves but at a higher level than under a time system. When a piece system is then introduced, using the level of production achieved under bonus, the standard is again raised. The payment system further supports and reinforces the higher standard. Again, a stable pattern develops with standards accepted at a higher level. But again, with the introduction of a bonus system with its ranking of workers, the pace of the fastest worker becomes the standard for the group and the bonus reinforces the standard.

The movement from piecework back to time rate on the unwrapping operation resulted in 25 percent decrease of production. While this is a substantial drop, it would take a 110 percent decrease to return to the original productivity obtained under time rate in first eight weeks. The group standards dropped when piecework was abandoned but were still retained at a relatively high level.

Some behavioral factors associated with the three systems that affected productivity were systematically observed by the researchers. These are summarized in Table 10-6.

At times, the workers left the room to attend to their personal affairs. The least lost time occurred under a piece rate and the most under bonus. Three aspects of friction and conflict were observed. These were when a worker disturbed the others, when two or more workers exchanged words, or when workers complained about materials and conditions of work. Under

[35]Ibid., p. 24.

TABLE 10-6[36]   Effects of Reward System on Work Behavior

Work Behavior	Time Rate	Reward Systems Bonus Rate	Piece Rate
Relative degree of lost time	medium	highest	lowest
Average number of disturbances each week	20.1	16.6	11.3
Average number of quarrels each week	1.4	6.7	4.2
Average number of complaints each week	2.9	7.1	10.8
Relative amount of talking	1.0	.8	.7
Sense of fairness of system	lowest	medium	highest
Interest in work	lowest	medium	highest
Competition among members	lowest	highest	medium

the time-rate system, distracting forms of behavior were comparatively frequent, while quarrels and complaints were relatively infrequent. The workers talked freely and were inclined to be playful and frivolous; they were generally on friendly terms and there was a notable absence of friction. Instances of envy or jealousy because one worker happened to be doing more than another were rare, and whenever an argument or dispute arose it was usually about events outside the factory. There was little desire to do as much as possible; consequently, minor difficulties or interruptions that interferred with progress seldom gave rise to complaints.

After the introduction of the bonus method of payment, behavior changed and unpleasant incidents occurred fairly frequently. Some of the workers accused the others of being "mean" and "hurrying," and jealousy was shown whenever an unusually high level of output was attained. Abusive and insulting remarks were fairly common, and friendships were sometimes strained or broken. The slower and less capable workers were generally responsible for these incidents. On the whole, the workers were more irritable and sensitive to any factor, whether real or imagined, that was likely to impede output. During this period, the taffy was repeatedly said to be too big for the tins, string seemed to develop a tendency to break, and wrapping paper was blamed because it was thin and liable to tear. The material was exactly

[36]Ibid., p. 36.

the same as that used during the time-rate system, when such complaints were seldom heard. The bonus method of payment revealed unpleasant personal tendencies that had remained dormant under the time rate.

During the piece-rate period, most of the undesirable characteristics observed under the bonus scheme were continued, but they were less numerous and intense. The workers were still inclined to find fault with the material and the conditions of work, and anything that seemed to interfere with productive activity was resented. Outbursts of jealousy, spite, and abuse were, however, less conspicuous than under the bonus scheme. Talking was highest under time rate and lowest under piece rate. The time rate was regarded as unfair because the slacker received the same wage as the hard worker. Since there was no relation between earnings and output, it was considered foolish to work at a high rate. Interest in work was negligible, the day seemed long, and boredom was pronounced. Only in cases of natural incapacity or temporary indisposition was a time rate favored.

The bonus scheme, although regarded as a great improvement on the time rate, was disliked by some workers because it imposed an upper limit to earnings, and rewards were not proportional to individual output. At the same time, a competitive element was prominent and the workers showed a high interest in one another's performance. Time passed more quickly than under the time-rate system, and the work was less monotonous.

The flat piece rate made the strongest appeal to interest and activity, and it was generally felt to be fair because the reward was proportional to the work done. The operatives regarded each unit of output in terms of its equivalent pay, and thoughts were more often directed to work and its possibilities. The expenditure of energy was maintained, the mind was less absorbed with the unpleasant aspects of work, and boredom tended to be replaced by fatigue.

In summary, where the work pace was entirely under the control of the worker, the incentive method sharply affected both the productivity and behavior. The changes through time demonstrate some of the dynamic aspects of systems of payments. Moving from time rate to bonus, to piecework, and back to bonus resulted in sharp increases in productivity with each change. Further, while a move back to time rate from a piece rate resulted in a partial decline in output, the productivity still was high compared to the original base.

The workers got along better under the time-rate system but had the highest level of boredom. The bonus system increased productivity but created high stress among group members. Individual incentive systems obtained the highest productivity, the most job interest, moderately good group relations, but the most complaints about materials and working conditions. The high motivation of the workers caused them to be impatient with the system that caused any delays. The experiments provide strong support for the theory that the payment system along with associated standards constitutes a powerful influence over worker behavior.

Reward Systems, Work Flow, and Panic. Aside from the effects that incentive systems have on productivity, they may affect behavior patterns in a wide variety of contexts. Mintz theorized that the nonadaptive behavior of people in panic can be traced to the nature of the reward systems rather than to the personality characteristics of individuals or the emotional intensity of the situation.[37] His contention was that many situations provide an incentive to place one's own interest over the interests of others; when many people take this approach, as in a fire, the resulting behavior often harms everybody. He devised a number of experiments to test the degree to which the reward system or the emotionality of the setting affects the nature of the behavior patterns.

In one experiment, fifteen to twenty-one members in each group were given the task of pulling an object out of a glass bottle. Each was given a piece of string to which the object was attached in the bottle. The small opening required close coordination among the individuals if they were to avoid traffic jams at the bottle neck. A number of the groups operated under a reward system where they had a small monetary incentive of ten to twenty-five cents if they succeeded but were penalized one to ten cents if they failed to get their object out of the jar in the specified time. When the groups weren't given the opportunity to devise a plan for action, they failed to pull out the objects in the given period of time even though, in practice sessions prior to setting up the reward system, they had easily removed the objects in the time period. Even where the individuals had an opportunity to discuss and develop a plan, serious traffic jams still developed in the majority of the cases. Where no individual incentives were offered and the experiment was described as a cooperative exercise, serious traffic jams were avoided in most cases. Thus, where an interdependent work situation exists and close cooperation is required among individuals, their efforts are disrupted by an individual incentive system.

In summary, institutional reward systems when contrasted with individual systems provide consistent results. Individual systems generate higher productivity. Both the absolute size and relative size of individual incentives influence behavior. Partially differentiated rewards are more effective in increasing production than extreme differences in rewards allocated to relative performances. Equal rewards initially exert the same influence as no rewards, but production under equal rewards goes up in a second time period while no-reward conditions cause productivity to go down.

Changing from one reward system to another influences productivity.

[37]Alexander Mintz, "Non-adaptive Group Behavior," *Journal of Abnormal and Social Psychology*, 46 (1951), 150–59.

By moving from a straight hourly based method, to forced rating and individual bonus, to a piece rate causes productivity to rise with each change. Group processes are sharply affected by each method, with piece rate adversely affecting group relationships while eliciting highest sustained application. An hourly rate generates the most positive group processes but results in least application.

Incentive systems sharply affect cooperation patterns in large groups. Where close coordination is required, individual systems disrupt the group processes that support cooperation.

Reprinted courtesy Mell Lazarus and Publishers-Hall Syndicate, Copyright 1973, Field Enterprises.

PART 4

FIELD STUDIES

Numerous case studies and surveys of experiences with incentive plans have been done. There are, however, several problems with relying on case studies and surveys of management experiences. Typically, incentive systems are introduced along with other changes such as a systematic study of methods, setting of higher standards, or introduction of new tools, machinery, or other supportive equipment. The reports usually attribute improvements in behavior, efficiency, and productivity to the incentive system even though the associated changes could be made independently. Further, the comparison between daywork and piecework jobs is confounded by the selective process by which management decides which jobs will be placed on piecework. When an operation cannot be put on piecework due to irregular flow of work, faults in the materials that need special attention, or other limitations that reduce the productivity of the worker, the job is normally paid on time rate.

One of the problems of interpreting case studies is highlighted by a report by Wyatt, Langdon, and Marriott in 1938.[38] They studied six groups of men and eight groups of women in six firms. After the introduction of a new individual incentive system, output increased from 15 to 65 percent in the first nine months, with a leveling off in the output for the latter part of the period. However, coincident with the introduction of the incentive system, machines were speeded up, unproductive time was reduced, subsidiary operations were shifted to unskilled labor, daily sheets were posted on production, and those who didn't obtain the standard were circled with red marks, less efficient workers were removed, and management emphasized the importance of achieving higher level standards. Thus, the contribution of the incentive system apart from these other factors was undetermined.

One of the functions incentive systems serve is to elicit a variety of associated changes in management and employee practices. The studies are fairly consistent in their conclusion on the advantages and disadvantages that flow from individual and group incentive plans and the factors that contribute to success and failure.[39]

Individual incentive systems typically increase productivity and generate higher earnings with reduction or maintenance of unit costs. These results are achieved by increasing pressure for *both* management and employees to do a better job. Incentive systems stimulate the systematic study of factors affecting work flow and efficiency, contribute to establishment and acceptance of explicit standards, stimulate quick exposure of operating problems, and direct management's attention to them. An incentive system also provides a postively graded incentive that supplements the negative sanctions of discipline and discharge, permits greater flexibility in adjusting to changing conditions in the labor market and increased competition in the product market, and reduces the pressure to substitute capital for labor.

On the employee side, incentive systems encourage worker inventiveness and improvision to increase efficiency, stimulate increased application of employee effort, contribute to greater satisfaction, attraction, and retention of a harder working labor force, reduce the need for close supervision of operating personnel, reverse traditional relations and move initiative from management to operating personnel, and create an environment that is more consistent with the needs of employees.

Effects on Productivity, Earnings, and Costs.   Incentive plans contribute to higher level earnings without increases in per unit cost.

[38]Reported in Marriott, *Incentive Payment Systems,* p. 117.

[39]Several books have summarized some of the advantages that flow from incentive systems. A couple of the better reviews are Brown, *Piecework Abandoned;* Marriott, *Incentive Payment Systems;* and Wolf, *Wage Incentives as a Managerial Tool.* A good book of edited essays is Tom Lupton, ed., *Payment Systems* (Suffolk, England: Richard Clay, 1972).

Value of Incentives: A Skeptical View

One author takes a skeptical view of wage incentives, their appeal to workers, and the fairness of a system that doesn't reward employees in direct relation to savings that they generate. Although this is done, "tongue-in-cheek," it nicely illustrates a viewpoint that is probably broadly held.[40]

Incentives—'Jealousy and Friction'

An incentive is a carrot held before the donkey's nose. If you want the maximum number of bassoons to be made in your factory it is desirable to hold an adequate carrot before the noses of your employees.

It is becoming increasingly difficult to write about incentives. Before it was necessary to be a humane employer, one made no bones about it. If people didn't work hard enough, one just sacked them. But nowa-

---

[40]Nigel Balchin, *How to Run a Bassoon Factory,* (Boston: Houghton Mifflin Co., 1936), pp. 62–65. Copyright 1934 Nigel Balchin.

days, of course, we don't want to *sweat* anybody. We only offer incentives because people are really much *happier* if they work hard and of course, with business in the state it is, unless production cost is reasonably low . . .

You follow me? I think you do.

There are two main sorts of incentive—the sort where people get something nice if they work hard, and the sort where they get something nasty if they don't. In these enlightened days we only use the first sort. (Of course we still fire people who don't work hard enough but we don't usually consider that an incentive any more.)

Money

Don't, I implore you, run away with the idea that people will do anything for money. They won't. Only the other day I heard a very eminent person say (with some surprise) that he had discovered that men won't work themselves to death even to earn four pounds a week. On the other hand all the books on incentives agree (albeit with gentle regret) that if you want a man to work harder, the easiest way to get him to do it is to offer him more money. I'm afraid that fact—the appalling cupidity and lack of idealism of the working-class—is one of the cruel disillusionments you'll have to face. But I wouldn't *worry* about it. It's a pity people won't make more bassoons for you just for the love of it, but there it is. And a number of very snappy ways have been evolved by which you can make people *think* you are paying them more, while actually you are paying them less. Which serves them right for not being Idealists. Thus: supposing you decide to pay a man 2/- for each bassoon he makes. He makes twenty-five bassoons a week, so you pay him fifty shillings. Well, if you are a really progressive employer, you then go along to him and say, 'See here, Bill, fifty shillings a week isn't much.' And he says, 'That's so, boss.' So you say, 'Well, look here, Bill, I like you and I have your welfare at heart, so if you like to make thirty bassoons a week, instead of twenty-five, I'll pay you fifty-five shillings, and if you make forty, I'll even pay you three pounds.' And Bill, not being good at arithmetic, and thinking another five shillings would be nice, says, 'Well, that's very good of you, boss,' and works like blazes. And of course, he gets more money and you get the job done for one and six a bassoon instead of two shillings. That's what is called an Incentive. For donkey read Bill, for extra five shillings read carrot . . .

Surveys on experiences under incentive plans report a high level of effectiveness in terms of increased earnings of 20 to 25 percent above ordinary rates, sharp increase levels of performance, a tendency for accidents to decrease, quality to be maintained, and maintenance of the plant to be improved, and higher interest on the part of the workers. Others have reported reduction of absenteeism, increased employee morale, fewer grievances, better teamwork, better cost standards, and more efficient man-power utilization. These opinions reflect management convictions in a wide variety of countries.[41]

Statistical results gathered by governmental agencies reveal similar patterns.[42] Surveys in the United States, Australia, and Belgium report a wide range in increases in productivity and reduction of costs; one large survey in the United States showed production increases of nearly 39 percent, unit labor cost reductions almost 12 percent, and average take-home pay 18 percent higher. The survey by the National Labor Office in 1951 showed that earnings and ouput in the countries surveyed almost invariably increased. In Australia, on the average, workers earned 30 percent above their time rates in eighty-seven firms surveyed. In Belgium, a survey of twenty-four industries showed that increased earnings ranged from 10 to 40 percent under individual systems and from $1\frac{1}{2}$ percent to $27\frac{1}{2}$ percent for group systems.

One of the earliest studies of the effects of payment systems in industrial setting was made by a social scientist in Great Britain during the First World War.[43] The output of two groups of girls, with one group composed of seventeen members, the other three members, was recorded for one week under a time wage and the following week under a piece wage. Average increases were 24 and 28 percent on the day shift, 40 and 48 percent on the night shift.

The Hawthorne studies are perhaps the most well-known experiments dealing with effects of incentive systems and other factors on productivity. Elton Mayo and colleagues at Harvard carried out a series of investigations between 1927 and 1932 into the importance for work behavior and attitudes of a variety of physical, economic, and social variables.[44]

In stage 1, five women assembling telephone relays were transferred from the factory floor to a special test room. Their output of relays was recorded for over two years during which a large number of alterations were made in working conditions. These alterations included a less variable assembly task,

[41]Various reports are summarized in Marriott, *Incentive Payment Systems*, pp. 107–10.

[42]Ibid., pp. 110–13.

[43]Health of Munition Workers Committee, *Industrial Efficiency and Fatigue*, Ministry of Munitions, Intern Report (London: Her Britannic Majesty's Stationery Office, 1917), related in Marriott, *Incentive Payment Systems*, p. 116.

[44]Fritz J. Roethlisberger and William Dickson, *Management and the Worker* (Cambridge, Mass.: Harvard University Press, 1939). The reports have been broadly criticized. For a review of these charges and criticisms, see Delbert Miller and William Form, *Industrial Sociology* (New York: Harper, 1951), pp. 74–83. For a defense, see Henry L. Landsberger, *Hawthorne Revisited* (New York: Cornell, 1958).

shorter hours, rest pauses, freer and more friendly supervision, and a group incentive system. At the end of two years, the women's output had increased by about 30 percent.

In stage 2, the aim was to reproduce the testroom situation only in respect to the one factor of method of payment, using another group of operators. Since the method of payment was to be the only variation from the normal situation, any marked changes in output could be related to this factor. Five women were employed on the same type of task as assigned the women in stage 1. They were given a group incentive system where the earnings of each woman were based on the average output of the five. The women's output increased by 12.6 percent. When the experiment discontinued after nine weeks, the output of the five women dropped by 16 percent.[45]

Influence of Incentive Systems on Management. Wage incentives exert pressure on management to rationalize the work flow to minimize disruptions. The international labor office concluded that while the incentive provides a spur to the effort of the workers, it is an equal or greater spur to management to provide a well-organized human and technical organization. While the increases in output may be due, partly, to greater effort by the workers, they appear, mainly, to be due to "the improved organization of work and the elimination of lost time and other sources of inefficiency and waste" and because "both supervisors and workers are provided with a positive incentive to improve working methods and increase output."[47]

Where the work flow is poorly rationalized, there is a continual reordering of priorities. Instead of jobs being run to completion, the work flow is regularly disrupted by giving priority to "emergency" orders. Once a cycle is established of giving priority to special cases, these cases increase as deadlines are passed and schedules are deviated from. The employee on the wage incentive resists these disruptions since they sharply reduce his efficiency unless equivalent allowances are paid. In either case, management is under pressure to avoid the disruptions. The measurement of work, time study, arranging the work in logical sequence, and improving techniques reduce wasted time and enable the management to supervise more effectively.

A comprehensive set of studies in the boot and shoe industry illustrates the importance of management's role. Forty-three factories were studied where

---

[45]A third experiment was introduced to further test the effects of the incentive systems. While their conclusions were that incentive systems do not affect productivity and these conclusions have been broadly accepted, cogent criticism has highlighted that the results are of little scientific value.[46]

[46]Alex Carey, "The Hawthorne Studies: A Radical Criticism," *American Sociological Review*, 32 (1967), 403–10; A. J. M. Sykes, "Economic Interest and the Hawthorne Researcher," *Human Relations*, 18 (1965), 253–63.

[47]International Labour Office, *Payment by Results: Studies and Reports*, Report no. 27 (Geneva: International Labour Office, 1951), p. 150.

the productivity of dayworkers and pieceworkers on various operations was compared. Pieceworkers almost invariably had higher productivity than dayworkers and had lower labor costs per unit. The researchers concluded that the main reason for the low productivity of dayworkers was that their work was rarely as well organized as it was for pieceworkers.[48]

Systematic Study of Work Flow. While some incentive systems are established without systematic work study, this leads to many problems as employees improvise and sharply increase their earning potential or press management to make changes to eliminate delays or bottlenecks in work flow. Establishment of stable standards depends upon some degree of standardization of the work. While historical averages of productivity can be used as a standard, these may be as much as 30 to 200 percent below what could be achieved with changes in work flow and higher employee effort. Moreover, different jobs lend themselves to different degrees of improvement; thus the wage structure can quickly get out of line where historical patterns of productivity are used. For these reasons, the introduction of wage incentive is nearly always preceded by systematic work measurement.

Incentive systems encourage acceptance of performance standards where previously standards were undefined or only vaguely specified. Conflict typically centers on the level of the standards that are set but not the principle of whether they should be specified. Since incentive wages are based upon some base of a normal day's work, this standard must be made explicit. The standard may be loosely established by taking the average level of past production or more systematically by time study. In either case, explicit standards are set when incentive systems are introduced. In turn, these standards periodically are updated through time as the product is redesigned or as work conditions changes. This is in contrast to most hourly or salary payment systems where explicit standards could be set but typically aren't.

Attention Directed to Operating Problems. Incentive systems contribute to a common cause between employees and management to pinpoint and solve operating problems that affect efficiency. Many factors are outside the control of operators, such as availability of work tools and blueprints, efficient repair and maintenance of machines by service groups, and consistent quality of materials used. The operators typically must rely on supervisors or staff specialists to solve problems in these areas. Where an operator is on an hourly or salary system, he is less concerned than when his pay is directly affected. Employees exert pressure on management to solve the problems by drawing attention to them and by asking for allowances to compensate for reduced output where problems aren't solved. Management is pressed to provide more expeditors and service personnel to enable operating workers to be more efficient.

[48]Reported in Marriott, *Incentive Payment Systems,* p. 121.

Graded Set of Incentives Provided. Incentive systems provide a graded set of positive incentives that complement the negative sanctions of discipline and discharge. Increased rewards are directly related to greater application. This provides a broader range of incentives compared to straight wage or salary systems. Wage or salary increases are typically slower to be applied and are often unrelated to increased effort. There is greater reliance on the negative sanctions of discipline and discharge to motivate. The experience of Glacier Metal Company illustrates the point. When the company changed from a piecework to daywork system in a repair and special-order shop, the company had to rely to a greater degree upon penalties.[49] The change took place under good conditions. A proposal to drop the piecework system was initiated by management but discussed at length with employees, union representatives, and the workers; the agreement was then ratified by the workers. Management agreed to set day wages at the average level achieved under the incentive system (157 percent), and union representatives and workers agreed to maintain that level of production.

During and immediately after the change to the new system, production dropped sharply; the level of production recovered in part and stabilized at about 11 percent less than existed under incentives. There was also about 20 percent greater variability around the mean production rate under the new system. The experienced skilled workers generally maintained their pace after the change to daywork, while the unskilled tended to decrease their work pace, with some individuals' level falling sharply.

Both the union and the management took action to maintain the productivity level. They first had the superintendent and shop committee chairman talk with those whose production had fallen off. This had little effect so the union agreed to have the employees' supervisor and superintendent talk with the employees *without the union representative being present.* This was further strengthened two months later when the union issued a statement where they explicitly recognized that "in instance of continuing abnormal (low) productivity, management must have a right to take disciplinary action." In this way, the incentive to produce was gradually replaced by emphasizing penalties if workers didn't produce. With the cooperation of the union, the company experienced only about an 11 percent drop in productivity.

Adjustments to Changing Environment. Incentive systems provide greater flexibility in adjusting to labor and product market conditions. As competitive pressures increase, it is difficult to lower wage rates, particularly when they have been incorporated into union contracts. Under incentive systems, there are numerous ways that labor costs can be reduced. In estab-

---

[49]Elliot Jaques, A. K. Rice, and J. M. M. Hill, "The Social and Psychological Impact of a Change in Method of Wage Payment," *Human Relations*, 4 (1951), 315–40.

lishing or revising rates, the areas where judgment enters, such as giving allowances for downtime, providing time for setup, and evaluating the pace the employee is working when being timed, offer considerable discretion for tightening up standards. When skilled personnel can be easily hired, employees are likely to accept these adjustments even though they have to work harder for the same or less pay. It is also possible to move wages up when government controls restrict wage increases by the same methods. It is thus possible to attract or retain a higher skilled work force during periods of wage controls.

A study by Butler in Australia highlights the way in which an incentive system may result in a different type of employee being employed and retained. An incentive plan was introduced in a small textile mill to solve the problems of high labor turnover and low productivity. Despite various explanations and joint consultation, twelve of the fifty-eight workers refused to accept the system and were dismissed; a new group was hired. Production increased 63 percent from 1948 to 1954, without important changes in machinery or production methods. The supervisor reported that the mill could attract and hold a better class of labor of the type "who wished to work under incentives and who readily fit into the life of the mill."[50] A similar study was done by Wootton on 190 workers in a factory in Australia. The company was faced with a high turnover, with a small proportion of the labor force leaving at a fast enough rate to generate a 200 percent turnover figure per year. The introduction of an incentive system caused the rate to fall to 15 percent. Weekly output rose 5 percent the first year, 10 percent the second year, and 21 percent the third year.[51]

Effects On Employee Innovation and Self-Direction. Wage incentives also stimulate innovation. Operators typically can improve their efficiency in numerous ways, such as by eliminating unnecessary motions, redesigning steps in doing the work, inventing or improving jigs, clamps, and fixtures, using more efficient machine speed, tool feed, and cooperating with service personnel by performing routine servicing of machines. Wage incentives stimulate employees to make these innovations. This can also contribute to problems when management retimes the operation and establishes a higher standard to absorb the increased efficiency brought about by employee innovations. This is discussed at a later point.

Incentive systems reduce the need for close supervision and surveillance and place the burden of initiative, direction, and control upon the employee rather than the supervisor. The latter becomes more of a service agent and mediator among the worker, higher level management, and specialists and other groups in the work flow. The burden of responsibility for efficiency is

[50]Reported in Marriott, *Incentive Payment Systems*, pp. 117–18.
[51]Ibid., pp. 118–19.

shared between the workers and their supervision. Close surveillance isn't necessary and is less feasible. The employee must operate within the minimum requirements to keep his job, but there are wide variations in pace, effort throughout the day, balance between free time and working hard, and talking with fellow workers that may be taken. The employee both assumes responsibility for these factors and sharply resists efforts by the supervisor to direct his approach.

In summary, incentive systems typically increase productivity and higher earnings while reducing unit labor costs. These advantages are achieved by stimulating the employee directly and management indirectly to do a better job. These advantages are realized for many organizations, but for others the system deteriorates and costs gradually increase to the point where the organization isn't competitive.

Demoralization of Incentive Standards

The operation of wage incentives involves numerous problems. Many of these already had been identified in the nineteenth century.[52] The problems that are associated with incentive systems can be discussed under four headings:

1. Problems of setting standards
2. Difficulties of maintaining a balanced wage structure
3. Deterioration of quality, extravagant use of materials, and careless use of tools and machines
4. Inhibition on making technical changes

Setting Standards of Output. For each job, a standard and a piece rate normally is set by time study. The ideal is to set a standard and rate that are considered fair by employees and yet that are high enough to induce about

[52]David E. Schloss, *Methods of Industrial Renumeration*, 3rd ed. (Oxford: Williams and Norgate, 1898), pp. 6–86. There have been numerous restatements, illustrations, and amplification of these criticisms in the last seventy years. See W. D. Stearns, "Wage Payment Systems in Machine Shops," *Machinery*, 25 (August 1919), 1115–16; Charles B. Going, *Principles of Industrial Engineering* (New York: McGraw-Hill Book Co., 1911), pp. 120–25; W. D. Forbes, "Why Piece-Work Is Not Satisfactory," *American Machinist*, 52 (March 18, 1920), 612; Harrington Emerson, "My Objections to the Piece-Rate Method of Wage Payment," *Industrial Management*, 57 (June 1919), 470–72; National Industrial Conference Board, *Some Problems in Wage Incentive Administration and Wage Incentive Practices*, Studies in Personnel Policy, nos. 19 and 68 (New York: American Management Association, 1945); Donald Roy, "Quota Restriction and Goldbricking in a Machine Shop," *American Journal of Sociology*, 58 (1952), 427–42; Mangum, "Are Wage Incentives Becoming Obsolete?" pp. 73–91; Wolf, *Wage Incentives as a Management Tool;* Summer H. Slichter, James J. Healy, and E. Robert Livernash, *Impact of Collective Bargaining on Management* (Washington, D. C.: Brookings Institute, 1960); T. Lupton, *On the Shop Floor: Two Studies of Workshop Organization and Output* (Oxford: Pergamon Press, 1963); Brown, *Piecework Abandoned;* Pym, "Is There a Future for Wage Incentive Schemes?" pp. 379–97; Opsahl and Dunnette, "The Role of Financial Compensation in Industrial Motivation," pp. 94–118.

30 percent or higher productivity than would be achieved by the *average* worker who applied himself at a normal effort. There are several difficulties in achieving this end. Time study provides a degree of systematic consideration of relevant factors involved in setting the standard. However, the time study specialist must make several critical judgments in the process including: (1) What pace the worker being studied is working. If it isn't normal, what percentage below or above normal is he working? The judgment of the time specialist results in upward or downward adjustments in the standard. (2) The time specialist must judge the degree to which delays occur that are outside the workers' control so that allowances can be made. If fewer allowances are given than actually occur, the employee is assigned a high standard that makes it more difficult to earn extra wages. If the allowances for delays are greater than actually occur, the worker receives benefits without having to apply greater effort. (3) What is a fair standard? Employees and management have different perspectives on what a fair standard is.

There is plenty of room for reasonable men to disagree on these points, and typically the workers exert pressure for lower standards and higher rates and management for higher standards and lower rates. The result is a continuing strain and tension that often erupts into a conflict among employees and management, time specialists, and method engineering personnel.

Workers employ a number of techniques to obtain or retain low standards including deception, slowdowns, wildcat strikes and strikes at contract renewal time, overloading the grievance procedure, and output ceilings. Management counters these by restudying operations that are out of line, disciplining workers on a slowdown or wildcat strike, and refusing to move on grievances. When a job is being studied, workers typically try to hide shortcuts they have devised and to introduce unnecessary steps into the process or work slower than necessary. The workers often become skilled at deceiving time study personnel. However, where higher standards are set that workers feel are inequitable, workers may undertake a slowdown or wildcat strike, overload the grievance procedure—including pressing numerous cases to arbitration, or keep the issues alive until contract renewal and bargain for the items then. These are difficult tactics to counter since disciplinary measures often further contribute to conflict.

One of the most pervasive factors regulating production is the establishing of restrictions on output and minimum and maximum ceilings by the workers.[53] Management is usually more concerned with the norms that

---

[53]Studies that have identified restrictive practices of organized and unorganized workers are as follows: S. B. Mathewson, *Restriction of Output Among Unorganized Workers* (New York: Viking Press, 1931); Health of Munition Workers Committee, *Industrial Efficiency and Fatigue;* C. S. Myers, *Mind and Work* (London: University of London Press, 1920).

restrict production than those that maintain production levels. Any stable group tends to evolve a standard of appropriate production. Even though workers could produce substantially more, they restrict their effort to produce at some stable level. Restriction occurs both by organized and nonorganized employees; it is a defensive method designed to assure stability of employment, maintenance of wage rates, protection of slower workers, and to avoid the pressures of doing more work for the same pay. Methods of stabilizing production include building "banks" of inventory of completed items and turning these in for payment when production is below the norm of the job. The employee may work several hours intensively and then stop or slacken pace to a slower level to arrive at the established norm. Where the employee has both loose and tight standards, he may report more time spent on jobs with low standards and less on jobs with higher standards to protect the low-standard jobs from restudy and imposition of higher standards. By using such methods, workers try to maintain achievable standards and minimize management's restudying and setting of higher standards.

The dilemma that faces management is that rapid development in tools and methods, changes in design, and organization of work affect the amount that an individual working at a normal pace can produce. These changes may be initiated by management or technical experts or the employee. The result is that a substantially greater output can be obtained for the same level of work. If the individual is under a piece-rate system, earnings go up sharply, even though per unit costs are maintained or actually decline. If management adjusts its piece rate or standards each time these small changes occur, the employees become suspicious. However, if management does not, then the series of small changes over a period of time results in substantial earnings over the basic rate. When the operations are restudied and earnings are reduced sharply, the employees react in a predictable hostile, suspicious manner. Marriott observed some situations where over a period of years small changes in layout, tools, and other methods resulted in earnings rising 70 percent or more above the basic rate.[54]

If employees are represented by a union, they press for contractual provisions that restrict the conditions under which management can restudy the operations. These clauses usually prohibit restudy of operations unless there are changes in design or methods. This is unlikely to solve the conflict or restrict management discretion very much. If operations are reorganized each year when new models are introduced, the work may be retimed. In the old days, if earnings rose to what was considered to be too high, the rate was cut; today, it is done "scientifically" by altering the method or procedure.

[54]Marriott, *Incentive Payment Systems,* p. 143.

Problems of Maintaining the Wage Structure.   The effects of individual
or group incentives on intergroup relations have been explored in case studies. Sayles observed that several types of relations develop among groups
where traditional wage structures are substantially modified. Wage structure
in a plant is generally accepted where it reflects the relative skill and importance of the jobs in the production process. The differences among positions
are considered to be the proper order of things. Traditionally, high-seniority,
high-skilled personnel receive the highest per-hour wage and have the largest
take-home pay. Incentive systems, however, jeopardize this social system
by enabling less-skilled, lower-seniority personnel to earn more than the
higher-skilled personnel. Although those receiving the higher wages are
happy at this turn of events, all other workers tend to be unhappy. Relatively
speaking, the skilled personnel go down in status and feel both abused and
underpaid. Sharp conflict may arise among the workers and between skilled
workers and management. Both the union and management come under
pressure to redress the pay structure either by extending the incentive system,
transferring higher seniority employees to incentive jobs, or in other ways
redressing wages to bring back the relative wage structure.

Similarly, conflicts may develop among incentive groups. Where some
groups are operating with loose rates and others with tight rates, frictions
develop in respect to who is to be assigned to the jobs with looser rates. If a
group's earnings get out of line with other groups, this creates an intergroup
problem. Other groups are likely to be jealous of the higher earnings and to
fear that jobs in that area and other areas will be restudied and standards
generally tightened up. This is particularly true among departments on
different shifts, adjacent work units, or those that are particularly visible to
other groups.[55]

Another difficulty in arriving at a standard is the different perspectives
workers and management have on what is a "fair" standard. If the workers
are assigned a standard where past production levels are considered low, the
workers normally feel that the standard is unfair and improper. For example,
if a standard is set that in effect says workers have been working at a 60
percent level, workers are unlikely to readily accept the point of view of the
time specialist and management. Management, on the other hand, usually
considers a fair standard to be that established by the time specialist. Standards at less than the 100 percent level for a normal worker are likely to be
judged as promoting featherbedding, laziness, and lack of commitment on
the part of the workers.

A third problem in maintaining a balance in wage structure comes from

---

[55]Leonard R. Sayles, "The Impact of Incentives on Intergroup Work Relations—A Managerial and Union Problem," *Personnel*, 28 (1952), 483–90.

the different perspectives that management and employees have on the basis on which incentives should be paid. Management's point of view is that employees should receive higher wages when greater skill is developed and greater effort expended. The employees' perspective is that effort, skill, and *creative ingenuity* should be rewarded. During the normal course of working at his job, the employee may streamline the job to eliminate unnecessary motions, process the material in a different and more efficient manner, and invent various aids that substantially reduce time taken. Through his creative efforts, the employee may become substantially more efficient and make it possible to earn higher wages with the same level of effort. When these processes are restudied and higher standards established, the affected worker considers this unfair since his earnings drop unless a substantially greater effort is made. That is, management appropriates the savings developed by the employee's ingenuity. Management's point of view is that the new standards are fair since it isn't employee effort but changes in manufacturing methods that have resulted in the higher productivity.

Management's View on Encouraging Employee Innovation

Arthur Rath provides us the perspective of a top management's view of what is being paid for in an incentive system.[56]

Since the goal of good management is to do each job in the best way, there is every desire to take advantage of ideas of employees. At the same time, there should be no procedure of pay for work not done—which would be the case, for example, if an operator were to make some improvement on his own that would greatly step up his output. In such a case, consistent with the principle of changing standards when methods are changed, the standards should be changed. However, a good incentive system will include a well-operated award system, providing for prompt and liberal rewards to employees for all useable ideas. These can then be adopted as standard practice for all operations affected. Far from stifling individual initiative, a sound incentive system, especially encoupled with high-caliber supervision, can be made to stimulate a high order of individual ingenuity and initiative.

---

[56]Arthur A. Rath, "The Case for Individual Incentives: Management's Most Potent Motivational Tool," *Personnel Journal*, Part II, 39 (1960), 217.

A third difficulty arises where management innovates materials or processes that permit greater productivity with the same skill and effort. Management feels that it is justified in restudying the operations and eatablishing a higher standard. The employee's focus is more on the number of pieces he must produce for a given amount of pay, so he considers the higher standards as a "speedup." Management considers this simply as a move to bring standards in line with the effort-skill bargain that underlies the incentive system.

Deterioration of Quality and Uneconomical Use of Materials and Facilities. Incentive systems are often associated with a lower quality of the product, reduced care of tools and equipment, and unnecessary materials waste. Workers may increase their speed by paying less attention to the quality of their work. Equipment and tools may be used in a manner that shortens their lives, such as neglecting time-consuming but necessary maintenance. If the worker is paid a relatively high rate during downtime, he may be able to earn higher wages by running equipment at a faster pace than it was designed for. While this may increase the amount of downtime when machines or tools are being replaced or repaired, an employee may be able to earn higher total earnings by combining incentive earnings and downtime than if he worked a regular pace. Similarly, while management may wish to conserve materials, the incentive system may encourage the employee to make extravagant use of materials. He may be able to increase his pace by disregarding the amount of waste material that is generated.

Inhibiting Technical Change. Wage incentive systems inhibit capital investment and technical changes. The emphasis in wage incentives is to use labor more intensively and is an alternative to labor-saving capital investment. Further, capital investment and technical change are inhibited because of worker resistance to changes and management's reduced control of the labor force. Where capital investments are made, or technical changes initiated by management or its specialists, work processes are restudied, new standards set, and the amount that can be earned reduced where standards have become loose. Workers on operations using new methods often cannot initially produce at the previous rate. While interim standards and allowances are typically set so that familiarity and skill can be developed, the interim period is often characterized by suspicion, controlled pace, and jockeying around for a better position for the day when standards are finalized. Thus, capital investment and technical innovation are often associated with conflict; as a consequence, management becomes more cautious or may entirely abdicate its initiative in introducing new up-to-date equipment.

In summary, the laboratory and field experiments demonstrate that for individual rewards to stimulate individual effort to a 30 percent or higher increase in productivity is a reasonable possibility. The broad-scale testimony of practicing managers on the power they attribute to individual systems to motivate high-level performance is supported. While most of the laboratory studies have been done over a few days or a few weeks of time, a few have lasted several months and have supported the findings of the motivational influence of rewards indicated by shorter studies.

However, short-term advantages of incentive systems may be offset by longer term problems. The incentive system may gradually deteriorate in effectiveness. The problems of setting standards, maintaining a balanced wage structure, introducing up-to-date equipment and technical innovations, and maintenance of quality, material control, and proper use of tools and equipment may gradually get out of control. This often results in high costs and loss of a competitive position.

We have numerous case studies of incentive systems operating in a wide variety of contexts that encountered an extensive set of problems. Through time, the systems were undermined or demoralized where the result was low motivation, high cost, high conflict among individual workers and among groups, conflict among workers, specialists, and operating management, discouragement of investment, and serious loss of competitive position. There also are many studies of successful systems that have been maintained over a period of many years with employees, organized labor, and management enthusiastically supporting the continuance of the systems and attributing efficiency, good employee-union-company relations, and satisfaction on the part of all concerned to the incentive system.

It is apparent that a set of conditions creates an appropriate climate for the introduction, maintenance, and adaptation of incentive systems. What are these conditions that enable the resolution of the difficult problems of restudying methods, retiming and establishing new standards, and dealing with problems of a changing social order and that permit accomodations to the changed roles of specialists, management, and workers?

PART 5

CONDITIONS AFFECTING THE MAINTENANCE OF INCENTIVE SYSTEMS

The factors that affect the stability of incentive systems include the structural aspects of the work situation, variability of work conditions, and structural characteristics of the incentive system. These contribute to the maintenance or demoralization of a system and are outlined in Table 10-7.

TABLE 10-7. Factors Affecting Maintenance or Demoralization of Incentive Systems

Structural Aspects of the Work Situation	Maintaining a System	Demoralization Pressure on a System
Size of a group	Under 50 members in a group system	Over 50 members in a group system
Work flow	Independent work flow	Interdependent work flow
Degree skill/effort of worker affects his productivity	Worker can substantially influence productivity (i.e., increase it at least 20% or more by greater skill and higher effort)	Worker has little effect on productivity (i.e., has less than 20% impact); other factors such as nature of equipment, materials, or other groups' actions determine productivity
Ratio of overhead to total costs	High: over 50%	Low: less than 50%
Labor market conditions	Loose labor market: employees easy to hire	Tight labor market: employees difficult to hire and have good alternative opportunities

Variability of Work Conditions	Maintenance	Demoralization
Consistency of quality and materials, reliability of tools and machines	High degree of consistency in materials used in the work and highly reliable tools and machines	Varies broadly so that the worker's pace is affected substantially by factors outside his control
Batch size and length of production cycle	Large batches with associated long production cycle of 6 months or longer	Small batches with the associated short production cycles of less than 6 months
Stability of production methods and homogeneity of products produced	Stable methods and homogeneous products manufactured; changes occur in discrete steps after 6 months or more stability	Erratic or continuous small changes in production methods and production of multiproducts
Uniformity of work and degree performance can be objectively measured	Work is standardized and objective measures of performance on 80% or more of this work can be made	Work is nonstandardized and performance measures are difficult to obtain and are controversial

Characteristics of Incentive System	Maintenance	Demoralization
Complexity of system	Worker can compute earnings and can relate his effort to output	System is so complex that only staff personnel can compute the earnings

TABLE 10-7 (Cont.)

Characteristics of Incentive System	Maintenance	Demoralization
Immediacy of payment	Payment is closely related to work done: pay period no longer than biweekly	Payment for work done is delayed to a point where the relationship between work done and payment is unconnected
Consistency of incentives with relative importance of quality and quantity and economical use of materials	Incentives encourage quantity and quality in relation to their relative importance	Incentives are weighted so that they support an over-emphasis either on quality or quantity
Percentage of workers covered	High: 70–100% Low: 1–30%	Moderate: 31–69%
Suggestion system	A suggestion system that is well developed and administered rewards employee innovation	No suggestion system exists or it is poorly administered
Level of standards	Average worker should be able to exceed standards by 20 to 40% by applying himself at a greater but sustainable effort	Standards are either so low as to encourage soldering (can earn higher wages without effort regularly) or so high they discourage workers from trying to obtain incentive wages (can earn less than 20% by extra effort)
Level of base rate when not on incentive	Base rate of 90–100% paid when worker off of incentive	High base rate of 110% or above paid when worker isn't on incentive (e.g., before standards are initially set, downtime, etc.)
Quality control system	Quality standards are clearly specified and a regular check is made on quality of work done	Quality standards are diffuse and/or quality checks are infrequent

Structural Aspects

Structural aspects of the work situation include size of the work groups, the degree to which work flow is interdependent, the degree to which skill and effort exert a substantial influence on productivity, the ratio of overhead costs to direct labor costs, and the nature of the labor market.

Size of Group.   The size of the group, particularly with group incentives, determines, in part, the effectiveness of the system. Marriott reports that satisfaction with the group system decreases as the size of the group increases. He found out the productivity decreased when the group size was fifty or more but increased until that point. In this case, the size effect influences the majority of the group and its productivity. While the reward system also influences the productivity, it is apparently overwhelmed by the size effect. Probably some interaction between size and incentive system exists that needs to be explored.

Work Flow.   Similarly, the incentive system is easier to implement where little specialization exists among workers, i.e., where work flow isn't interdependent among members of a group and among groups. Where the work flow is interdependent, it is difficult to establish measures of quality at each step or to maintain a steady work rate. An interdependent work flow contributes to pressures and strains among the workers. An individual incentive system adds to those stresses. A group incentive system would be most compatible with an interdependent work flow. But again, the interaction between a work flow and group incentive system needs to be explored.

Relation of Skill and Effort to Output.   The relation of skill and effort to output is another element affecting the probable success of incentive systems. In some jobs, it is possible for the worker by greater effort and by developing a higher level of skill to substantially increase his output. Contrarily, he may be in a situation where his level of skill and his effort level may have little influence on productivity. Output may be more directly determined by variations in the quality of materials, inputs from other groups, quality of the machinery and tools with which he works, weather conditions, and many other factors. An incentive system has little influence over productivity if, in fact, the individual has little control over the factors that go into it. It is doubtful that an incentive system can be effective unless the employee can increase productivity by application of greater skill and effort by at least 20 percent. Where effort is rewarded with less, the worker is likely to be discouraged and not apply himself.

Ratio of Overhead to Total Costs.   Where overhead is a large percentage of total costs and direct labor is a low percentage, this structural feature contributes to maintenance of an incentive system. Where 80 percent or more of costs are due to overhead, for example, any increase in productivity of labor results in substantial reductions in per unit costs even where the employee receives total direct savings that flow from the incentive systems. An example illustrates the point. Assume that production is doubled under the incentive system.

Effects on Unit Labor Costs if Production is Doubled Under an Incentive System

	Before Incentive	After Incentive	Overhead Costs Before Incentive	After Incentive
Fixed cost per unit	$10.00	$5.00	$2.00	$1.00
Direct labor cost per unit	2.00	2.00	10.00	10.00
Total cost per unit	12.00	7.00	12.00	11.00

This example highlights the fact that if you start out with a high fixed cost per unit and double productivity, the per unit cost drops sharply. In contrast, if a low fixed cost exists with a high direct labor cost, increased productivity results in a small change in per unit costs. Management is in a better position to incur the costs of properly maintaining a system and to reward in direct relation to the increased productivity. If the employee doubles his production, it is possible to pay him double his wages, particularly in the high-overhead cost situation.

Labor Market Conditions.   The relative tightness of the labor market and the difficulty of obtaining the skilled and unskilled personnel affect the incentive system. The difficulty is that management often makes short-term adjustments to make the jobs more attractive in a tight labor market. Thus, earnings are permitted to creep up by delaying restudy of jobs when changes occur, and standards are set at a level where the employee can earn relatively high wages. These changes also occur when labor wages are frozen by government decree. The problem develops when the competitive conditions change and management attempts to reestablish a reasonable relationship between effort and earnings. The employees and union aren't willing to give up gains gradually won over a period of time; they reject the thesis that the only way in which increased competitive conditions can be met is through lower earnings on the part of the employees. In this way, major conflicts, tensions, and ultimately the incentive system itself come under attack. Contrarily, if labor is relatively easy to obtain, management is more willing to take the actions to maintain the system—restudying methods, reducing allowances, and in other ways balancing the earnings of the employees for a given amount of effort.

Variability of Work Conditions

The variability of work conditions include consistency and quality materials, reliability of machines and tools, size of orders or job lots, length of production cycle, stability of production methods, heterogeneity of product mix, and objectivity of the work measurement.

Quality of Materials and Equipment. The consistency and quality of materials and reliability of machines and tools determine, in part, the importance of the incentive system for productivity. Wide variation in the quality of raw materials or parts being used or unreliable machines and tools penalize the worker; these factors are outside of his control. The quality of materials must be consistent, or appropriate allowances must be made for low-quality, inadequate machines and tools. Unless a set of conditions exists whereby the employee's effort is the principal factor that influences the output, the motivational influence of incentives is reduced.

Length of Production Cycle. The size of the batch and the length of the production cycle are relevant factors affecting the maintenance of an incentive system. Batch size is relevant since large production runs reduce the percentage of time that is involved in setting up, learning a rhythm in a new job, establishing methods and standards, and working out a pace appropriate to the job. Small batches mean essentially a short production cycle. The workers are continually involved in switching jobs, making adjustments to new conditions, and reacting and evaluating the allowances on set-up time, other allowances, and adequacy of the standards. Small batches and short production cycles contribute to a high level of conflict between workers and management representatives. It is probable that a production cycle must last six months or longer without endemic conflict among those associated with the system.

Stability of Production Methods. The stability of production methods and homogeneity of products or services produced are important determinants of the stability of standards, work rhythms, and the capacity to develop a routine. The greater the changes in production methods and the more heterogeneous the products, the more complex the conditions that the union, the workers, and management face. If the system is relatively stable but changes occur in discrete steps with stability between changes, it is possible to establish a set of standards and methods that apply for the various periods of time. Where the products are heterogeneous or where there are continuous small changes in production methods, management must continually evaluate methods and standards, accepting the associated tension, conflict, and distrust that go with these reviews.

Objectivity of Work Measurement. The uniformity of work and degree performance can be objectively measured also affects the stability of an incentive system. If work is standardized and objective measures of performance level can be made, issues are less likely to develop between management and union. Probably, if 80 percent of the work is standardized and objective measures of the work can be obtained, conflict is minimized. Where the work isn't standardized and performance measures are controversial, continuing issues arise on the proper level of standards and whether adequate allowances are allowed.

Characteristics of the Incentive System

Some of the characteristics of the incentive system that influence its stability and effectiveness include the complexity of the incentive system, the immediacy of payment for work done, the degree to which incentives are consistent with the relative importance of outputs (quantity and quality of the product manufactured, economical use of materials, and importance of minimizing scrap), the presence of a sound suggestion system, the percentage of workers covered, the level of standards, the level of the base rate for those not on incentives, and the quality control system.

Complexity of the Incentive System. The complexity of the incentive system and how soon payment is made for work done are important dimensions affecting the viability of an incentive system. The more difficulty the employee has in computing his earnings or relating his effort to earnings, the less likely he will be to accept the system as being fair. Similarly, if delays occur between the time that he has worked and the time payments are received—and the two are not traceable to each other—it undermines the confidence in the incentive system and its motivational effects. The payment for work done should be included in a weekly or biweekly check the employee receives in order to maximize motivational influence. The design of the system should permit the employee to understand the way in which the earnings are computed.

Consistency of Incentives with Ends. Incentives should be consistent with the relative importance of quality and quantity. The incentive system may be designed to encourage the employee to produce a larger quantity without a consideration of the effects upon quality or vice versa. If only the quality produced is rewarded and management relies on some form of check to govern quantity, then the control system and incentive system exert pressures in the opposite directions. The incentive system would contribute to continuing stress between the management and the workers. A properly designed system weighs the relative importance of quality and quantity; the system is designed to motivate the employees to concern themselves with both. Thus deviations in quality result in declines in earnings as well as lack of commitment to produce a larger amount.

Similarly, if management wishes to encourage economical use of materials and minimize scrap, the incentive system should be designed so that the employee profits by attention to these factors. The incentive may be designed so that those who maximize the use of materials receive a bonus or those who use a disproportionate amount of materials and create an unacceptable level of scrap are penalized. In any case, to the extent that these factors are important, they should be included as part of the design of the system weighing the basis for earning greater pay.

Suggestion System. A suggestion system is an essential complement to an incentive system. The suggestion plan recognizes the employee's creativity, and the incentive plan is designed to reward his effort and skill. One of the perennial problems of an incentive system is who is to profit by the shortcuts and other innovations developed by the employees. The incentive system stimulates the employee to apply himself to generate ways of improving his efficiency. If management has the job restudied after the innovations are developed and appropriates the saving to the company by raising standards, it *discourages* initiative. If the job isn't restudied, then it is possible for the worker to earn high wages with only partial effort. This creates a couple of problems that undermine the stability of the incentive system. The wage structure rapidly becomes out of line, and the other employees exert pressure to have their standards reduced, allowances increased, or in other ways to redress the wage structure so that the relative earnings are maintained. If the jobs aren't restudied and high wages through low effort are possible, this becomes a divisive factor among the workers. They seek to obtain the better assignments by winning favor with their supervisors or, if they are senior employees, to be transferred to the higher paying jobs.

One method of partially solving this problem is to have a well-designed and well-administered suggestion system. In this manner, the employee wins recognition and a one-time payment for his innovative ideas. It is possible to pay a large bonus to employees where their innovations apply to other, similar jobs.

Percentage of Workers Covered. The percentage of workers covered is an important dimension of the system. Where 80 to 100 percent of the workers are on an incentive system, it minimizes problems of coercive comparison of those earning incentive-level earnings and those on a straight hourly or day rate. Otherwise, there is continued pressure to expand the percentage covered. The relation between service personnel and incentive workers is particularly difficult. When the former are not covered, stresses are built into the system. The group of workers under incentives commits itself at a high level but is served by another group of workers that has a lower level of commitment. Similarly, if unskilled workers are covered in an incentive system that enables them to earn relatively high wages and skilled workers are not covered, this creates a form of coercive comparison that upsets traditional relationships and contributes to grievances on the part of skilled personnel.

The specific percentage of workers that needs to be covered to minimize the problems isn't clear. There probably is a changing relationship, with the greatest problems being caused when around 60 percent of the workers are covered and the rest are not. The problems are not so great when either a small or large percentage is on incentive. If the incentive system is concentrated on one group of workers, such as those on assembly line, the absolute percentage probably is less important than when different groups scattered throughout the organization are on different methods of payment. In the case of moderate percentage, such as where 30 to 60 percent are covered or when the groups are widely scattered, ample opportunity exists for the coercive comparison to develop among and within the groups in the organization. Where only a small percentage is covered or the bulk of the workers are covered, it is easier to rationalize the wage differentials.

Level of Standards.   The standards should be at a level that encourages the worker to improve and apply himself. This means that standards should be set at a level at which the normal worker, by applying himself, can achieve 20 to 40 percent higher wages. Standards should not be so low that the worker can obtain higher wages. This encourages workers to set restrictions on their productivity; limits are set that are sharply below their potential and that encourage workers to soldier on the job. This creates an imbalanced wage structure, which contributes toward the problems of coercive comparison among individuals and groups. Contrarily, if standards are excessively high, employees are discouraged from trying to earn incentive wages. In this case, the thrust of the employees is focused on management to move off of the standards, increase allowances, or otherwise provide a base for higher level earnings. Productive effort is discouraged rather than encouraged.

The Level of Base Rate When Employee Is Not on Incentive.   The base rate that is set for downtime and other nonincentive periods also affects the operation of an incentive plan. Downtime, which is when machines are being fixed or when an individual is on a nonincentive job, is a period when the worker is off incentive and is paid a guaranteed rate. If the base rate is relatively high, such as 100 percent (where a normal incentive earning would be 130 percent), it may be possible for the employee to earn greater wages by increasing downtime. If he works at a high level under incentive part of the time but is off of incentive and drawing base rates for the rest of the time, he may be able to take home greater paychecks than if he worked hard all the time on the incentive system. The level of base rate should discourage the employee from seeking greater downtime where he is under a non-incentive base.

Quality Control System. A well-designed quality control system contributes to the maintenance of an incentive system. If quality standards are clearly stated and a regular check is made upon the quality of work done, this counters the tendency to achieve greater production by paying less attention to quality. If quality standards are diffuse, if infrequent quality checks are made, or if the system doesn't enable accountability to be fixed, a logical consequence is for quality to deteriorate.

SUMMARY

The laboratory studies that compare group and individual reward systems find inconsistent effects on behavior and productivity. The level and nature of standards and degree of specialization confound tracing out the relationship. When institutional and individual systems are compared, piecework systems consistently increase productivity but adversely affect group processes. Moving from institutional systems to individual systems increases sustained application and productivity; moving from piecework to institutional systems causes some decline in productivity but the level of productivity is sustained at a higher level than develops when only an institutional system is used.

The field studies reveal that numerous advantages are associated with some piecework systems, while other systems incur costs that undermine their effectiveness. Where a system is operating well, productivity is increased and earnings are higher while unit labor costs are lower. Both management and employees operate at a more efficient level in dealing with problems. More rapid adjustments are made to changing conditions in product and labor markets. Other advantages are that employee innovativeness is encouraged, greater effort is applied, greater satisfaction is obtained, and a more work-oriented work force is attracted. Management, unions, and employees are happy and support a smoothly functioning incentive system.

A number of problems must be resolved if an incentive system is to be maintained. These include the issues of setting standards, maintaining a balanced wage structure, introducing technical change, maintenance of quality, economical use of materials, and careful use of tools and equipment. Many organizations fail to solve these problems with results that the advantages fade away and are replaced with disadvantages: productivity declines, unit labor costs rise, and union and management confront each other over pervasive problems associated with the piecework system. Management becomes locked into arrangements where it cannot adjust to changing conditions. Employee and management innovativeness is discouraged, and the parties become disillusioned with the incentive system.

Some conditions support an incentive system and other conditions undermine its operation. Several structural aspects of the work situation that exert strains on the functioning of incentives are where the systems are applied in large groups and where work flow is interdependent; when factors outside worker control principally determine production rate; when total costs are made up of low overhead and high direct labor costs; and when tight labor markets exists. These create problems or pressure to make short-run adjustments that have long-term adverse consequences.

High variability of work conditions also adversely affects the functioning of an incentive system. Low consistency in quality of materials, equipment, and tools makes it difficult for the worker to control his production rate; small batches reduce the length of the production cycle and increase the associated problems of setting up, developing rhythm, and adjusting to changing standards. Changing production methods and heterogeneous items produced adversely affect worker rhythm, acceptance of standards, and stability of the group. Any factor that interferes with the degree to which standards can be objectively set increases controversy and conflict. This set of work conditions determines that a high rate of problems will flow regularly from the work situation and adversely influence relationships among the parties.

The characteristics of an incentive system also determine its maintenance. A highly complex system where the worker cannot relate his efforts to earnings undermines motivational effects; where payment is delayed so that the connection between work done and earnings is unclear, the value of incentives is reduced; where incentives are applied that are inconsistent with desired goals—whether the goals are high quality, economical use of materials, or other ends—the system's pressure is in a different direction than sought by management; where groups of workers aren't covered by incentive systems, they feel discriminated against and press for costly adjustments; where a suggestion system isn't designed and administered to complement the incentive system, conflicts over updating standards are a pervasive part of the system; where standards are low, soldiering is encouraged, while standards beyond the attainment of the average worker contribute to withdrawal, absenteeism and turnover, and reduced commitment.

Similarly, relatively low or high base rates paid to workers *not* on incentive either increase discontent with the system or discourage application of effort. Failure to specify quality standards or other standards for important features of output—and failure to institute a procedure for evaluating the degree to which standards are met—causes the system to motivate in directions inconsistent with the goals of the organization. These features of incentive systems undermine the systems' functioning and maintenance. A system still may function effectively with many of these conditions, but it requires a higher level of competence on the part of management, union representatives, and employees to make the system work.

SECTION IV

DISCUSSION QUESTIONS

A.   *Standards*
1.   Distinguish between direction, intensity, and duration of effort and provide an illustration of each.
2.   In what sense are formal standards "low" or "high"? How would standards be evaluated as "low" or "high" by a management and the employees where the bases used are: (a) Past performance of the group, (b) Performance levels of similar groups, (c) Time study, (d) Self-set standards?
3.   What level above present performance would you set standards to motivate greatest improvement? At what point would you increase these to induce even higher levels of performance?
     Does the base (referred to in question 2) used to set standards affect the practical problems of raising them further when and if performance increases?
4.   Provide examples of single standards; of multiple standards. What are the performance implications of setting formal standards on some aspects of performance and not establishing them on others?
5.   Develop what influence, if any, the following aspects of formal standards have on the *direction, intensity,* and *duration* of effort.
     a.   Level at which standards are set
     b.   Whether single or multiple standards are set
     c.   The base used to justify the standards
          1.   Past performance levels of the group
          2.   Performance levels of other groups
          3.   Time study
6.   To what extent are the effects of formal standards dependent upon feedback on how well one is doing in the short run? In the longer run?
     At what point in relation to formal standards does the sharpest rise in performance develop? What does this imply about the necessity to provide feedback on how performance is measuring up to formal standards?
7.   In what way are formal standards conceptually different from internalized standards? What relationship between these two contribute to stable performance levels?
8.   Provide examples in the classroom, sports, or your work place of each of the following relationships:

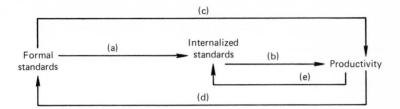

a. Formal standards eliciting higher internalized standards; lower internalized standards.
b. Level of internalized standards increasing productivity; decreasing productivity.
c. Level of formal standards influencing productivity directly without affecting internalized standards.
d. Level of productivity resulting in formal standards being increased; being decreased.
e. Level of productivity causing internalized standards to rise; to fall.

9. You have been brought in as consultant to advise the management of a small plastics plant on the establishment of a set of standards for production employees. The industry is competitive where both quality and costs are important. Manufacturers are in "similar" position and competitive position is determined by the relative efficiency of the organization.

The production department is made of five groups of employees, 15 to 20 employees each, and a maintenance unit of 12 employees. They vary in the stability of production rates, efficiency, and the quality of product. Each of the units produces a complete item.

Recommend to management a set of standards that would provide appropriate direction, intensity, and continuity of effort on the part of the production and maintenance employees.

10. The *Wall Street Journal* (10/24/74) described the "woes" a construction company encountered in building a planned community of 516 houses on Staten Island, New York. The company's operations were based in Southern California; it had planned to expand by undertaking large scale developments on Long Island, Chicago, and Washington, D.C. along with the project on Staten Island.

While the houses were moderately expensive—ranging from $41,000 for a duplex to $73,000—they offered a number of attractive features: A modern style imported from Southern California with natural siding, cathedral ceilings, large glass areas and amenities, community clubhouse, tennis courts, parks, and other facilities that would be supported by a small membership fee of all residents. They also were offered liberal terms that required only 5% to 10% down with 30 year mortgages.

The firm encountered numerous problems in building the community, including:

—Severe weather conditions required storm windows to cover the wide expanse of glass. These costs added another $1000—much to the chagrin of residents.

—The furnaces were undersized for the nature of the houses and the weather.

—New York had an interest rate ceiling of $8\frac{1}{2}\%$. When prime interest rates rose to 12% and mortgages to $10\frac{1}{2}\%$ the firm lost $8,000 for each $50,000 mortgage it financed.

—Features that residents paid extra for weren't delivered in many cases. For example, some who paid an extra $400 to obtain $3\frac{1}{2}''$ insulation received regular $2\frac{1}{4}''$ insulation instead.

—Subcontractors didn't perform as specified, and cut corners; for example, door and window casings were improperly installed, fireplace facings were poorly supported; one knowledgeable resident compiled a list of 81 defects on his house due to faulty workmanship and material, or failure to install agreed-upon features.

—High rate of vandalism and stealing occurred, including ripping siding off houses.

—A subcontractor was spotted by a resident hauling away appliances from the firm's warehouse. When he reported the apparent theft to a local official of the firm, he was told to "mind his own business."

—A windstorm blew many of the frames down on one section of houses that were started, delaying schedules and increasing costs.

—The firm was charged by subcontractors for work not done, or not done up to standards. It lost substantial money bringing the houses up to agreed specifications, or in refunding money to residents for services paid for but not received.

As further background, it is a common practice for a contractor to assume responsibility for the entire house, but most work is done by subcontractors—plumbers, electricians, cement workers, bricklayers, painters, etc.

These operations must be sequenced and scheduled carefully or costly delays occur. It is also costly to go back and fix any inadequacies whether in the structure, wiring, plumbing, or any other feature once the house is largely built.

Any subcontractor who isn't paid may place a lien against the house and a clear title isn't possible until the lien is paid. Construction financing is usually 2 to 5% higher than long-term mortgages.

Building trades are strongly unionized and any craft may be able to shut down the entire project.

The builder is considering closing down the project after completing 144 of the 516 houses in the Staten Island development and abandoning plans for other developments outside Southern California. If he follows through on this he faces a $10,000,000 lawsuit by the unhappy homeowners from Staten Island for failure to complete the development.

You have been brought in as a consultant to advise this builder on how he could restructure the organization to better deal with these problems. If he were to continue with his projects, analyze for him the nature of the situation as it existed in Southern California and as it exists now that he has expanded. Consider how his situation has changed (particularly with respect to the primary variables). Given these factors, advise him on what formal authority system and control system he should establish. Deal with at least the following points:

—Assume the headquarters is in San Diego and is considering setting up both specialist departments in San Diego and regional departments for the four areas.

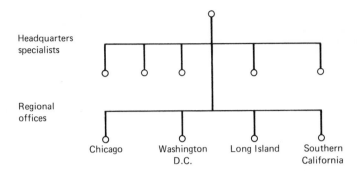

a. What specialists, if any, do you plan on locating in San Diego?

b. Do you plan on having a high degree of centralization at headquarters level, or decentralization to the regional departments? How do you obtain this degree of centralization or decentralization?

—Do you wish to have a high degree of centralization or decentralization in the regional divisions? How do you obtain this?

—Where do want the operating decisions to be made—at the headquarters, regional offices, or by supervision and craftsman on the building sites? Does this vary by specialized area? Where do you need coordination? Are these features consistent with your design?

c. What formal control system do you want to establish at the divisional level? At the operating level? Be specific on how you would formulate the standards, if any, in terms of their level, base you could use, single or multiple criteria, and changes through time.

—What form of reward system would you establish at the regional level?

—At the operating level for your supervision? At the operating level for the craftsman? (Note: Are your actions restricted in this respect?)

Summarize how your formal authority and control systems are appropriate, given the conditions facing the firm, and could contribute to solving of the firm's problems.

B. *Departmentation*

1. Define the difference between autonomous and interdependent departmentation and provide examples of each.

2. Develop the advantages of autonomous departmentation. Develop the disadvantages of interdependent departmentation.

3. Develop what implications, if any, each of the following factors has for the choice of functional vs. product departmentation. Refer to research studies that support your positions.

a. Provide greater emphasis on a long-term management perspective; support on longer perspective in dealing with operating problems

b. Develop broad-scale management talent for higher level positions

c. Contribute to greater interaction and coordination among diverse specialists

d. Contribute to greater control of specialists in their contact and dealings with outside individuals/groups

   e.   Reduce the conflict among service groups and units relying upon the service such as maintenance and production

   f.   Increase satisfaction in their work, with their peers and the organization

   g.   Support the stability and cohesion among members in the department

4.   A dean of a business school has asked you to advise him on the best way to departmentalize the college. He has mathematicians, statisticians, psychologists, sociologists, lawyers, and economists on his staff. He also has finance, marketing organization, production, and accounting specialists with a broad variety of backgrounds. He wishes to achieve several goals:

—Similar specialists to interact with each other to a high degree to support each other

—Diverse specialists to help each other and bring the perspective of their different disciplines to bear in the applied areas so that interdisciplinary work in teaching and research could develop

   a.   Suppose you gave priority to the second goal, how would you organize the personnel? What problems would the dean have to consider in appointing a department head? If he asked for a recommendation from the faculty, do you predict they could achieve consensus on an individual within or outside the department?

   b.   What do you predict in terms of intragroup and intergroup tension and conflict?

C.   *Reward Systems*

1.   Define an institutional reward system; develop how it differs from a group reward system; illustrate each.

2.   The usefulness of individual incentive plans has been challenged on several grounds. Summarize the Maslow-Herzberg thesis. What conclusion does this approach logically lead to if you are designing a system to induce higher performance?

3.   A problem in research design is to isolate the effects of one variable. In the following examples indicate whether standards, rewards, or both are being changed. One set of groups is operating under individual incentives, another set is under group incentives, and a third is under hourly wages.

   a.   The base used to determine changes in productivity for the three sets of groups are average productivity for the last six months. This provides data for total pay for these on incentive.

   b.   The base is the same as above except that those under individual and group incentives are asked to improve productivity during the next period by 10%; those under hourly pay are asked to do their best.

   c.   Level of rewards of those under individual incentives is based upon their comparative performance in their group; those under group incentives are rewarded on the basis of relative performance among groups; those under hourly wages are given a set amount per hour, but are requested to do their best.

4.   In reviewing and comparing the results of studies on reward system, what relevance, if any, do the size of the groups, interdependence of work flow, nature of standards, and past relationships of members have for the reliability of the generalizations?

5.   A number of laboratory studies have focused upon the impact that individual

and group incentives have upon group processes and performance. Compare the findings of Deutsch, Hammond and Goldman, and Zander and Wolfe.

6. Other variables may mediate the influence of a reward system on group processes and performance. What, if any, interaction do the research studies demonstrate between the following:

Reward system and specialization?

Reward system and personality?

Reward system, personality, and peer ranking?

7. What is the distinction between the *absolute* level of hourly payment or incentive rate and the *relative* level of payment?

8. If you were relying upon the results of Tseng's study to design a reward system to induce the best combination of high productivity, quality, cooperation, and minimize tension, what combination of features would you choose?

9. What would explain increasing levels of productivity as a reward system changed from time rate, to bonus system given for relatively high performance, to a piecework system? What happens to group processes? Can you speculate on why these processes develop?

10. What are some changes that the introduction of incentive systems induce in management practice and organizational design that improve the functioning of the organization?

11. Discuss the problems of setting standards, maintaining a balanced wage structure, making technical changes, maintaining quality, and using tools and machines responsibly under individual incentive systems.

12. Why can't men of good will work out these problems and retain the advantage of individual incentive systems?

13. Develop the importance of the following factors in deciding whether to establish or try to maintain an individual incentive system:

a. Size of group

b. Degree of interdependence of work flow

c. Degree worker skill and effort can influence productivity

d. Ratio of overhead to total costs

e. Looseness of labor market conditions

f. Variability of work conditions

g. Ease of understanding the system

h. Consistency of incentives with the relative importance of standards on quality and efficiency

i. Percentage of workers covered

j. Presence of a suggestion system

k. Level of standards

l. Level of base rate when not on incentive

m. Nature of quality control system

14. Which of the above factors would you speculate to be of prime importance, which of moderate importance and which of least importance in deciding whether to set up an individual incentive system?

15. You are brought in as a consultant to advise management on the appropriate form of structure to use. They want you to consider *only* the following conditions in your analysis.

a. A high degree of specialization exists among plants (i.e. the parts/components plants produce parts for each other and for final assembly plants).
b. The plants are physically dispersed into several parts of the country.
c. The company produces a single product (electronic calculators) but with many variations. Both the manufacture and assembly are relatively simple.
d. The company is moderately large with 10,000 employees, but the plants are relatively small—200–600 employees each.
e. They wish to emphasize a high quality of a standardized product and high efficiency/low costs to meet intense competition.

Develop for them:

1. The form of departmentation to use at the first level.
2. The degree of delegation down to the first level and within the departments down to plant level.
3. The nature of the standards to establish for departmental and plant managers.

Explain why this combination of factors will result in the desired balance of quality and efficiency.

V

LEADERSHIP STYLE

11

LEADERSHIP THEORY:
The Major Approaches

The extensive body of literature on leadership has been reviewed and summarized back to 1900 by several persons.[1] Several major themes characterize the leadership literature. "The Great Man" theme develops the personal traits that are associated with the exercise of leadership. A second theme explores the functions or activities that a leader undertakes in the

[1]Some of the authors who have reviewed the literature are H. L. Smith and L. M. Krueger, "A Brief Summary of Literature on Leadership," *Bulletin of the School of Education,* 9, no. 4 (1933), pp. 1–13; W. O. Jenkins, "A Review of Leadership Studies with Particular Reference to Military Problems," *Psychological Bulletin,* 44 (1947), 54–79; R. M. Stogdill, "Personal Factors Associated With Leadership: A Survey of the Literature," *Journal of Psychology,* 25 (1948), 35–71; C. A. Gibb, "Leadership," in G. Lindzey, ed., *The Handbook of Social Psychology,* 2 (Cambridge, Mass.: Addison-Wesley Publishing Co., 1954),877–920; C. A. Gibb, "Leadership," in G. Lindzey and Elliot Aronson, eds., *The Handbook of Social Psychology,* 2nd ed., 4 (Reading, Mass.: Addison-Wesley Publishing Co., 1969), 205–82; R. D. Mann, "A Review of the Relationships Between Personality and Performance in Small Groups," *Psychological Bulletin,* 56 (1959), 241–70; Robert Dubin, "Supervision and Productivity: Empirical Findings and Theoretical Considerations," in Robert Dubin et al, eds., *Leadership and Productivity* (San Francisco: Chandler Publishing Co., 1965), pp. 1–50; A. P. Hare, *Handbook of Small Group Research* (Glencoe, Ill.: Free Press, 1960), pp. 291–321; D. A. Erickson, "The School Administrator," *Review of Educational Research,* 37 (1967), 417–432.

process of exercising influence. A third theme develops the consequences of a particular leadership style in different contexts—or, more specifically, the interaction between leadership style and context. We will briefly summarize these approaches, indicate their present status, and compare the approach taken in this book with previous efforts.

Personal Traits of Leaders. The personal traits approach has broad intuitive appeal among both laymen and professionals. It seems eminently sensible that particular traits would permit an individual to lead effectively. This orientation occupied the interest of most researchers up to about the Second World War. This literature has been well surveyed by Smith, Stogdill, and Mann.[2]

Unfortunately, different studies using the trait approach have arrived at contradictory findings. Further, the summaries and critical reviews of the personality traits of leaders have emphasized the low relationship between selected traits and leadership. Each of these reviews, however, noted the need for research designs that identify leadership and the nature of the context. Writers over forty years ago stressed that cultural and situational factors may determine leadership.[3] A similar theme has been developed by nearly every major review of the literature since then.

Leadership Traits : A Critical View

Mann provides a brief statement on the status of the traits approach to leadership and shows how the traits perspective complements other approaches.[4]

Viewed historically, the study of leadership has stimulated more than its share of controversy. The trait approach to leadership, the view that leadership is an attribute of the individual, has received the harshest treatment throughout the years. To have spoken of an individual as possessing a measurable quantity of leadership was perhaps an unfortunate choice of words. The clear implication of such a statement is that since leadership is specific to the individual, it will remain constant for the individual regardless of the situation in which he finds himself. Investigations of the actual consistency with which an individual maintains leadership status in different groups and under varying conditions have yielded results sufficiently equivocal to permit a new

---

[2]Smith and Krueger, "Literature on Leadership;" Stogdill, "Personal Factors Associated with Leadership;" and Mann, "Personality and Performance in Small Groups."

[3]G. Murphy and L. B. Murphy, *Experimental Social Psychology* (New York: Harper, 1931); G. Murphy, L. B. Murphy, and T. M. Newcomb, *Experimental Social Psychology,* rev. ed. (New York: Harper, 1937); M. H. Krout, *Introduction to Social Psychology* (New York: Harper, 1942).

[4]Mann, "Personality and Performance in Small Groups," pp. 246–47. Copyright 1959 by the American Psychological Association. Reprinted by permission.

bifurcation of the field. On the one hand, the trait approach has been modified to imply that an individual's achieved leadership status is a function of his personality. On the other hand, sufficient evidence has been accumulated to give impetus to the situational approach to leadership, which maintains that leadership is an emergent phenomenon, created through the interaction of individuals (leaders and followers), and that the selection and stability of any leadership pattern is a function of the task, composition, and culture of the group. From all this work has emerged some such summary formulation as that an individual's leadership status in groups is a joint function of his personality and the particular group setting. There is an interesting parallel here to the controversy over the role of heredity and environment in determining behavior, that each factor sets limits for the operation of the other; and researchers turned to studying the relative importance of and the interaction between the two major factors.

One variation on the traits approach continues to receive wide attention and has stimulated numerous empirical studies. Fiedler early in 1950 developed a scale to measure the characteristics that a "least preferred co-worker" (LPC) possesses.[5] Instead of measuring the traits of the supervisor directly, one measures the traits the leader *leasts* likes in those with whom he works. The traits include degree of pleasantness, friendliness, enthusiasm, coldness, self-assurance, and other similar personality characteristics.

This model postulates an interaction between the compatibility of the context with the leader's personality. The focus upon both selected dimensions of the context and leadership traits is superior to the older traits approach followed so long. Unfortunately, this rather old way of describing leadership traits makes it difficult to tie the approach to other efforts in the area. An even more awkward aspect is that the research shows little relationship of LPC scores and selected contextual factors—that are supposed to be supportive of a particular style—with the leader's effectiveness.[6]

Leadership Functions. The reviews of the leadership trait theme emphasized the necessity to explore the leadership traits in a particular context but resulted in the nearly complete abandonment of the direct study of leadership traits. Another major theme that has replaced the interest and focus upon leadership traits explores what the leader does, that is, what functions he performs in a group or in an organizational context. There have been

---

[5]Fred E. Fiedler, *A Theory of Leadership Effectiveness* (New York: McGraw-Hill Book Co., 1967).

[6]George Graen, Kenneth Alveres, and James B. Orris, "Contingency Model of Leadership Effectiveness," *Psychological Bulletin*, 74 (1960), 285–96; Samuel C. Shiflett, "The Effects of Changing Leader Power: A Test of Situational Engineering," *Organizational Behavior and Human Performance*, 7 (1972), 371–82.

several major centers of influence. A set of studies of children's groups at the University of Iowa has broadly influenced subsequent work. A sequence of studies at Ohio State done largely in military and educational settings has generated much additional work. Parallel in time to the Ohio State studies, a set of projects at the University of Michigan was undertaken.

The University of Iowa studies were conducted in the late 1930s by Lewin and Lippitt.[7] Working with children's groups, they explored the way in which leadership style influenced the behavior of group members. The experiment was on the way in which "authoritarian, democratic, and laissez faire" styles affected the group. The three types of leaders were differentiated on the degree to which they gave orders, disruptive commands, destructive criticism, and guiding suggestions; also, on the extent to which they provided information, stimulated self-guidance, provided praise and approval, assumed a jovial and confident manner, and the matter of fact way in which approval and criticisms were given.[8] In other words, a multiple set of dimensions described the similarity and differences among the laissez faire, democratic, and autocratic approaches to leadership.

Lewin and Lippitt did a fine, sensitive piece of work with detailed observations, and it has been one of the germinal studies in the area. The design of the study, however, only permitted the authors to generalize on the overall style of leadership. Little attention could be directed to individual factors that made up overall style.

A second theoretically significant development was made by a group at Ohio State University. Using a combination of empirical and theoretical materials, they developed a concept of leadership. They first collected eighteen hundred specific statements on how supervisors structured their roles. Independently of these they conceptualized the eight following dimensions of leader behavior.[9]

Initiation—How often a leader originates, facilitates, or resists new ideas and new practices
Membership—The degree to which a leader mixes with the group, stresses informal interaction between himself and members, or interchanges personal services with members

[7]Kurt Lewin and Ronald Lippitt, "An Experimental Approach to the Study of Autocracy and Democracy: A Preliminary Note," *Sociometry*, 1 (1938), 292–300; K. Lewin, R. Lippitt, and Ralph K. White, "Patterns of Aggressive Behavior in Experimentally Created 'Social Climates'," *Journal of Social Psychology*, 10 (1939), 271–99; Ronald Lippitt, "Field Theory and Experiment in Social Psychology: Autocratic and Democratic Group Atmospheres," *American Journal of Sociology*, 45 (1939), 26–49; R. Lippitt, "An Experimental Study of the Effect of Democratic and Authoritarian Group Atmospheres," *University of Iowa Studies in Child Welfare*, 16 (1940), 43–195.

[8]Ronald Lippitt and Ralph White, "An Experimental Study of Leadership and Group Life," in Eleanor Maccoby, Theodore Newcomb, and Eugene Hartley, eds., *Readings in Social Psychology* (New York: Holt, Rinehart & Winston, 1958), p. 499.

[9]Carroll L. Shartle, "Studies in Naval Leadership," in Harold Guetzkow, ed., *Groups, Leadership and Men* (Pittsburgh: Carnegie University, 1951), p. 124.

Representation—The extent to which individual behavior is subordinated, pleasant group atmosphere encouraged, conflict reduced, and individual adjustment to the group promoted

Organization—The degree to which a leader structures his own work, the work of other members, or the relationships among members in their work

Domination—The frequency that the leader restricts individuals or the group in action, decision making, or expression of opinion

Communication—The degree to which a leader informs members, seeks information from them, supports exchange of information, or shows awareness of the group's affairs

Recognition—The extent to which a leader expresses approval or disapproval

Production—The degree to which a leader sets levels of effort, achievement, or prods members for greater effort or achievement

The statements that described leadership behavior were screened and placed under the above headings. This gave the researchers ten to twenty operational measures of each factor. These eight items were then grouped into three larger categories; ultimately only two categories were used—consideration and initiation.

Other centers where studies on a functional approach to leadership have been actively carried on include the University of Michigan, University of Southern California, and National Institute of Industrial Psychology in London. Each has had a coordinated and sustained program of research. While the approaches have developed largely independently of one another, they have converged in identifying a similar set of leadership processes.[10]

The studies using leadership functions are running into problems similar to those that resulted in nearly complete abandonment of the focus upon leadership traits. Korman, in reviewing the leadership studies done using the Ohio State approach, found that the leadership profile permitted low-level predictability.[11] He concluded that despite the broad acceptance of "consideration" and "initiating structure" as useful measures of leadership, little is now known as to how these variables predict work group performance and the conditions that affect such predictions. Similar conclusions have been arrived at by other reviewers.[12]

Leadership in an Environmental Context. It has become increasingly clear that it is necessary to explore the way in which leadership affects behav-

[10]D. G. Bowers and S. E. Seashore, "Predicting Organizational Effectiveness with a Four-Factor Theory of Leadership," *Administrative Science Quarterly*, 11 (1966), 238–63; D. A. Butterfield, "An Integrative Approach to the Study of Leadership Effectiveness in Organizations" (Ph.D. diss., University of Michigan, Ann Arbor, 1969); James Taylor, "An Empirical Examination of a Four-Factor Theory of Leadership Using Smallest Space Analysis," *Organizational Behavior and Human Performance*, 6 (1971), 249–66.

[11]Abraham K. Korman, "'Consideration,' 'Initiating Structure,' and 'Organizational Criteria'—A Review," *Personnel Psychology*, XIX, no. 4 (1966), 360.

[12]L. R. Anderson, "Leader Behavior, Member Attitudes, and Task Performance of Intercultural Groups, "*Journal of Social Psychology*, 69 (1966), 305–19; J. P Campbell et al., *Managerial Behavior, Performance, and Effectiveness* (New York: McGraw-Hill Book Co., 1970).

ior or output in a particular environment. Those reviewing trait leadership made this point. Those reviewing the literature on the way in which the leader functions also emphasized the necessity to study leadership in particular settings. This was highlighted by Korman's review of the Ohio State studies,[13] by Erickson's review of a similar set of studies between 1964 and 1966 on the school administrator,[14] and by Robert Dubin's review of the literature on supervision and productivity.[15]

Two closely related points need emphasis. A high degree of interaction may exist between leadership style and the particular context. Or in the developing the effects of leadership style, the changes in the dependent variable (e.g., group efficiency) may be due to contrasts in contextual factors rather than leadership. This important distinction is often omitted. Korman, in his review of the Ohio State studies, stated:[16]

> While a few of those actively involved in this area have emphasized constantly that the effects of "Consideration" and "Initiating Structure" on performance would depend on various situational variables, in most cases the researchers have made little attempt to either conceptualize situational variables which might be relevant and/or measure them. Instead, the researchers have tended almost always to follow the two-variable design which consists simply of correlating the test variable with the criterion variable, with little appreciation of the possible situational variables which might be moderating these relationships.

This statement may mean that the contextual variables exert an independent influence over behavior and output, or leadership and contextual variables interact in exerting their effects. Most researchers who direct attention to environmental variables believe a high interaction exists between leadership and the situation. This may be true, but even if interaction effects don't occur, ignoring the influence of environmental variables, the findings in these studies are often misleading.

Despite the recurring calls to delineate the situational variables, most researchers have failed to do so. This can be traced largely to the absence of relevant theoretical models. While some factors have been suggested,

[13]Korman, "'Consideration,' 'Initiating Structure,' and 'Organizational Criteria'—A Review," p. 355.

[14]D. A. Erickson, "The School Administrator," pp. 417–32.

[15]Dubin, "Supervision and Productivity," pp. 1–50.

[16]Korman, "'Consideration,' 'Initiating Structure,' and 'Organizational Criteria'—A Review," p. 355.

most researchers have little familiarity with the broader models that are available. In our review of leadership studies, we will use the framework of structure variables to identify contextual variables to reconcile some of the apparently contradictory results. We will focus upon the holder of the formal office and ask how different ways of undertaking the supervisory role affect behavioral patterns.

Leadership Process: Adjusting to Organizational Demands. A leader operates in an organizational context where multiple pressures are exerted on his office. The supervisor is the center of conflicting demands, particularly in large, complex organizations. These demands flow from his boss, from other groups, and from his subordinates. This is true of all levels in an organization including the presidential level, although demands at that level flow from external groups such as community organizations, customers, stockholders, bankers, etc.

An important dimension of supervisory effectiveness is the supervisor's response to these various demands. In describing a leadership pattern, we will develop how a supervisor relates to his subordinates, superiors, and higher level management including staff groups. In small groups, no higher level group, management, or other parallel groups are present. However, in complex organizations, these relationships predominate along with superior-subordinate relations.

A number of important dimensions of leadership determine the effectiveness of a supervisor. A supervisor can be described by how he carries out the representation function, encourages participation, adheres to rules, and uses resources of his office; the closeness with which he supervises; and the use he makes of rewards and penalties to motivate. The leadership style is described by the way in which the supervisor undertakes these processes. In practice, a supervisor's approach to his job is represented by a profile.

	Democratic		General				Directive	
	1	2	3	4	5	6	7	8	9
Representation	Upward							Downward
Rule Enforcement	Lax							Strict
Participation	Extensive							Limited
Direction	Loose							Close
Inducements	Rewards							Penalties
	1	2	3	4	5	6	7	8	9

FIGURE 11-1. Leadership profile of two supervisors

These dimensions are defined in later chapters where the influence on behavior of each is explored. We will be particularly concerned with the interaction among these aspects of leadership, and between leadership style and the situation in which a supervisor operates.

Leadership Scale

The following scale captures some other leadership characteristics. Can you recognize why the scales have no scientific value?

Leadership Behavior	1 ——— Out-standing	3 ——— High Satisfactory	5 ——— Satisfactory	7 ——— Low Satisfactory	9 ——— Unsatisfactory
Competence	Belongs in general management	Belongs in executive ranks	Belongs in supervision	Belongs in rank and file	Belongs in board of directors
Planning	Too bright to worry	Worries about future	Worries about present	Worries about past	Too dumb to worry
Organizing	So capable he doesn't need to organize	Organizes work of others	Organizes his own work	Thinks about the need to organize	So incapable he isn't able to organize
Communicating	Talks to employees on all occasions	Talks above employees' level on all occasions	Talks about employees on all occasions	Talks below employees level on all occasions	Talks to himself on all occasions
Controlling	Acts to influence all developments	Acts as if he controls all developments	Acts to protect himself from all developments	Acts to control his panic from all developments	Panics on all developments
Staffing	Hires those who are as competent as himself	Hires those who have high promise	Hires those who have some promise	Hires those who make promises	Hires those who are as incompetent as himself

	Leaps tall buildings with a single bound	Leaps tall buildings with running start	Leaps only small buildings	Leaps into buildings	Leaps out of buildings
Achieving					
Adaptability	Walks on water in emergencies	Swims in water	Washes with water	Drinks water	Passes water in emergencies

SUMMARY

This chapter provides a brief introduction to the extensive leadership literature. Two major themes have occupied the attention of researchers in this area. One line of investigation identifies the traits that outstanding leaders possess. This approach was largely abandoned around 1945 and has been replaced by an exploration of the effects of carrying out leadership functions. The new line of investigation is encountering the same problem as the traits approach but has promise of providing a basic understanding of why supervisors vary in effectiveness.

The difficulty is that while repeated calls have been made to study leadership in a particular context, the operational frameworks to implement this advice have been formulated only recently. The approach to leadership in this book is to explore how carrying out a set of processes in various ways affects the behavior of subordinates and others. We shall be concerned with the structural factors that may confound the results of investigations or that may interact with leadership to influence behavior.

12

REPRESENTATION:
Balancing Conflicting Demands

Representation is a concept that is useful in discussing the conflicting demands that are made upon supervisors. In an organizational setting, groups and individuals exert pressure to have greater resources allocated to their unit; they may press for policy changes, try to minimize the demands other units make upon them, seek changes that give them greater status in the organization, and generally promote their welfare vis-à-vis others in the organization. On the other hand, other units make demands on their unit, seek to obtain compliance with their needs, and generally try to increase the attention paid to them. These demands may come from other parallel work groups, specialist groups such as engineering, methods groups, or higher level management. Conflicting pressures are part of organizational life. An important aspect of leadership is how a supervisor deals with these pressures.

REPRESENTATION DEFINED

Representation is the degree to which a supervisor acts as spokesman, buffer, and defender of his group before others. He may take his clues principally from higher level management and other groups, or he may primarily represent his subordinates' interests to other groups and higher management. In the capacity of a spokesman for subordinates, for example, he tries to obtain resources needed by them and promote action on their grievances where others have the authority to make decisions. In acting as a buffer, he screens out pressures exerted by upper management or other groups on his unit. Further, the leader challenges decisions made by other groups or higher management where the group's welfare is adversely affected. As a basic orientation of upward representation, the supervisor promotes the interest of his groups to other groups and higher management.

"Take a couple of days off, Wendell, and when you come back, keep in mind that between the hours of nine and five, Miss Brewer is a no-no."

On the other hand, when he represents higher management and other groups, the supervisor transmits orders as given and supports the positions of his superiors; he interprets and helps to implement demands of superiors or other groups on his subordinates. Further, the supervisor screens out pressures and demands that his group makes on higher management and other groups.

Measurement of Representation:
Upward to Downward

Representation is defined as the act of being a spokesman and a buffer (defender) for the group vis-à-vis superiors and other groups, or the reverse, acting as a spokesman and buffer for higher management and other groups vis-à-vis subordinates.

1	2	3	4	5	6	7	8	9
Upward—							Downward—	
represents his							represents	
subordinates							superiors and	
							other groups	

1. Does your superior stand up for the interests of your work group on important job-related issues (such as overtime, raises, promotions, job classifications, transfers, and getting fair hearing on grievances)?

1	2	3	4	5	6	7	8	9
Almost always	Usually			Often		Sometimes		Seldom

2. Does your supervisor stand up for the interests of your work group in trying to obtain adequate resource support (such as personnel, new equipment, materials, and supplies)?

1	2	3	4	5	6	7	8	9
Almost always	Usually			Often		Sometimes		Seldom

3. Does he try to build up the group's image in dealing with management and staff (such as keeping them informed on what the group is doing, soundness of its program, and competence of its personnel)?

1	2	3	4	5	6	7	8	9
Almost always	Usually			Often		Sometimes		Seldom

4. When organizational demands conflict with professional rights of group members, does your supervisor emphasize the need to make adjustments to the organizational pressures?

1	2	3	4	5	6	7	8	9
Seldom		Sometimes		Often		Usually		Almost always

5. When he must decide between supporting higher management or his work group, does he go along with management (such as by allowing his decisions to be overruled without protest)?

1	2	3	4	5	6	7	8	9
Seldom		Sometimes		Often		Usually		Almost always

6. When the interests of other work groups and your group are in conflict, does your supervisor respond to the pressures of the other groups?

1	2	3	4	5	6	7	8	9
Seldom		Sometimes		Often		Usually		Almost always

VIEWS ON REPRESENTATION

Lyndall Urwick, an early writer in management, held that it is essential that the supervisor perform a buffer function:

The second aspect of leadership is the full acceptance by the leader of his own·responsibility. The responsibility of a superior for the acts of his subordinates is absolute. This does not mean that a subordinate can never make a mistake or that his chief should never discuss him with his own superiors as a human being, with limitations as well as virtues. It does mean that a chief should never allow a subordinate to

> be criticised or penalised, except by himself, for any action taken by that subordinate within the chief's area of responsibility. Only with a complete appreciation of and adherence to that principle on the part of the chief can he expect loyalty and confidence from those working under him.[1]

Leonard Sayles was one of the first modern writers to emphasize the importance of lateral relationships and the implications these relationships have for leadership. Typically the emphasis has been upon superior-subordinate relationships, but Sayles provided a broader perspective of complexities of the leadership role. He described some of the relationships that dominate the manager's job. Several of these are work flow, trading, advisory, and auditing relations.[2] Work flow relations are contacts with groups that precede and follow the part of work flow under the jurisdiction of the supervisor. Trading relations include arrangements to exchange goods, services, or personnel with other units. Advisory relations are giving advice or information to other groups, or requesting advice and information from them. Auditing relations are evaluating or responding to the evaluation of other groups. The supervisor in varying degrees must deal with these relationships. The formal relations, policies, and rules are designed to minimize the extent negotiations and relative bargaining power dominate the nature of these relationships. Only a highly static organization, though, possesses the stability that entirely eliminates negotiation and bargaining.

In the industrial setting, the foreman's role has been profiled in sharp relief as subject to pressures from below, above, and from specialist groups.[3] In complex production organizations, the foreman has responsibility for his unit to meet standards of quantity, quality, and other multiple goals such as keeping waste down, minimizing accident rates, keeping a clean, orderly appearance in the area, and actively showing equality in treatment of males and females, races, religions, and nationalities, In the face of multiple responsibilities, the foreman only has residual authority. He is bound by the initiative, instructions and policies of top management, his immediate supervisor, and specialists who structure his work and limit his action.

At the same time, the foreman is in direct contact with operating personnel; he fields their complaints and deals with their stresses and initiatives.

[1]Lyndall Urwick, *The Elements of Adminstration* (New York: Harper & Brothers, 1943), pp. 50–51.

[2]Leonard R. Sayles, *Managerial Behavior: Administration in Complex Organizations* (New York: McGraw-Hill Book Co., 1964), pp. 49–50.

[3]Fritz J. Roethlisberger, "The Foreman: Master and Victim of Double Talk," *Harvard Business Review* (spring 1945), pp. 283–98.

He is expected by them to respond to their requests and grievances but is handicapped by having little discretion to act. He is a "man in the middle." While the foreman has the least discretion and the most immediate pressures, all managers are faced with similar conflicts. The supervisor over development engineering, for instance, has to balance the demands for greater attention to immediate problems instead of for longer term development in dealing with top management and his subordinates.[4]

The supervisor's position parallels that of the representatives of union and management in labor union negotiations. Each representative must manage the bargaining that takes place within a group in arriving at a position as well as representing his group in dealing with his counterpart. The outcome of the intragroup bargaining influences the flexibility and outcomes of intergroup bargaining. The negotiator is the "man in the middle" who is faced with the pressure of trying to move his group to a position that will enable agreement to be achieved with his opponents.[5]

Value of Upward Representation

In a brief excerpt, Sayles develops a rationale for representation and suggests the consequence of weak representation of subordinates.[6]

When a hierarchy has more than two levels, subordinates are concerned with their ability to influence leaders with whom they do not have regular contact. They quickly become aware of reality: Their own superior does not control all rewards and punishments or the channels by which these are imparted.

Subordinates are quick to distinguish managers who "aren't afraid to stand up to those guys in the front office when our interests are at stake" from those who cower before superior status. Thus, for many day-to-day problems, it is not sufficient to encourage initiative from subordinates. Many times the leader cannot satisfy the request or solve the problem because it lies outside the resources or decisions he controls. As has been demonstrated in employee counseling programs, the

---

[4]Louis B. Barnes, *Organizational Systems and Engineering Groups: A Comparative Study of Two Technical Groups in Industry* (Boston: Harvard Business School, 1960), pp. 36–45.

[5]H. Turk and M. J. Lefcowitz, "Towards a Theory of Representation Between Groups," *Social Forces*, 40 (1962), 337–41; Richard J. Klimoski, "Intragroup Forces and Intergroup Conflict Resolution" (Ph.D. diss., Purdue University, 1970); Richard J. Klimoski, "The Effects of Intragroup Forces on Intergroup Conflict Resolution," *Organizational Behavior and Human Performance*, 8 (1972), 363–83.

[6]Leonard R. Sayles, *Managerial Behavior: Administration in Complex Organizations* (New York: McGraw-Hill Book Co., 1964), pp. 154–55.

employee wants more than a chance to be heard; he also wants action to follow. Thus the leader must initiate action by others (who may not be readily responsive to him, since they are superior in status).

Where the leader does not carry on such negotiations as a representative of his group of subordinates or of a particular individual, he will find it increasingly difficult to gain adequate responses to his own directions. Representation is not an easy administrative action because the leader is often aware that those who outrank him are unfavorably disposed to the matter in question. Obviously, only deserving requests for representation are honored. However, because of the many ambiguities surrounding the question of who is deserving and of how much, the leader who does not represent his group will find that an increasing share of the benefits being distributed by top management is going to other parts of the organization.

Melville Dalton, in his study of a large industrial organization, describes the complex relationship the supervisors and managers face. He profiles the department head as a "claims adjustor" who must reconcile the complex outlooks and compromising techniques of his superiors with the relatively direct and uncompromising approaches of his juniors. As the claims of each mount on him, he shares their respective burdens.[7] "This forces him into the nebulous role of liaison semanticist: He translates the irregularities below him into decorous reports for his chiefs, and liberally interprets their directives to his subordinates."

Field Studies of Lower Level Managers. Dalton provides an intensive case study of the shifting relations between a maintenance department and production units in a large manufacturing firm. The company had created high pressure on department heads to meet or excel difficult cost standards. Many factors affected the efficiency and costs over which the foremen had little control including machine breakdowns, material variations, and delays in installing and repairing new equipment. The speed of the maintenance unit in processing its orders for repairs or service directly affected the ability of the foremen to meet their cost standards. The formal procedure was for the maintenance unit to process the orders on a first in, first out basis. In fact, it did not work that way. Some units had backlogs of fifteen hundred uncompleted orders; others had no back orders at all. The backlog belonged almost entirely to the less aggressive supervisors. Once their orders and worn equipment were delivered to the shops, they assumed that the work would

[7]Melville Dalton, *Men Who Manage* (New York: John Wiley & Sons, 1959), pp. 248–49.

be done as soon as possible, and they waited until their requests were completed. If they inquired at the shops, they did so without pressuring the maintenance foremen. On the other hand, the aggressive supervisors checked constantly on the progress of their orders and expedited it by use of friendships, bullying, and by subtle threats. An inverse relation existed between a supervisor's personal influence and his volume of uncompleted repairs.

A supervisor who wanted his work expedited appeared in person to tell the maintenance foreman that certain maintenance requests were holding up production. A supervisor might threaten to stop his flow of support of maintenance including (1) cooperation to "cover up" maintenance errors, or at least to share responsibility for them; (2) defense for additional maintenance personnel; (3) opposition in meetings to staff recommendations that maintenance opposed; (4) representing to top management that maintenance needed resouces to meet the needs of the operating groups.

When he was confronted by an aggressive executive, the maintenance foreman looked about his shop for jobs that could be delayed with least danger of getting into trouble. He would stop work on a partially repaired job of a less demanding supervisor and replace it with the pressing job.

In effect, some department heads pressed aggressively for priority treatment for their units. Where the supervisor exerted pressure or exchanged favors, he received efficient service. This, however, was at the expense of those who depended upon the system to function without them representing the interest of their units. The supervisors perhaps should not have exerted pressure on maintenance; it was a fact that the aggressive supervisors did. Dalton contends that this form of competition and conflict is a part of organizational life. Those supervisors who don't recognize it and make their accommodations measure up poorly and are judged as weak and ineffective.

A field study by Patchen provides some further insights on effects of representation.[8] He explored the influence of several factors on the development of "group performance norms"—a measure of commitment and group relations. Two of the factors explored were representation and the level of standards. This study was conducted in a manufacturing company employing 700 people. The firm had seven production departments that performed specialized functions in the manufacture of plastic materials. Within each department, there were two or three rotating shifts for a total of eighteen groups.

Table 12-1 presents the results of how these factors affected group norms or performance levels. The higher scores represent lower norms.[9]

---

[8]Martin Patchen, "Supervisory Methods and Group Performance Norms," *Administrative Science Quarterly*, 7 (1962), 275–93.

[9]Ibid., reordered from pp. 283–84.

TABLE 12-1. Relation of Standards and Representation to Group Performance Norms

Foreman "goes to bat" for his men	*Foreman encourages efficiency*	
	Much	Little
	11	12
	2.20	
	2.35	
	2.38	
	2.49	2.59
Much	2.55	2.61
	2.55	2.74
	M = 2.42	M = 2.65
	21	22
		2.33
		2.43
Little	2.74	2.46
	2.80	2.60
	2.86	2.63
	M = 2.80	M = 2.49

High score means lower group performance norms. Means of cells 11 and 21 are significantly different at .01 level of *p* (1-tailed test) ; means of cells 21 and 22 are significantly different at .01 level of *p* (2-tailed test).

The data show a high interaction between standards and representation. Low representation of subordinates combined with high standards results in lower performance norms (cell 21); when low representation and low standards are combined, though, performance norms are higher (cell 22).[10] When foremen go to bat for their men and encourage efficiency (cell 11), this is associated with the highest production norms. However, these norms are nearly identical when low standards and low representation are combined (cell 22). The lowest norms are shown by groups whose foremen encourage efficiency but don't go to bat for their men (cell 21). While it makes sense that high standards and high representation contribute to high group commitment and cooperative relations, it is unexpected that the same results hold when low standards and low representation exist. It is likely that some other elements of leadership or differences in the units are affecting these results.

External Representation: The School Principal. Some recognition has been given in the research literature to the importance of representation of

[10]This analysis sharply differs from the interpretation by Patchen. See Ibid. for comparison.

external groups. In the school setting, parents and other community groups exert pressure upon the school system and teachers; teachers and students also make demands. The principal is the center of a set of conflicting pressures. The same is true of grammar schools, high schools, or universities. Groups in other organizations such as hospitals, prisons, industrial organizations, and other institutions also set up conflicting demands. Some organizations are more open to the pressures from external groups than others. In these cases, dealing with these external groups may be a key part of leadership activity.

Multiple Demands in the School System

The importance of external representation is developed by Jean Hills.[11] He describes in some detail the set of conflicting pressures that occur in schools, but principally he is concerned with the pressures that impinge upon the organizations from external groups.

Multiple demands for the output of the school pose problems. The possibility of serving both internal and external demands, either simultaneously or sequentially, is limited by scarcity of resources, limitations of time, and intraschool consequences of incompatible goals. One cannot serve one demand at the expense of other demands, without risking tensions both among consumers of the school's product and among members of its staff. A common example may be seen in the dissatisfaction of industrial arts teachers in upper-income suburban schools with what many consider an overemphasis on college-preparatory programs.

A cardinal principle of stability, therefore, is that careful steps must be taken to establish priorities among the demands placed on the school. This is a matter of external integration; that is, decisions concerning priorities among external demands serve to integrate the contribution of the school with those demands.

The administrator is faced by a twofold problem. On the one hand, the consumers of the educational product have a legitimate right to expect that their demands will be met and a legitimate reason for being disturbed when they are not met. In the case of an enterprise that provides a nonessential product, or one for which a suitable alternative is available, failure to adjust to demands is of little concern to the consumer. Where the function is an imperative one, however, for which no competing product is widely available, the consumer cannot readily

---

[11]R. Jean Hills, "The Representative Function: Neglected Dimension of Leadership Behavior," *Administrative Science Quarterly*, 8 (June 1963), 87–89.

change products—although this happens sometimes, as the existence of parochial and private schools indicates—but can change administrators.

Teachers, on the other hand, tend to view administrative accommodations to external pressures and demands as defections from professional standards. The administrator who accedes too readily to parental or interest group demands is, from the teacher's point of view, guilty of corrupting the goals of the institution. If he fails to "back up" teachers in disputes with outsiders, defending them against interference and defending the integrity of professional values, the administrator may be viewed as the worst kind of self-seeking "politician."

To compound an already complicated relationship, not only are the administrator's tenure and reputation at stake in the performance of his external integrative and disposal functions, but also the resources and support granted to the school. Despite the fact that revenues are partly determined by legislative action at higher governmental levels, the school depends for a large proportion of its resources on the local district, i.e., on the immediate consumer.

In sum, there are multiple and often conflicting demands which the school must meet if it is to be well supported. Decisions of the administrator (and board of education) that attempt to integrate the school's output with external demands may conflict with the beliefs and values of teachers and be seen as defections from professional standards.

Furthermore, teachers do not share a single, common set of values and beliefs; they too place multiple and conflicting demands on the administrator. Teachers of academic subjects have values that are not entirely in accord with those who teach vocational subjects. While a decision to add advanced placement courses to the curriculum may be warmly received by the teachers of academic subjects, teachers of vocational subjects may—particularly if their share of resources is threatened—look upon it as catering to the interests of an influential minority.

Also, even though adequate support for the school is contingent upon the integration of the product with external demands, and even though the administrator can accede to those demands at the risk of creating dissatisfaction among the staff, teachers consider it a prime responsibility of the administrator to secure for them the greatest possible amount of resources. In this respect the administrator is exposed to another danger: he can attempt to procure too much, i.e., taxes can be made too high.

If then we take the perspective of staff members as a point of reference—the case in the present study—attention is focused on the "protection" or the "defense-of-institutional-integrity" aspects of the problem. On the other hand, if the school is viewed as a subsystem of a more inclusive system, namely, the community, and one takes the perspective of the more inclusive system as a point of reference, attention is focused on the problem of integrating the contribution of the school with relevant community demands.

Becker's study of teachers in the public school system also illustrates the importance of representation.[12] He focused on the teachers' relations with the parents and principals. He describes teachers as striving to maintain their legitimate sphere of authority in the face of challenges. The teacher views herself as a professional with specialized training and knowledge in her field. To her the parent lacks such background and is unable to understand her problems properly. As a logical corollary, parents are not considered to have a legitimate right to interfere with the work of the school. The teacher tries to avoid disputes over authority with parents. She feels this can best be accomplished when the parent does not get involved in the school's operation beyond some minimum way. To some extent the teacher can handle the situation herself, but she also is dependent upon the principal to act as a major buffer. Representation by the principal is considered to be one of the most effective defenses against attacks on authority from parents and pupils. The principal is expected to "back the teacher up"—support her authority in all cases of parental "interference." The teachers view this as one of the major criteria of a "good" principal.

Teachers have a well-developed conception of how and toward what ends the principal's authority should be used. These expectations are clear on the teacher's relationships with parents and pupils, where the principal is expected to uphold the teacher's authority regardless of circumstances. This expectation of support is independent of the legitimacy of the teacher's action; the latter can be punished later without parents knowing about it. The principal is expected to use any means necessary to preserve authority, including lying himself or supporting the teacher's lies. Becker quotes one teacher on the point: "If a parent came to school hollering that a teacher had struck her child, Mr. D ____ would handle it. He'd say, "Why, Mrs. So-and-So, I'm sure you must be mistaken. I can't believe that any of our teachers would do a thing like that."[13] He would promise to look into the matter and do what was necessary. The teacher would be punished later when he would call her to the office for a tongue lashing. "But he never failed them when it came to parents."

[12]Howard S. Becker, "The Teacher in the Authority System of the Public School." *Journal of Educational Sociology*, 27 (1953), 128–41.

[13]Ibid., p. 134.

Not all principals live up to this expectation. Their failure is attributed to cowardice or an orientation to see the parents' side of a question.

Teachers expect the same kind of support and defense in their dealings with pupils without regard for the justice of the complaint. When students find the principal a friendly court of appeal, control over them is weakened. Challenges to classroom control are directly related to the principal's strictness. Where he fails to be "tough," the school develops a restless atmosphere, and control over pupils is difficult to maintain. The opposite is true where the children know that the principal will support teachers' actions.

In summary, the principal is expected to provide a defense against parental interference and student revolt by supporting and protecting the teachers' authority if it is challenged. In his supervisory role, he is expected to respect the teachers' independence. Failure to do so generates conflict. Both parties have effective means of controlling the other's behavior, so that the ordinary situation is one of compromise when disputes arise, with penalties applied only when the agreed-on boundaries are overstepped.

SUMMARY AND CONCLUSION

The representation aspect of leadership explores how a supervisor handles the conflicting sets of pressures that are a part of every leadership position. Principal attention may be given to protecting the group from the demands and pressures of other parts of the organization and aggressively pursuing the group's interests. In contrast, the supervisor may press the group to minimize its demands and respond positively to pressures of higher level management, specialists, and other groups.

Leonard Sayles suggests that a leader who fails to carry on these negotiations for his group will find his subordinates unresponsive to his leadership. Melville Dalton provides an extensive case study of line supervisors dependent upon maintenance services. Those supervisors who relied upon the formal arrangements and policies soon found their work relegated to the bottom of the work pile. They were competing against supervisors who aggressively pressed their demands or negotiated favored treatment with maintenance. The case is of general interest since complex organizations have the general feature of a high degree of specialization. Each specialized unit is dependent upon many other units for information, services, and other resources. Dalton's study suggests that representation is a critical activity determining the extent to which a unit will measure up in performance vis-à-vis other units.

Jean Hills highlights the importance of external representation where the organization is subject to pressures and demands from outside groups. He sees a need to achieve a fine balance of partially accommodating and adjusting to external demands and partly responding to the demands of internal groups for absolute protection. If the supervisor accedes entirely to the pressures of either group, the supervisor and the organization are exposed to withdrawal of essential support. Howard Becker's study looks at representation from the perspective of the teacher. The maintenance of the teacher's influence and control in the classroom is seen to rest on the strong representation by the principal when parents and students challenge their actions.

In total, representation is one of the more important aspects of leadership in complex organizations. The handling of conflicting pressures has important effects upon relationships with superiors, other groups, and subordinates.

13

RULE ORIENTATION: The Reliance on the Formal System

Most complex organizations have a network of policies, procedures, and rules that either are broadly understood to exist or have been formally written and distributed. They cover authority and responsibilities that define the formal limits that members are expected to observe in their offices.

RULE ORIENTATION DEFINED

Supervisors vary in their attitudes toward observing the policies, procedures, and rules prescribed by higher managements, other groups, or that they specify themselves. The supervisor may permit, or encourage, deviation from the rules and other prescriptions when they restrict getting the job done. On the other hand, a supervisor may require adherence to rules and policies and seldom permit deviation regardless of the reasons for waiving enforcement.

When the supervisor disregards the formal restrictions that have been imposed on his office and those below him, this may be done by (1) explicitly authorizing—either verbally or in writing—his subordinates to ignore certain policies and rules that have been set forth, (i.e., the supervisor

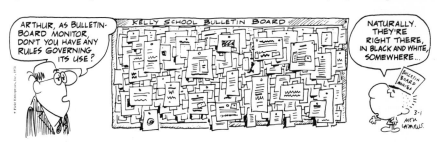

Reprinted courtesy of Mell Lazarus and Publishers-Hall Syndicate, Copyright 1973, Field Enterprises.

directly assumes the responsibility for waiving the formal restrictions), or (2) allowing subordinates to deviate from the formal restrictions even though they aren't given explicit permission to do so. Where the supervisor emphasizes rule and policy adherence, subordinates are prohibited from deviating from the rules and prescriptions. Rules are only deviated from when a formal authorization for such variation in writing is provided by a superior or by those who initially formulated the rules and regulations.

One aspect of rule observation concerns the use of resources that are under the formal jurisdiction of each office. These resources may include personnel, materials, equipment, or financial resources. The supervisor may only loosely control the use of these resources or, in contrast, carefully rationalize their usage. The supervisor can de-emphasize controls by, in effect, saying, "If this office can provide assistance, this is our function; the facilities are at your disposal." Little attention is given to establishing priorities and controls to allocate use of given facilities. In dealing with the opposing approaches of satisfying the demands for freedom and the need for control, the attitude of the supervisor is to minimize the risks associated with the unrestricted use of equipment and resources.

On the other hand, a tight control orientation may be taken. In effect, the official states, "This equipment and other resources have been assigned to the office for the use of subordinates and other departments in the organization. The resources are limited and it is the supervisor's responsibility to see that they are allocated in the fairest manner and only for authorized purposes." The control-oriented individual is concerned with the risk of potential abuse for unauthorized projects. He sees controls as a solution and tries to increase and maintain these controls. Only limited resources exist, and these need to be rationed among competing demands; the supervisor's function is to establish and administer a system for allocating the resources. He develops a list of priorities so that when competing demands are made for the limited resources, the requests can be placed in a queue. Those who request resources are required to make formal applications setting forth their needs and justifications. The supervisor might interview them personally to determine the priority the project has. He carefully considers whether each requirement falls within the jurisdiction of his office, whether the task should be done by another office, or whether a special decision is needed to permit an exception.

The supervisor considers himself a gatekeeper. To ensure that priorities are observed, he requires that the use of resources be formally authorized first by his office. Thus, those needing assistance must first obtain formal clearance instead of going directly to a resource such as a typing pool. To ensure that resources are utilized as authorized, detailed reporting procedures are required on the progress made, what happened at the end of the project, and whether the expenditures of time and money or other resources were utilized as approved.

Measurement of Rule Orientation: Lax to Strict

Supervisors vary in their attitudes toward observing the policies, procedures, and rules that are established from lax to strict.

1	2	3	4	5	6	7	8	9
Lax								Strict

1. Does your supervisor enforce formal policies, procedures, and rules on the work group?

1	2	3	4	5	6	7	8	9
Rarely		Sometimes		Often		Usually		Almost always

2. In dealing with his superior, other supervisors, or staff groups, is the emphasis of your supervisor on observing the restrictions of policies, procedures, and rules?

1	2	3	4	5	6	7	8	9
Rarely		Sometimes		Often		Usually		Almost always

3. Does the supervisor take a "can do it" approach when policies or rules impede getting the job done and find a way (rather than a "cannot do it" approach and quote the policies or rules that prevent action)?

1	2	3	4	5	6	7	8	9
Rarely		Sometimes		Often		Usually		Almost always

4. Does he maintain tight control over office resources (such as on the use of supplies, personnel, or equipment) to ensure they are used only for authorized purposes?

1	2	3	4	5	6	7	8	9
Rarely		Sometimes		Often		Usually		Almost always

5. Where there is some freedom, does he assume a flexible position on moving
    budgeted funds from one category to another when it would help the overall
    group?

1	2	3	4	5	6	7	8	9
Rarely	Sometimes			Often		Usually		Almost always

THE CONTRADICTIONS OF RULE
ADHERENCE AND RULE DEVIATION

Some authors argue that high rule adherence is harmful. They believe
that organizational flexibility and deviations from policies are a necessary
part of organizations functioning. Bendix develops the view that large-scale
organizations depend for their effectiveness on a clearly understood hierarchy of authority.[1] Yet, they break down if every official follows all regulations to the letter and consults superiors whenever these rules don't provide
sufficient guidance. This type of "bureaucratic" behavior interferes with the
functioning of the organization at every point. All organizations depend on
the ability and the willingness of their employees to act on their own initiative to deal with unanticipated problems.

Robert Merton points out that if a bureaucracy is to operate successfully,
it must attain a high degree of reliability of behavior.[2] This is achieved
where conformity with prescribed patterns of action develops to a high
degree. Close adherence to prescribed patterns supported by strong commitment to do one's duty, and a keen sense of the limitation of one's authority and competence create stability of behavior. The stability of the
organization depends upon the participants developing these attitudes and
sentiments.

The problem is that sentiments to conform may become the ends rather
than the means to the ends of the organization. The tendency is to shift
from attention to goals of the organization to the particular details prescribed by the rules; an instrumental value becomes a terminal value. This
is accompanied by rigidities and inability to adjust to variations in the situation; formalism and ritualism ensue. This may reach a point where the
principal concern is conformity to the rules rather than providing service.
Merton's analysis suggests that a balance between rule adherence and interpretation of the rules must develop for the organization to be effective.

[1]Reinhard Bendix, "Bureaucracy: The Problem and Its Setting," *American Sociological
Review* (October 1947), p. 503.

[2]Robert K. Merton, "Bureaucratic Structure and Personality," *Social Forces*, 18 (1940),
560–68.

The Order of Bird: For Those Who Know How to Follow Rules[3]

Facing a big policy decision? Consider the principles of "creative bureaucracy":
"When in charge, ponder. When in trouble, delegate. When in doubt, mumble." Then refer the whole problem to a coordinating committee for review.

That's the advice of no less an expert than James Boren, founder and chief finger-tapper of the National Association of Professional Bureaucrats. NATAPROBU (every self-respecting Washington group must have an acronym) is devoted to paper shufflers everywhere "who, by their steadfast dedication to the principles of dynamic inactivism, have kept things from happening, and thereby prevented mistakes from being made." Its emblem: a scrawny bird strangling in red tape, initialed-memos and gobbledygook.

Jim Boren, formerly a State Department official and now a Washington consultant, created NATAPROBU in 1968 as a vehicle for giving proper recognition to bureaucratic inaction. For a while all was well. But now NATAPROBU is perilously close to violating its own commitment to the status quo: Ominously, it is beginning to accomplish something.

Veteran ponderers here blame this largely on the "Order of the Bird." This an award, a metal statue of an "unfeathered, potbellied bird," presented by NATAPROBU to those exhibiting excellence in bureaucratic excess. The first winner was a regional Internal Revenue Service official, for his detailed memorandum outlining lengthy requirements for employee sideburns. Another recipient was a State Department analyst who wrote a foreign-policy paper on "the qualitative quantitive interface."

Mr. Agnew Declines an Award

The scheduled winner at NATAPROBU's 1969 awards banquet (delayed until December 1970 by red tape), was Vice President Spiro Agnew, for his alliterative achievements in communications. But Mr. Agnew declined the honor, responding in a telegram that "in all meiotic modesty" there were others "possessing prolusionary processes more deserving." ("Prolusionary" actually is Mr. Boren's word and appar-

---

[3]Ronald G. Shafer, "No Bureaucrat Wants Award of 'The Bird,' Not Even the Winners," *The Wall Street Journal*, December 21, 1971. Reprinted with the permission of The *Wall Street Journal*, © Dow Jones & Company, Inc. (1971).

ently is his version of "prolusory"; he admits to sometimes making up words as part of his philosophy of "adjustice responses.")

At any rate, therein lies the problem. No one wants to get the bird. Consider, for example, a recent case in which the Social Security Administration, citing regulations, denied a total-disability rating to a handicapped Korean war veteran in Wichita, even though he had suffered a third heart attack. Informed of the ruling, Mr. Boren dispatched a letter and press release. Both nominated the officials involved for the Order of the Bird, "in recognition of constant devotion to punctillious and amblyopic interpretation of Social Security rules."

Shunning personal recognition, however, the officials subsequently granted the veteran the disability rating after all. Shocked by such decisive action, Mr. Boren withdrew his nomination.

He frets that such embarrassments are occurring increasingly. Early this year, the Federal Aviation Administration threatened to fine a Denver inventor for failing to get FAA clearance before flying his tethered, homemade helicopter six inches off the ground. But when Mr. Boren wired congratulations and a nomination to regional FAA officials (as duly reported in the Denver press), the FAA Los Angeles office bucked the matter to Washington, which bucked it back to the Los Angeles office, which dropped the case.

NATAPROBU is even attracting the attention of that most prestigious ponderer of all, Congress. Last summer Mr. Boren was a star witness at hearings by a House Public Works subcommittee into ways to reduce government red tape. Mr. Boren, however, staunchly defended the growing blizzard of paper and carbon copies. Indeed, the 46-year-old Oklahoman testified with his usual deadpan eloquence:

"To deny a dedicated finger-tapper an adequate supply of paper on which to record the results of his prodigious pondering is to deny him the tools of creative nonresponsiveness."

Mr. Boren's solution for controlling government bureaucracy is, of course, to create another bureaucracy. It would be called the Department of Adjusted Procedures and Orchestrated Clearances, or DAPOC. It would include such sub-agencies as Office of Orderly-Overruns, Permeations and Statistics (OOOPS) and Governmental Linguistic Obtusity Bureau (GLOB).

When pressed for his true motives, Mr. Boren has been known to frantically begin rubber-stamping and initialing papers on his desk. But yes, he admits, "I have a serious purpose. I'm trying to use satire to obtain some constructive changes in bureaucracy."

Mr. Boren contends effective government action too often is delayed by important-sounding presidential commissions, inordinate paperwork and overadherence to bureaucratic rules. "There are good people in government," he says, but "the doers are frustrated by the nit-pickers."

Field Studies: Rule Adherence in Bureaucracies

Melville Dalton develops the theme that conflicting pressures and paradoxes exist in organizations that create an unstructured, ambiguous context. In the excerpted selection, he develops the consequence of supervisors being flexible on rules versus rule oriented.[4] He uses the terms "strong" and "weak," respectively, for these two types.

The weak are fearful in conflict situations and absorb aggressions to avoid trouble. Having a low tolerance for conflict, they do not fill their offices. They hesitate to act without consulting superiors, and take refuge in clearly formulated rules whether adequate or not for their footing at the moment. Following their fairy-tale image of the organization as a fixed thing, they suffer from their experience that it is not. This, of course, aggravates their difficulty in grasping the tacit expectations that associates do not wish to spell out when events are troublesome. When regulations are changed, the weak adjust slowly and often fail to make passable use of the new directives. In their life outside the firm, where conflict is less or different, they may function acceptably, yet fail when trapped among competing claims peculiar to the plant. When they do fall short, they are likely to advertise the fact. In their distress they involve associates in trouble by blunders that disclose departmental secrets. As they seek to escape dilemmas, their unfitness to act outside the haven of understood rules invites aggression from the strong who are searching for shortcuts in the network of official routes.

The strong, on the other hand, tolerate dilemmas, and even make a game of them. Pulled between official and unofficial claims on themselves, they are less morally disturbed than the weak because they and their followers variouly influence the system and profit from it. They flee neither necessary conflict nor the responsibility for charting new routes. They quickly turn ambiguous situations to their needs. By resolving contrary demands on themselves they aid both superiors and subordinates and thus expand their office. Where the weak look for protection in the letter of rules, the strong find essential meanings in formal precepts by their free and unanswerable interpretations. They know when to avoid decisions, and they are able to mark time and wait for

[4]Melville Dalton, *Men Who Manage* (New York: John Wiley & Sons, 1959), pp. 247–48.

developments with minor frustration. More able to anticipate and interpret developments, they are more likely to have the reserve which
enables them to meet the situation, and to refrain from driving subordinates toward some abstract end they are fearful of missing. If
they fail to adjust quickly to reorganization, they at least meet change
with minimum distress for themselves and plant goals. They use failures
to reorient themselves in the maze of events.

In short, the weak are prone to lose sight of goals in concentrating
on procedures. Hence in unstable situations not yet covered by rules,
or where rules are outdated or will never be detailed, they cannot improvise. Against this, the strong are so unconcerned with procedure—
except when it is a clear aid or can be interpreted to their advantage
or is a necessary symbol—and so accustomed to moving directly
toward goals that they readily devise new methods in doubtful situations.

The two types are spontaneously identified by associates and subordinates. In general, the weak are spoken of being "unable to cut the
buck," being a "foul ball," as having "no guts," "no savvy," and as being
"boneheads," etc. The strong, as "a guy you can count on," or "who
won't let you down," as having "a lot on the ball," as "doing what's
necessary," as being "on the beam," as one who "really stacks up," "a
damn good man," etc.

Ralph Turner presents a number of useful insights based on his study of
the Navy disbursing officer. He suggests that conflict between the regulations and orders from superiors is part of every organizational structure.[5]
Official supervisor behavior and commands may often counter the rules. In
the small organization with only a few employees, rules may be largely
unformulated and procedures passed verbally down the hierarchy as
required. No conflict develops since orders are supreme. In the opposite
extreme, authority is expressed solely through a code of rules, and each
employee is left to apply the rules without supervision. This can be imagined
but isn't realized in an actual situation. Both rules and supervisory authority
are present in all organizations; both are utilized with the result that the two
channels of authority often are in conflict.

Bureaucracies differ in their emphasis on the chain of command or rules.
Some organizations vest greater anthority in the chain of command and
minimize rules; other organizations such as government bureaucracies
develop an extensive set of rules, policies, and procedures and minimize the

[5]Ralph H. Turner, "The Navy Disbursing Officer as a Bureaucrat," in Robert Dubin,
Human Relations in Administration, rev. ed. (Englewood Cliffs, N.J.: Prentice-Hall, 1961), pp.
96–103.

discretion of the office holder. In the armed services, these are the standard regulations (SR's) and army regulations (AR's) that detail how to carry out every job. The extent to which a conflict exists between orders and rules may be related to the level; for the lower ranks of enlisted men, the conflict may hardly exist because the men often are explicitly denied the right to make decisions on their own. At the higher levels, the official is confronted with fewer and broader orders so that in top ranks the conflict arises less frequently. The conflict between orders and regulations is most acute at the intermediate levels.

Inadequacies or conflicts in the procedures and goals, incompetent bureaucrats, pressures related to an exchange system, and friendship patterns exert pressure for deviation. Turner's focus is on the Navy disbursing officer, but his points are relevant to most complex organizations. The training given the disbursing officer teaches him that he should be a "can do paymaster" in contradistinction to the type of officer who cites the paragraph in the official manual that prevents any particular action from being taken. The "can do" officer finds a way to respond to requests of his superiors; if one is a rule book reader, he will be held in low esteem.

In any organization, it is awkward for an office holder to disregard requests or orders that counter rules. Various penalties may be applied if a positive response isn't made to superiors, subordinates, or other groups. Subordinates are not typically in a position to impose penalties directly, but their cooperation and commitment to some extent must be won. Failure to show flexibility can result in subtle sabotage. Three forms of relationships found in the Navy—and in most organizations—are old friendship patterns, simulated friendships, and exchange relations. These are relatively enduring patterns.

This is true especially aboard ship where a relatively small group of officers live and interact in a small space. "Say Pat, I sure could use about twenty dollars for payday," or, "Isn't there some way I could get flight pay this month?" is the sort of appeal that comes constantly from friends.[6] The officer wants to help his friends; aside from that, the penalty for brusque dismissal of requests is social ostracism.

Simulated friendships may be less enduring but at the same time exert pressures for personal consideration. These take several forms. An officer may treat one of lesser rank as equal; he may compliment the disbursing officer on the good reputation of his office; he jokes and relates as an old friend. The aim is always to be regarded as a person rather than an applicant in the disbursing officer's eyes and to be defined favorably.

A more pervasive factor is obligations that flow from the exchange system. Anyone who has personal or office resources to distribute is in a position to

6Ibid., p. 100.

participate in the exchange system. The officer who assigns staterooms aboard ship finds it easy to get extra food in the galley. The ship's photographer who makes personal pictures for the supply officer gets his first choice of the next shipment of supplies. Such exchanges are not usually verbalized as such by officers, but the officer who does another a favor expects a return.

The exchange system extends so far that it is often difficult for a man to secure those services and equipment that are essential to his job unless he can promise some return. These exchanges affect the ability of an officer to elicit cooperation from others: "Needless to remark, any resort to strictly formal procedure impairs the disbursing officer's potentially exceptional good position in the system of mutual benefits."[7] An individual who puts legal technicality ahead of reciprocity is spoken of with moral indignation. The system is not wrong or crooked: it is a moral system of its own, and anyone who puts legality first is considered a hypocrite. The most successful officers are those who are "realists."[8]

They see regulations as illogical; procedures, restrictions, and interpretations are frequently ambiguous, sometimes contradictory, and often, when strictly applied, defeat the purpose for which they were constructed. The most successful career men of the supply corps include many of this type. They assume the regulation facade with those who aren't fortunately placed in an informal exchange relationship or those of low rank; they know how any payment may be made "legally" if the request comes from an important enough source.

A field study by Aiken and Hage on professionals in sixteen social welfare agencies explored three dimensions of structure and leadership and their effects upon behavior.[9] They explored how rule observation affected attitudes toward the job and relationships among members ("alienation from work" and "alienation from expressive relations"). They found that rule observation was substantially related to both measures of alienation. About one-third of the adverse intragroup relationships and job dissatisfaction were caused by rule emphasis.

Peter Blau, in generalizing on the findings of his study of a governmental agency, developed some of the implications of supervisor rule adherence and subordinate representation.[10] A lenient foreman or supervisor allows subordinates to violate minor rules, for example, to smoke and talk even though it is prohibited by management. This permissiveness increases his power by furnishing him with legitimate penalties that can be used when leverage is

[7]Ibid., p. 101.

[8]Ibid., p. 102.

[9]Michael Aiken and Jerald Hage, "Organizational Alienation: A Comparative Analysis," *American Sociological Review*, 31 (August 1966), 497–507.

[10]Peter M. Blau, *Bureaucracy in Modern Society* (New York: Random House, 1956), pp. 70–72.

needed. If subordinates displease him, he can punish them by enforcing the rules. "Cut out the smoking: Can't you read the sign?" If he always enforces the rules, this leverage isn't available to him. It is rarely necessary to be so crude in applying penalties. The knowledge that the rule exists and is enforced elsewhere instills a sense of obligation to superiors and induces greater compliance with their requests.

Factors Mediating Effects of Rule Adherence. Four additional factors provide additional perspective of the conditions that partially determine the consequences of rule adherence. Charles Page, in his study of the Navy, emphasizes that the acceptance of rule deviation may be closely related to the pressures on the organization.[11] As the military units move closer to combat or are isolated from American communities and other military bases, greater deviation from formal procedures develops. He suggests that a high degree of interaction exists between rule deviation and the pressures to get the job done. A rule-oriented posture under fluid conditions has adverse consequences; contrarily, close adherence to rules and procedures may be acceptable in a routine situation.

Alvin Gouldner points out that rules may be initiated by outside groups, jointly initiated by management and employees, or imposed by either the employees through their union or by management.[12] He develops the thesis that adherence to rules has different behavioral implications depending on the way they are initiated. Where rules are imposed on the group by some outside agency, neither workers nor management may accept them, such as when a "no-smoking" rule is required by an insurance company on production workers. Enforcement of the rule violates the value of "equality" of employees and management since office workers could still smoke. When rules aren't followed, it is explained by "uncontrollable" needs or characteristics of "human nature." People smoke because of "nervousness." Rule deviation enhances status of both workers and management. Violation of the no-smoking rule, for instance, minimizes the visibility of status by preventing the creation of a privileged group of smokers. In summary, where rules are imposed on the group, they aren't enforced by management or obeyed by workers. Evasion of rules is supported by the sentiments of both participants.

Both groups may jointly initiate the rules and view them as their own, such as when pressure is exerted by union and management to develop a safety program. Workers and supervisors modify the program periodically. Enforcement of the rules is consistent with both groups' values. Rule deviation is explained by ignorance or well-intentioned, but careless, acts. It is an

[11]Charles Page, "Bureaucracy's Other Face," *Social Forces* (October 1946), pp. 88–94.

[12]Alvin Gouldner, *Patterns of Industrial Bureaucracy* (Glencoe, Ill.: Free Press, 1954), pp. 215–28.

accident if a worker gets a hernia and is attributed to ignorance of proper lifting technique. Deviation from the rules impairs the status of superiors and subordinates, while conformance supports their status. A safety program increases the prestige of workers' jobs by improving the cleanliness of the plant and enables workers to initiate action for their superiors on safety. It helps management realize its production goals and provides it with a rationale for extending control over workers. In summary, where rules are jointly initiated by both employees and management and enforced by management and obeyed by workers, some tension is generated but little overt conflict occurs. Rules are supported by sentiments, participation, initiation, and education of both workers and management.

Where rules are unilaterally initiated by *either* workers or management, the reacting group views the rules as imposed by the other. If a union initiates a bidding system, supervisors typically see this as a program that the company is forced to accept. Enforcement of the rules violates the values of only one group—either superiors or subordinates. The bidding rules threaten management's use of skill and ability as criteria for recruitment, promotion and transfers. Rule deviance is attributed to deliberate intent. Rule conformity leads to status gains *either* for workers or supervisors, but not for both. The bidding system allows workers to secure jobs and promotions without dependence upon the supervisor. In summary, the rules are initiated by one party and opposed by the other. Rules are enforced by one group and evaded by the other; the process of rule initiation and enforcement is accompanied by tension and conflict. The threat of punishment and the sentiments of either workers or management support enforcement.

Richard Carlson comments on both rule making and rule observation based on his study of school administrators.[13] New administrators are more preoccupied with rules and rule making. Rule making creates an image that the administrator is busily engaged in vital organization activities. This may be important to administrators when they aren't clear on what role they are going to play in the organization. It requires members to direct attention to the administrator's office. Rule making identifies the new man, since the rules are clearly his and signal that he has arrived and that things are going to be different.

Rule making provides the new man an opportunity to assess the reaction to change. It provides him with some idea of the possible sources of support and where resistance is likely to be greatest. As a successor continues in office, his preoccupations with rules decline. As he becomes established, he no longer needs to rely upon rule enforcement.

Carlson also observes that different groups may have varying responsiveness toward rules and their enforcement. In the school setting, rule enforce-

---

[13]Richard O. Carlson, *Executive Succession and Organizational Change* (Chicago: University of Chicago, Midwest Administration Center, 1962), pp. 23–40.

ment on the teachers is sharply restricted. It is easy to make rules on what teachers should do and how it should be done; however, it is practically impossible to enforce rules on teachers since surveillance is nearly impossible. Teachers work in closed rooms where they can be observed only with difficulty. Further, teachers strongly claim professional autonomy. These factors suggest that teachers are relatively invulnerable to rules; thus it is difficult to influence them by the use of rules.

Administrative personnel directly under the principal, on the other hand, are more responsive to rule making since they are in vulnerable positions where penalties can be easily brought to bear, are more easily watched, and don't have the same claims for professional antonomy.

Melcher and Beller deal with one special area of rule adherence—the use of formal channels in the formal decision process.[14] They develop the thesis that it is appropriate only to utilize the formal channels on routine, relatively simple or broadly acceptable decisions. Where disagreement exists on goals or means of achieving goals, it is desirable to explore areas of common interest or conduct bargaining on the informal level. Once consensus is reached at least among key individuals, the formal channels and decision process are useful to legitimize an agreement.[15]

Their thesis is that criticism on low level of participation in decision making in organizations is based upon misunderstanding of the separate functions that formal and informal action play. Low attendance and nominal participation in general meetings or committees where important decisions are made in unions, universities, government, hospitals, and other organizations may reflect a viable organization. For instance, when decisions are made with little more than pro forma participation and little discussion, it may indicate an appropriate use of the informal level before the agreement is formalized. Controversial proposals may be screened out or modified in informal negotiations so as to be made generally acceptable.

They further suggest that active participation in meetings may indicate an unstable organization or misuse of the formal channels. The administrator may be attempting to achieve consensus on the formal level rather than legitimatizing decisions informally achieved. If open confrontations between contending groups or individuals occur, this contributes to inflexible attitudes and positions. It may result in such harm to the interpersonal relations that action cannot be undertaken even on noncontroversial issues. A formal decision under conflict conditions may result in loss of status that creates ill feelings that are difficult to overcome for many years. To be effective, an administrator needs to choose carefully the occasions when he is willing to

[14]Arlyn J. Melcher and Ronald Beller, "Toward a Theory of Organization Communication: Consideration in Channel Selection," *Academy of Management Journal*, 10 (March 1967), 39–52.

[15]Ibid., pp. 44–45.

accept formal confrontations; other administrators may be ineffective largely because formal conflicts occur often enough to disrupt the social fabric essential to cooperation in any organization.

SUMMARY AND CONCLUSION

In summary, most of the material reviewed indicates that rigid adherence to policies, procedures, and rules influences behavior adversely even though the formal organization is intended to restrict the discretion that employees and supervisors exercise. Both Bendix and Merton emphasize that when rules are followed closely and inflexibly, the achievement of organization ends is subverted. Dalton and Turner supplement this view by noting the complex pressures for rule deviation. Dalton profiles the organization as being fluid and unstructured with conflicting demands being exerted on supervisors. Those seeking security in rules and regulations find themselves held in low esteem by their colleagues. Turner notes the conflict that exists in varying degrees in all organizations between orders and requests of superiors and others and, on the other hand, formal rules and policies. Immediate superiors and other higher level supervisors may exert pressure to waive or favorably interpret policies handed down from above. Aside from these contradictions, friendships, simulated friendships, and an intricate exchange system often exist that exert pressure to accommodate peers and other groups. Individuals who take a formal posture may find it difficult to obtain the cooperation necessary to carry out their assigned activities. Dalton's focus was on large industrial organizations and Turner's was on the United States Navy. They arrived at similar conclusions.

The findings and conclusions of Aiken and Hage and Peter Blau, who studied other types of organizations, parallel this thesis. Rule adherence adversely affects the satisfaction professionals in social welfare agencies have with their jobs and their colleagues. Blau stresses the leverage a supervisor obtains by permitting rule deviation: it creates a set of credits that can be used to elicit cooperation later.

Page, Gouldner, and Carlson qualify when rule deviation is effective. Page develops the thesis that when stress is exerted on the organization and demands for performance are high, rule observation is less acceptable and dysfunctional. Gouldner suggests that the consequences of rule enforcement are dependent upon who develops the rules and the extent to which member values are supported or violated by the rules. Carlson suggests that when a supervisor moves into his office, rule making and enforcement may be a useful strategy in making his presence felt, particularly by those under his direct control; when he is established, it may then be useful to relax the rule emphasis. But rules are effective only for those who can be observed and who can be penalized.

Melcher and Beller develop the view that one aspect of the formal structure—channels for communicating and decision making—should be used to formalize and legitimatize communications and decisions. Where there are controversial issues and contending groups, though, problems should be dealt with on the informal level, where discussions and negotiations can take place. The effective administrator partially follows formal procedures and partly deviates from them, depending on the nature of the action to be taken.

Casual observation suggests that a high interaction exists between personality types and rule observation. Those who seek a highly structured context probably accept rule adherence even where they are goal oriented. Those who can tolerate ambiguity find rule adherence intolerable where it doesn't aid in getting the job done. Dalton's analysis supports this thesis.

14

PARTICIPATION:
Consulting with Subordinates

Greater attention probably has been given to participation as a leadership dimension than nearly any other element of leadership style. The University of Iowa studies in 1941 paid major attention to participation. This aspect of leadership subsequently has been popularized by writers such as Rensis Likert, who has equated broad use of participation with effective management.[1]

Participation Defined. In reviewing the literature, several conceptual problems confound the interpretation of research results.[2] One of these problems is the distinction between "delegation of authority" and "participation." A low or high degree of authority may be delegated in the sense that decisions are centralized or decentralized. Independent of the degree of delegation is the extent to which a leader uses participation in making decisions.

---

[1]Rensis Likert, *New Patterns of Management* (New York: McGraw-Hill Book Co., 1961); Rensis Likert, *The Human Organization: Its Management and Value* (New York: McGraw-Hill Book Co., 1967); Robert C. Albrook, "Participation Management: Time for a Second Look," *Fortune* (May 1967), pp. 166–70, 197–200.

[2]One problem in unraveling the effects of participation is that the term is used diffusely or equated to democratic approaches to leadership. We consider it as only one of the building blocks that make up a democratic leadership style. An additional problem is that one can look at participation as a leadership style, or one can ask what the factors are that result in one participating in an organization. In the first case, participation is the independent variable and we are concerned with the effects of involvement in the decision process; in the second case, participation is the dependent variable and the concern is with causes of individual commitment to the organization. Many writers who focus on unions are concerned with the question of what influences the level of membership attendance at meetings or other activities in the union, i.e., their level of participation. We will not explore this element of participation because it is unrelated to leadership style.

A body of literature also develops the effects of lecture versus discussion on opinion and behavioral changes. This is often referred to as the use or nonuse of participation. However, no decision is reached by the group that becomes binding on the members. We will limit our discussion of participation to where the decisions that are reached affect the entire group. This excludes the literature on the effects of lecture versus discussion on behavior.

Reprinted courtesy of Mell Lazarus and Publishers-Hall Syndicate, Copyright 1973, Field Enterprises.

In an academic organization, for instance, decisions may be broadly centralized at the university level with relatively little decentralization down to the college or department level. In a centralized organization, little potential exists for meaningful participation at lower levels in an organization. However, there may be broad or limited use of participation at the central level. In effect, the degree of delegation determines the parameters limiting the maximum of participation that can potentially be used at each level.

Table 14-1 highlights the difference between delegation and participation.

TABLE 14-1. Some Possible Combinations of Delegation and Participation

| | Delegation | |
Participation	Decentralization	Centralization
High	11	12
Low	21	22

In cell 12, the supervisor retains the right to make final decisions even though he does not usually exercise it; he broadly consults with those involved or affected by the decision. In cell 11, he broadly delegates the decisions to the subordinates; on those decisions that he retains, he uses broad participation. In cell 21, authority is broadly delegated, but low use is made of participation on remaining decisions. In cell 22, we have both low delegation and low use of participation.

Specifically, participation is defined as consulting and involving subordinates or other groups that are affected by decisions in the making of decisions. This varies from extensive to limited involvement. On the one hand, the supervisor involves subordinates or other groups that would be affected by decisions. They are involved both in the deliberations and the final making of the decisions. For example, committees might be formed or meetings held with all those directly affected to consider actions to be taken. Decisions are reached by majority consesus. In relating to higher level supervisors or the groups that are making decisions affecting his group, the supervisor initiates suggestions and otherwise attempts to participate and exert influence on the decision process.

On the other hand, decisions are made by the supervisor without consultation or participation of those affected by the decision. Instead, the decision is made simply by the supervisor and transmitted to others to implement. Where suggestions or other initiatives are offered by subordinates or other groups, these are *not* systematically considered.

Participation: A Ripple Effect?

We need to address ourselves to the question of when participation is most effective and to what extent involvement in some decisions carries over into a more positive attitude and orientation generally. George Strauss raises a series of questions along these lines.[3]

It is often said that, if a worker is permitted to participate in making decisions, he will work harder. But work harder at what? At making the decision? At implementing the decision? Or at implementing *other* decisions? Suppose, for example, workers are permitted to decide for themselves *when* coffee breaks should be taken (though management still determines how long they should be). The discussion itself may well be quite lively. But will the mere fact of participation lead to workers taking their breaks only at the times agreed upon? Will they be less likely to take breaks which are excessively long? And will they also produce more on the job? And, to consider a related question: when will decision making within the small group lead to greater support of the goals of the entire organization? Many managers assume that participation in regard to a relatively trivial problem will lead to higher productivity generally. Perhaps this will occur at times. But when? Why? This is what I would call the problem of *generalization*—the question of when the impact of participation in one area carries over into another area.

I know of no empirical research which squarely attacks this difficult question, and the most I can do here is raise it as a problem and suggest a few hypotheses worthy of further research:

1. It would seem that the effects of participation would be most easily generalized where this participation serves to *reduce resistance* to

---

[3]George Strauss, "Some Notes on Power-Equalization," in Harold J. Leavitt, ed., *The Social Science of Organizations: Four Perspectives,* © 1963. Reprinted by permission of Prentice-Hall, Inc., Englewood Cliffs, New Jersey.

higher production (in Lewinian terms, reduces restraining forces or reduces the negative valence attached to a high production level). Specifically, the effects of participation in regard to one area, for example, coffee breaks, may carry over into another, for example, productivity, when the following conditions prevail:

a. Where participation tends to reduce the subordinates' resentment which may arise from excessive one-way initiation on the part of higher management (in other words, where participation tends to establish a more balanced interaction pattern).

b. Where participation permits catharsis and a reduction in generalized resentment against management. In the example given, this would be *particularly* true in the fairly unlikely case where productivity was low because the poor timing of coffee breaks led employees to become emotionally disturbed.

2. Participation may also set up an exchange relationship, for example, workers may feel that they should work harder in exchange for management's concession regarding coffee breaks.

3. As suggested previously, participation may increase an individual's attraction to the group and make the group more cohesive. To the extent that this occurs, the individual will be more strongly influenced by group norms, regardless of whether these norms directly relate to the questions about which the original participation occurred. This does not mean, from a strictly management point of view, that it would be wise to promote cohesion or participation willynilly. Participation may lead an individual to accept the *group* norms ("group" here referring to the face-to-face primary aggregation of individuals); but, if these norms are not congruent with those of the larger organization, then participation in group decisions may actually render the individual less receptive to the values of the larger organizations. For example, if the group promotes "bogies" or "ceilings" restricting output, then participation may result in lower production.

4. To the extent that the larger organization permits individuals to participate in organizational decisions (for example, regarding coffee breaks), these individuals may feel that their status in the organization is enhanced. Thus, they may value the organization more highly and feel more favorable toward its norms (for example, regarding productivity). Participation does raise certain dangers. As group members become more involved in group processes and as cohesion increases, the group may learn to expect to be consulted about every problem which arises. Since in a large organization it may not be possible to consult everyone about every problem, expectations will often be frustrated, and perhaps it might be better not to get the members so involved.

5. Motivation for achievement may be most difficult to generalize. Participation in decision making in one area may lead an individual to feel that doing well in this area provides a test of valued skills. But there is no a priori reason why it should lead him to want to do equally well in other areas.

Let me summarize my position. Most of the writing about participation has emphasized *personal involvement*. Without denying the real importance of this factor, I should also like to emphasize two other factors: First, participation changes *interaction patterns* and thus may reduce resistance to change introduced by management (including changes in work levels), even where subordinates do not initiate these changes on their own hook. Second, group participation may be viewed as a means of "negotiating" an implicit (or even explicit) contract among the individual, the group, and even the larger organization. On the whole, I believe that, at least for hourly workers, participation is more likely to be a hygienic factor (in the Herzberg sense) than a positive motivator to work.

Finally, let me mention again four possible dysfunctional aspects of group participation: (1) individuals whose opinions have been rejected by the group may become alienated from it; (2) participation may lead to greater cohesion, but it may be cohesion against management; (3) participation may set up expectations of continued participation which management may not be able to satisfy; and (4) participation often takes a great deal of time, can be frustrating to those involved, and frequently results in watered-down solutions.

Popular Conceptions of Effects of Participation. Perhaps one of the most broadly accepted ideas in organizational practice is that participation should be widely used. Even where the supervisor makes little use of participation, he seldom defends the practice; rather he will point to areas where he uses it to some degree. McGregor develops the thesis that broad use of participation incorporates the values of Theory Y. Participation is used as a method to express confidence in the potentialities of subordinates, to show management's awareness that it is dependent downward, and to avoid the negative consequences of using personal authority.[4] "It is consistent with Theory Y—with management by integration and self-control."

McGregor holds that one of the major consequences of the use of participation is that it encourages the growth of subordinates and improves their ability to accept responsibility. He contends that it provides oppor-

[4]Douglas McGregor, *The Human Side of Enterprise* (New York: McGraw-Hill Book Co., 1960), pp. 125–26.

tunity for employee satisfaction and increases motivation towards organizational objectives by integrating employees into the organization. He further sees this as contributing to a sense of independence, a sense of controlling one's destiny, and gaining satisfaction and recognition from peers and superiors. Participation also enables personal needs to be satisfied and made consistent with working toward organizational objectives.[5]

This form of listing could be expanded by drawing upon other books with the human relations viewpoint. It is an imposing list of values without any apparent appreciable risk. We need to examine more closely the studies on which these generalizations have been built and critically assess whether this degree of optimism is justified.

Operationalization of Participation

Participation: Extensive to Limited. In arriving at a decision, the supervisor may seek broad involvement from those affected by the decision or may make consultations.

1	2	3	4	5	6	7	8	9

Extensive								Limited

1. Does your supervisor make personnel decisions (hiring new staff, promoting personnel, or adopting new personnel policies and programs) without asking for advice and comments of your work group?

1	2	3	4	5	6	7	8	9

Rarely	Sometimes		Often		Usually		Almost always	

2. Does he ask for comments and suggestions from your work group on job-related matters (setting goals, changing methods, solving job problems, or making important changes in the working arrangements)?

1	2	3	4	5	6	7	8	9

Almost always	Usually		Often		Sometimes		Rarely	

---

[5]Ibid., p. 131.

3. Does he *discourage* open discussion of issues and problems (such as by acting defensively, becoming critical, or otherwise acting as if he is personally being attacked)?

1	2	3	4	5	6	7	8	9
Rarely	Sometimes		Often		Usually		Almost always	

4. Does he encourage "majority rule" (such as by insisting the *minority* abide by the *majority* in cases of disputes, and generally supporting the majority position)?

1	2	3	4	5	6	7	8	9
Almost always	Usually		Often		Sometimes		Rarely	

5. Does he ask for advice and comments of others (his superior, relevant staff personnel, or supervisors of other work groups) on issues and problems on which *they* are likely to be concerned?

1	2	3	4	5	6	7	8	9
Almost always	Usually		Often		Sometimes		Rarely	

FIELD STUDIES OF PARTICIPATION

Consultation at the Top Levels. A classic study on the uses and limitations of participation was done by Nyman and Smith, who investigated the Pequot Mills, a textile firm, for a period of over four years in the early 1930s.[6] The mills employed approximately twelve hundred employees located in five departments. The company was under market pressures to introduce labor-saving technological changes but was faced with a strong, well-organized union. In the face of a deteriorating competitive position, the company resisted the demands of the union for improvements in wages and other protections. The company's resistance caused internal problems within the

[6]C. Nyman and Elliott D. Smith, *Union-Management Cooperation in the "Stretch Out": Labor Extension at the Pequot Mills* (New Haven, Conn.: Yale University Press, 1934).

union; factional groups formed and dissatisfaction with the union leadership developed.

The business agent was a man of imagination and foresight. He proposed a plan of organized union-management cooperation to provide a basis for joint adjustments to the competitive conditions facing the company. The plan was accepted by the firm.

Under this plan, the management, in addition to agreeing to recognize the union "as both desirable and essential to the successful operation of the company," and to "maintain good working conditions, fair wages, and continuity of employment," agreed also to meet regularly with the union officials to discuss labor relations problems.[7] This plan enabled the union to participate in conferences where it could exert influence on company policies—an objective that it had previously sought to reach through collective bargaining.

Monthly conferences were held where problems of mutual interests were discussed. At first, a fairly large-scale meeting was held with about thirty-five representatives of the company and union. Later, these were held infrequently, and only the mill officials and a few workers generally participated. The workers were consulted informally, or, when an issue was pending, a general meeting of the union was held. In effect, the system permitted close consultation between top union and management officials in the plant; however, lower echelon management and employees were not involved.

The participation was effective in that the union leadership developed an understanding of the problems facing the company and an acceptance that the union and the workers had to make adjustments to acute competitive conditions. The union leadership supported management efforts in these directions. While the understanding was achieved at the upper level, it wasn't achieved by lower level supervision or operative employees. The lower level management saw participation as a device to elicit acceptance of changes the company wanted to implement. They did not see it as a joint decision process or joint consultation on decisions. The workers felt that consultation was a device for "speedup." As management increasingly consulted with top local union officials, it became less acceptable to the workers.

Relations deteriorated between the company and union membership and a strike was called under adverse economic circumstances despite the strong opposition of the union leadership. Factionalism within the union along with the discrediting of the union leadership made it difficult to settle the strike. Ultimately, an independent union was formed with new leadership.

The study illustrates some of the powers of cooptation that are attributed to participation. It also suggests that the value is limited to those who are actively involved in the consultative process. The failure to involve lower

[7]Ibid., p. 8.

level personnel split the leadership and the followers both on the union and management side.

The Ahmedabad Studies: Consultation at the Bottom Levels. Another study in the textile industry, but in this case located in India, illustrates the power of participation to win acceptance of technical change in an organization. Rice studied the introduction of technical changes and reorganization in a small textile plant in Ahmedabad, India.[8] The plant was part of a larger company that employed approximately eight thousand workers. The study covered a period of several years.

As a professional consultant, Rice approached the company to establish a collaborative relationship with the Tavistock Institute—a research group in England. The top management approved of the idea and worked out an approach for organizational changes. The reorganization, in effect, permitted the organization of small, integrated work groups. The elements of the idea were proposed to lower level supervision who, in turn, proposed them to the workers. The workers accepted the idea and immediately proceeded to implement it along the lines they saw as most useful. They organized the experimental groups with size and membership following the new plan. The move was successful in that productivity increased and, in particular, the basic change in traditional working relationships was immediately accepted.

Rice replicated the experiment in a somewhat different setting in the same company.[9] An experimental group of seven workers was formed, later enlarged to eleven workers. This time, Rice planned out the form of structure and task arrangement. Neither the operating managers nor the workers were initially consulted in the planning of the system. When problems developed, though, Rice discussed the difficulties with the workers, and out of the discussions came modifications in the plan. These meetings operated on an open-ended basis where expression of viewpoints spontaneously developed. The meetings allowed broad participation and involvement on the part of supervision and the workers. A cohesive group developed with considerable enthusiasm for the new arrangements.

The acceptance of the changes in many respects was remarkable. The changes occurred during a period when there was broad resistance against what is termed "rationalization" in India, i.e., introduction of labor-saving methods. Permission had to be obtained from union officials and the workers to introduce the changes. The experiment became a center of agitation in the city and region from those who opposed both the introduction of automatic

[8]A. K. Rice, "Productivity and Social Organization in an Indian Weaving Shed," *Human Relations*, 6 (1953), 297–330.

[9]A. K. Rice, "The Experimental Reorganization of Non-Automatic Weaving in an Indian Mill," *Human Relations*, 8 (1955), 199–250.

machinery and the increased productivity of individual workers. Still, the change was maintained in spite of the hostile environment.

The Rice studies are confounded by a number of factors. The workers had volunteered to participate in the experiment. Further, the experimental shed was located in an area that had been a main thoroughfare through the mill. This permitted anyone concerned to observe what was going on. An open invitation was given to officials of the trade union to observe, and many others visited the operation.

The "Hawthorne effect" probably occurred since both experimental units became the center of attention of the larger plant and of management. Still, technical changes, whether they are desirable or undesirable from either union, employees, or management standpoint, are often actively resisted. While the small-sized units, the use of volunteers, and the attention given the group were supportive factors, the broad use of participation contributed to acceptance of change under unfavorable conditions.

The Pajama Factory Studies : Participation in Goal Setting. A famous set of studies took place at the Haywood Manufacturing Company.[10] One study dramatically demonstrated the value of participation in changing a stereotype.[11] In the plant, a broadly held conviction was that women over thirty were slow in developing speed in production, were frequently absent, had a shorter working life, and were difficult to teach. French, who was employed as a psychologist in the plant, tried to convince management that their conclusions about older women weren't true. He could not, so he devised a method to educate management and the workers. A simple study was designed that the management carried out to determine the relationship of women's ages to productivity as well as other relevant factors. The idea was that if management participated in the study, they would accept the conclusions more readily. When the top management found that, in fact, the older women were reliable employees, they changed their opinion and were ready to modify hiring policy.

Those who did not participate in the study, however, weren't persuaded by the opinions of top management or the plant psychologist. A series of meetings was held to acquaint them with the evidence and to discuss their reservations and the general nature of stereotypes. Group consensus developed that an experiment in training older workers should be tried. In this

[10]Al Coch and John R. P. French, Jr., "Overcoming Resistance to Change," *Human Relations*, 1 (1948), 512–32; John R. P. French, Jr., et al, "Employee Participation in a Program of Industrial Change," *Personnel*, 35 (1958), 16–29; Norman Maier, *Psychology in Industry* (New York: Houghton Mifflin, 1965); Alfred J. Marrow, David G. Bowers, and Stanley E. Seashore, *Management by Participation* (New York: Harper & Row, 1967).

[11]Alfred J. Marrow and John R. P. French, Jr., "Changing a Stereotype in Industry," *Journal of Social Issues*, 2 (1945), 33–37.

way, the new policy became broadly accepted. A number of other studies followed.

We have a relatively unusual situation in the Haywood organization. The firm was a small, family-owned manufacturer of textiles, located in the small town of Marion, Virginia. The plant mostly employed women (500 women and 100 men in 1948). The workers were recruited from the rural, mountainous areas surrounding the town and normally were without previous industrial experience. The average worker was twenty-three, with eight years of grammar school. In the late thirties, the management of the company was turned over to the owner's two sons, one a psychologist (A. Coch) · and one an engineer. The Haywood firm became a center of behavioral research when Kurt Lewin began working with the plant management in 1939 and brought in co-workers, including Alex Bavelas and John R. P. French, Jr., to carry out projects. These studies proportedly demonstrate the values of participation in changing basic beliefs, making individuals more responsive to technical change, increasing productivity, and contributing to more positive employee attitudes.

The fact that the studies have been broadly quoted justifies a close look at their design. In one study, Coch and French explored whether participation influenced acceptance of technical change.[12] The company's experience with technical change had been poor; employees had a high quit rate or were slow in achieving previous levels of productivity when technical changes were implemented. The research design was to contrast three groups, one defined as the "no-participation group," one as "participation through representation," and one as "total participation."

The no-participation group went through the usual factory routine on implementing changes. The production department modified the job, and the new piece rate was set. A group meeting was held in which the group was told that the change was necessary because of competitive conditions and that a new piece rate had been set. The new piece rate was explained by the time-study man, questions were answered, and the meeting dismissed.

In the group with participation through representation, a meeting was held where the need for change was explained and dramatized. Management then presented its plan. This involved making a study of the job as it was being done, eliminating unnecessary work, training several operators in the new methods, setting the piece rate by time studies, explaining the new job and rate to the operators, and training operators in the new methods. The group then selected the operators to be specially trained. Additional meetings were held with these operators where the changes were discussed. The selected operators then trained the other group members on the new job.

[12]Coch and French, Jr., "Overcoming Resistance to Change."

A total-participation group went through the same steps as the group with participation through representation except that the group was smaller and all the operators were given the special training. In both participation groups, suggestions were solicited and recorded by a stenographer. The differences between the groups were partly in participation but mostly in variations in training to adjust to the change and an unknown degree of methods change. Participation in these cases was the opportunity for the employees to present suggestions and choose members for training. Management made the decisions on what was going to be done and how it was to be done and trained the employees to do it.

The results were that the no-participation group had lower level productivity, higher level conflict with supervisory and staff personnel, and a greater rate of turnover as compared with the other two groups. Little difference developed between the total-participation group and the group with participation through representation.

Ten years later, a replication in the same plant of the experiment had most of the same characteristics and results.[13] Another replication of the study was done in a Norwegian manufacturing plant.[14] They sought to determine how participation in planning technical changes affected employee productivity and behavior. The study involved nine 4-member groups. Participation was practically unchanged in two groups and only moderately changed in three other groups. The other four groups were set up as controls.

The authors hypothesized that increased participation affects production, labor-management relations, and job satisfaction only to the extent that four conditions are present: (a) the decisions are important, (b) the content of the decisions is relevant to production, labor relations, or job satisfaction, (c) participation is considered legitimate, (d) reactions to the methods of managing change are either neutral or positive.

This is a useful listing of preconditions, but the experimental design only partially provided evidence related to these premises. Taking nine groups out of a larger group of nearly 400 employees and in a minor manner increasing their participation limits the potential influence on behavior and productivity. In fact, participation didn't affect productivity of the workers or behavior in any consistent way. In effect, the group norms defined level of production, and participation didn't touch these norms.

The work done by Bavelas at Haywood also has won wide attention even though his work has been reported second hand by others. In one experi-

---

[13]French, Jr. et al, "Employee Participation in a Program of Industrial Change," pp. 16–29.

[14]John R. P. French, Jr., Joachim Israel, and Dagfinn As, "An Experiment on Participation in a Norwegian Factory," *Human Relations*, 13 (1960), 3–19.

ment, he explored how participation in goal setting influenced production.[15] Bavelas met with one group of workers to discuss the establishment of goals. The goals were set at a high level and were subsequently reached. Another group also met with Bavelas for interviews. "They received the same attention and friendly encouragement, but no production goal was decided upon."[16] In this group, no change in production occurred. This study was replicated in another midwestern garment manufacturing plant. While the results were not as clean-cut as those achieved by Bavelas, the results as interpreted by French and his co-authors generally supported that participation in goal setting improved subsequent productivity.

While these results indicate that participation was the relevant factor, a closer look suggests that standards—not participation—were the key variable. In effect, we have a research design where cells 11 and 21 of Table 14-2 are explored—not 11 and 12, or 21 and 22.

TABLE 14-2.   Some Possible Combinations of Goal Setting and Participation

| | | Participation | |
		Some Participation	No Participation
Goals	Set	11	12
	Not Set	21	22

There are always problems in field studies in sorting out the effects of the variable under study from other possible causal factors. In the case of the Haywood organization, the management has actively supported the intensive study of their organization over a period of thirty years. The major figures reporting their studies are committed to an intellectual position that participation is a pervasive force affecting behavior. One has to view the findings with some skepticism since other variables are confounding the results.

Participation as we have defined it—and as it usually is used—is being changed only in a mild degree. Other factors are changing sharply. Employees under "participation" conditions receive training; those under "no participation" don't. Goals are set for a participating group but not for a nonparticipating group. The authors consistently ignore other variables that also affect behavior and productivity. In the last reported study of the Haywood organization, a great number of changes in technology, formal structure, control systems, and information systems occurred when the firm

[15]Maier, *Psychology in Industry*, pp. 160–62.
[16]Ibid., p. 161.

took over another plant. Yet, the sharp changes in behavior and productivity have been attributed to greater participation.[17]

Numerous other studies conclude that participation importantly affects behavior. We shall want to check whether these generalizations are borne out by somewhat narrower but better controlled studies.

Interaction of Participation and Personality. Several studies provide us with some of the effects of participation and necessary conditions for it to be effective. Victor Vroom explored the extent to which personality mediates the influence of participation on behavior.[18] This was a field study of supervisors of two branches of a parcel post firm located in New York and Chicago. His concern was with how participation interacted with personality to affect job attitudes of subordinates and job performance. His measure of participation included two questions directed at how much influence the subordinate had over the supervisor and two questions that measured the extent the supervisor consulted with the subordinate and was responsive to the subordinate's suggestions.

Two measures of personality—a measure of the need for independence and a measure of authoritarian qualities—were used. Neither personality nor participation *alone* had much influence over attitude toward job, but participation and the two measures of personality together influenced attitudes.[19] High participation combined with high need for independence resulted in the most favorable job attitude; low participation and high need for independence caused the lowest job satisfaction. Low participation in combination with low need for independence provided more favorable results than low participation and high need for independence. The same relations held with interaction of authoritarian qualities and participation except the influences were smaller.[20]

In summary, we find that one of the better studies finds that participation alone has little affect on behavior. However, those high on independence and low on authoritarian qualities react more positively to greater participation. This study doesn't support the more optimistic statements of the effects of participation. If participation is effective, a supervisory force should be responsive toward different levels of participation. We find only mild differences in behavior in this study.

---

[17]Marrow, Bowers, and Seashore, *Management by Participation.*

[18]Victor H. Vroom, *Some Personality Determinants of the Effects of Participation* (Englewood Cliffs, N.J.: Prentice-Hall, Inc. 1960); The study is also briefly reported in Victor H. Vroom, "Some Personality Determinants of the Effects of Participation," *Journal of Abnormal and Social Psychology,* 59 (1959), 322–27.

[19]Ibid., p. 83.

[20]Ibid., p. 326.

Participation in Goal Setting. French and his colleagues focused on management in a division at General Electric.[21] The firm had an appraisal system where individual performance levels were periodically evaluated in terms of formal standards. One part of the appraisal interview was the establishment of goals for the next period. The researchers were concerned with the question of whether different degrees of participation in setting goals affected achievement in the next time period. They also explored how participation affected various aspects of superior-subordinate relations and job satisfaction.

The experimental design varied the degree of participation in setting performance goals and planning of how to achieve these goals. One-half the employees participated to a high degree and the other half very little. In the high-participation group, the manager asked each individual to write out a set of goals for improving future performance, methods for achieving goals, and measures of evaluating progress toward them. Following this, a meeting was held where the employee presented and discussed the goals with his manager and modified or added to them. The manager tried to elicit additional goals from the subordinate.

In the low-participation group, the manager presented the goals to the subordinate, the means for achieving them and the ways to measure his progress. He then secured the subject's agreement; he reluctantly modified key goals, where relevant points were raised, and accepted the subordinate's suggestions with minimum discussion and emphasis.

Consistent differences existed between the high- and low-participation groups *before* goal planning sessions were set up.[22] If this is taken into account, participation in goal setting had little effect on behavior either immediately after the goal planning session or ten to twelve weeks later. The only exception was somewhat greater acceptance of goals under higher participation.

However, degree of threat, participation, and degree of influence interacted in their influence on behavior.[23] One of the factors that was included in the design was the "usual level of participation." This was operationalized as the amount of influence the subordinate exerted. Where high threat in the first appraisal interview was coupled with the subordinate's judgment that he had *low influence*, increased participation caused goal achievement to deteriorate from 72 to 49 percent. This contrasted with where an individual felt he had high influence. Under the high-threat condition, increased participation caused goal achievement to rise from 46 to 75 percent. The high-threat condition created anxiety that those with low influence felt unable to handle. Providing them with greater opportunity to participate

[21]John R. P. French, Jr., Emanuel J. Kay, and Herbert H. Meyer, "Participation and the Appraisal System," *Human Relations*, 19 (1966), 3–20.

[22]Ibid., p. 13.

[23]Ibid., p. 14.

only increased it further since they felt they had little influence over goals that were set.

In summary, our analysis of French's data indicates that participation in establishing goals has little effect on the three dimensions of behavior. The establishment of goals, in contrast, generally improves behavior. When two other dimensions are introduced, the results are somewhat modified. Where the degree of threat in the first appraisal interview and the degree of influence are held constant, then higher level participation improves performance. However, a high degree of interaction exists among these three dimensions. If high threat in the interview is combined with participation in goal setting, performance attainment is high; when participation is increased under this circumstance, goal attainment is reduced sharply.[24]

Short- and Long-run Implications of Participation. Lawler, Heckman, and Scheflen explored in a field -experiment the effects of participating in planning to reduce absenteeism in a firm providing maintenance services.[25] Three groups designed a plan with the researcher providing expert advice. They developed a bonus plan where $2.50 a week would be given for perfect attendence, i.e., no unauthorized absenteeism; management applied an identical plan on two other groups after explaining its purpose and goals. The problem of absenteeism was discussed with two other groups, but no bonus was offered for reducing absenteeism. The result was that absenteeism dropped 6 percent in the participation group in the three months after the plan was instituted. Absenteeism was unchanged where the plan was initiated by management and in the groups with no incentive.

However, one year later, a different pattern had developed.[26] Management had terminated the plan in two of the groups that had formulated the plan working with the researchers. Absenteeism rose to its previous level when the plan was abandoned. In the participation group, where the plan was retained, the level of improved attendance was maintained. In the two groups where management had initiated the plan, while no change in absenteeism had occurred in the first three months, absenteeism had dropped 4 percent by one year later. In summary, the use of participation influenced how fast employees responded to the incentive of the $2.50 a week bonus. With participation, the plan immediately affected absenteeism; without participation, the employees took somewhere between three months and a year to respond to the incentives.

---

[24]This analysis departs fairly sharply from that provided in the article. Readers are encouraged to read the original articles to evaluate the usefulness of the interpretation.

[25]Edward E. Lawler III and J. Richard Heckman, "Impact of Employee Participation in the Development of Pay Incentive Plans," *Journal of Applied Psychology*, 53 (1969), 467–71.

[26]Kenneth C. Scheflen, Edward E. Lawler III, and J. Richard Heckman, "Long-term Impact of Employee Participation in the Development of Pay Incentive Plans: A Field Experiment Revisited," *Journal of Applied Psychology*, 55 (1971), 182–86.

In chapter 13, we examined Gouldner's thesis that the way rules are initiated determines, in part, the response to them. In this case, a plan for reducing absenteeism was initiated by the employees and an outside researcher and supported by higher level management. The plan was effective in achieving its goals but was abandoned by management within a year. Where the plan was initiated by management, the plan was maintained, but employees' response to its incentive feature was delayed and two-thirds as effective. Gouldner's thesis is supported in this study, but the response to rules is more complex than Gouldner visualized. Participation is a method of making a plan, policies, or rules the property of both employees and management when *both* are involved in consideration and formulation.

SUMMARY AND CONCLUSION

In summary, broad attention has been given in the literature to participation as a leadership dimension. We have a couple of dramatic but loosely designed field studies that demonstrate that participation has a powerful effect. The more rigorous studies suggest that participation is effective only under certain conditions. The value of participation is limited to those who are actively involved in the consultative process. While plans can be initially formulated, their acceptance is dependent upon an open forum where objections can be voiced and changes made. The independence and authoritarian aspects of personality interact with participation. Those with a high need for independence react favorably to high participation; on the other hand, low participation and low need for independence combined are consistent with job satisfaction. Where appraisal threats and low influence are combined with high participation, performance declines. Under the same conditions, if individuals see themselves as having high influence, performance rises. Limited evidence supports the view that short-term consequences of participation vary from longer term implications. Participation facilitates immediate acceptance of changes; management's initiatives are accepted over the longer term without participation, but the impact on behavior is lessened.

Wilensky, in a review of research in 1957, developed the thesis restricted participation (or what he calls anthoritarian leadership) is acceptable and effective when conditions support leadership initiation.[27] These conditions include: (1) goals are clearly defined, (2) division of labor is clear-cut, (3) the group has the necessary skills, (4) outside pressures threaten the group, (5) the members perceive that speedy action is necessary, and (6) individuals have previous experience in operating in structured environment, such as in an authoritarian family.

[27]Harold L. Wilensky, "Human Relations in the Workplace: An Appraisal of Some Recent Research," in Conrad Arensberg et al, eds., *Research in Industrial Human Relations* (New York: Harper & Brothers, 1957), footnote, pp. 34–35.

This suggests the following combinations when high and low participation would be effective:

TABLE 14-3. Conditions That Support High and Low Participation

	Participation	
Conditions	*High*	*Low*
Goals	Ambiguous	Clearly defined
Division of Labor	Overlapping and limited	Clear-cut and extensive
Group process skills	Developed	Undeveloped
Outside pressures	Low	High
Need for speedy action	Low	High
Family background	Democratic	Authoritorian

As investigations are made of participation under these various conditions, we will have a better base for generalizing when participation contributes to better functioning groups and organizations.

15

DIRECTION:
The Closeness of Supervision

INTRODUCTION

The classic experiments by Lewin, Lippit, and White in 1939–1949 directed attention to leadership style. Among the nine different ways in which the leadership style differed, a number of these fell under what we are calling direction.

Direction Defined. The approaches to direction may vary from loose supervision to the other extreme of close, detailed direction. Loose direction is primarily a hands-off policy. Ends or goals are broadly specified, but the means for achieving these ends are largely left to the group or individual to develop. Subordinates must rely upon their own counsel and ability to handle problems. Requests by subordinates for direction and guidance are referred back to the individual or group to make their own decision. Few direct or indirect orders are given; there is little use of the imperative tone of voice or the use of explicit instructions to "do this" or "don't do that." The leader seldom issues disruptive commands or orders which directly countervene the activities or orientation of the group members.

On close supervision, in contrast, a supervisor's orientation towards subordinates or other groups is to establish detailed direction that specifies both ends and means of achieving these ends. The individuals are closely observed to determine the extent to which prescriptions are followed. The tendency is to give direct orders and to use the imperative tone of voice where suggestions are offered. Disruptive commands are more frequent; that is, orders are given that directly countervene the activities and orientations of subordinates or others with whom the supervisor is working. Steps are specified one at a time; as a consequence, the subordinate has to continually seek additional instruction at each stage of the job. The supervisor's posture towards his superior is to seek detailed direction and to systematically report on the extent to which the instructions are followed.

Operationalizing Direction

The approach to direction may vary from loose to close detailed instructions. The differences are defined by the extent to which the supervisor instructs in specifying both means and ends.

(1)	2	3	4	(5)	6	7	8	(9)
Loose				General				Close

1. In directing your work group, which of the following best describes your supervisor:

1. *Loose direction*—he outlines the job to be done and leaves it up to individuals or groups to decide how to do it.
5. *General direction*—he outlines the job to be done and gives general instructions on how to do it, leaving the details for the individual or group to work out.
9. *Close direction*—he issues detailed instructions on what to do and how to do it. These are given step by step so that he gives instructions as the job proceeds.

(1)	2	3	4	(5)	6	7	8	(9)
Loose				General				Close

2. In checking on your work group, which of the following best describes your supervisor:

1. *Loose checking*—he hardly ever checks on how well the job is going and seldom checks on how well the completed job is done.
5. *General checking*—he regularly checks on the general progress of the group and nearly always checks on how well the completed job is done.
9. *Close checking*—he checks regularly to see that his instructions are followed, how each step is proceeding, and how well the completed job is done.

(1)	2	3	4	(5)	6	7	8	(9)
Loose				General				Close

3. In ordering, requesting, or giving suggestions, is your supervisor's method best described as:

1. *Adaptive*—his suggestions and comments complement the problem-solving approach and flow of activities being carried on by individuals or the group. He doesn't impose different ideas and approaches on the group.
5. *Directive*—his comments and directions partly amplify and partly modify the approach being followed by individuals or the group. Occasionally, he will substitute his judgment for theirs and order them to implement his approach.
9. *Nonadaptive*—the supervisor generally substitutes his approach over that being taken by individuals or the group; his concern is with implementing his ideas rather than developing further the ideas and approaches initiated by others.

(1)	2	3	4	(5)	6	7	8	(9)
Adaptive				Directive				Nonadaptive

4. Is your supervisor's "style" to request assistance, ask for help, and give suggestions (such as "Would you do this? . . . or "Why don't you look at the problem another way? . . .")

(1)	2	3	4	(5)	6	7	8	(9)
Almost always	Usually			Often		Sometimes		Rarely

5. Does your supervisor try to persuade his superior and staff groups to issue broadly stated policies and procedures so as to leave flexibility for the work group (rather than detailed instructions that clarify exactly what the group is supposed to do)?

(1)	2	3	4	(5)	6	7	8	(9)
Almost always	Usually			Often		Sometimes		Rarely

Effects of Close Direction: The Human Relations View.   What are the consequences for behavior of different degrees of direction? Many supervisors in industry and other organizations subscribe to the viewpoint that close supervision contributes toward more productive employees. Douglas McGregor described this conception of supervision by highlighting what he felt were its underlying basic assumptions. He called these assumptions "the Theory X approach to management."[1] The assumptions he abstracted were the following:[2] (1) The average human being dislikes work and will avoid it if he can. (2) Most people must be directed and threatened with punishment to get them to apply adequate effort toward organizational objectives. (3) The average person prefers to be directed, wishes to avoid responsibility, has little ambition, and wants security above all. McGregor challenged this view of man. He subscribed to the Herzberg thesis that a hierarchy of needs exists and close supervision impedes the satisfaction of some of the strongest needs. He contended that when people cannot fulfill their needs at work, it stimulates indolence, passivity, refusals to accept responsibility, resistance to change, receptiveness to the demagogue, and unreasonable economical demands.

Mason Haire has described a close supervisor as a special kind of bird:

The White-shirted Hoverer clearly falls in this province, assigning a task and then standing over it to see that it is done. His effect is probably not as devastating, however, as that of the Pin-striped Oopster, the bird which, as soon as the task is delegated, feels he must follow every step of the operation, saying "Oops! Oops!!" at regular intervals.[3]

While these comments suggest that close supervision is unnecessary, and unfruitful, the reality is that many supervisors judge that it is essential to obtain employee application.

Research Studies: The Reaction of Professional Personnel. A field research project by Aiken and Hage on sixteen welfare agencies explored how close leadership affected the behavior of professional staff members.[4] They explored how direction, participation, and rule adherence affected satisfaction with the job and satisfaction with the immediate supervisor and fellow workers. They found that close direction caused dissatisfaction with the job, but direction had little impact on interpersonal relations.

[1]Douglas McGregor, *The Human Side of Enterprise* (New York: McGraw-Hill Book Co., 1960), pp. 33–43.

[2]Ibid., p. 42.

[3]Mason Haire, *Psychology in Management* (New York: McGraw-Hill, 1956), p. 57.

[4]Michael Aiken and Gerald Hage, "Organization Alienation: A Comparative Analysis," *American Sociological Review*, 31 (1966), 497–550.

Methodogical Problems in
Leadership Research

Many of the studies have had serious problems of research design. This reflects the early development of the area. To illustrate the problems, we have identified some difficulties in a study by Aiken and Hage.[5]

They conducted a field research project on sixteen welfare agencies. The research reflects both operational and conceptual problems of developing the effects of supervision. The authors explored how participation in decision making, rule observation, "hierarchy or authority," and "job codification" affected "work alienation" and "alienation from expressive relations." Hierarchy of authority and job codification were operationalized as we have defined direction, as indicated below:

The index of hierarchy of authority was computed by first averaging the replies of individual respondents to each of the following five statements:
1. There can be little action taken here until a supervisor approves a decision.
2. A person who wants to make his own decisions would be quickly discouraged here.
3. Even small matters have to be referred to someone higher up for a final answer.
4. I have to ask my boss before I do almost anything.
5. Any decision I make has to have my boss' approval.
Responses could vary from 1 (definitely false) to 4 (definitely true.) The individual scores were then combined into an organizational score as described above.

The index of job codification was based on the following five questions:
1. I feel that I am my own boss in most matters.
2. A person can make his own decisions without checking with anybody else.
3. How things are done here is left up to the person doing the work.
4. People here are allowed to do almost as they please.
5. Most people here make their own rules on the job.
Replies to these questions were scored from 1 (definitely true) to 4 (definitely false), and then each respondent's answers were averaged. Organizational scores were then aggregated as described previously.

In effect, "hierarchy of authority" measures one end of a scale and "job codification" measures the other end. The authors, however,

[5]Aiken and Hage, "Organization Alienation," pp. 497–507.

inverted the scales, with one ranging from definitely false to definitely true and the others varying from definitely true to definitely false. Answers to both sets of questions should receive the same number on the scale. Aiken and Hage conceptualized and analyzed the data as if these were two separate variables, even though they are operationally defined as one variable. Given these conceptual problems, the interpretation of the statistics and conclusions are misleading and untenable. In other respects, the field study is well designed and carefully controlled. The authors do not, however, report the original data that would permit an independent analysis and interpretation of the results.

They found a simple correlation of .49 and .51 between these two factors and alienation from work. We expect nearly identical relationships since there is actually only one variable. But in developing the relation of "hierarchy of authority" and "job codification" with alienation from expressive reactions, they found a correlation of .45 and .23. That is, these two nearly identical measures of direction are reported as affecting satisfaction with the boss and peers differently. The coefficients of partial correlation between hierarchy of authority and job codification with alienation from work are −.01 and .67 This is as one would expect given the way the variables are operationalized, i.e., adding the second variable doesn't contribute to the explanation of variance. In contrast, the coefficient of partial correlation between these two factors and alienation from expressive relations was .27 and .30. One of these coefficients should have been near zero for exactly the same reasons as above. In other words, the authors unwittingly operationalize one variable under two headings and somehow find that the identical variable had different effects on interpersonal relationships.

Women in a Simulated Organization. A widely known study by Day and Hamblin developed the effects of both close and general supervision and high- and low-punitive style of supervision on women.[6] In general supervision, eight essential instructions were given; also, certain degrees of obvious hovering and watching as well as repetitions of previous instructions were practiced. Punitive supervision was operationalized by making negative, status-deflating remarks. In the high-punitive situation, forty remarks were made; in the low-punitive situation, none were made.

[6]Robert C. Day and Robert L. Hamblin, "Some Effects of Close and Punitive Styles of Supervision," *American Journal of Sociology*, 69 (March 1964), 499–510.

Close supervision was associated with greater feelings and expression of dissatisfaction toward the supervisor, co-workers, and the task. The combination of nonpunitive, general leadership elicited lower aggression than the combination of punitive, close supervision. Close supervision caused lower productivity; when close leadership was combined with nonpunitive leadership style, productivity decreased the most. The researchers found that these results were unrelated to the self-esteem aspect of personality. In summary, close supervision increased aggressiveness and reduced productivity. The combination of punitive supervision and close supervision generated the most adverse effects on behavior and productivity.

Direction, Communication Nets, and Type of Task. Shaw explored how leadership style and communication nets affected several measures of productivity and job satisfaction.[7] Close supervision was operationalized by having the leader act in a directive manner; the general leader was to be more responsive to the group. A leader acting in the close style of leadership gave orders rather than suggestions, received suggestions critically, and in general made it clear that he was the boss. The general leader offered and accepted suggestions if he thought they were good ones and behaved in a cooperative manner. The task assigned to each four-person group was to solve a simple problem where the information for the solution was distributed among the members.

It took a longer time to solve the problem with general leadership. A higher error level occurred under general leadership, particularly in recording and transmitting information. Job satisfaction was lower under close leadership style. In summary, the group's efficiency under close leadership was higher, but satisfaction was lower compared with general leadership.

Shaw explored this theme further in a later study.[8] He was interested in whether leadership style interacted with the type of task the group was performing. Three different tasks were assigned that varied in the degree to which a structured, well-defined answer was possible. He operationalized leadership similarly to the previous project. Relatively little difference developed on the degree of leader directiveness (on a 1–5-point scale, the directive manner had an average value of 4.1 compared with 3.5 for nondirective manner). Still, the close leadership was more effective than general leadership on a structured-type activity. In contrast, on unstructured and

[7]Marvin E. Shaw, "A Comparison of Two Types of Leadership in Various Communication Nets," *Journal of Abnormal and Sociol Psychology*, 50 (1955), 127–34.

[8]Marvin E. Shaw and J. Michael Blum, "Effects of Leadership Style Upon Group Performance as a Function of Task Structure," *Journal of Personality and Social Psychology*, 3 (1966), 238–42.

semistructured tasks, close leadership stimulated higher productivity. Satisfaction, cooperation, group performance, and satisfaction with leadership performance were all higher with nondirective leadership. Shaw concluded that directive leadership is more effective than nondirective when the task is highly structured, that is, when there is only one solution and only a few ways of obtaining the solution. Where the leadership possibilities for helping are limited, nondirective leader actions interfere with the problem-solving process. However, on tasks that require greater information and varied approaches, nondirective leadership is more effective. On such tasks the leadership possibilities are greater since all members can be encouraged to contribute. This requires motivating, advising, and giving support to them to apply themselves, rather than specifying what they are to do and how they are to do it.

Direction and Standards.   The findings from a study by Rosenbaum are only partially consistent with Shaw's conclusions.[9] He studied whether high or low standards interacted with close or general supervision in small groups on satisfaction and productivity. Structured problems were assigned four-member groups. High standards were set by informing the groups that their performance was to be compared with similar college groups. Low standards were implemented by telling them the task was designed to be interesting; no reference was made to expected level of performance. Under high standards, close leadership motivated greater performance; under low standards, general leadership elicited higher performance. However, the group members were equally satisfied with both types of leaders. They were willing to accept either general or close leadership style. This finding is inconsistent with other studies. It may be that the leadership styles were differentiated enough to affect group processes but not enough to elicit a difference in attitudes toward the leaders.

Vigilance Performance Studies.   One line of studies has focused upon what are referred to as "vigilance performance" activities. A routine task is assigned that requires close attention and commitment to detect signals. The nature of the experiment is to determine how many errors or failures to detect signals occur. In one experiment, Fraser found that when the experimenter remained in the testing room, the operators performed significantly better than when he was absent.[10]

Bergum and Lehr followed up these results to determine whether the

[9]Leonard L. Rosenbaum and William B. Rosenbaum, "Morale and Productivity Consequences of Group Leadership Style, Stress, and Type of Task," *Journal of Applied Psychology,* 55 (1971), 343–48.

[10]D. C. Fraser, "The Relations of an Environmental Variable to Performance in a Prolonged Visual Task," *Quarterly Journal of Experimental Psychology,* 5 (1953), 31–32.

presence of a higher level supervisor resulted in a similar reaction.[11] Close direction was operationalized by having an officer visit each group four times during the test. Failures to detect the signals were pointed out to the individual, but conversation was held to a minimum. Visits were made according to a prearranged but apparently random schedule. Under the permissive condition, the individuals were told it was important to detect as many signals as possible; they were free to do anything they wanted that didn't interfere with this process. Performance was 26 percent higher in the first time period under close direction. Performance fell through time under both close and loose direction, with 43 percent deterioration under the permissive approach and 25 percent deterioration under the close supervision.

In a somewhat more complex design, Kidd and Christy explored the way in which direction and work demands influenced productivity of two-man units.[12] Teams of two and a supervisor were responsible for the guidance of aircraft through the preliminary stages of a landing approach. Two levels of workloads were imposed, with three different forms of direction. Under the loose form of direction, the supervisor acted as a passive monitor of the operation. He was available for consultation and responded to direct questions but gave no assistance.

The "active monitor," or general form of supervisor, observed the operation, anticipated difficulties, and watched for controller errors. When problems developed, the supervisor gave instructions to the controller on how to correct the situation. The closest form of supervision was by a "direct participant" approach. In this case, the supervisor took over the job of the controller when the latter erred, and made direct contact with the subordinates instead of instructing them to take corrective action. Four measures of productivity were used that, in effect, evaluated the efficiency in getting the plane in landing position and the number of errors made in the process.

The experiment found a tradeoff between efficiency and error level. The laissez faire supervision produced the highest efficiency and most errors. General supervision elicited the lowest efficiency and lowest error rate; the closest supervision resulted in the middle ratings on efficiency and errors. The varying forms of direction communicated the different importance of quality and quantity of output and affected group processes that contributed to these ends.

Individuals Under Stress. Stanley Milgram explored the conditions that influence a person to carry out directions when he is ordered to hurt

---

[11]Bruce O. Bergum and Donald J. Lehr, "Effects of Authoritarianism on Vigilance Performance," *Journal of Applied Psychology*, 47 (1963), 75–77.

[12]J. S. Kidd and R. T. Christy, "Supervisory Procedures and Work-team Productivity," *Journal of Applied Psychology*, 45 (1961), 388–92.

another person.[13] Specifically, Milgram explored how much of an electric shock a person would administer to another person when so ordered. The general context was that this was a learning experiment where increasing levels of shocks stimulated the learner to remember. Individuals volunteered to participate in a learning experiment. The experimenter introduced two volunteers (one of whom was not a volunteer, but an individual planted by the experimenter) by giving them a general talk developing the subject of how little scientists knew about the effect of punishment on memory. Subjects then were told that one member of a pair would serve as a teacher and one as learner. A rigged drawing was held where the volunteer always ended up as the teacher, and the accomplice, the learner. The learner was taken to a room next door and strapped into an electric chair. The volunteer was told that his task was to teach the learner a list of paired words, to test him on the list, and to administer punishment of increasing levels whenever the learner erred on the test.

In effect, a series of errors was programmed, and the volunteer was told to give the learner a set of increasingly severe shocks. The individual being shocked responded, in turn, by a predetermined set of protests. The volunteer was caught between the pleas of the learner to discontinue the experiment and the commands of the experimenter that he must continue and ignore the learner's protests. Thus the subject had to decide whether to follow the orders of the experimenter or respond to the pleas of the learner. Milgram modified the experiment in a number of ways to determine which conditions would affect obedience. One of these conditions was how close the experimenter was to the volunteer. In one variation the experimenter sat a few feet away; in a second situation, after giving initial instructions, the experimenter left the laboratory and gave his orders by telephone; in still a third, the experimenter was never seen—he provided instructions by means of a tape recorder.

Obedience dropped sharply as the experimenter was removed physically from the laboratory. In the first situation, where the experimenter was present, almost three times more subjects obeyed the command compared to the second situation, where the experimenter gave his orders by telephone. Subjects were able to take a far stronger stand against the experimenter when they did not have to face him. Moreover, when the experimenter was absent, they lied more often to him. Though they continued the experiment, some volunteers administered lower shocks than ordered without telling the experimenter. Some specifically assured the experimenter they were increasing the shock level according to instructions but, in fact, were using the lowest shock on the board. They found it easier to handle the conflict by lying to the experimenter rather than openly breaking with his authority and quitting

[13]Stanley Milgram, "Some Conditions of Obedience and Disobedience to Authority," *Human Relations*, 18 (1965), 57–76.

the experiment. Another condition was created where the experimenter was initially absent at the beginning but appeared when the volunteer refused to give a higher shock that the experimenter demanded on the telephone. The experimenter's appearance frequently forced further obedience.

SUMMARY AND CONCLUSION

The human relations literature suggests that close direction violates individuals' basic needs and results in an array of undesirable behavioral consequences. It is common practice, though, to exercise close supervision, and it is often justified as necessary to get the job done.

The experimental studies by Day and Hamblin support the view that close supervision contributes to aggressive feelings toward one's superior and co-workers, task dissatisfaction, and lower productivity. In contrast, the studies by Shaw suggest some of the distinctions that need to be made in tracing out the influence of direction. In one study, under a less directive approach, productivity was less but errors were lower and job satisfaction was higher. In a second study, a less directive approach was associated with greater job satisfaction, cooperation, and higher group performance in unstructured and semistructured tasks. It was only under a highly structured task that closer supervision was associated with higher group productivity. Satisfaction, cooperation, and satisfaction with the leadership were lower. These findings are striking since the followers' perception of the different leadership styles was that one was only slightly more directive than the other. This suggests that subordinates have a high degree of sensitivity and responsiveness to the closeness of supervisors.

The vigilance performance studies parallel these findings. With a structured task, close direction contributed to greater productivity. However, a tradeoff develops between quantity and quality of production. In the unstructured task, productivity was lower, but fewer errors were made under close supervision.

The Milgram experiments suggest that close supervision and surveillance are necessary where employees are being pulled between the demands of the organization and counterdemands from adversely affected individuals. In a modern bureaucratic organization, many situations exist—such as demotion, other disciplinary measures, evaluations, allocation of resources along new directions, and cutting of previous allocations—where an employee or supervisor is expected to act even though someone is hurt. In general, an individual is expected to assume an "affectively neutral," unemotional position in dealing with other members of the organization. It is common rather than unique that conflicting demands are faced. Dalton's studies indicate that where individuals have a choice, they will act to fulfill their needs, desires, and ambitions rather than the theoretical rationale of what contributes toward organizational goals. Milgram's experiment suggests that the further removed or loose the supervision, the greater the tendency to respond to the special needs and favored treatment demanded of those who have access to those making decisions.

The view of human relations literature that close leadership adversely affects individuals' attitudes and behavior is partially supported. A number of conditions, though, determine which style of leadership gets more results. The less the task is structured, the greater the emphasis on quality rather than quantity; the less individuals are pulled between the conflicting demand of doing their job and responding to other pressures, the greater the value of a less directive approach. Or looking at the problem from the behavior side, when greater value is placed on job satisfaction, intergroup cooperation, and favorable relations between superiors and subordinates, general direction contributes to this end.

16

INDUCEMENTS:
The Use of Rewards
and Penalties

INTRODUCTION

This chapter focuses on alternative methods of influencing behavior. The germinal studies by Lewin, Lippit, and White sharply delineated different approaches that a leader may take. A number of the elements dealt with the use of criticism or supportive-type actions. This may be viewed as the extent to which reliance is on the use of rewards or on the use of penalties. We are calling this element of leadership the use of inducements. The Ohio State group referred to this variable as "recognition" in their initial conceptualization of leadership.

Inducements Defined. Primary emphasis may be on the use of rewards to motivate. On the other hand, heavy emphasis may be placed upon applying penalties when performance isn't up to expectations. Where the supervisor primarily relies upon rewards to orient and motivate subordinates and others, he emphasizes achievements, sets goals to solve problems, and generally develops the way in which problems can be solved. The emphasis is upon reinforcement through rewarding with money, status symbols, or simple encouragement to keep up the good work.

Another approach is to use penalities to induce desired performance. Where poor performance develops, penalities are invoked, such as taking away privileges, demoting, transferring, firing, and so forth. When the supervisor discusses his evaluations with subordinates or others, he concentrates on inadequate performance. The supervisor disciplines publicly to make clear to all the nature of his dissatisfactions and the penalties that are being applied. His general posture is that a satisfactory level of performance is expected in all areas, and he concentrates only on those elements where performance is below standard.

Rewards need not be emphasized at the expense of penalties; that is, it is possible to vigorously reward performance *and* apply penalties for inadequate

"Ulcers, nonsense! My motto is: Give 'em, don't get 'em!"

Dun's Review and Modern Industry, (March, 1957).

performance. In practice, it appears that one is emphasized over the other. To simplfy the approach, we will concentrate on the consequences where one approach or the other is used.

Operationalization of Inducements

Inducements. Different ways of motivating performance are by use of rewards and penalties. On the one hand, primary emphasis may be on the use of rewards and counseling to motivate. On the other hand, heavy emphasis may be upon applying penalties when performance isn't up to expectations.

Rewards		Rewards & Penalizes					Penalizes	
1	2	3	4	5	6	7	8	9

1. Does your supervisor rely upon rewards such as personal recognition, raises, promotions, and persuasion to motivate members of your work group (rather than on orders and threats of punishment)?

1	2	3	4	5	6	7	8	9
Almost always		Usually		Often		Sometimes		Rarely

2. In dealing with his superior and staff groups, does your supervisor try to get them to emphasize rewards (such as liberal promotions and raises) to motivate work groups?

1	2	3	4	5	6	7	8	9
Almost always		Usually		Often		Sometimes		Rarely

3. Does he discipline in personal terms (such as declaring individuals lack ability, are slow, clumsy, or incompetent)?

1	2	3	4	5	6	7	8	9
Rarely		Sometimes		Often		Usually		Almost always

4. Does he discipline by focusing on elements of the job (such as pointing up areas of poor performance and setting goals for correction)?

1	2	3	4	5	6	7	8	9
Almost always		Usually		Often		Sometimes		Rarely

5. In disciplining, does he discuss subordinates' behavior and performance in private (rather than in front of fellow workers and others)?

1	2	3	4	5	6	7	8	9
Almost always		Usually		Often		Sometimes		Rarely

6. To obtain cooperation of other supervisors, does your supervisor rely upon persuasion, trading arrangements, and good personal relations (rather than upon appeals to higher level supervision or other pressure methods)?

1	2	3	4	5	6	7	8	9

| Almost always | Usually | | Often | | Sometimes | | Rarely | |

The Use of Penalties: The Human Relations View. A popular theme in human relations literature is that applying penalties is destructive of employee morale and ineffective in motivating performance. Telling the employee that he is doing poorly or unsatisfactorily undermines his confidence and commitment. Likert develops the view that even reviewing with the employee his performance rating seriously deflates the employee's sense of importance and personal worth. It also damages the relationship between the employee and his superior and adversely affects the quality and quantity of the work. "It is virtually impossible to tell an employee either that he is not as good as another employee or that he does not measure up to a desirable level of performance, without having him feel threatened, rejected, and discouraged."[1] Likert considers performance rating and review procedures as fundamentally flawed because they compel the superior to behave in a threatening, rejecting, and ego-deflating manner with his people. This adversely affects his relationship with them, prevents the employee from working effectively, and reduces the capacity of the superior to function effectively.

Douglas McGregor, in his famous little book, *The Human Side of Enterprise*, summarizes the rationale for using punishments. Managers believe that the average human has an inherent dislike of work and will avoid it where possible to do so: " . . . *most people must be coerced, controlled, directed, threatened with punishment to get them to put forth adequate effort towards achievement of organizational objectives.*"[2] Dislike of work is so strong that the use of rewards isn't enough to overcome it. People will accept the rewards, demand more, but won't apply the necessary effort. Only the threat of punishment works. McGregor's book and much of the human relations literature challenge this viewpoint.

---

[1]Rensis Likert, "Motivational Approach to Management Development," *Harvard Business Review*, 37 (1959), 75.

[2]Douglas McGregor, *The Human Side of Enterprise* (New York: McGraw-Hill Book Co., 1960), p. 34.

On Cruelty and Clemency: Is it Better to Be Loved or Feared?

Machiavelli, that dispassionate observer of mankind, arrived at conclusions in his study of history that are sharply different from the human relations viewpoint. A brief passage presents his views on consequences of use of rewards and punishments.

I say that every prince must desire to be considered merciful and not cruel. He must, however, take care not to misuse this mercifulness. Cesare Borgia was considered cruel, but his cruelty had brought order to the Romagna, united it, and reduced it to peace and fealty. If this is considered well, it will be seen that he was really much more merciful than the Florentine people, who, to avoid the name of cruelty, allowed Pistoia to be destroyed. A prince, therefore, must not mind incurring the charge of cruelty of the purpose of keeping his subjects united and faithful; for with a very few examples, he will be more merciful than those who, from excess of tenderness, allow disorders to arise, from whence spring bloodshed and rapine; for these as a rule injure the whole community, while the executions carried out by the prince injure only individuals. And of all princes, it is impossible for a new prince to escape the reputation of cruelty, new states being always full of dangers. . . . is (it) better to be loved more than feared, or feared more than loved? The reply is, that one ought to be both feared and loved, but as it is difficult for the two to go together, it is much safer to be feared than loved, if one of the two has to be wanting. For it may be said of men in general that they are ungrateful, voluble, dissemblers, anxious to avoid danger, and covetous of gain; as long as you benefit them they are entirely yours; they offer you their blood, their goods, their life, and their children, as I have before said, when the necessity is remote, but when it approaches, they revolt. And the prince who has relied solely on their words, without making other preparations, is ruined; for the friendship which is gained by purchase and not through grandeur and nobility of spirit is bought but not secured, and at a pinch is not to be expended in your service. And men have less scruple in offending one who makes himself loved than one who makes himself feared; for love is held by a chain of obligation which, men being selfish, is broken whenever it serves their purpose, but fear is maintained by a dread of punishment which never fails.[3]

[3]From *The Prince*, by Niccolo Machiavelli, translated by Luigi Ricci, revised by E.R.P. Vincent. By permission of the Oxford University Press.

Punishment is widely used to induce conformity and change. Many with a religious background contend people are good only because they "fear the loss of heaven and the pains of hell"; employers and supervisors feel the necessity to wave the big stick. Parents traditionally adhere to the dictum of "spare the stick and you spoil the child." While popular folklore isn't necessarily true, it has some elements of truth in it. In a loosely done case study, a personnel director wrote up the experience his company had had in the use of rewards.[4] His thesis was that the firm had abandoned penalties for a program of "discipline without punishment" and had achieved remarkable improvements in behavior. In fact, though, the firm replaced one system where penalties were increased, through several steps, with one where individuals received increasingly sharp warnings of approaching discipline and then "the employee's services are terminated." In some cases, the offense was dealt with by skipping the warnings.[5] The exception to this procedure was that "in case of discovery of criminal behavior or in-plant fighting, termination results without preliminary steps. Such behavior is taken as conclusive evidence of lack of adequate self-respect and discipline even if it happens only once." In the topsy-turvy world of current fads, the program was considered consistent with the current human relations philosophy.

Psychologists have found it difficult to systematically assess the effects punishment has on behavior. In 1913, Thorndike thought that both reward and punishment had simple and clearly predictable effects: "When a modifiable connection between a situation and a response is made and is accompanied or followed by a satisfying state of affairs, that connection's strength is increased; when made and accompanied or followed by an annoying state of affairs, its strength is decreased."[6] His position remained unchanged twenty years later on the effects of rewards. On punishment, however, Thorndike was confronted with many cases where punishment didn't affect the response: "Rewarding a connection always strengthened it substantially; punishing it weakened it little or not at all."[7]

Thirty years later, Church, in a review of the literature arrived at a similar position: "Much experimental evidence indicates that punishment decreases the probability of occurrence of a response or increases its latency, but there is also much conflicting evidence."[8] In some experiments, punishment

[4]John Huberman, "Discipline Without Punishment," *Harvard Business Review*, 42 (July 1964), 62–68.

[5]Ibid., pp. 66–67.

[6]E. L. Thorndike, "The Psychology of Learning" *Educational Psychology*, 2 (New York: Teacher's College, Columbia University, 1913), 4.

[7]E. L. Thorndike, "Reward and Punishment in Animal Learning," *Comparative Psychological Monograph*, 8, no. 39 (1932), 58.

[8]Russell M. Church, "The Varied Effects of Punishment on Behavior," *Psychological Review*, 70 (September 1963), 369.

temporarily suppresses a response or has no influence; in other experiments, punishment increases the strength of the response.

Punishment: A Psychological Interpretation

In the following excerpt, Collins and Guetzkow present an explanation of why rewards may be more effective than punishment in influencing behavior.[9]

We have written implicitly as though punishment were merely the inverse of reward, a kind of "negative reward." But, in many ways, punishment and reward are psychologically distinct processes, not merely reverse images.

Several factors contribute to the fact that learning through punishment is more complex than learning through reward. In the first place, punishment tells the individual only what not to do; it does not provide an alternative or substitute for the punished behavior. If there was a "reason" (motive) for the punished behavior, some alternative must be discovered which meets the needs previously satisfied by the punished behavior. Until this happens, there will be psychological forces supporting the behavior while it is being punished. For example, embarrassing a conference member for displaying his self-oriented needs does not eliminate the needs. They can manifest themselves again in some other form such as substantive disagreement which is quite irrational on the surface.

Second, while only the desired responses need be reinforced, it is necessary to punish all undesired behavior. Since the range of undesired behavior is frequently larger than the range of desired behavior, the agent will have to use more punishment or spread it thinner. Miller and Butler reported that punishment was less effective than reward, possibly for this reason.

In the third place, punishment teaches the person to avoid the punished situation, and this leads to at least two complications. The individual may learn to avoid the whole issue rather the specifically punished behavior. The participant punished for irrelevant comments may soon learn to avoid all participation, rather than to eliminate merely sidetracking remarks. Furthermore, avoidance learning prevents the individual from gaining further information about the situation he is avoiding. When the group member remains silent, he may never

[9]Barry E. Collins and Harold S. Guetzkow, *Social Psychology of Group Processes* (New York: John Wiley & Sons, 1964), pp. 131–32.

learn the acceptability of his ideas. Avoidance learning is particularly troublesome when the environment is rapidly changing. The individual learns to avoid some part of the environment and thus does not get any information about the changes because he avoids further opportunity to learn.

In the fourth place, punishment works through a learned drive of fear. An individual comes to fear the situations in which he is punished; this creates several problems. Fear is particularly hard to extinguish and may last long after it is appropriate. Fear is an emotion, and excessively high states of emotional involvement decrease the efficiency with which the organism can solve new problems. Perhaps a reason why there is so much controversy about the use of groups in decision making derives from traumatic experiences individuals encountered in particularly intense and important conferences.

Research Studies Supervisor's Reaction to Criticism. In a field study done in the General Electric Company, Kay, Meyer, and French explored the effects of praise and criticism on the individual's defensiveness, relationship with his boss, and subsequent job performance.[10] Trained observers sat in on appraisal sessions and classified the supervisor's remarks that were threatening or approving in character and observed the degree of defensiveness of the individual being evaluated.

Those who received a low number of criticisms in an interview were less defensive. Those with more than the average number of threats in their appraisal discussions offered defenses to about two-thirds of the threats; those who received less than the average number of threats reacted defensively to only one-third of the threats. The more criticisms that were made, the more the individual reacted defensively to each of them.

Those who had relatively high self-esteem reacted about the same as those with a low self-esteem score. The reaction to criticism, though, was affected by the extent of criticism and the constructive tone that was set early in the conference.[11] If the manager pointed up a few areas of needed improvement early in the discussion, the appraisees were less defensive. The number of threats, however, had no effect on attitudes towards the manager. While praise was expected to have the opposite effects of threat, it had no significant effect on degree of defensiveness, goal achievement, or attitude toward the manager.

[10]Emanuel Kay, Herbert H. Meyer, and John R. P. French, Jr., "Effects of Threat in a Performance Appraisal Interview," *Journal of Applied Psychology*, 49 (October 1965), 311–17.

[11]Ibid., p. 314.

The effects of threats on goal achievement were somewhat more complex. The number of threats had little effect upon perception of goal achievement of those who had high self-esteem. However, those who had low self-esteem and were criticized, perceived they had attained 32 percent fewer goals compared to the group that hadn't been criticized. The highest level of goal was achieved by those who had low self-esteem and received few threats. In summary, if the individuals had high self-esteem, it didn't matter much whether they received a low or high number of threats on subsequent goal achievement. But if they had low self-esteem, it made a sharp difference, with penalties reducing goal acheivement.

Public Response as a Defensive Play. Collins and Guetzkow specify two conditions when punishment influences behavior. One can affect behavior when (1) the conditions of punishment are clearly specified and (2) compliance can be observed.

The mere fact that an agent can punish a person does not insure that the agent will influence the behavior of the person. The person must understand what he can do to avoid punishment. Furthermore, if punishment is to be effective as a threat, the person must have learned that the agent can punish him. . . . not only must the conditions to a punishment be clearly specified, but it is also necessary that the agent be able to observe the conformity of the low power person. If the agent cannot see whether or not there is compliance, he will be unable to administer punishment for not conforming. Several studies have demonstrated that public compliance occurs in the face of punishment, but the public compliance was not accompanied by private opinion change. The high power person can observe the public conformity and could punish nonconformity; but the agent cannot observe a private opinion and, therefore, he cannot punish private nonconformity.[12]

In summary, one may not respond to another's attempts to influence. A subtle but common method of resistance is to respond publicly but to conceal actual attitudes. In this case, previous patterns are reverted to rapidly.

Ring and Kelley contend that a teacher or trainer must provide a consistent schedule of reinforcements rewarding correct behavior or punishing incorrect behavior to effectively induce the desired response.[13] The trainer should

[12]Collins and Guetzkow, *Social Psychology of Group Processes,* p. 134.

[13]Kenneth Ring and Harold H. Kelley, "A Comparison of Augmentation and Reduction as Modes of Influence," *Journal of Abnormal and Social Psychology,* 66 (1963), 95–96.

consider both how his reinforcement motivates learning and the orientation to conceal responses. Concealment and subsequent learning are affected by size of rewards and punishments. Two possible cases are large rewards for desired behavior but only small punishments for errors, or small rewards for correct responses and large punishments for errors. Standards may be low and easy to achieve or high and difficult to meet.

In the case of rewarding behavior, the trainee will present evidence on his compliance with the trainer's instructions if it is a required condition for his reward. If, however, the trainer punishes the learner when he errs, the trainee is stimulated to conceal his behavior or make it difficult to monitor. The trainee is pressed in this direction since he can avoid punishment by complying or concealing. He will choose concealment if he has difficulty in complying, or when he rejects the standards.

To test out their thesis, Ring and Kelley placed individuals in a context where their opinions were supported in one situation and criticized in another. Further, one group was reinforced in the direction they were initially oriented in and the other was pressed in an opposite direction. The stated purpose of the study was to find out what conceptions students had of mental illness. The students were given a set of cards that had two statements that described symptoms of maladjustment and were told to choose which statement showed the greatest degree of mental illness. Under a reward condition, the trainer supported the students' correct answers by appropriate praise, passed off errors lightly, and corrected in a friendly fashion. Under the penalty condition, correct statements were given token praise while the trainer sharply criticized errors or made deflating remarks and was sarcastic.

The statements on the cards indicated an anxiety-type or a depression-type statement. Previous research had shown that depression statements would be selected as indicating mental illness about 65 percent of the time. The experiment then was to determine to what extent supportive remarks versus criticism would influence the subjects to incorrectly choose anxiety statements as symptoms of mental illness.

The design is of general significance, since it focuses on the implications of different methods to motivate. While this is a simple laboratory design, it parallels actual situations where a supervisor tries to influence the subordinate's initial orientation or, in contrast, violates the individual's sense of correctness. The methods used may vary from emphasis upon support or criticism.

A high degree of interaction occurred between the subject's initial orientation and the methods used to influence him. It didn't matter whether rewards or penalties were used when the person's views were reinforced.[14] Refusals to state an opinion, the extent to which a subject picked up clues

[14]Ibid., pp. 95–102.

on the trainer's opinions, and how much a subject disagreed with the trainer were about the same whether support or penalties were used. When the trainer supported or contradicted the subject's initial opinions and used *rewards* to influence, little difference developed on concealment of opinions or perception of trainer's opinions. The exception was that the subjects disagreed with the trainer more when he contradicted their initial views.

Where the supervisor penalized errors, refusals to state opinions increased from 8 to 23 percent of the time. The understanding of the trainer's opinion decreased from 78 to 63 percent of the time, and disagreements with the trainer rose from 13 to 37 percent of the time. In summary, penalizing errors and contradicting initial opinions resulted in a higher rate of refusals to state opinions, lowest understanding of the trainer's views, and greatest differences in opinions between the subjects and the trainer.

EFFECTS OF CONSISTENCY OF SUPPORT OR CRITICISM OF GROUP MEMBERS

Berkowitz, Levy, and Harvey focused on the way in which supportive or negative feedback to either individuals or groups as a whole affected the relationship among group members and the group's effectiveness.[15] Airmen in basic training were divided into three-man groups. They were assigned a task that involved a miniature three-man aid-defense warning center. Their job of defending target areas against an attack by enemy bombers required the coordinated work of the three-man team.

The groups were divided into high- and low-standard groups. After a practice session and a trial, they were given individual performance evaluations that varied from where (1) all three members were favorably evaluated (FFF); (2) two were favorably evaluated and one unfavorably (FFU); (3) one member was favorably evaluated and the other two unfavorably (FUU); and (4) all three were unfavorably evaluated (UUU). These evaluations were on broad attributes such as understanding the problem, utilizing resources, and level of cooperativeness. When the group had set high standards, team members were considered as desirable work partners when they *all* were favorably evaluated or *all* unfavorably evaluated. Where one or two members were unfavorably evaluated, they judged fellow members as less desirable as work partners. However, where low standards were set, the nature of feedback had little consistent impact on judgment of fellow members. The members even valued one another slightly more where all three received unfavorable feedback compared with when all three received favorable reports.

[15]Leonard Berkowitz, Bernard I. Levy, and Arthur R. Harvey, "Effects of Performance Evaluations on Group Integration and Motivation," *Human Relations*, 10 (1957), 195–208.

The initial standards affected the relationships. Those who had set low standards were more dissatisfied with their partners than those who had set high standards whether all were favorably or unfavorably evaluated. This study suggests that it is incidental whether leadership style is supportive or nonsupportive as long as it's done on a consistent basis among members. When, however, some individuals are supported and others are criticized, this adversely affects group relationships. Work groups are evaluated regularly by their superiors and this information is given to the groups, so the experiment has general significance.

Interaction of Past Performance and Use of Rewards and Penalties.

Pollack and Knaff explored the effects of rewarding, punishing, or taking no action upon individual commitment and performance.[16] They constructed a routine dull task and evaluated the way in which these factors motivated commitment. They also evaluated whether past performance on similar tasks when combined with these methods of motivating affected performance. More specifically, volunteers were assigned a simple monitoring task that required close attention. Failure to closely observe the instrument panel resulted in errors. They were placed under three different standards: (1) No rewards or punishment—they were told to do the best they could. They had previously done this type of observation so it had some meaning. (2) Reward (high standards with incentive)—a perfect score in seven of the periods or the greatest improvement over previous scores was rewarded by an extra hour's pay. (3) Punishment—errors were penalized by half-second blasts of a truck horn.

All groups achieved the highest performance where errors were punished. Those groups who had had the highest performance in the past produced 5 percent more under the reward conditions and 12 percent more under punishment, compared with the neutral support group. The group that had had the lowest performance in the past declined 7 percent under reward conditions but increased its performance by 75 percent under punishment. The group that had had moderate past performance improved 11 percent under rewards and 38 percent under punishment.

The implications of this experiment are that when dealing with a low-motivated group, punishment achieves short-term results. Providing rewards results in small improvement in performance for both high- and low-skill groups. If a group is highly motivated, it is incidental whether rewards or punishment are used, although the latter gives slightly better short-term results. This experiment was not concerned with longer term consequences or with the effects upon group relationships or possible side effects of general

[16]Irwin Pollack and P. Robert Knaff, "Maintenance of Alertness by a Loud Auditory Signal," *The Journal of Acoustical Society*, 30 (November 1958), 1013–16.

dissatisfaction of individuals. The results show that punishment contributes most to short-term performance.

Interaction of Use of Penalties and Close Direction. The Day and Hamblin study that was summarized in chapter 15 on direction is also relevant to the inducements aspects of leadership.[17] In review, the aspects of leadership that were explored in the experiment were "close" and "punitive" aspects. Punitive supervision had some effect: aggressive feelings towards supervisors slightly increased; a somewhat better feeling developed toward the co-workers; task dissatisfaction increased; and overt aggression was more pronounced. Where a general style of supervision and a punitive approach were combined, the amount of aggression towards supervisors and co-workers and dissatisfaction with the tasks fell sharply.

Rewarding and Penalizing. In a follow-up study, Day explored the separate and combined effects of close and "punitive" leadership. He separately operationalized high and low penalties and high and low rewards.[18] We have treated these two aspects as alternative approaches to inducing performance, but they can be combined with a supervisor using *both* high rewards and penalties or low rewards and penalties. The combinations of high and low rewards and penalties and high and low direction were operationalized as in the first study by varying the number of instructions and derogatory remarks. Individuals were assigned a simple construction task and worked separately in four-person groups on their projects; the different groups were supervised by a trained individual who used the various combinations of leadership styles.

Greater penalties elicited the most dissatisfaction with the leader but stimulated productivity from 2 to 8 percent. Higher leadership support improved attitudes toward the supervisor, but productivity fell 0 to 15 percent. Under close supervision, the combination of high penalties and high rewards elicited dissatisfaction with the leader and 5.5 percent greater production compared to low penalties and low support. The relationships were partly reversed under general direction. In this case, the combination of high penalties, high support created the same effect on dissatisfaction with the leader but 9 percent *less* productivity. Increasing support combined with those leadership styles adversely affected productivity probably because of inconsistent leadership clues to the workers on whether they were doing a good job. With close supervision, numerous instructions are given; with

[17]Robert C. Day and Robert L. Hamblin, "Some Effects of Close and Punitive Styles of Supervision," *American Journal of Sociology*, 69 (1969), 499–504.

[18]Robert C. Day, "Some Effects of Combining Close, Punitive, and Supportive Styles of Supervision," *Sociometry*, 34 (1971), 303–27.

punitive leadership, workers receive criticism on the way the job is done. Supportive comments then are inconsistent with other leadership clues. The combination of high penalties, few supportive comments, and close direction caused greatest dissatisfaction with the leader but highest productivity. The combination of low penalties, close direction, and either high or low support stimulated medium dissatisfaction with the leader and *lowest* productivity. In summary, applying penalties creates dissatisfaction with the leader but high productivity—at least in the short run. Providing support and emphasizing the positive improve relationships with the leader, but adversely affect productivity. However, the closeness of direction confounds the effects of support. Under general direction, higher support causes the largest drop in productivity; but under close direction, greater support elicits only small, or no, change in productivity and attitudes toward the leader.[19]

Dealing with An Extreme Case:
Autistic Children

The excerpt deals with the training of autistic children. These are severely disturbed children who show no signs of warmth towards others, don't enjoy being held, don't play with others, don't respond to noise or verbal commands; many walk into objects and cannot speak, or have distorted speech habits. One of their most difficult features that interferes with working with them is that they throw terrible tantrums, and many engage in self-mutilation or physically attack others. In an interview, Professor Lovaas discusses how they use reward and punishment to eliminate such behavioral patterns in his clinic.[20]

    Lovaas: Autistic kids are like blind kids. If a blind child is not given a special environment, if you try to treat him in the same way that you treat sighted children, he will look autistic: he will rock himself a lot, injure himself and so on. But if you handle things correctly, you can make a blind or deaf child look very nearly normal. All you have to do is figure out how to make his environment instructive.

    Chance: A blackboard is not a useful part of the environment of a blind child, and a radio is not a useful part of the environment of a deaf child. And autistic kids are missing something which likewise prevents them from developing in an ordinary environment. What are they missing?

    Lovaas: Right now it looks as though they have overselective attention. Give an autistic child more than one kind of sensory input and he will pick

---

[19]This analysis varies from that provided by Day. Readers should look carefully at his data to evaluate the appropriateness of these interpretations.

[20]Paul Chance, "After You Hit a Child, You Can't Just Get Up and Leave Him; You Are Hooked to that Kid," *Psychology Today*, 7 (January 1974), 79–80.

up on only one of them. Attention is always selective, but with these kids it seems to be extreme. For example, if you tell an autistic child to open the door, he may not hear the words at all; he may focus so intensely on the movement of your lips that he will not hear the sound of your voice. It is very often the case that if they see you they do not hear you, and if they hear you they do not see you. It is as though they receive input on only one channel at a time. We don't know for sure if this is the deficiency that is responsible for autism, but the evidence looks very good.

Chance: Don't they also acquire certain behaviors that interfere with learning?

Lovaas: Yes. They have tantrums, and believe me they are monsters, little monsters. And they spend a lot of time in repetitive behaviors that we call self-stimulatory behaviors. For example, they rock themselves back and forth or they spin around in a circle. All kids have tantrums and engage in self-stimulatory behaviors, but with autistic kids it is extreme; they can do it for hours. Before you can get very far with developing normal social behaviors, you have to eliminate these aberrant behaviors. Some of them will bite other people or injure themselves. You can't teach a child to speak if he is injuring himself or bitting his teacher. They don't bite their teachers very often in our clinic.

Chance: How do you get rid of behaviors like that—biting a teacher?

Lovaas: Spank them, and spank them good. They bite you and you just turn them over your knee and give them one good whack on the rear and that pretty well does it. This is what we do best; we are very good at controlling these kinds of behaviors. This is also the way we handle self-destructive behavior. In fact, self-destructive behavior was the problem that we first started on. We had these kids that we tried to teach and they were so loaded down with self-destructive behaviors that we couldn't do very much with them. Some of these kids were severely self-mutilating.

Chance: When you say "self-mutilating," just what do you have in mind?

Lovaas: Well, there were some kids who would bite their fingers off. One kid had actually bitten off a finger—I think it was the little finger of her right hand–down to the second joint. She had started to chew the little finger of her left hand and had severe biting wounds all over her hands. She also pulled her fingernails out with her teeth. Another child chewed most of his right shoulder off. He would put his head sideways, lift his shoulder toward his mouth and chew his shoulder. He had actually chewed enough of his shoulder away that you could see the bones. We had other kids who broke their noses with their knees. Others would bang their heads against the wall or against the edge of a metal filing cabinet. Not all autistic kids engage in self-mutilative behavior but many do. The treatment used to consist of putting them in full restraints. We saw kids who were ten years old who had been in restraints for six or seven years.

Chance: By "put in full restraints," what do you mean?

Lovaas: Bound to a bed. The child would be bound to a bed spread-eagled so that he could not get to himself. We discovered how to handle self-destructive behavior in a very accidental way. When we first started to treat autistic kids we began with only one child. I would pick up Beth at her parents' house at nine in the morning and I would drop her off at three, so we had her for about six hours a day, five days a week. You spend that much time with someone and you get to know them pretty well. In fact, I saw more of her than I did of my own children. Well, what happened was that she ceased to be a patient for me—she was simply a child, just like one of my own children.

Beth did very well in some ways; she learned very quickly. But she was also very self-destructive. One day I was talking with her teacher and Beth began hitting her head against the edge of a steel cabinet. She would only hit steel cabinets and she would only hit them on the edge because, you see, she wanted to draw blood. Well, I think because I knew her so well, I just reacted automatically, the way I would have with one of my own children. I just reached over and cracked her one right on the rear. She was a big fat girl so I had an easy target. And I remember her reaction: She turned around and looked at me as if to say, "What the hell is going on? Is this a psychiatric clinic or isn't it?" And she stopped hitting herself for about 30 seconds and then, you see, she sized up the situation, laid out her strategy and then she hit herself once more. But in those 30 seconds while she was laying out her strategy, Professor Lovaas was laying out his. At first I thought, "God, what have I done," but then I noticed that she had stopped hitting herself. I felt guilty, but I felt great. Then she hit herself again and I really laid it on her. You see, by then I knew that she could inhibit it, and that she would inhibit it if she knew I would hit her. So I let her know that there was no question in my mind that I was going to kill her if she hit herself once more, and that was pretty much it. She hit herself a few times after that, but we had the problem licked. One of the things that this taught me was that if you treat these kids like patients, you are finished. The best thing you can do is treat them like people.

So then we sort of specialized in treating self-mutilative kids. We took in some of the worst cases that the state hospitals could provide. We used electric shock and spanking as punishment. The procedure was simple—we just set up a contingent punishment for self-mutilative behavior.

    Chance: When you say "contingent punishment" you mean that you shock them only when they self-mutilate?

    Lovaas: Right. We stay close to them and when they hurt themselves we scream "no" as loud as we can and we look furious and at the same time we shock them. What typically happens is this—we shock the child once and he stops for about 30 seconds and then he tries it again. It is as though he says, "I have to replicate this to be sure." Like a scientist. He tries it once more and we punish again and that is pretty much it. So we can cure self-destructive behavior—even long-standing, self-destructive behavior—in a matter of minutes.

We know the shocks are painful; we have tried them on ourselves and we know that they hurt. But it is stressful for the person who does the shocking too. You may have used shock successfully with a hundred kids, but you are still apprehensive about it; you always think that maybe this kid will be the exception; maybe you will hurt him and it won't do any good. But then when you shock him and you see the self-destructive behavior stop, it is tremendously rewarding.

I remember a kid named John who had been in restraints for years. We took him out of restraints at 9:00 a.m. He hit himself in the face and we shocked him. He hit himself a few more times and each time we shocked him; that was the end of his self-injury. Then he just sat in a corner until about 9:30, when he got up and looked out the door into the hallway. Then he darted back to his corner. About 10:00 he walked over to the door again and then returned to his corner. About 10:15 he moved around the room again, but this time he didn't run back to his corner. By 10:30 he actually stepped out into the hallway and by 11:00 he moved about the room freely.

Then he discovered several nice things. He had been in restraints for so long he had forgotten how good it feels to scratch yourself. So he spent about half an hour scratching himself—his stomach, his butt, his head, his back. Sheer luxury. Then he jumped up and down several times to stretch his muscles. About 12:00 we decided to give him a bath. You can't give the severely self-destructive child a bath because he will hit his head on the bath tub and when the blood hits the water it looks awful. So they just get sponged down in bed. Now that John was no longer self-destructive, he could have a real bath. He loved it. He lay completely submerged in the water with his eyes open, just loving it. After the bath we gave him food and he fed himself; in restraints he had to be spoon-fed. So you see, after we got rid of the self-destructive behavior, John could start to do things he hadn't done for years. He had a ball. It is because of experiences like that that I can't wait to get at self-destructive kids.

Chance: How do you avoid having the child become afraid of you?

Lovaas: That is a good question. No one punishes who isn't prepared to devote a major part of his life to that child. Nobody punishes a child who doesn't also love that child. As soon as you suppress self-mutilation you start building appropriate behaviors. You reward the child for doing other things instead of hurting himself.

Chance: If he is not busy banging his head against the wall, he can be be doing other things.

Lovaas: Oh, yes. And if he doesn't, you prompt him. But the nice thing about punishment is that it not only gets rid of the self-mutilative behavior, it also affects the adults who administer the punishment. Once you lay your hands on a child it morally obligates you to work with that child. You see, that is one of the reasons that people stay away from the use of punishment—they don't want to commit themselves. After you hit a kid you can't just get up and leave him; you are hooked to that kid.

Chance: What has always seemed peculiar to me is that you can stop a child from hurting himself by punishing him. The way these kids injure themselves you'd expect them to enjoy being shocked.

Lovaas: I know. I am not sure exactly why it works, but it works. What typically happens is that the child hits himself and someone comes in to love him and take care of him—and he knows this is what happens. See, we are all made of this kind of wool; a child in pain is a child that we attend to and love. It just seems natural to us and a kid soon learns that this is the way it works. The same thing happens, perhaps less clearly, to parents with normal children. Sometimes parents will only pay attention to their children when they misbehave. So, what happens is that the child misbehaves a lot and gets lots of attention. The parents don't see that what they are doing is rewarding bad behavior. When an autistic child injures himself and you give him lots of attention, you are rewarding him for injuring himself. You are actually teaching him to self-mutilate. What you have to do is to give him plenty of love, but for good behaviors, not for self-mutilation. The theory that says that these kids hit themselves because they feel they are unlovable dictates that you give them lots of love, especially when they injure themselves. The theory sounds great, but it doesn't work that way. What is different about our clinic is that while we are treating children we are also collecting data. We don't rely on our subjective impressions of what our results are; we record the child's behavior accurately and objectively so that we know what effect the treatment has. And what we find is that when we love kids for self-mutilation, the rate of self-mutilation increases; when we punish it, the rate decreases.

SUMMARY AND CONCLUSION

The currently popular view represented in textbooks and popular trade journals is that the use of penalties is ineffective in inducing behavioral change and has other undesirable side products. A persuasive psychological explanation can be offered as to why this outcome is to be expected. Widespread current practice on use of punishment, popular folklore, and astute observations of others suggest that punishment is effective.

A field study at General Electric suggests that a number of factors mediate the effects of criticism. While a limited amount of criticism is received constructively, a good deal of criticism generates defensive reactions. While praise is supposed to be superior to criticism, this study found it had little effect either positively or negatively on degree of defensiveness, attitude toward the manager, or goal achievement. The self-esteem aspect of personality interacts with the number of threats on the extent to which goals are achieved; those people low on self-esteem achieve substantially fewer goals under the high-threat condition. The number of threats makes little difference, though, for those with high self-esteem.

The use of rewards and penalties may cause individuals to move publicly in the desired direction, but privately they retain their previous attitudes. Behavior rapidly reverts back to old patterns in this case. Collins and Guetzkow suggest that punishment only influences behavior where the conditions for punishment are clearly specified and compliance can be observed. Ring and Kelley found that when the change was in the direction in which the subject was originally oriented, the emphasis on rewards or penalties made little difference. But when the subject's beliefs were contradicted, the use of penalties resulted in greater opinion concealment, less awareness of the trainer's attitudes, and less change.

Berkowitz, Levy, and Harvey showed that group relations are affected by whether group members receive different evaluations. Little difference develops in group relations when all favorable or all unfavorable evaluations are received. Different evaluations, however, contribute to deterioration of group relations. Pollack and Knaff found that individuals doing a routine task developed greater productivity when punishments were used to penalize failures in performance. Those who had had low commitment in the past (as implied by poor past performance) sharply inproved their performance; those who in the past were highly committed responded about the same under no-reward, reward, and punishment conditions.

Day and Hamblin's first study indicated that it mattered little whether a punitive or nonpunitive approach was used. However, if a punitive approach was combined with general supervision, the effect was to increase aggression toward supervisors and co-workers and heighten dissatisfaction with the task. In their second study, Day and Hamblin found that penalizing errors elicited the most productivity and the greatest dissatisfaction with the leadership style. Providing support or rewarding posture generated more favorable attitudes to the leader but lower productivity. The relationship is further confounded when close or general leadership is combined with degree of support and penalties. The combination of penalties for mistakes, minimal support, and general direction elicits greatest dissatisfaction with the leader but highest productivity. Minimizing of penalties combined with close direction elicits moderate dissatisfaction with the leader and lowest productivity.

Our conclusion on how rewards and penalties affect behavior is that "It all depends . . . " It is affected by:

—How many penalties are used. A little goes a long way in influencing behavior. As penalties increase, they rapidly exert a negative influence.

—The degree of self-esteem. The lower the self-esteem, the greater the necessity to limit the use of penalties.

—The potential for concealment and passive resistance. If individuals can readily conceal actual attitudes and behavior, penalties are less effective than rewards.

—The sharpness of change. If individual orientations are sharply contradicted, i.e., considerable change is sought, then penalties are less effective than rewards.

—Amount of commitment to do a good job. The less the commitment, the greater effect penalties have in inducing change, at least in the short term.

—How closely the supervisor directs subordinates. Close supervision when combined with emphasis on penalties creates an adverse effect that neither factor causes alone.

SECTION V

DISCUSSION QUESTIONS

1. Develop the nature of the following approaches to study of leadership:
   a. Personal traits of leaders.
   b. Leadership functions.
2. Develop the implications for developing meaningful generalizations about leadership if the context is ignored.
3. Assume that you are examining the leadership profile of two leaders, Ralph and Dick, and you find they have the following characteristics:

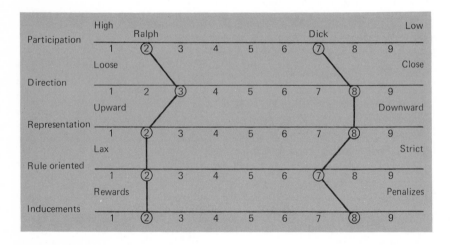

Develop the approach Ralph has to supervision noting separately how each aspect of leadership is carried out. Illustrate the approaches with examples for each aspect of leadership.
4. An experimenter designed an experiment where he evaluated how representation in various groups influenced productivity of groups. He studied a plant which had 39 unit supervisors. He measured their representation style and found 13 represented employees upward, 13 took an in- between approach, and 13 downward. He found that the first 13 were in large departments, the second 13 in medium-sized departments, and the last 13 in small departments; all other factors were similar among departments. Relative efficiency in the three departments was:

Upward representation	140%
Medium representation	110%
Downward representation	80%

Draw a matrix and develop the appropriate generalization.

5. Subsequently, he investigated some additional departments. He found in 15 small departments the supervisors had upward representation and efficiency of 80. And in 15 large departments supervisors had downward representation style and efficiency of 140. Combine this data with the date in question 4 and generalize on the factor(s) influencing efficiency. What is the influence that size exerts? What influence does representation exert? If the context had been ignored, would the researcher have arrived at accurate conclusions?

6. A supervisor or manager is faced with conflicting pressures; external pressure, downward pressure, upward pressure, and lateral pressure. The form of representation and degree of rule adherence are two methods of dealing with these pressures.

   a. Illustrate these types of pressures in organizations in which you have worked.

   b. What style of supervision are most people likely to develop as they adjust to these pressures? What risks are associated with upward representation and rule deviation?

   c. Develop how the form of representation and degree of rule adherence affects the relation of the supervisor to his subordinates, his superiors, and other groups. Refer to studies that support your position.

   d. List several factors that support rule adherence; that support rule deviation.

7. What pressures in an organization are there to closely supervise subordinates? To loosely supervise subordinates? Which style is one more likely to adopt as he adjusts to these pressures?

8. The human relations literature develops the thesis that close direction violates individuals' basic needs and results in undesirable behavior. Discuss the way in which the following studies support, reject, or modify this thesis:

   a. Day and Hamblin's study.

   b. Shaw's studies.

   c. Vigilance Performance studies.

   d. Milgram's studies.

9. What pressures in an organization are there to use high participation? To use low participation? As one adjusts to these pressures, what style is he likely to adopt?

10. What is the distinction between delegation of authority and use of participation? Is it possible to have the following combinations: Cell 11, 12, 21, and 22 in the matrix?

	Participation	
	Low	High
Centralization	11	12
Decentralization	21	22

11. Provide illustrations from your work of these combinations—if they exist. Where would the following examples go in the cells? A faculty senate in a university that makes recommendations to the president; a representative committee that makes budget recommendations to the president; a representative committee

that decides who is to be promoted; a regularly scheduled meeting of department heads with the president where he communicates to them his views and gives them instructions; where broad policies orient lower level supervisors who meet regularly with their personnel to communicate share their thinking and decisions; where an organization has numerous committees at all levels to consider the best way to implement detailed policies, procedures, and rules that are formulated by headquarters personnel.

12.   The text raises the question "When is participation most effective, and to what extent does involvement in some decisions carry over into a more positive attitude?"

Develop what insights each of the following studies provide on this point:
a.   Nyman and Smith study of Pequot Mills.
b.   The Almedabad studies.
c.   The first of the Pajama Factory studies (of Haywood Mfg. Co.).
d.   The Pajama Factory studies of participation on goal setting.
e.   Vroom's study on supervisors.

13.   To what extent are moderately satisfactory performance levels likely to receive little attention and errors, or drop in performance likely to receive considerable supervisor attention? What does this suggest in terms of relying upon rewards or punishment?

14.   Evaluate whether the human relations perspective on the use of rewards or the hard line Machiavellian approach on punishment elicits more appropriate behavioral patterns. If results depend upon special conditions, what are they?

15.   In what way might the following elements of leadership modify the influence of the following structural variables:
1.   Centralization and rule orientation?
2.   Centralization and participation?
3.   Decentralization and direction?
4.   Large size of organization and representation?
5.   High standards and representation?
6.   Unprogrammed tasks and use of rewards and penalties?
7.   Spatial-physical barriers and participation?
8.   Interdependent Work flow and representation?

16.   You have been brought in as a consultant to analyze the factors contributing to high level of conflict among departments. Upon investigating, you find the following information on the firm. Eleven departments have a high incidence of conflict and antagonism among groups.

The departments vary in size from 18 to 20 people, and are highly specialized; 8 departments manufacture parts that require close tolerances even though they are using older, unreliable equipment. Two departments assemble the product and a service department does repairs and maintenance work for the other departments. The management insists that inventories be kept to a minimum, so supplies of parts are maintained at a level where only one half day's production can be maintained at the assembly stage if parts manufacture stops.

All units except the service department are on an individual incentive system. The company believes in democratic management and has decentralized broadly down to the departmental level. Standards are high, competitively based, and periodically raised as performance increases. Leadership style of department heads is predominantly upward representation, high participation, loose direction, low enforcement of policies, and emphasis on rewarding for good performance.

Personnel are satisfied with their own units but unhappy with higher level management and other units. Management has been pleased by the productivity of the plant in the past but is concerned that intergroup relations will undermine this efficiency in the future.

Provide management a set of recommendations on resolving or reducing intergroup conflicts while retaining the sense of morale, satisfaction, and production of the units.

Initially, assess whether the leadership style is appropriate given the nature of the context. Next, evaluate whether any changes in delegation, standards, or reward system are appropriate. Would any other changes help to achieve management's goals?

17. Select a complex case from one of the case books. Analyze the influence that the variables covered in this course exert over behavior in the case. Use the following format:

    a. Describe the behavioral patterns (individual, group, and intergroup) and how they have changed through time, or contrast among departments.

    b. Analyze the influence that the primary variables (size, work flow, spatial-physical barriers, and task complexity) exerted on behavior.

    c. Analyze the influence that the mediating variables of standards, delegation, departmentation, and rewards exerted over behavior.

    d. Analyze the influence that leadership exerted over behavior.

    e. Comment on what changes, if any, of the mediating variables and leadership style would reduce the problems that occurred. Specifically relate your answer to the primary variables that existed that would justify changes.

MECHANICS

—Set your paper as a consultant report. It is a formal document and should meet the tests of proper spelling, grammar, organization, and cogency of thought.

—Your instructor may encourage an individual or group approach. One method is to work together in discussing the case or the strategy on how to approach it. However, when you write it up, do it independently.

VI

CONCLUSION

17

SUMMARY AND APPLICATION: The Practicality of the Model

In the second chapter, the general framework was set forth. The approach identifies structural features of the context that exert pressure over behavior in organizations and a set of leadership processes that mediates the influence of structure. The factors exert pressures on individuals and groups. The personality of members and character of the groups may either moderate or reinforce the impact of these pressures. A brief overview of the chapters provides some perspective on where we stand in our understanding of the systematic factors shaping behavior in organizations. An application of the approach in diagnosing and proposing ways to improve the situation illustrates the practicality of the approach.

The primary variables of size, work flow, spatial-physical barriers, and task complexity exert an important influence over individual and intra- and intergroup behavior. Worthy's conclusion in an early study of the importance of size that "there is no more important influence on attitudes and morale than sheer size of organization" overstates the importance of the pressure of numbers but gives it the attention it deserves. Absenteeism and accident rates increase and job satisfaction decreases with increased size of organizations; vertical communication and intragroup relations are inversely related to size of the organization. Severity of disputes between unions and management rises with size of the organization; small plants are more likely to have a cohesive work force, fewer strikes, to be nonunion, and to have a plant atmosphere that supports close contact between workers and management. Increasing the size of a group affects organization processes of interaction, nature of the relationships, level of participation and active involvement, communication blockage, and formation of informal subgroups.

As formal specialization increases, the degree of interdependence rises. Historically, the thrust in large-scale organization and industrial civilization has been to increase the specialization of organizations and the jobs within organizations. This achieves economies in training workmen and in the amount

© King Features Syndicate 1973.

410

of materials wasted during training, reduces time moving from one operation to the next and from one tool to another, and enables the workman to develop the rhythm and skill for top efficiency. It also increases the opportunity to simplify and improve methods and allows better selection, training, and placement of personnel. However, a number of problems must be solved where specialization takes place: separate operations must be coordinated; separate workmen and work groups must cooperate to complete the total operations; individuals must be motivated to perform at a stable, reliable level in respect to quality and quantity of the work. The advantages associated with specialization may be offset by emergent individual, group, and intergroup patterns of behavior that are incompatable with requirements of specialization unless dealt with in the further structuring of the context or by leadership processes.

Spatial-physical barriers influence interaction patterns, particularly among workers who are only casually acquainted. Increasing barriers reduces interaction and the intensity of relationships and reinforces neutral relationships. Spatial-physical barriers between groups increase the interaction *within* groups and reduce the interaction *between* groups. Increased interaction amplifies existing relationships, with endemic conflict further increased and existing cooperation and group identity further reinforced.

Evidently, the interaction that exists between size of groups, degree of specialization, and spatial-physical barriers reinforces the factors' effects. If we take the polar values of each of these variables and explore the combinations in Figure 17-1, we can see more clearly the impact of the variables.

		Size		
	Small		*Large*	
	Spatial-Physical Barriers		*Spatial-Physical Barriers*	
	Concentrated	*Dispersed*	*Concentrated*	*Dispersed*
Low	11	12	13	14
	Simple			
High	21	22	23	24
				Complex

Specialization

FIGURE 17-1. Combination of three variables

Cells 11 and 24 provide the biggest contrast with all the variables different. Size and spatial-physical barriers both contribute to similar effects in respect to individual, intragroup, and intergroup behavior (cell 11 contrasted with cell 14). Both contribute to isolation of individuals with size contributing to subgrouping and spatial-physical barriers shaping the composition of groups formed. Both are passive factors in influencing neutral relations and reduce the intensity of existing relations. Both contribute to the breakdown of the formal group into sets of informal subgroups. The effects of either can be partially but not completely offset by opposing changes in the variables (e.g., reducing the size of formal groups to offset increased spatial-physical barriers or vice versa).

Size, spatial-physical barriers, and specialization probably interact to create an amplified influence on behavior when they all move in the same direction. The change from low to high specialization is more likely to be different when the group is small and spatial-physical barriers are absent than when the group is large and spatial-physical barriers exist (cell 11 compared with 21 and cell 14 compared with 24). The effects are likely to be different because satisfaction with the group and the social satisfaction of being a member of a group can substitute for satisfaction with the work. When the group is small and concentrated, group esprit de corps is supported. Even though the job may be monotonous, the individual often derives high satisfaction at work from group relations. Contrarily, where the group is large and spatially-physically dispersed, such as on the typical assembly line, little opportunity exists for social groups to develop. Without satisfaction in the work or membership in a supportive work group, individuals are less likely to like the job, the formal group, or the company.

The complexity of the task influences the individual, intragroup, and intergroup behavior. Problems may be unsolvable in that individuals lack knowledge of the way in which a solution can be obtained, or the state of knowledge may be such that there is no solution. The distinctive character of an unprogrammed situation is that individuals lack structure or an anchor to reality. This makes it difficult to cope with the requirements of the situation. Ambiguities in either the steps to take to solve problems or in the structure of the group contribute to stress on individual, intragroup, and intergroup relations. As a group is faced with problems that don't yield solutions, frustration mounts and intragroup relations deteriorate. Members overreact to irritations; expressions of antagonism and hostility increase; milder forms of reaction such as withdrawal of help, withholding of positive support, and increased criticism and backbiting rise. Increases in self-oriented behavior such as expressions of disgust and anxiety occur.

Size, work flow, spatial-physical barriers, and task complexity are important determinants of the complexity of the environment within which individuals operate. Size of the group and spatial-physical factors influence the degree to which individuals interact and have the opportunity to work out problems. Degree of interdependence influences the stress placed on the relationships and the degree of monotony and routine that exists in their work. The difficulty of problems and the degree to which a satisfactory solution cannot be worked out amplify any stresses that exist from the work flow. These four factors exert pressures upon individual behavior and intragroup and intergroup relations that generally adversely influence the functioning of the organization.

The mediating variables of authority relationships, control systems, and information systems are formal methods to offset the disintegrative influences. However, both functional and dysfunctional consequences are associated with changes in these factors. With a simple organization defined in terms of size, work flow, spatial-physical barriers, and tasks, the functional consequences of decentralization, interdependent departmentation, low standards, and institutional reward systems are more important than the dysfunctional consequences. As the organization becomes more complex, greater coordination and external incentives are needed to offset the influences that develop with increased complexity. Then the functional consequences of centralization, autonomous departmentation, high standards, and individual-reward incentive systems become more important than the dysfunctional consequences.

Increases in the degree of centralization provide the formal means for increasing coordination and moving decisions down to the operating level by providing the framework of policies, procedures, and rules. The policies and rules provide the common premises for decisions even though many individuals make decisions. This reduces the ability of the organization to adjust to local situations, inhibits the development of personnel, and contributes to a greater stability and rigidity of the organization. These are costs associated with obtaining coordination in a complex organization.

Formal groupings have implications for organization processes by determining the size and number of units and their interdependency. A functional grouping reduces interdependency within departments but creates it among departments; project forms of departmentation create interdependency within a department and reduce or eliminate it among departments. That is, functional departmentation shifts the problem of coordinating departments to top management while project departmentation shifts it to within the department. As the organization becomes more complex, one way of reducing the problems of coordination among departments is to move from functional to project departmentation. This results in utilizing manpower sources less efficiently, reduces coordination within each specialized area, and decreases professional reinforcement of skills. However, project departmentation has the advantages of relating departmental goals to company goals, increasing communication among diverse specialists, and training managers with a company-wide viewpoint and long-range perspective. The focus of conflict becomes intradepartmental rather than interdepartmental and greater control and coordination is achieved over contacts with outside personnel. While professionals feel less comfortable and less satisfied with their department and the firm, project departmentation increases the possibility for subgrouping and development of informal groups within the department.

The formal control system of standards, measurement instruments, and the reward-penalty system affects the direction, intensity, and duration of motivation and influences the nature of intragroup and intergroup relationships. The extent to which a worker performs his tasks up to the limits of his powers depends upon inborn traits of character, his interests, and temperament and upon the extent to which the conditions under which he works stimulate the release of energies and ability with which he is born. Important conditions affecting this release are the elements of the formal control system —standards, measurements, and method of rewarding.

Experimental work back to 1945 has found that increasing the level of standards improves performance where goals are within reach. Standards influence the internalization of goals and level of aspiration. Specific, achievable standards have greater impact on performance than diffuse, "do your best"-type standards.

Where it is desired to obtain several types of goals such as high quality, efficiency, and low waste of materials, establishing standards on each of these results in a balanced emphasis on performance. Establishing multiple standards makes the tradeoffs explicit rather than leaving it up to the workers to make the tradeoffs by neglecting the areas where standards haven't been established.

Other effects of higher standards are less desirable. Higher standards exert pressure for increased performance, but they also exert stress on some workers who find it difficult to adjust or respond to the pressure. Increased standards often build counterpressure from employees to resist management's actions as standards are moved up. Intergroup friction is elicited, particularly where competitively based standards are difficult to achieve and penalties of lower earnings or discipline accompany falling short of the goals. Short-term problems of meeting the standards at each measuring period dominate over the longer term orientation of building an organization that would be capable of higher performance. In total, making explicit standards and increasing them sharply improves performance while also creating a changed social structure in the organization and changed relationships within and between groups. The effects are observable at all levels in the organization and supported by both laboratory and field studies.

The reward system directly complements and reinforces the standards that are established. In combination with standards, the reward-penalty system is one of the most powerful structural variables influencing individual, intra-, and intergroup behavior. The laboratory studies consistently show that performance increases as one moves from an institutional reward system to group and individual incentives.

The application and degree of success that is achieved in actual practice in industrial and other type organizations depend upon a complex set of factors. The reward-penalty system affects the nature of the social system that develops. It is thus necessary to plan the entire remunerative system rather then take a sectional approach. Some conditions such as short-production runs and rapid technical change create problems of maintaining and updating standards. Still, if reasonable attention is given to the design and maintenance of an individual or group incentive system, the system will constitute a powerful force for a productive organization.

The leadership processes either complement or counter the pressures created by the structural variables. The degree of participation used in a centralized organization is likely to offset some of the dysfunctional consequences of a centralized bureaucracy or autocracy. Further, if a high degree of delegation is used but the supervisor closely supervises his subordinates, then the formal delegation of authority is less meaningful. An organization may be established with a relatively bureaucratized structure with formal policies, rules, and procedures covering most problems. The degree to which supervisors and managers emphasize rule observation determines how reasonable these restrictive characteristics of the formal structure are considered to be. Similarly, the formal incentive system is reinforced or moderated to the extent the supervisor emphasizes the use of rewards or penalties in trying to elicit desired behavior.

Representation can be a key element in determining the response employees have to the structured environment. If the supervisor plays an important role in mediating these pressures, the structure may have a substantially different influence on behavior.

Personality mediates the influence of all of these variables. The research is more suggestive than conclusive, but where research projects have focused on the personality of those operating within a particular structured context, a variation in reaction has occurred. This reaffirms our initial statements that it is the combination of structural variables, leadership process, and personality that determines the behavioral patterns in an organization.

Personality, cultural background, and prior relationships, for example, influence the use of spatial-physical barriers. Some personalities are comfortable with greater distance in interpersonal relationships while others seek a close physical contact. Psychological and physical disabilities influence the reaction to spatial-physical barriers, with the psychologically disturbed or physically ill being affected to a greater degree.

Personality mediates the influence of work flow. Some personality types are able to adjust to the routine and monotony of highly specialized work; others are bored and dissatisfied with the entire context of their job and interpersonal relations. A high degree of specialization creates interdependence within groups or interdependence among groups. Those who are comfortable in a highly structured context are disturbed by the variability implicit in this interdependency. Similarly, in an unprogrammed situation, some individuals are able to structure the situation and work systematically toward a solution. Those with a more stable, more controlled personality are able to continue to work on a solution in the face of apparently insurmountable odds.

Similarly, personality interacts with each of the mediating structural variables. Some individuals are uncomfortable in the heterogeneous context of a project department. An authoritarian-type personality is comfortable in the structured environment of a centralized bureaucracy. High standards and individual reward systems are compatible with some personalities and not with others. Particular forms of leadership are acceptable to some personalities.

This framework provides the basis for consideration of a larger perspective. Other variables also need to be included in increasing our understanding of behavior and organizational processes. It may be that in most organizations, the variation that is typically found in factors such as comfort conditions (heat, light, humidity, cleanliness, and other such factors) exerts little effect. Other factors such as group heterogeneity (combination of backgrounds in terms of race, sex, nationality, age, years of seniority with the organization) exert little effect or are reflected in different personality types. This, however, is an empirical question and can only be determined by systematic review of the literature and rigorous research. While the model presented isn't the final statement on factors influencing behavior, it should nevertheless be an important consideration in systematically approaching the prediction and understanding of behavior in all types of organizations. An application of the approach highlights the diagnostic value of a systematic framework.

APPLICATION

In large manufacturing firms and large service-type organizations such as insurance firms, retail establishments, finance units, and similar organizations, the local branches or divisions are organized semiautonomously. The local branch is subject to a multiple set of pressures created partly by the local context and partly by the relationship between the local office and the home office. An understanding of these pressures and the way in which they influence behavior in the local unit is essential in predicting and dealing with problems that develop and in restructuring the organization for improved performance.

This case concerns a local office in a large brokerage firm engaged in many facets of the investments field.[1] The firm is primarily noted for its commission business, which accounts for a sizeable portion of the total trading done on the floors of the securities exchanges. The company is also active in the over-the-counter market, the various commodity markets, dealing in government bonds, and underwriting new security issues. The home office is located in the heart of the New York financial district, with branch offices spread throughout the country and in many foreign countries as well. The primary focus of this analysis is on that part of the firm's business dealing with buying and selling securities.

The firm can be used as a model representing the type of pressures that may be found in large organizations with many small branches. The model illustrates that the local office is a focus of many pressures—some resulting from the local environment and some from the home office. These pressures are focused partly upon the operative employees but even more directly upon the manager of the local office. His leadership style moderates or increases the pressures on his subordinates. The behavioral patterns that emerge directly affect the productive output of the local unit.

A number of factors interact in influencing the behavioral patterns in the local unit. The factors highlighted are the influences of the local environment, several structural variables (size of the firm and the local unit, spatial-physical relations, work flow, task complexity, centralization, nature of the control systems, and the information network) and leadership processes of the local supervisor. The behavior set focused upon is the nature of intra-group relations and the individual level of motivation, commitments, and satisfaction. This relationship is represented diagrammatically in Figure 17-2.

The firm in its earlier years of development achieved rapid growth through numerous mergers; pattern of growth was primarily internal for twenty years. The growth rate had slowed sharply at the time of the study as measured by the company's share of the odd-lot business (purchases or sales in less than 100-share lots) and round-lot business (sales or purchases of 100-share units). The firm's share of the odd-lot volume nearly doubled from 1947 to 1957 but in the next ten years had barely been maintained. Its percentage in the industry of round-lot volume had been highly stable for the previous twenty years, neither growing nor declining. The firm had not been so successful as to erode the position of competitors but had been able to maintain its position in an expanding industry.

A number of factors roughly indicate the nature of behavior patterns. The firm had a training program for the key position of account executive (A/E). A large portion of those who went through the program stayed with

---

[1]Adapted from a study by David Hawk, "Pressures on the Local Branch: A Systems Analysis" (Kent State University, Kent, Ohio).

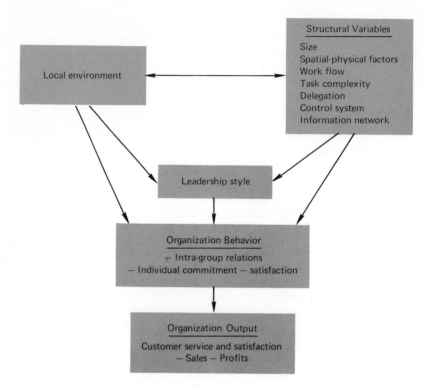

FIGURE 17-2. Systems model of determinants of behavior in a local unit

the firm. There was a high level of application on the part of both managers and account executives. Some evidence of conflict existed at the local level among the personnel and between the supervisor and his subordinates, but this conflict seldom reached the degree where outright formal confrontations and direct challenges occurred. Several indications existed of high anxiety and a morale problem in the local office studied.

One indication of the anxiety level is suggested indirectly by the medical problems of the manager and A/E's. The manager had an allergy and was constantly taking medicine. Six of the ten A/E's also had some recognized medical problem that could be related to stress. For instance, an A/E in his late thirties had a seizure while playing golf that kept him in the hospital for two weeks. Another A/E in the same age group developed an ulcer and subsequently had to drink milk constantly.

Some signs of job and company dissatisfaction were also evident. The local manager did much of the paper work that he was required to submit to the home office by working two to three hours at home each night. His reaction to this was, "Sometimes I wonder if it's worth it. I'm bushed before

I ever get started in the morning." The A/E's were responsible for getting new business through a systematic process of prospecting, much of which was done in the evening. The home office was constantly sending out memorandums on ways of obtaining new accounts. The younger A/E's often responded as they viewed the activity as a means of increasing their income. Older A/E's resented the pressure. Indicative of a general feeling, one of the A/E's who had been with the firm for over twenty-five years remarked, "I won't do it! I am just too tired by the end of the day to go out in the evening. If I didn't have a boy in college . . ." Others were resentful because they had to work as hard as when they had entered the business five, ten, or fifteen years earlier. Despite the resentment over the pressure, both the A/E's and the manager had a high level of commitment to their jobs. We shall attempt to unravel the factors that contributed to this commitment as well as the less constructive behavioral patterns.

The local environment, interdependent work flow, and unprogrammed tasks created stresses that adversely affected interpersonal relations, individual morale, and commitment. The size of the local unit and spatial-physical relations exerted, on balance, a positive effect over behavior. The control system, information network, and degree of centralization contributed both positively and adversely to the behavior and productivity of the organization. These factors interacted to create the context in which the local supervisor operated. The model provides both the perspective to evaluate the factors influencing behavior and the means to restructure the context to be more supportive of the organizational processes that contribute to an effective organization. These points are developed in the following sections.

EFFECTS OF LOCAL ENVIRONMENT

The local branch operated within a context determined partly by the organization and partly by the nature of the investments industry. The term "local environment" is used to characterize the form of pressures that emanate from the industrial setting. The local environment exerted pressure both on the local unit and on all levels of the firm's operation. The significant dimensions of this environment were the factors that affected the variability in the workload. They were volume of transactions, inflexible work hours and work week, and number of orders received at once or near closing hours.

The organization was equipped and staffed to handle a normal number of transactions each hour and each day. As the workload increased, some organizational slack existed that could be used to adjust to increased demands. However, the point was rapidly reached where the organization did not cope adequately with the additional burdens placed on it. The form of behavioral patterns that emerged further increased the problems faced by the employees. Trading on the floor of the exchange took place only within a prescribed 5½-hour period for the New York and the American exchanges. A customer's order to buy or sell a security had to be executed promptly within the time limit. Pressure developed when several orders were received at the same time. Under high stress, errors occurred at all points in the work flow. The switchboard operator was under pressure to get the calls through to the responsible A/E; the salesman was under pressure to handle the customer rapidly without seeming to brush him off and at the same time to make sure that the order was correct in all details such as whether to buy or sell, the stock symbol, exchange, limit or market order, the customer's name, and the correct account number—which could be one of several for the same customer. Finally, the teletype operator in the local unit had the responsibility to transmit the orders both rapidly and accurately The same type of situation developed when orders were received near the close of the day's trading as the employees tried to execute the order on that day.

In this industry, a high degree of variability in the volume of shares traded occurs. During periods when the economic outlook is unfavorable and the stock market is depressed, trading volume on the New York Stock Exchange is normally quite light, with 30 to 40 percent of normal volume. As the economic outlook improves and develops to the point where speculation begins to take place, trading volume may reach the level where an 80 to 100 percent increase in shares traded occurs. High trading volume exerts stress on the switchboard operator, the A/E, and the teletype operator to handle the orders and on the cashier to collect and handle additional money and securities. Continued high volume also exerts pressure on the home office to handle physically the funds and the transfer of securities. Additional employees are usually added, but their inexperience typically results in a higher percentage of errors such as lost certificates, crediting cash receipts to wrong accounts, and an increased time lag involved in transferring a stock certificate from the seller to the buyer.

Customer dissatisfaction manifests itself by complaints, adding further pressure on the salesman, the cashier, and the local office manager. Unanswered complaints often result in letters to the home office and to the various governmental regulatory agencies. These are forwarded back to the local manager and then to the responsible account executive, who is then faced with the additional demands of responding to the charges.

In summary, changes in volume of transactions, inflexible work hours and work week, and number of orders received at one time and near closing hours all create variability in working conditions. While acceptable adjustments can be made for moderate increases in unstable conditions, these adaptations rapidly become inadequate as conditions become even more unstable. The customer exerts direct stress on the account executive, and this stress is transmitted along to the other personnel through the work flow.

EFFECTS OF SIZE, SPATIAL-PHYSICAL FACTORS, WORK FLOW, AND TASK COMPLEXITY

While the local environment exerted stress on the local unit, some organizational factors created a positive influence over behavior. The small size of the local unit and the spatial-physical concentration of personnel of the branch exerted a positive influence for a close-knit, supportive work group to develop.

Size of the Firm and of the Local Unit. The firm employed about three thousand employees. This included the home office and 165 branches scattered over one hundred cities and towns. Except for the offices in New York and Los Angeles, most of the offices were of modest size. The branch office studied employed ten account executives and ten supporting personnel supervised by a local manager.

Spatial-Physical Relation. Most of the branches were broadly dispersed in relation to one another and to headquarters. In contrast, the employees in most local offices and in the one studied were located in one building on the same floor. This permitted easy face-to-face interaction. Figure 17-3 outlines the layout.

Work Flow. There was a highly interdependent work flow within each office and between the central headquarters and local offices. There was little flow of work among the local offices. Within the local office, there were A/E's, sales assistants, and operating personnel. The operation of the branch office was organized around the A/E who dealt directly with the customers. The key transaction was a customer order to buy or sell. The flow of an order was generally through the switchboard operator, the sales assistants (in the form of supplying information and keeping records), the A/E, and the teletype operator, who transmitted the order to the proper exchange and the central office. When this transaction was completed at the home office, the local office was notified. The operating employees billed the customers, collected payments, sent out certificates, and completed the other details.

Task Complexity. The A/E had to induce those with financial resources to invest in stocks by suggesting that they could obtain capital gain, greater earnings on capital, or both. While the A/E's had available the best information and advice in the industry, the movement of the stock market was unpredictable. Some investors accepted this and concentrated upon fundamental factors such as industrial and company prospects over several-year periods, the general trends of the economy, and broad considerations such as governmental, fiscal, and monetary policy. They accepted the ups and downs that occurred on a daily, monthly, or yearly basis and sought long-term gains. Others looked for tips into new stock prospects or took a technical

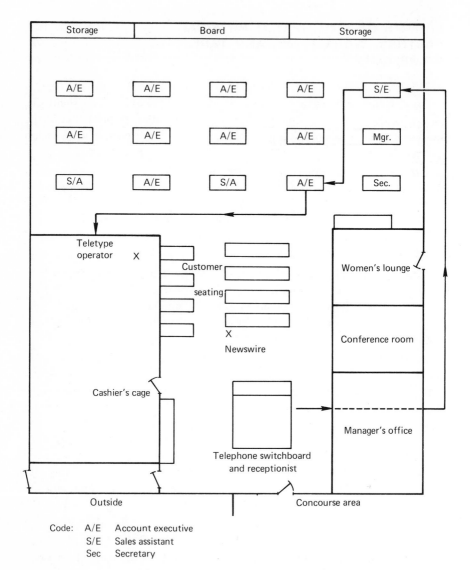

FIGURE 17-3. Office layout with illustrative flow of work starting with customer order

approach that essentially rested upon discovering what others were doing and following up their leads. Most investors adhered to the technical approach to some degree so were concerned about short-term fluctuations in the market and the groups of stocks in which they had invested. The difficulty was that it mattered little which approach was taken since the fluctuations were similar to a random walk—going up and down without predictable patterns. Since few A/E's and even fewer investors accepted this, they were faced with trying to make reasonable predictions that would result in customer gain. Customers reacted favorably to a rising market and unfavorably to one that was declining and tended to blame the salesman when a recently purchased stock went down in price; customers wished they had never bought, and other customers who had bought earlier felt the A/E was responsible for not telling them to sell. This type of pressure could occur regardless of the overall market. An individual stock or group of stocks can and often does move independently of the overall market. Further, substantial variations in prices occur during the day in many stocks. Such fluctuations in the daily trading range could cause conflict between the customer and the A/E if the customer had bought on the high of the day or sold on the day's low.

The implications of these factors can be briefly commented on at this point. While the firm was of substantial size, it was divided into small, semi-autonomous subunits. There was little work flow or other relations among the offices. The significant relation was among personnel within the branch and the relation of the home office to the branches. The individuals within these units performed specialized functions, so they were highly dependent on one another. This created stress among personnel, but the size was small enough and sufficiently physically concentrated to readily permit face-to-face interaction. Were only these factors to be considered, one would expect the interpersonal relations to be congenial, personal satisfaction and commitment to be high, and each individual to support his co-workers in dealing with external stress imposed upon the group! Although this was a formal unit of a large firm, many of the behavioral characteristics of a small informal group should have developed. However, other factors had various disintegrative and debilitating effects.

The fluctuations in stock values created a changing flux of support and criticism. The feedback the personnel received from customers and the workers' self-image were affected by the rising and falling market. The unstable work flow created further pressures on their organizational processes.

A set of factors that exerted a mixed influence was the control system, information network, and degree of delegation of authority to the local unit.

EFFECTS OF CONTROL SYSTEM, INFORMATION NETWORK, AND DECENTRALIZATION

A significant variable was the control system. Operating personnel worked in the cashier's department and were held accountable for the securities and money handled by the firm. They were compensated on the basis of a straight salary with a year-end bonus based upon length of service and the firm's profitability for the year. Educational and experience qualifications were low with mostly clerical skills required. Few formal standards for measuring performance existed, and the departmental supervisors made a qualitative judgment on the personnel's level of achievement. In this local branch, this judgment was largely delegated to the cashier who had little training in the area. He was responsible for hiring, training, scheduling, and dismissing operating employees. The majority of these employees had been with the firm for several years. No basis existed for rewarding differential performance levels other than continued employment with the firm and equal participation in the year-end bonus.

The A/E's and the local manager were on a modified individual incentive system. Each salesman was paid a base salary; in addition, he was paid an adjusted compensation based upon length of service, the firm's profitability, and individual productivity. This latter standard was made up of total dollar amount of commissions produced, number of new accounts opened, number of portfolios sent by each salesman to the research department for review, and the number of errors made in entering orders and any dollar losses incurred. These items were divided into categories such as commodities, new stock offerings, over-the-counter stocks, listed stocks, etc. The total set of items was entered into a computer program designed to provide monthly totals and accumulations. The information that constituted the standard was provided to the sales manager at headquarters, the manager of the local office, and to the salesman himself. The local manager then had the discretion of weighing these various items for final adjusted compensation. He could, for example, disregard errors or penalize the A/E by reducing his "adjusted compensation." Different A/E's could be compared with one another by length of time with the firm. The performance of the other A/E's provided a competitive standard against which the individual salesman could be compared.

The design of the reward-sanction system contributed to high commitment and conflict between the A/E's and operating personnel during high volume and among A/E's during low volume. The unstable work conditions, interdependent work flow, unprogrammed tasks, high standards, and a combination individual-institutional reward system created a stressful context. The control system provided an incentive for one part of the work force to increase its pace and make appropriate adjustments but did nothing to encourage the operating group to make similar adaptations. When the overall volume level of trading rose, the demands on each A/E increased. The A/E had a direct incentive to handle the increasing volume and pressure because he experienced higher income. Due to the interdependent work flow, each A/E made increasing demands on the operating personnel. They had to respond to some degree but did not have the incentive of direct customer contact, explicit standards, or additional pay for higher productivity. This contributed to friction between the A/E's and operating personnel. The operating personnel resented the pressures of the increased workloads flowing from the A/E's. While few direct confrontations developed between the operating personnel and the A/E's, friction sharply increased as market volume rose.

The incentive system and competitive standards increased the degree of conflict among A/E's as market volume dropped. During those periods, greater emphasis was given to holding old accounts and obtaining new ones. During periods of low market activity, the home office and local manager urged the salesmen to prospect aggressively through mailing promotions, making cold calls, following up on calls, giving speeches, and developing investment programs and market forums.

Various problems developed as a consequence of this activity. Some letters in a mailing campaign, for example, inadvertently went to the customers of other A/E's. Customers assigned to one A/E sometimes attended market forums and investment sessions of another A/E. The aggrieved A/E often regarded this as an attempt to steal his accounts. Age and seniority differences among the A/E's added their divisive influences. Younger A/E's often were more active and aggressive. This contributed to a strain on the relations among the A/E's. As expressed by one of the older men, "I don't know what I am going to do; these young fellows can get out and hustle around."

The discretion given the manager on the weight to give various errors and omissions in arriving at adjusted compensation contributed to conflict between A/E's and the manager. Since salary was an expense against sales, the manager was under pressure to penalize the A/E's when they made various errors. His alternative was to allocate higher adjusted compensation to one A/E and to penalize one or more of the others. While this was done only in a limited way, the effect was to create pressure upon the A/E to cater to the supervisor. This created a divisive factor on the A/Es' relations with one another and a pressure to be nice to the local manager. It encouraged such behavior as an A/E's informing the manager of local business news while withholding the information from other A/E's.

A similar set of standards and reward system was applied to the office manager. All direct expenses incurred by the local unit plus a percentage of administrative overhead were charged against the revenues or commissions generated at the local level. The local office manager was held responsible for the net profit of his branch. The branches were grouped into units of five based upon commissions generated. This afforded top management with a control system based upon competitive standards. The manager was compensated in proportion to the profitability of his branch. He was under constant pressure to improve any areas in which his branch made an unfavorable comparison. The leadership section details some of the adjustments the manager made to these pressures.

Delegation of Authority to the Branch Office. There was a sharp contrast between the official position on the relationship and the actual formal relations that existed. On the one hand, a top management member stated:

> We believe in decentralization, and great latitude is given to all our managers. They, of course are required to operate under our basic policies, but they are permitted and encouraged to work out their own local problems as they best can.

A close examination of the local branch and the headquarters relationship indicated the "great latitude" was actually little discretion. Several interacting factors affected the way in which the central office was related to the local offices. Several service departments were located at the headquarters level including all the bookkeeping and accounting. A research department with specialists in different industries developed investment analysis and recommendations and provided up-to-date data on developments. Sales promotion and advertising policies and programs were developed centrally; the budget for charitable contributions had to be centrally approved. The branch manager had to have local advertising approved by the home office and make periodic reports on the effectiveness of various advertising campaigns conducted by the firm. The manager was required to seek legal opinions from the home office on legal matters and to explain and to justify any legal proceedings in which he became involved. The sales department sent out directives and standards on increasing new business; for example, each salesman was expected to make a given number of promotional mailings per month. The manager was then required to report on such mailings and evaluate their effectiveness. Authority was largely retained in the home office and wielded by a staff of specialists. While there were various reasons for the form of structure, including economic, historical, and regulatory as imposed by the SEC, the effect was to create a highly centralized firm. The extensive influence exercised by the various staff departments as well as the formal exercise of authority for control purposes resulted in little discretion at the local office level.

The Information System. The local units were located in centers of financial activity and thus were physically separated from one another and from the home office. Normally, this would prohibit the development of a highly centralized firm such as has been described were it not for the interaction of the formal information system. A financial institution such as this firm is a service institution. To increase its competitive position, this firm had successfully provided excellent service by increasing the speed by which it could process orders and make available securities information to customers. The company had evolved a highly complex information system connecting the home office and the local units. Several wires were leased for the company's own use so orders, requests for research opinion, and short messages could be wired directly. For involved communications, the firm used a leased wire to set up an appointment for a telephone call. An automatic switching mechanism at the home office routed incoming wires to the proper destination. A wire was used for receiving confirmation of orders placed and research opinion on companies, which was retrieved from a computer storage system. A news service and a Dow Jones news service existed in most offices. The firm used a leased wire to operate its electronic quote boards and "ticker tapes" that were located in most offices. It also subscribed to a computer retrieval system with several input devices in each office. The total system made it possible to obtain instantaneously high, low, and last price, volume, price/earnings ratio, dividend, yield, and yesterday's closing price on all listed stocks and a number of stocks that were traded over the counter. The billing procedure and the portfolio review procedure were both computerized.

Besides providing a high level of service for customers, this complex information system enabled a detailed control of operations to be maintained by the home office. Management could receive at any time a complete rundown on current performance of any A/E or standing of any branch. By utilizing competitive standards or norms established for the group, management could continually evaluate the performance of any given individual salesman or manager. Through various reports the central office could ensure that policies were followed at the local level. The information system, competitive standards, and reward system brought to bear on the local office high incentive to maintain an efficient operation. These factors interacted to create a high-pressure situation. The local manager was held closely accountable for sales and profits of the local unit, but the unit was expected to operate within sharply circumscribed policy parameters and direction from specialists at the central office. In other terms, the local manager was held responsible for the profit of the unit, but his authority on how to do this was sharply restricted.

We can examine the response of the manager to these demands and the degree to which these pressures were screened out or passed on to subordinates.

LEADERSHIP STYLE OF THE LOCAL
MANAGER

The manager of the local unit had held his position for about twenty years. Working in a centralized context where it was necessary to continually obtain approval from various home office staff specialists, the manager was highly conscious of the impression he conveyed to them. Any independence he had once had had been displaced largely by a desire to please his superiors and staff specialists at the central office. Disagreeable policies were passed off by the manager as something he had to do because "New York" required it.

Occasionally a sharply punitive approach was taken. In one incident, an A/E who was handling a commodity account was fired. The customer who speculates in this area—to use the manager's description—is "the guy who's in the market for a fast buck." Commodity prices often change rapidly, and since the accounts are typically highly leveraged, quick action is required to establish or eliminate a position. The A/E tried to contact the customer, but when he could not, he entered an order in the customer's name. When substantial losses developed over a two-month period, the customer initiated court action to be released from the transaction. The local office made an out-of-court settlement that cost the branch several thousand dollars, and the A/E was dismissed. These incidents seldom developed but were critical in establishing the relationship between the manager and his subordinates. A more common incident was when the customer became dissatisfied with the advice or service of an A/E and asked to be transferred to another A/E. Where the customer experienced losses or failed to achieve gains at the speed he desired, the A/E could easily be blamed. The manager's typical posture was to readily make the transfer rather than attempt to mediate the dispute and risk the loss of the account to another branch or another firm. Unwillingness to represent the A/E's contributed to friction among the A/E's and between the manager and A/E's.

The manager represented the A/E's to some degree by permitting some deviation from home office policies, such as not requiring the A/E's to turn in call sheets on their customer contacts. In this instance, he permitted some flexibility. In most cases, however, he made it a practice to enforce home office policies and rules, especially those that were checked by the headquarters auditor on his inspection trips to the branch. To protect himself, when the home office issued new instructions or emphasized the importance of implementing old policies, the manager circulated memorandums and required each A/E to initial and return them.

The manager made few attempts to bridge the psychological and administrative distance between himself and his subordinates. The manager seldom interacted with his men. At regional sales meetings, some of the A/E's would get together for dinner or cocktails following the meeting. The manager seldom attended these informal gatherings. Similarly, while the manager often introduced the A/E's at investment classes and stock market forums sponsored by the firm, he would not stay for the conclusion to interact socially with his staff following the meeting.

Little systematic attention was given to mitigate the tensions and personal antagonisms that developed among the A/E's and between the A/E's and the operations personnel. One formal dinner party for the sales and clerical personnel was held each year at Christmas where the branch office and home office absorbed the expenses. The manager viewed this as a formal requirement rather than as an opportunity to promote social integration. The activity was treated in a pro forma manner. One of the A/E's was assigned the responsibility of making the arrangements, and the manager gave little attention to the project.

Although the manager stimulated hostile reaction by his close supervision, he felt one of his principal areas of responsibilities was to maintain control over operations. To effect this, he reviewed all customer orders written by A/E's to prevent any deviations from firm policy; he reviewed and initialed all outgoing letters soliciting business from customers; he reviewed all wires requesting information from the research department at the home office and generally closely supervised the work of the A/E's where it was possible.

The supervisor was little concerned with methods of cooptation or other means of increasing voluntary cooperation. Since the firm was highly centralized, there was limited opportunity to involve the A/E's in policy formulation. The manager, however, did not even consult with the A/E's or discuss with them the approach to take in implementing these policies. In areas where authority was delegated to the local office, such as in administrating the bonus system and keeping expenses down, the manager's approach was to order and instruct. Even though the unit was small and compact, the A/E's professionally trained, and with similar interests and goals as the manager, the manager apparently saw no advantage in actively involving them.

The manager relied almost completely upon his authority, the reward-penalty system, and coercive methods to motivate subordinates. The reward-penalty system was well designed to induce a high level of commitment on the part of the A/E's even in the absence of any supervision and permitted a coercive approach to motivation. The discretion that the manager had in determining the total size of the bonus, the authority to transfer accounts from one A/E to another, the detailed reporting system that provided up-to-date information on the activities of the A/E's, and the authority to discharge permitted the manager to take an autocratic approach to supervision.

The failure to represent the A/E's when he could, the lack of skill in involving the A/E's in local office decisions, the discouragement of interaction between himself and A/E's, a few dramatic incidents of a punitive approach to discipline, and a general attitude that policies, rules, and regulations set forth by the home office must be implemented practically eliminated the possibility of eliciting cooperation and commitment through exercise of personal influence. The attempts to use persuasion and influence were outweighed by the general reliance upon authority and coercion.

The result of the interaction of the pressures created by the context and leadership style of the local manager was to place the A/E's and to some extent the operating personnel in a cauldron of high stress. It is little wonder that symptoms of conflict, low morale, and anxiety emerged. The A/E's could not readily leave the firm after a few years despite their dissatisfactions. The accounts they had so diligently cultivated would largely be lost if they moved to another firm, and they probably had little hope that conditions would be much different in another company.

In summary, the local environment and unprogrammed tasks created a set of stresses on the local unit. Some of the organizational factors created favorable conditions in dealing with these pressures. In particular, the branch was small so that individuals were grouped together so they could regularly meet face to face. However, disintegration pressures were exerted by other factors. The degree of specialization created an interdependent work flow within the local office and established the need for close coordination and high cooperation. The control system elicited a high commitment on the part of the A/E's to meet the pressures but a lower level commitment from the operating personnel. There was little opportunity for creative efforts and innovation in adjusting to these pressures. The high degree of centralization meant that the activities of the local office were highly structured. The sophisticated communication network that permitted efficient service to the customers also enabled the central office to achieve close surveillance on the extent to which policies and procedures were implemented.

The manager of the local unit could have mitigated some of these pressures on his subordinates. Instead, however, the leadership pattern that emerged contributed additional pressures. This pattern of leadership had many undesirable dimensions. Even so, the pressures exerted on the local manager's position were such that a similar pattern could be expected to evolve in most offices of this firm. An individual who was committed to a more supportive style of supervision might retain this approach, but the pressures were in the opposite direction.

The firm, by innovating its service to customers and devising this set of pressures, maintained its position in the industry. Whether the emergent behavior patterns contributed to the long-run effectiveness of the firm, however, is questionable. Unnecessary conflicts had been designed into the system. Local initiative, experimentation, and adaptability were restricted sharply. The system elicited an attitude of conformity, subservience, and managerial weakness at the local level.

Recommendations. Several structural changes would go far in solving these problems:

1. The reward-penalty system should be redesigned to provide an incentive to supportive personnel in the offices to increase their work pace when customer demands increase.
2. Explicit standards should be established for operating personnel.
3. Greater authority should be delegated to local offices from the main office.
4. A leadership program should be implemented that provides insights into effects of an authoritarian leadership approach in this context.
5. As a longer term solution, a systematic program of research should be implemented to determine personality types that adjust well to a high-stress environment.

Each of these points is developed briefly below.

1. *Reward-Penalty System*—The firm operates in an unstable environment with work demands changing sharply during the day, the week, and cyclically over periods of months. The reward-penalty should be designed to provide incentives for all individuals to adjust their work pace to these demands. At present, the "customers" personnel have an incentive to do so, but the supportive personnel haven't any incentive to respond since they are paid on an institutional basis. An incentive system should be introduced whereby their pay goes up directly with increased business. This could be either a bonus system paid each week or an adjustable salary scale. This would provide an incentive to increase work pace with changes in business conditions and contribute to greater group cohesion and unity of effort on the part of all personnel at the local level.

2. *Explicit Standards*—Explicit standards should be developed for operating personnel that are related to fluctuations in level of work. Establishing standards on a comparative basis and evaluating performance in terms of these standards would place the operating personnel under similar pressures as the A/E's in the office.

3. *Greater Delegation*—The areas that can be delegated are limited by the necessity to follow uniform approaches, particularly where legal issues are involved. Still, a greater emphasis can be given to managerial discretion at the branch level on nonsensitive areas by putting greater emphasis on end results and less on means of achieving these ends. This would mean that the staff groups at central level would need to partially abandon their line relation, where they make detailed policies in their specialties that must be applied at the local level. Instead, central-level staff would need to provide services for the local manager to use if they fit his situation. Areas such as how much to contribute to charity, building layout and decor, and other decisions that have only local implications should be delegated to the local level.

4. *Leadership Program*—A leadership training program should be implemented that provides feedback to supervisors on their approach and the implications their approach has for behavior and functioning of the organization. This would involve (a) providing a profile of leadership style either by questionnaire, interview, or by combination; (b) training sessions with role playing, tapes, and lectures that develop the consequences of various approaches to carrying out a leadership role; (c) personal counseling with the joint setting of goals on leadership changes. By using the profile of present leadership styles as a beginning point, joint goals between trainers (operating out of the central office) and managers would be set. A year later, a follow-up assessment would be made and new goals established.

5. *Research Program*—A longer term program of research should also be implemented to determine the form of personality that reacts most favorably to the stresses of the environment. It is evident that many of the individuals operating under the high stress were deteriorating emotionally, physically, and professionally. Some individuals, however are able to accomodate to stressful job situations. A long-term program would need to (a) identify those adjusting well to high stress and those adjusting poorly, and (b) determine if there were a common personality type among the adapters and low adapters. If there were common features that differentiated high and low adapters, these would then be used in screening candidates hired by the firm in the future and in promoting people to managerial positions.

APPENDICES

OVERALL PERSPECTIVES OF THE STRUCTURAL-PROCESS MODEL

FIGURE A-1. Structural-process model: Overall relationships

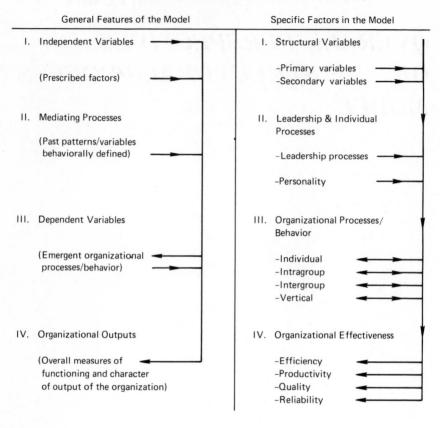

General Features of the Model	Specific Factors in the Model
I. Independent Variables	I. Structural Variables
(Prescribed factors)	–Primary variables –Secondary variables
II. Mediating Processes (Past patterns/variables behaviorally defined)	II. Leadership & Individual Processes –Leadership processes –Personality
III. Dependent Variables (Emergent organizational processes/behavior)	III. Organizational Processes/ Behavior –Individual –Intragroup –Intergroup –Vertical
IV. Organizational Outputs (Overall measures of functioning and character of output of the organization)	IV. Organizational Effectiveness –Efficiency –Productivity –Quality –Reliability

FIGURE A-2. Classification of organizations in terms of complexity

A. PRIMARY STRUCTURAL VARIABLES

Simple Organization						Complex Organization	
1	2	3	4	5	6	7	8	9

1. Size: Small .... Large
2. Work Flow: Independent .... Interdependent
3. Task Complexity: Programmed .... Unprogrammed
4. Spatial-Physical Factors: Concentrated .... Dispersed

B. SECONDARY STRUCTURAL VARIABLES

1	2	3	4	5	6	7	8	9

1. Formal Authority Relationships:
   a. Delegation: Decentralized .... Centralized
   b. Departmentation: Interdependent .... Autonomous
2. Formal Control System:
   a. Standards: Low .... High
   b. Rewards-Penalities: Institutional .... Individual

C. LEADERSHIP PROCESSES

Democratic				General			Directive	
1	2	3	4	5	6	7	8	9

1. Representation: Upward .... Downward
2. Rule Adherence: Low .... High
3. Participation: Extensive .... Limited
4. Direction: Loose .... Close
5. Inducements: Rewards .... Penalizes

FIGURE A-3. Hypothetical behavioral profile of two departments in an organization

Individual Behavior

1. Job involvement
2. Commitment to standards
3. Work-goal commitment
4. Job initiative
5. Self improvement
6. Satisfaction
7. Sense of achievement
8. Job attendance
9. Job commitment

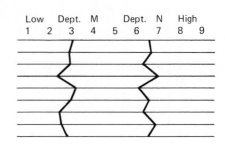

Low	Dept.	M		Dept.	N	High	
1	2	3	4	5	6	7	8	9

Group Relations: Lateral

10. Confidence and trust
11. Job related communication
12. Non-job related communication
13. Cooperation
14. Group unity

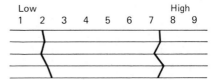

Low							High	
1	2	3	4	5	6	7	8	9

Group Relations: Vertical

15. Trust downward
16. Trust upward
17. Requested information upward
18. Communication screening
19. Job information upward
20. Human relations information upward
21. Teamwork
22. Acceptance of immediate superior's decision

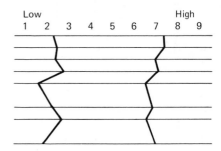

Low							High	
1	2	3	4	5	6	7	8	9

Intergroup Relations: Lateral

23. Confidence and trust
24. Information accuracy
25. Cooperation
26. Acceptance of decisions

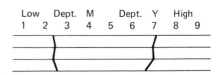

Low	Dept.	M		Dept.	Y	High	
1	2	3	4	5	6	7	8	9

FIGURE A-4. Structural-process model: Brief definition and summary of measures of each variable

Variable	Abbreviated Definition	Measurement—Scaling

I. PRIMARY STRUCTURAL VARIABLES

A) Size — No. of individuals assigned to a formal group

Small ____ Large
1 ————————— 9

Size	1–5	11–15	21–25	31–35	41–
	1 2	3 4	5 6	7 8	9
Level 1	1–5	11–15	21–25	31–35	41–
Level 2	1–30	61–90	121–150	181–210	241–
Level 3	1–125		251–325 etc.		

B) Work Flow

Independent/Interdependent — Input-output dependence among *positions* within each formal group

1 ————————— 9

Specialization	Low	High
	1 —————	9

Average of two scales

1) Intragroup — Short-term means for adjusting to varying work load

Buffers	Extensive	Limited
	1 —————	9

2) Intergroup — Input-output dependence *among groups*

Specialization among groups	Low	High
	1 —————	9

C) Task Complexity

Programmed/Unprogrammed — Predictability of outcomes of decisions, or actions

1 ————————— 9

Predictability	Almost always	Seldom
	1 —————	9

Resources for help	Available	Unavailable
	1 —————	9

FIGURE A-4. (Continued)

Variable	Abbreviated Definition	Measurement—Scaling			
D) *Spatial-Physical Factors*					
Concentrated Dispersed					
1 9					
1) Intragroup	Barriers that separate individuals and groups	Average of 2 scales			
	Barriers that exist among *group members*	Distance & walls	Little 1	Direct	Extensive 9
		Spatial orientation		1	Indirect 9
2) Intergroup	Barriers that exist *among groups*	Distance & walls	Little 1		Extensive 9
				1	9
II. MEDIATING STRUCTURAL VARIABLES					
A) *Formal Authority Relations*	Formal right to make decisions; defined in terms of delegation and departmentation	See below			

1) Delegation

Decentralized		Centralized
1		9

Distribution of authority among levels

% of decisions delegated	99%	0–11%
	1	9
Degree of discretion	Extensive	Restricted
	1	9
% of decisions referred to higher levels	0–11%	99%
	1	9

2) Departmentation

Interdependent		Autonomous
1		9

Degree departments are interdependent

Specialization among departments	Little	Extensive
	1	9

B) *Control System*

1) Standards

Low		High
1		9

Formal system to motivate performance defined in terms of formal standards and rewards

Performance standards specified for individuals

Standards	Low	High
	1	9
Stability	Maintained	Increased
	1	9
Base	Historical	Comparative
	1	9

FIGURE A-4. (Continued)

Variable	Abbreviated Definition	Measurement—Scaling
2) Rewards-Penalties Institutional Individual 1 — 9	Formal system for rewarding, penalizing individual performance	Relation of rewards to performance Little 1 — Extensive 9 Relation of penalties to performance Little 1 — Extensive 9
III. LEADERSHIP	The way in which the supervisor deals with subordinates, superiors and other groups Described in terms of five processes	See below
A) *Representation* Upward Downward 1 — 9	The degree a supervisor defends the interests of his group	Four questions that relate to: Job related issues Image building Resource support General issues
B) *Rule Orientation* Low High 1 — 9	The degree that the supervisor emphasizes literal adherence to policies, procedures, and rules	Three questions that relate to: Rule enforcement Commitment to means or ends Use of resources

C) Participation

High	Low
1	9

Degree that those affected by decisions are consulted and involved in decision process

Four questions that relate to:

Personnel issues	Breadth of involvement
Job issues	Group process

D) Direction

Loose	Close
1	9

Degree that the supervisor specifies the ends to be achieved and the details of how to achieve these ends

Three questions that relate to:

Specification of ends and means
Checking on progress
Domination in problem solving

E) Inducements

Rewards	Penalties
1	9

Degree that the supervisor relies upon rewards rather than penalties to induce performance

Four questions that relate to:

Reliance on rewards	Reliance on reciprocity rather than formal authority
Reliance on penalties	

IV. PERSONALITY

Predisposition to react to a given stimulus in a particular manner

Any standardized personality measure such as Rokeach measure of open-closed mind, Adorno's F scale, etc.

MEASUREMENTS
OF THE VARIABLES

PART 1

BEHAVIOR: PERCEPTUAL MEASURES OF INDIVIDUAL PATTERNS, INTRAGROUP, AND SUPERVISOR-SUBORDINATE RELATIONS

Instructions

Below are questions on the behavior of work groups. Please fill in the space on the answer sheet which best describes your behavior and that of the group. For example, on the first question the number is filled in on the answer sheet that best describes your level of commitment on the job.

1. JOB INVOLVEMENT. To what extent are you committed to your work (like trying to do the job well and taking pride in your work)?

1	2	3	4	5	6	7	8	9
0–11%	22%	33%	44%	55%	66%	77%	88%	99%

| of the time you feel committed to doing a good job. | | | | of the time you feel committed to doing a good job. | | | of the time you feel committed to doing a good job. | |

Behavior

Individual

1. JOB INVOLVEMENT. To what extent are you committed to your work (like trying to do the job well and taking pride in your work)?

2. COMMITMENT TO STANDARDS. What percentage of the time do you try to meet work standards, or other measures of a full day's work?

3. WORK-GOAL COMMITMENT. To what extent do you automatically increase your work pace and shorten work breaks as work pressure increases?

4. INITIATIVE. To what degree do you assume job responsibility (such as trying to improve methods and solve work problems)?

5. SELF-IMPROVEMENT. Do you try to develop your skills and abilities to do a better job?

6. SATISFACTION. What percentage of the time do you feel contented, (rather than frustrated) in trying to do your job?

7. ACHIEVEMENT. To what degree do you have a sense of achievement in performing your job (such as getting a kick out of doing good work)?

8. ATTENDANCE: What percentage of the time are you on the job?

9. JOB COMMITMENT: To what extent do you think of staying on your job (that is, you aren't thinking of quitting, or asking for a transfer)?

Intragroup

10. CONFIDENCE AND TRUST: What percentage of the members in your work group do you have confidence in and trust?

11. JOB RELATED COMMUNICATION: To what degree do you have useful discussions with other group members on *job related* subjects (such as on work problems, how to resolve personal conflicts, and so forth)?

12. NON-JOB RELATED COMMUNICATION: To what extent do you have discussions with other group members on *non-job related* subjects (such as politics, sports, etc)?

13. COOPERATION: What percentage of the time do members of your group help you when assistance is needed without being asked?

14. GROUP UNITY: To what degree do you identify with your work group (such as feeling part of the group, and wishing to remain in the group)?

Vertical

15. TRUST-DOWNWARD: To what extent does your *supervisor* show he has trust and confidence in you?

16. TRUST-UPWARD: To what degree do you have trust and confidence in him?

17. REQUESTED INFORMATION: When information is *requested* by your supervisor, to what extent do you provide accurate and complete data?

18. COMMUNICATION SCREENING: What percentage of the time is it *unnecessary* for you to withhold and distort information from your supervisor for your own self-protection?

19. JOB INFORMATION: To what extent do you bring job problems to his attention?

20. HUMAN RELATIONS INFORMATION: To what degree do you volunteer useful information to him on personnel problems, group conflict, and other types of human relations problems?

21. TEAMWORK: To what extent do you have a sense of being a part of your supervisor's team?

·22. ACCEPTANCE OF DECISIONS: What percentage of the time do you accept decisions of your supervisor? (For example, do you implement his orders and requests by interpreting both what his intention is as well as what he actually says?)

PART 2

STRUCTURAL VARIABLES: PERCEPTUAL MEASUREMENTS

Structural Variables

Simple 0–11%								Complex 99%
1	2	3	4	5	6	7	8	9

The following questions relate to important aspects of the organization. Please fill in the number on the answer sheet that best describes your group, (that is, the formal unit to which you are assigned).

Work Flow: Intragroup

23. SPECIALIZATION: What percentage of your work are you dependent upon other members of your work group (that is, it is necessary to coordinate your job with what they are doing)?

24. BUFFERS BETWEEN POSITIONS: Inventories or other buffers between positions may permit one to continue to work when breakdowns occur or others are absent. Under normal conditions, what percent of your work is so interrelated that you *cannot* continue to work for one day or longer when individuals are absent from the group or breakdowns and other stoppages occur?

Spatial-Physical Barriers: Intragroup

25. PHYSICAL RELATION OF GROUP MEMBERS: What percentage of members of your work group are located so far away that you *cannot* carry on a normal conversation without shouting or going out of your way?

26. DIRECT EYE CONTACT: What percentage of members are located so you don't have direct eye contact with them unless you turn around or move from your regular work position or office?

Task Complexity

27. PREDICTABILITY OF OUTCOMES: In some jobs, things are unpredictable—if you do something to solve a problem, you don't know what will happen. What percent of the time are you unsure on how things will work as expected?

28. ASSISTANCE ON PROBLEMS: What percent of the time are you at a loss about whom to go to for reliable help when you cannot solve a problem?

Delegation

29. DELEGATION OF AUTHORITY: For what percentage of decisions in regard to your job are you supposed to check with, or obtain approval from, higher level supervisors (rather than making decisions using guidelines of policies and procedures)?
30. DISCRETION TO MAKE DECISIONS: What percentage of the time do the formal policies, procedures, and rules limit *decisions related to your job* so you don't have flexibility to adjust to local conditions and special situations and discretion to try out new ideas?
31. LEVEL OF DECISIONS: Where you don't have the authority to make decisions, what percent of the time is your supervisor authorized to make decisions (rather than being required to refer them to higher levels)?

Standards

32. LEVEL OF INDIVIDUAL STANDARDS: What percent of performance standards (such as time, cost, quantity, or quality) are relatively high and difficult to meet?
33. STABILITY OF STANDARDS: To what degree are standards increased as performance rises (rather than being maintained at some level)?
34. BASE USED IN SETTING STANDARDS: To what degree are standards based upon comparative levels of performance of similar groups (rather than related to past performance or some standardized benchmark)?

Reward-Penalty System

35. RELATION OF REWARDS TO PERFORMANCE: What percentage of salary increases, promotions, special recognition, and privileges are related to performance levels over which the *individual has control*?
36. RELATION OF PENALTIES TO PERFORMANCE: What percentage of penalties (taking away of special privileges, salary reductions, demotions, and firing) are related to poor performance *over which the individual has control*?

Size

37. SIZE OF WORK GROUP: How many full-time and part-time employees are assigned to the unit in which you work?

1–5	*6–10*	*11–15*	*16–20*	*21–25*	*26–30*	*31–35*	*36–40*	*41+*
1	2	3	4	5	6	7	8	9

PART 3

LEADERSHIP: PERCEPTUAL MEASUREMENTS

Leadership

Democratic				General				Directive
1	2	3	4	5	6	7	8	9
99%	88%	77%	66%	55%	44%	33%	22%	0–11%

The following questions relate to important aspects of a supervisor's leadership approach. Please fill in the number that best describes your supervisor. For example, interpret question 38 as follows:

(Sample)
38. What percentage of the time does your supervisor stand up for the interests of your work group on important job related issues (such as overtime, raises, promotions, job classifications, transfers, and getting fair hearing on grievances)?

1	2	3	4	5	6	7	8	9
99%	88%	77%	66%	55%	44%	33%	22%	0–11%
of the time							of the time	
he stands up							he stands up	
for the inter-							for the inter-	
ests of your							ests of your	
work group							work group	

Representation

38. What percentage of the time does your supervisor stand up for the interests of your work group on important job related issues (such as overtime, raises, promotions, job classifications, transfers, and getting fair hearing on grievances)?
39. What percentage of time does he try to obtain adequate resource support for your group (such as added personnel, new equipment, materials, and supplies)?
40. When dealing with management and the staff, what percentage of time does he try to build up the group's image (such as keeping them informed on what the group is doing, praising the quality of group's work and competence of its personnel)?
41. When he must decide between supporting higher management or his work group, what percentage of the time does he support the work group (such as by challenging adverse decisions)?

Rule Orientation

42.   What percentage of the time is he flexible in enforcing policies, procedures, and rules on the work group?

43.   Does he take a "can do it" approach when policies or rules impede getting the job done and find a way (rather than a "*cannot do it*" approach and quote the policies or rules that prevents action)?

44.   What percentage of the time does he permit resources under his control (such as supplies, personnel, or equipment) to be liberally used to get the job done?

Participation

45.   What percentage of time does he ask for comments and suggestions when making *personnel* decisions (such as hiring new staff, promoting personnel, or adopting new personnel policies)?

46.   What percentage of time does he ask for comments and advice on *job-related matters* (such as setting goals, solving job problems, or making changes in the working arrangements)?

47.   What percentage of time does he encourage discussion of issues and problems (such as by evaluating criticism objectively and encouraging suggestions and comments)?

48.   What percentage of time does he encourage "majority rule" (such as by supporting the position which has the broadest agreement)?

Direction

49.   In directing, what percentage of the time does your supervisor loosely direct by *outlining* the job to be done and leaving it up to those doing the work to decide how to do it (rather than giving detailed instructions step-by-step as the job proceeds on what to do and how to do it)?

50.   In following up on your work group, what percentage of the time does he leave the group alone (that is, he *hardly ever* checks on how well the job is going, and *seldom* checks on how well the completed job is done)?

51.   In ordering, or giving suggestions, what percentage of the time does he go along with the problem-solving approach and flow of activities being carried on by the group (rather than substituting *his* approach and implementing his ideas)?

Inducements

52.   What percentage of the time does your supervisor rely upon rewards such as personal recognition, raises, and promotions to motivate members of your work group (rather than relying upon orders and threats to motivate such as disciplinary warnings, layoffs, or firing)?

53.   What percentage of the time does he motivate by focusing on elements of the job such as pointing up areas of poor performance, and proposing ways for correction (rather than personalizing the issues such as by asserting poor performance is due to lack of ability, laziness, or incompetency)?

54.   What percentage of the time does he criticize poor performance in private (rather than in front of fellow workers and others)?

55.   To obtain cooperation of group members, what percentage of the time does he rely upon persuasion, trading of favors, and good personal relations?

PART 4

INTERGROUP: PERCEPTUAL MEASURES OF BEHAVIOR & STRUCTURAL VARIABLES

Intergroup Relations:

The following questions deal with the relation that your work group has to the others listed below. Fill in the space on the answer sheet that best describes what your relation is to these groups. For example, questions 1 to 5 ask, "What percentage of the time is there confidence and trust in each of these other groups?"

A "1" on the scale indicates that 11% or less of the time there is confidence and trust; in contrast, a "9" shows that 99% of the time trust and confidence exists. Question 1 deals with the relation of your work group to the group listed under *A*; Question 2 looks at how your work group is related to group listed under *B*, and so forth.

Please answer all questions.   Relation of your group (particularly how you feel) to: [The groups are specified before questionnaires are handed out.]

Intergroup Behavioral Patterns

	A	B	C	D	E
1–5 What percentage of the time is there trust and confidence in each of these groups?	1	2	3	4	5
6–10 What percentage of communications with each of these groups is accurate and complete?	6	7	8	9	10
11–15 In the normal working relationship called for by the job, what percentage of the time do each of these groups readily cooperate and provide assistance?	11	12	13	14	15
16–20 When your group is affected by decisions made by these other groups, what percentage of the time are these decisions accepted with good will (such as where necessary adjustments are made without protesting)?	16	17	18	19	20

Relation of your group (particularly how you
feel) to: — — — — — — — —

Structural Factors : Intergroup

	A	B	C	D	E
21–25 WORK FLOW What percentage of time are you dependent on each of these other groups to do your work (that is, is it necessary to coordinate your work with what they are doing?)	21	22	23	24	25
26–30 SPATIAL-PHYSICAL What percentage of members of each of these groups is located so far away that you cannot carry on a normal conversation without going out of your way?	26	27	28	29	30
31–35 DELEGATION To what extent are decisions of each of the groups limited by policies or procedures established by central staff groups or higher level supervisor?	31	32	33	34	35
36–40 STANDARDS To what extent are the standards of expected performance based upon the *comparative* level of past performance of these groups?	36	37	38	39	40
41–45 REWARD-PENALTY What percentage of time are rewards and penalties (salaries, promotions, etc.) based on the comparative level of performance of each of these groups?	41	42	43	44	45

46   How many full- and part-time employees are in the larger formal unit in
which your group works (that is, how many employees is your supervisor's
superior responsible for)?

1–30	31–60	61–90	91–120	121–150	151–180	181–210	211–240	241+
1	2	3	4	5	6	7	8	9

AUTHOR INDEX

SUBJECT INDEX